HOW TO PUZZLE CACHE

2nd Edition
Revised and Updated

by Cully Long

facebook.com/howtopuzzlecache

@h2puzzlecache

howtopuzzlecache@gmail.com

howtopuzzlecache.com

puzzlecachepractice.com

No patent liability is assumed with respect to the use of the information contained herein. Although every precaution has been taken in the preparation of this book, the publisher and author assume no responsibility for errors or omissions. Neither is any liability assumed for damage resulting from the use of information contained within.

This publication contains the opinions and ideas of its author. It is intended to provide helpful and informative material on the subject matter covered. It is sold with the understanding that the author and publisher are not engaged in rendering professional services in the book. If the reader requires personal assistance or advice, a competent professional should be consulted.

The author and publisher specifically disclaim any responsibility for any liability, loss or risk, personal or otherwise, which is incurred as a consequence, directly or indirectly, of the use and application of any of the contents of this book.

Version 2.0

ISBN #: 978-0-9973488-9-7

 **ontents**

What is a Puzzle Cache?

Call it a sport, a hobby, a game, or even an art... but geocaching has exploded in popularity in the past few years. What started as a simple game of placing a box in the woods and sending people on a nice hike has expanded and grown in ways that the originators probably never anticipated.

Puzzle caches, or mystery caches, are a subset of geocaching where rather than publishing the co-ordinates of the location of the cache, the cache owner (whom I'll refer to as the CO from here on out) publishes a set of false coordinates and the geocacher must solve a puzzle in order to learn the true placement of the cache.

Puzzle caches have been a part of the game since nearly the beginning The oldest active puzzle cache is GC70, "Octopus Garden," by AdventureTom. It also happens to be the oldest active cache in North Carolina, placed toward the end of September, 2001. GC58, "Pyramid Point," by a cacher named Kluso, was published in September 2000 and has the puzzle icon but *geocaching.com* does not recognize it as a puzzle cache because the text of that cache page has been changed, so we no longer know what the puzzle actually was, if indeed it actually was a puzzle. Regardless, puzzle caches now they make up a significant portion of the geocaching landscape.

Puzzle caches are polarizing: some people love them, some people hate them. For some cachers the solving of a good puzzle is just as good as finding the cache in the woods; others view the puzzles as an obstacle to get past in order to find the cache. Puzzle caches also intimidate quite a number of cachers, but as an avid puzzle cacher, who enjoys both hiding and finding, I hope that after you read this book you will no longer be one of those cachers!

Puzzling Start

So what are puzzle caches exactly? That's not actually as simple a question as it seems. Puzzle caches are a wide and varied topic and they cover a lot of different aspects of caching. There are as many variations on puzzle caches in the world as there are variations on traditional caches.

In truth, the "Puzzle or Mystery Cache" category has become sort of a catchall for things that don't easily slot into the other cache types. Many different things, including night caches (caches that can only be done at night), offset caches (caches where you have to project a waypoint), and challenge caches (caches where you have to accomplish a task or achieve a goal before you are allowed to log the find), have all been shoehorned into the category. There are also caches with locks on the container, or a physical puzzle box that you must solve in the field in order to get at the logs that fall into this category. In this book I'll be focusing on the most typical variation of puzzle caches, wherein you must solve a puzzle in order to learn the coordinates. The puzzles I'll be discussing are typically the "armchair" or "solve at home" variety, though you might come across variations of these intended to be solved in the field as well.

projection
See Chapter 5 for an explanation of waypoint projection!

Puzzle caches have a few things in common, of course. All puzzle caches start with false coordinates, sometimes known as "dummy coords." The dummy coords might be part of the puzzle, or a good parking spot, or it could just be a random location. There might be a clue at that location, by which I mean a clue to the theme of the puzzle, not a physical clue. For instance dummy coords in the parking lot of a music store might indicate that music is part of the theme of the puzzle. It's always worth the time to have a look at the dummy coords in streetview, to see if there is anything noteworthy there.

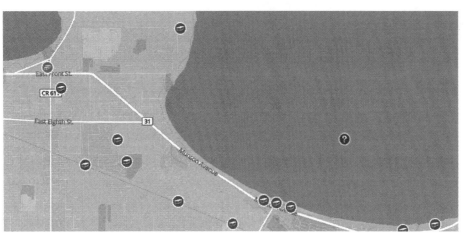

A puzzle cache in the middle of Grand Traverse Bay, in Michigan.

In general, 99% of the time, the cache is not at those coordinates (at least, not when there is a puzzle to be solved, most Challenge caches are actually at the initial coords.) You'll sometimes see that the dummy coords are in the middle of a body of water, on top of a building, or some other inaccessible place. But once you've solved the puzzle, you'll be rewarded with the coordinates to a regular geocache, just like the traditional "box in the woods!" That second location (where the actual cache can be found) is known as the "final."

And the puzzles? What are they? Well, again, much like traditional caches there are many types of puzzles. Some puzzles are very explicit: Go to this park, find this plaque, find this information, and then find the cache. I call those *Research Puzzles*. Since they are usually fairly straightforward, I won't be talking about them much, but you should be able to identify those just by reading the cache page.

research puzzles
For an excellent example of a research puzzle see GC1GTJK

Research puzzles are usually as simple as collecting information, either from the web, or from local sources. COs will typically give you a basic conversion, or a set of coords with missing information, like this: North 36° 40.ABC. Then telling you that "A" equals the numbers of letters in the fourth word on a plaque, or the number of park benches visible from a particular location, or some similar piece of information. This could also be accomplished at home, by telling you that 'A' will equal the number of seasons that *SportsNight* was on television, or the number of times that Man O'War won the Preakness. These are things that can easily be looked up on the Internet to gain the needed information.

Other puzzle types are just as explicit, based simply on familiarity. It could be a Word Search, a Crossword, a Maze, a Sudoku, or any number of familiar every day puzzles. I call those *Crossover Puzzles*. Again, these should be easy to identify.

Sometimes though… you just can't be sure *what* you are looking at. The page might contain nothing but a series of photographs, or a series of numbers. It might be a video clip, or nothing but a series of seemingly random letters. In fact, the cache page might appear to be entirely blank! In those cases, the only indication you might have that you are dealing with a puzzle cache is the big blue question mark at the top of the page. Before you can even get started, you have to find and ID the puzzle.

crossover puzzles
See Chapter 4 for tips on dealing with this puzzle type!

And that's what I hope to help with!

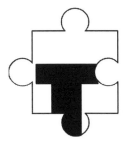 # his Book

First, be aware that I am writing this book with the assumption that you have done at least a couple geocaches, if not quite a few. You'll need to know the basic terminology and methods for caching. If you are unfamiliar with caching as an activity, I'd suggest seeking out a how-to on standard caching before you try to tackle puzzle caches, as they add an extra level of difficulty, and an extra layer of preparation onto caching.

The aim of this book is not to show you how to solve every geocaching puzzle in the world. Unfortunately, that simply isn't possible. Solving puzzles doesn't come down to knowing trivia, (except of course when it does). Solving puzzles is about a way of thinking, the ability to mentally turn pieces over in your mind and see differing combinations. Of course, it does help to have a base of knowledge to draw from. Think of it this way, reading nursery rhymes and reading Shakespearean sonnets take the same ability: the ability to put letters together in your head and recognize the words. An 8-year-old might be able to read Shakespeare, but she wouldn't have the personal experience to take those words and conjure connections between them, or see the subtle imagery and poetic combinations that convey a deeper meaning that might be more apparent to an adult.

What I hope to do with this book is provide you with a *toolbox*: a collection of ideas and methods that will at least give you a place to start. My hope is to get you on the trail of transforming from a reader of nursery rhymes to a reader of sonnets.

One of the most daunting aspects of puzzle caches is often simply determining what the puzzle *is*. My hope is that by the end of this book, if you can't actually identify the puzzle, you'll at least have some good ideas. A cache page that contains something like Maya numerals is going to stymie any cacher who hasn't been provided the proper clues, and has never *seen* Maya numerals. Again, I can't hope to show you every possible thing that you might come across, but I hope your knowledge base will be significant-

ly expanded.

The other aspect of puzzle solving that I hope to give you some training in is what is called the "Logical Leap." This is the moment in puzzle solving when it may not be entirely clear what you are supposed to do next, but suddenly something clicks--you see the next logical step that will get you over the hump. In a well-constructed puzzle this leap should make sense once you find it. In a poorly constructed puzzle, it may make no sense at all and would be impossible to guess without a hint or a clue. The more puzzles you do, the easier this step becomes, as you start to learn all the different ways that puzzle creators can manipulate you. Think of this in the way you think of "geo-sense." When you first started caching, finds were probably tougher, and you would arrive at ground zero with no idea where to look, right? As you cached more you developed that "geo-sense," the intuitive ability to know where a hider might have placed something. The Logical Leap is just like that.

The other end of the Logical Leap is sometimes called the "Aha! Moment," describing that feeling you get when your path suddenly becomes clear, and you can see the answer on the horizon. Many puzzle cachers describe this moment as being almost (and sometimes more!) rewarding than finding the actual cache.

Like regular caches, puzzle caches are rated by the CO according to their difficulty and terrain. It can sometimes be a little confusing (even to COs!) exactly whether the difficulty rating refers to the puzzle or the hide, and how to rank the difficulty of puzzles which might be simple for an experienced solver, but quite difficult for a newbie. My suggestion is to seek out some of the lower difficulty caches in your area to practice with. Learning how puzzle caches work will help you to generate a "puzzle sense," just like the geo-sense that you develop after caching for a while.

Each chapter in this book will be devoted to a specific taxonomy of puzzles: Crossover Puzzles, Math Puzzles, Ciphers, etc. I'll try and build a basic understanding with you of how each type works, and how to begin tackling them for a solution. At the end of each chapter I'll give you three puzzles. One will be a "walk-through" where I will show you step by step how I, as an experienced puzzle solver would tackle the solve. Hopefully this acts as a sort of training that will help you develop your own approach to puzzle solving.

The other two will be practice puzzles for you to solve on your own. The finals for the example and "solve it yourself" puzzles are NOT, in any way, real caches, and you should not go to the locations expecting to find a cache. Most of them are even in physically inaccessible places. I have tried to find interesting or humorous places to look at it in satellite view, however, so have a look at the places your answers take you!

Below each puzzle will be an image that provides the "Puzzle Stats" for that puzzle. This image provides the checksum that you will use as a geo-check. Checksums are exactly what they sound like, a "sum" that "checks" the answers. The CO will provide you with a number. If you add the digits of your

THIS AREA WILL DISPLAY THE CHECKSUM

THIS AREA WILL DISPLAY THE BEST WAY TO VIEW THE FINAL LOCATION

PUZZLE STATS

32 📷

CHECKSUM   BEST VIEW

HERE ARE THE POTENTIAL "VIEW" OPTIONS:

 STREET VIEW

 SATELLITE VIEW

 PHOTO VIEW*

*PHOTO VIEWS CAN BE SEEN AT THE BOTTOM IN GOOGLE STREET VIEW OR BY CLICKING NEARBY PHOTO ICONS IN GOOGLE EARTH!

coords together and have the correct answer, they should equal that number. So, if your answer is 40° 38.667, you would add 4+0+3+8+6+6+7, or 34. (See Page 29 for more.)

For purposes of this book, if the coordinates that make up an answer are in a different coordinates format (more on that in the next chapter!) you should use the coordinates in the format that they were in at the solve of the puzzle to check the answer. That means if the coordinates are 40° 42' 13.6" (decimal seconds format) then you would add 4+0+4+2+1+3+6 without converting the coordinates into the more familiar format used by *geocaching.com*.

The second is an image that will help you understand the best method to use to view the final. First is a human figure for "Street View" level viewing. This is the best for seeing statues or murals that are the final "cache."

Second is "Satellite View" for things like images, words, letters, or numbers written on the ground or on a roof and visible from above.

Finally there is "Photo View," which I use in areas where there is no street view available. These are often visible at the bottom of the screen in Google Maps, or as small blue circles on the satellite view map, and you use them just like you would use street view, by dragging the man from the menu into the small bubble.

Finally, each puzzle will be provided with 5 hints. Each hint is progressively stronger. Hint 1 is a general nudge to get you started. Hint 5 is nuclear and basically spoils the puzzle, so be careful!

Beside each hint level is a number between 1 and 150. In Appendix 1 you will find the corresponding hints. So, if you had the hint chart given here, you would go to Appendix 1 and check Hint 122 for the "light nudge," Hint 3 for a "medium" hint, and Hint 72 for the "nuclear level" hint.

Oh... one last thing. For hint levels 3 and above... they are Rot13 encoded. (See Page 138 for more information on what that means.) And unlike the *geocaching.com* website you won't be able to decode them just by clicking on them. You'll have to go to a website like *rot13.com* and retype the hint in order to decode it, so you'll have to REALLY want that hint, and do a little work to get it.

Where are the answers?!

One of the questions I get asked most frequently is why I do not provide you with the answers. Well... part of my goal here is provide an experience as close to actual puzzle solving as possible, and no CO is just going to give you the answer, are they?

Plus, I find that having the answer available is often just too much of a temptation for most people. If you know the answer is there you are much more likely to just skip to that answer rather than working to get it.

I did compromise a little in this new edition by providing hints, which were not provided in the previous edition.

What if I need more help?

On the title page I have provided multiple ways to get in touch. Feel free to drop me a line whenever you like!

Where To Start

Getting started on a puzzle cache is often the most intimidating thing, especially with those "Where's the puzzle?" style puzzles, where you can't even tell what the puzzle is supposed to be! Stumbling onto a cache page where there just doesn't seem to be enough information to get started can be frustrating and can put you off of puzzle caches entirely--especially when all you want is a set of coords so that you can get out into the woods! Understanding what the owners of cache puzzles can and can't do might give you a lever with which to get the puzzle moving.

A small note before we get started: In general, as *geocaching.com* is the most popular listing service, I'll be referring to the rules as if I mean the rules there; however, there are many other services that list geocaches and each listing service has their own standards. If you are looking for a puzzle cache that is listed somewhere other than *geocaching.com,* it will be useful to be familiar with how the rules on the other sites deviate. See the individual websites for information on that.

I will also be discussing some things that you can do with your Internet browser (the program you use to access the internet, generally Chrome, Explorer, Firefox or Safari), and I'll be referring to the directions as if I was talking about Chrome, as that is the most popular browser in the United States, with nearly 60% of us using it. In Appendix 9 you'll find a step by step breakdown for each of the four major browsers.

irst... the Rules

You may be asking why the rules for puzzle caches matter if you are only planning to *look* for a cache, not to place one. While knowing what the potential hiding places are probably won't be enough to solve the whole puzzle for you, it might help you narrow down some choices, and give you places to look.

There are two things about the rules at *geocaching.com* that you will want to keep in mind. First is that the final location of a puzzle cache is generally within 2 miles (or 3 kilometers) of the dummy coords. This rule was not always enforced for older caches; if a cache is from 2006 or earlier, it might be farther away. Local reviewers also have leeway in allowing some extra distance. If the CO has a compelling reason why they can't find a spot within 2 Miles, the reviewers might give them a pass. Areas with a high concentration of caches may also get a pass, since finding a spot to place the final may be difficult. Pay attention to the description and see if the CO mentions a distance between the final and the dummy coords, and adjust your calculations accordingly.

determining proximity

See Appendix 2 for some websites that will help you see what falls within the 2 miles surrounding a set of coordinates.

While a 2 Mile radius may not seem to narrow things down very much, it helps you know a couple things. Most importantly, it lets you know that the final coordinates are probably going to look very similar to the dummy coords because it won't be that far away. So if the north coordinates in your area generally start with 40° you can rest assured that your final puzzle solution will probably also start with 40°. (More on what goes into puzzle coordinates in the next section!)

Knowing that you probably won't go more than 2 miles (3.2 km) away, you may also be able to look at a map and see a park or forest that would be a prime location, and that gives you an even stronger idea what the final coordinates might look like. Programs like Google Earth allow you to draw lines and even circles measuring the distance around a cache, and there are several websites that will draw rings around given points on a map. Some even allow you to export that information to Google Earth.

Second, *geocaching.com* requires that the final, with its physical container, be subject to Geocaching's *528 Feet (or 161 meter) Rule* or the *Proximity Rule*. This rule states that it must be at least that far from any other physical cache in the area. Assuming that there isn't a physical object there, the dummy coords, are not subject to those proximity rules, but physical stages of a multicache *are* (at least in regards to other caches). So, if you used the 2 Mile Rule to narrow down your search area, knowing the 528 Feet Rule might help you narrow it even further, if there are other caches in the area. Keep in mind, though, that there might be other "hidden" waypoints that you aren't aware of: other puzzle finals or stages of multicaches.

Puzzle caches' immunity to the 528 Feet Rule has made them very popular in "Geo-Art," the creation of shapes or images on the caching map using cache icons. Since the initial coords for Puzzle caches can be placed basically anywhere, and the physical containers are found in other locations, it is easy to create Geo-Art using puzzle caches.

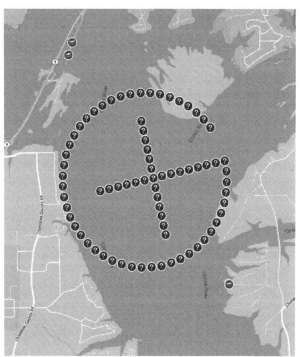

A Geo-Art in Alabama

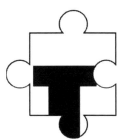

hen... the Page

When a CO builds the cache page at *geocaching.com*, there are a number of things that they have control over. The most obvious, of course, are the description, the main body of the cache page, and the name. These are certainly important. The description will contain the puzzle (usually), and the name might provide a clue (hopefully!). But there are many other areas that the CO also has control over, which might surprise you. These other areas allow COs to leave "breadcrumbs," a trail for you to follow to the puzzle, or even to the cache itself.

Starting at the top of the page we have the *"Placed By"* field (See A on Figure 2.2). Normally this is just the CO's name, but you might be surprised to know that they are free to enter anything they wish. It could be a variation on their own name that thematically links to the puzzle, as in the example. This CO usually caches under the name "mblatch," but in this case, going with the spy theme of the cache, he uses the name "Director mblatch." Or it could be anything! What would you think if the name here was "Alfred Vail?" A quick Internet search would tell you that Alfred Vail was instrumental in the invention of Morse Code! A clue! If you click on the name, you will be taken to the

Figure 2.2

profile of the CO, and will discover who truly placed the cache. Some cachers have even created whole new accounts to place a puzzle and leave hints in the profile for that user.

The next field that the cache owner has power over is the *"Date Hidden"* (See B on Figure 2.2). Although it defaults to the actual date, here again, COs have extreme power and can enter any date that they wish, as long as it is in the past. Does the date look unusual in any way? Is it very different from the publication date? Is it a famous date? A date of 4/12 for instance, might hint that the cache has something to do with the sinking of the Titanic. While it is possible to change the year as well, *geocaching.com* frowns on that as it alters cacher finder's statistics.

An often overlooked field is the *"Related Web Page"* (See C on Figure 2.2). *Geocaching.com* has removed this option for new cache creation, but prior to 2017 a CO can use it to place a link to a website. On the actual cache page, the link shows up just below the Terrain and Difficulty stars. There is just a blue hyper-link that says "Related Web Page." If the owner chose not to use this field, that area will simply be blank. If the puzzle you are looking at has one of these links, be *sure* to click it! The CO is going out of their way to tell you something about the cache. Related Web Pages are almost always clues, sometimes they are even

save the page

When a new cache gets published get into the habit of saving a copy of the cache page. Right click anywhere on the page and choose "Save As..." This saves the page as a file that you can open again later. If the CO changes anything on the page, you'll have your copy to check against and see what changed! There might be a clue to the puzzle in the changes.

links to the puzzle itself, that is being hosted elsewhere on the web.

With the invention and proliferation of Street View modes at on-line mapping services like Google Maps or Bing Maps, it has become very easy to look at the locations of coordinates to see what might be there. I suggest that you always have a look at the initial dummy coordinates in street view. Dummy coords (See D on Figure 2.2) might be nothing, but, of course, they might be everything. For instance, initial coords at a statue of someone famous, might suggest that they are involved in the puzzle somehow. Also note that just below the dummy coords are the UTM coordinates; this is another notation style (more on that in a moment!). I suggest visiting a website that converts coordinates (like *gpsvisualizer. com*) and looking at your local coords in several styles as the puzzle on the page might be written for a style other than the standard one that *geocaching.com* uses.

At the bottom of the page (just before the area for the logs) you'll find a space for *"Additional Waypoints."* Besides the possibility of physical objects being hidden at these different coordinates, other information could be found there. Have a look at the waypoints with a mapping program like Google Maps or Google Earth. Look for names of landmarks nearby, like businesses, streets or rivers. For instance, at N 32° 57.740' W -080° 08.227' you will find "Arithmetic Court." It might be a very useful hint to know that math is involved in the puzzle. Also look for shapes or images nearby. At N 48° 8.544', E 16° 57.464' you'll find a building shaped like the letter "P." With the whole Earth to search, an engineering CO could spell out anything or find almost any shape to incorporate into their puzzle.

Next, check to see if the CO added a background image. There is no currently no default background image at *geocaching.com*, so if you see an image (anything other than white) to the left and right of the cache description be sure to check it out. In Chrome you must either install a plug-in that allows you to view the background image separately or go through the source code to find the image (more on Source Codes in a few chapters). If you use Firefox and right-click on the area of the background, the menu that pops up will give you the choice to "View Background Image." Choosing that isolates the image so that you can view it without the rest of the cache page being in the way. Even if the background image looks white, take this step! Many clever puzzle COs have hidden a hint, or even the whole puzzle, by placing something in the background image.

white background

The default background at *geocaching.com*, is simply white. There is no associated file, the white is created through programming. If you view the background image and see a file linked, even though it is white, it could be an important part of the puzzle!

Also, check out the attributes (See E on Figure 2.2). These are there to tell you about any dangers you might face as a cacher: poisonous plants, thorns, or heavy muggle activity, or to tell you more information about the area: if there is water available, if camping is allowed, that sort of thing. But they can also be used as a clue. If the cache is named "Udderly Ridiculous," the initial coords point to a dairy, and the only attribute on the cache page is the "Livestock" attribute… what do these clues add up to in terms of the puzzle theme? The UV attribute indicates that you will use a black-light somewhere in the course of the cache, perhaps as part of a puzzle. Pay special attention to that puzzle-piece-shaped one. It indicates that there is a "Field Puzzle" to be solved, usually in the form of a Research Puzzle, as I discussed earlier.

Attributes

What are Attributes?

There is a second possibility for puzzles when it comes to attributes. When cache information is converted to GPX files, which is the file that your hand-held GPSr reads, the information on the cache page is also encoded in ways that look very differently than they do on the cache page. On the cache page, the attributes are represented by icons. But in a GPX file, the attribute icons are assigned numbers, rendering them in a way that is more understandable to the simpler processors in the GPSr. If the number is preceded by a minus mark, then it means that the attribute is not allowed or not present ("-32" would mean "No Bikes," for instance.)

With this knowledge, a CO could place an entirely black cache page, with nothing but the attributes at the side to act as the puzzle for the coordinates. The following attributes would give you coordinates for a famous location:

Consulting the chart on the previous page we see that these attributes give us the numbers 40, 41, 21, 74, 02, 40, and the coords 40° 41' 21", -74° 02' 40" or 40° 41.355, -074° 02.674.

A warning if you think you may be dealing with one of these puzzles, or you're considering placing a cache with this attribute style puzzle: These numbers are not widely known; it will take a pretty good deal of research to find them (if you don't have this book). You might be setting yourself up for a lot of repeated emails asking for hints, so beware! Groundspeak (the owners of *geocaching.com*) also changes the attributes on a fairly regular basis, and your puzzle might be inadvertently broken by a change outside your control.

For instance, Groundspeak recently altered the appearance of about 2 dozen of the attributes, simplifying some, removing color from all of them, etc. On the following pages are two charts of the attributes with the numbers indicated, one before the change and one after. The changed attributes are denoted with an asterisk. I don't think any of the changes were so dramatic as to break a puzzle, but you never know. The biggest change was "Kid-friendly," which went from a childish face to two figures, a child and an adult.

These changes are part of what makes this an unreliable puzzle route.

Next, take a look at the gallery for the cache, (See F on Figure 2.2). You can access that in two ways: one is by using the link I've indicated here. That method will show you not only all the images that the CO uploaded, but also all the images that people have placed in their logs. To see just what the CO put on the page look at the bottom of the description. Just before the logs, there will be a list of image links. The gallery allows the CO to upload images that could be used for the background, to entice the cacher to visit the area… or it could be a hint! You never know. If there is a picture in the Gallery that isn't used in the description, pay special attention to that one. Look for words or letters hidden in the background, or other hints.

We're almost done examining the cache page. The bookmark lists is another spot that the CO might be able to hide a puzzle. On the right of the cache page is a list of all the bookmark lists that contain the cache you are looking at. Check and see if any of those were created by the CO. Note that if the cache appears on more than 3 or 4 bookmark lists, they won't all appear on the cache page, you'll have to click through to see the full list. If the CO has created a list, you might want to look at the names of the other caches, the GC numbers, or even check the logs of the caches on that list to see if the CO of the puzzle you are trying to solve has logged those other caches. If they have logged them, check their logs. They could leave hints or images attached to those logs that might be relevant to the puzzle you are trying to solve.

Finally, have a look at the Trackables Inventory, (See G on Figure 2.2). The description of a Travel Bug, a Geocoin, or any other trackable can have a puzzle in it as surely as the cache page. Is there a trackable that has been in the cache since before it was published? Examine that one, especially.

another possibility

This same puzzle could be done using the attribute icons in the order that they appear on the page explaining them at *geocaching.com*, (*http://www.geocaching.com/about/icons.aspx*). Starting at the top you have dogs, bicycles, and motorcycles, so those would be 1, 2 and 3 respectively. Continue down the page in that manner.

Inventory

Rey Del Roble 2 Geocoin

View all Trackables
View past Trackables
What are Trackable Items?

Bookmark Lists

City Caches
by iandavid

I-95 Interstate Highway Challenge
by tiki-4

Active Caches Hidden in 2001 Volume 02
by ewenger

View all 6 bookmark lists…

	#	Attribute		#	Attribute
🐕	1	Dogs allowed		36	Snomobiles allowed
$	2	Access/parking fees		37	Horses allowed
	3	Climbing gear		38	Campfires allowed
	4	Boat required		39	Thorns!
	5	Scuba gear required		40	Stealth required
	6	Kid friendly		41	Stroller accessible
	7	Takes less than 1 hour		42	Needs maintenance
	8	Scenic view		43	Watch for livestock
	9	Significant hike		44	Flashlight required
	10	Difficult climbing		45	Lost and found (?)
	11	May require wading		46	Truck driver/rv accessible
	12	May require swimming		47	Is field puzzle
24/7	13	Available 24-7	UV	48	Uv light required
	14	Recommended at night		49	May require snowshoes
	15	Available in winter		50	Cross country skis required
	16	Unused		51	Special tool required
	17	Poison plants!		52	Night cache
	18	Dangerous animals!		53	Park and grab
	19	Ticks!		54	In abandoned structure
	20	Abandoned mine nearby	<1 KM	55	Hike shorter than 1km
	21	Cliffs/falling rocks nearby	<10 KM	56	Hike between 1km-10km
	22	Hunting area	>10 KM	57	Hike greater than 10km
	23	Dangerous area		58	Fuel nearby
	24	Wheelchair accessible		59	Food nearby
P	25	Parking available		60	Wireless beacon required
	26	Public transit available		61	Is a partnership cache
	27	Drinking water nearby		62	Seasonal access only
	28	Restrooms available		63	Recommended for tourists
	29	Telephone nearby		64	Tree climbing required
	30	Picnic tables available		65	In front yard (with permission)
	31	Camping available		66	Teamwork required
	32	Bikes allowed		67	Is part of a GeoTour
	33	Motorcycles allowed			
	34	Quads allowed			
	35	Off-road vehicles allowed			

	1	Dogs allowed		36	Snomobiles allowed
	2	Access/parking fees		37	Horses allowed
	3	Climbing gear		38	Campfires allowed
	4	Boat required		39	Thorns!
	5	Scuba gear required		40	Stealth required
	6	Kid friendly		41	Stroller accessible
	7	Takes less than 1 hour		42	Needs maintenance
	8	Scenic view		43	Watch for livestock
	9	Significant hike		44	Flashlight required
	10	Difficult climbing		45	Lost and found (?)
	11	May require wading		46	Truck driver/rv accessible
	12	May require swimming		47	Is field puzzle
	13	Available 24-7		48	Uv light required
	14	Recommended at night		49	May require snowshoes
	15	Available in winter		50	Cross country skis required
	16	Unused		51	Special tool required
	17	Poison plants!		52	Night cache
	18	Dangerous animals!		53	Park and grab
	19	Ticks!		54	In abandoned structure
	20	Abandoned mine nearby		55	Hike shorter than 1km
	21	Cliffs/falling rocks nearby		56	Hike between 1km-10km
	22	Hunting area		57	Hike greater than 10km
	23	Dangerous area		58	Fuel nearby
	24	Wheelchair accessible		59	Food nearby
	25	Parking available		60	Wireless beacon required
	26	Public transit available		61	Is a partnership cache
	27	Drinking water nearby		62	Seasonal access only
	28	Restrooms available		63	Recommended for tourists
	29	Telephone nearby		64	Tree climbing required
	30	Picnic tables available		65	In front yard (with permission)
	31	Camping available		66	Teamwork required
	32	Bikes allowed		67	Is part of a GeoTour
	33	Motorcycles allowed			
	34	Quads allowed			
	35	Off-road vehicles allowed			

Out of Control

In this chapter I focused on things that the CO can change on the page. But there are also a couple variables on the page that the CO can't change but still end up in puzzles from time to time.

The most obvious of those is the GC number. GC numbers are assigned when a cache is created, but the CO can get their GC number before publication.

even more?

For some less obvious ways to examine the cache page, see the next chapter!

GC numbers might be used as cipher keywords, as part of a formula on the page, or in other ways. See Chapter 11 for information on how to change the GC number into a standard decimal number mathematically, but the easiest method is there on the page: simply hover your cursor over the "Watch" link in the upper right, where you would click to add the cache to a watch list. After a few seconds, you'll get link that ends in "w=" followed by a number. That number is the decimal equivalent of the GC number.

If a CO uses a Travel Bug (or "TB") as part of their puzzle, the ID for the TB might come into play as well. This is a unique number, similar to the GC code, that gets assigned to each TB. If you click on any TB, you can see the number in two places: one is in the upper right of the page, the other is in the middle of the description for the TB where it says "Use XXXXXXX to refer to this item." Just like the GC code, hovering over the "Watch this item" on the upper right will get you a link that shows the decimal conversion of the TB code.

Finally, cachers themselves are also assigned unique numbers in the *geocaching.com* databases. On the cache page click on the CO's name. This will take you to their profile. On that page, towards the middle you'll see a link that says, "See the Forum Posts For This User." You'll get a link by hovering over that. The final numbers in that link, after "mid=" are the ID number for the cacher.

# hen Comes... Research

So, you've looked at all the things that a CO can change on the page, you've read through the description looking for Crossover Puzzles or Research Puzzles, but you still aren't sure what the puzzle is... what do you do next? The answer is almost always research. Remember, Google is your friend.

I can't really stress this enough: **GOOGLE IS YOUR FRIEND.**

But what exactly, you ask, are you supposed to be researching? Well... anything and everything. Start with anything that you don't recognize in the description. Are there words whose definitions you aren't sure of? Does the description mention any names you don't recognize? Places you are unfamiliar with? You can even search abstract things from the page that might eventually help. For instance, if you find a cache description that contains a seemingly random string of numbers and letters like "J 591.56 D" what would you be able to do with that? It might be a code. It might be a cipher. There are numbers in there, so it be part of the coordinates. Or it might be something else entirely... but if you don't research it, you will never know!

Word based searches

Let's take a closer look at that string of numbers and letters. Simply putting it into Google as J 591.56 D turns up a few things, but nothing that seems interesting at first. But did you know that there are ways to fine tune your search results to get something more useful?

By searching J 591.56 D you get over 2 MILLION results! But a very simple change will narrow that down significantly. By putting your search term in quotations, like this: "J 591.56 D" what you are telling Google is that you only want results that use those exact letters and numbers in exactly that order. Once you make that change you get just 6 results! That's a lot easier to look through, right? Looking at any of those 6 pages will quickly tell you that J 591.56 D is the Dewey Decimal call number for a book named "North." Well! That could certainly be the beginning of something, couldn't it?

There are several ways that simple changes in your search terms can help narrow down the returns. These are called "Search Operators." Some of my favorites are the minus sign, the tilde and the asterisk.

The minus sign tells Google to exclude something. Let's say that you want to research the word "Au." Au can mean many things. A quick google tells you that it is the abbreviation for Auburn University, Astronomical Units, *and* the chemical symbol for gold. That's a lot of things. But if you know offhand that you can eliminate Auburn University you can modify your search by adding a minus sign and the word "Auburn." Like this: **au -auburn**. That alters your search so that you get pages with "au," but NOT pages with the word "Auburn."

The tilde (this symbol: ~ , found left of the "1" on most keyboards) tells Google that you want not only the word you are searching, but also synonyms and related words. So **~sun** would return sun and solar, without you having to remember that solar is a connected word.

The most interesting by far though is the asterisk, sometimes known as the "wild-card" search. If your search term is "the bear went over the mountain" (include the quotation marks in your search), you will get pages with exactly that phrase, as I previously discussed. But if you search "the * went over the mountain" you will not only get the bear you'd expect, but any page with a variation on that phrase. Cows, beers, eagles, leopards, and even biochemists have all "gone over the mountain" and Google will show you that with a wild-card search.

Non-word based searches

Don't stop your research with just the words on the page, though. In the world of research, it is possible to search even the things that are *not* word based. With websites like *tineye.com* you can now search images on the web, and Google has also added that feature to their search engine. When you go to *google.com*, click "Images" at the top and you will get a new search window like the one at left, here. If you click the small camera icon inside the search box, you will get a new search window called "Search by Image."

In that search box you can enter the web address of an image. This should not be the full webpage that the image appears on, but just the URL, or web address, for the image only. To determine that, right click the image and choose "Open Image In New Tab." This will remove the rest of the webpage and show you only the image. Copy the URL from the tool bar at the top and paste that into the "Search by Image" search bar. Alternatively, you could download the image and upload it to the image search. (You'll have to use this method if

search operators
Search the phrase "search operators" to see other ways to modify your web searches, or to see how search engines other than Google allow you to modify searches!

you use Internet Explorer). Using Tin Eye is essentially the same process.

What will all this do for you? Magically, this type of search finds everywhere on the web that the image you have searched for appears, even if the image has been changed! This is the important thing. By comparing the image on the cache page to the versions of the image found elsewhere on the web, you may discover that the CO has added or altered the image. Someone who is good at Photoshop, or other image editing software, can change something in an image in ways that are completely undetectable to standard inspection, but you might be able to spot them if you compare the originals.

image issues

Not getting results with your image search? Try downloading the image, flipping it in an editing program, saving the new file and trying again. Some COs have learned this trick as a way to flummox image search engines, and to make the puzzles trickier!

Seeing the other web-pages that an image appears on will also tell you something about the image, even if it wasn't altered. For instance, if the cache revolves around identifying types of cars, finding the image online might help you more rapidly determine if the car in question is a '77 or '78 Mustang.

Another trick is to let your cursor sit on top of any images on a cache page for just a moment. This is called "hovering." When you hover a cursor over an image, sometimes a small message will pop up, this is called "alt text," and it could contain hints, or the puzzle!

Images can also act as web links, so click on the image to see if it takes you to another page. Of course, it may not be the whole image. It may be only a portion of the image that acts as a link. Move the cursor back and forth over the image to see if it changes, and if it does click there!

search types

Regardless of whether you search by word or by image, check the other search type before clicking away. Something may pop up in one that wasn't easily visible in the other.

If you have images on the page that you just don't know what to do with, have a look at Chapters 12 and 13 for more ways that images can be used in puzzle caches!

And then... an answer?

You've examined the cache page… you've done your research… but what else is there? How will you know when you… you know… have solved it? What does an answer *LOOK* like?

A lot of times solving a puzzle cache feels like trying to solve a jigsaw puzzle without having the picture from the box! But even if you don't know exactly what you are solving for, you have some clues. The biggest clue is that the answer to most (not all, but most) puzzle caches will be a set of coordinates. This is a geocache after all! There is an unwritten rule at *geocaching.com* that all geocaches must contain a "GPS element." In other words, coordinates and the use of a GPS receiver *must* come into play at some point in the cache. This is why the answer to a puzzle cache is almost always based on coordinates.

That helps you in a lot of ways. Most importantly you'll want to be on the look out for certain words or phrases: coordinate, north, west, waypoint, or cache are all words that might be part of the answer. And of course, numbers! After all, you can't have coordinates without numbers.

As geocachers, we use coordinates constantly, but how many of us really know what they mean? We all know longitude and latitude, the imaginary lines that crisscross the globe, marking off "degrees." The first set of numbers in a coordinate are referred to as the latitude, sometimes referred to as the "northing." The latitude lines themselves run E/W on the globe, but the number indicates how far north or south (from 0 to 90 degrees) you are from the equator, the line that runs around the center of the globe. The second set is referred to as the longitude, or "easting." These lines run N/S on the globe, and the number tells you how far east or west (from 0 to 180 degrees) you are from the Prime Meridian, which is an arbitrarily chosen line on the globe that runs through Greenwich England. The Prime Meridian acts as the zero point.

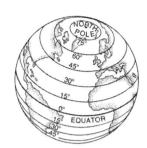

Latitude

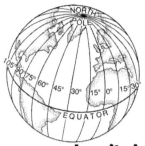

Longitude

To understand how coordinates are written, think of them as being similar to clocks. You can write a time as 12:30:45, stating the hour, minutes and seconds, which in this case would mean 30 minutes and 45 seconds past 12.

Coordinates are also expressed in three parts, starting with the largest component: degrees. A degree is treated like an hour, and like hours, the two smaller components of a degree are also called "minutes" and "seconds." Also like hours, 60 minutes make up a degree, and 60 seconds make up a minute.

When written out, degrees are followed by a degree symbol, just like degrees in temperatures. Minutes are followed by an apostrophe. Seconds are followed by a quotation mark.

N 50° 32' 12.00"
Degrees, Minutes, Seconds

A coordinate expressed as N 50° 32' 12.00" would indicate a location 32 minutes and 12 seconds north of 50°. The seconds may have a decimal place, but if they don't the CO may choose to just end with "12."

N 50° 32.200'
Degrees, Decimal Minutes

Back to our clock analogy, 12:30:45 could also be written as 12:30.750. This method combines the seconds into the minutes, and expresses them as a decimal. This is the way *geocaching.com* displays their coordinates and is known as "Decimal Minutes." Coordinates are written as XX° XX.XXX'.

N 50.53667°
Decimal Degrees

But there's one more way to do it! Just like Decimal Minutes eliminated the seconds, you can also eliminate the minutes and express those as a decimal portion of the hour. In this method, our time of 12:30:45 would be displayed as 12.575. Coordinates can also be written this way: XX.XXXX°. This method is known as "Decimal Degrees," and the number of places behind the decimal could be as many as seven, or as few as one!

If you want to see what your local coords look like in any of these other notation systems go to a website like *gpsvisualizer.com* and convert the coordinates. This will show you several different styles, so that you can become familiar with what numbers might be used in a puzzle in your area.

You will also want to look out for coordinates written in UTM. UTM, or Universal Trans Mercator, is an alternate form of coordinate grid developed by the US Army Corps of Engineers. You can look up the details of how it is different if you are interested, but for

negative associations

If you follow the convention that coordinates in the northern and eastern hemispheres are positive and coordinates in the southern and western hemisphere are written with a minus sign in front of them you can leave off the letter than denotes the direction (N, S, E or W) and still be understood.

			HP			
		HT	HU			
	HW	HX	HY	HZ		
NA	NB	NC	ND			
NF	NG	NH	NJ	NK		
NL	NM	NN	NO			
	NR	NS	NT	NU		
	NW	NX	NY	NZ	OV	
		SC	SD	SE	TA	
		SH	SJ	SK	TF	TG
	SM	SN	SO	SP	TL	TM
	SR	SS	ST	SU	TQ	TR
SV	SW	SX	SY	SZ	TV	

puzzle solving purposes, just know that besides the coordinates, a UTM style coordinate must designate a "Zone," so a UTM coordinate has 3 parts: the Zone, the easting, and the northing. The Zone is listed first and is a two digit number followed by a letter. In the continental US, it is a number between 10 and 19, and will be followed by the letter T. Some COs might omit the Zone, since it is unlikely that a cache will be far enough away to be in a new zone, so you might be solving only for the northing and easting.

Another method of writing coordinates is the "British Grid." This system was developed in the 1930's by the British Ordinance Survey, who devised a grid system that overlays England (Ireland has a separate grid). Coordinates are written one of two ways, using a pair of letters that reference the position of the grid, followed by two five digit numbers or by a pair of six digit numbers. The easting comes first in this system, followed by the northing. This system is more accurate for positioning in Great Britain because it references only the immediate area, and not the whole Earth. The distorted shape of the Earth means that long range measurements can become inaccurate, but shorter range ones are stronger. Several other countries have their own Grid system. If you are in North America, the first set of digits (the easting) will be preceded by a minus sign.

There are many websites online that will convert your coordinates between formats, so if you get an answer that feels right based on the puzzle but doesn't look like what you expected, try converting your answer to another format!

Geohashes

In the internet age a few other systems of writing coordinates have arisen. First was a system called "Geohash." Geohash has been embraced by several puzzlers. This system was invented by Gustavo Niemeyer and published at the website *geohash.org*. Geohash takes the standard latitude and longitude and puts them together into a single code created using an algorithmic hash, which is a fancy way of saying that it is encoded using a set system of transformations. For instance the coordinates N 36° 42.335, W 100° 56.235, which point to a place in the Oklahoma panhandle would be expressed as 9y80z459x8e7 by the Geohash.

coordinate conversion

See Appendix 2 for some websites that will help you convert coordinates between notation styles.

One of the useful things about Geohash is that the precision can be manipulated. For instance the example given above could have several letters knocked off the end, and be written just as "9y." That hash would point at the position N 37° 00.000, W 96° 00.000, which is a few hundred miles away. "9y80" brings us to N 37°0.000, W 101° 0.000. "9y80z4" brings us to N 36°42.600, W 100° 54.000... etc. etc. until the full hash takes you to the precise location.

This type of coordinate system could be used in a multicache puzzle to slowly move you, with more and more precision, closer to the correct location by giving you a few pieces of the coordinate at a time.

What 3 Words

Another immensely popular coordinate system in the puzzle world is the "What 3 Words" system. This one is interesting because it does not use numbers, but instead uses words. Creators Chris Sheldrack, Jack Waley-Cohen and Mohan Ganesalingam created a system that divided the surface of the earth into a grid of 3 meter by 3 meter squares. Each square was assigned three common English words that act as a unique identifier for that grid position. This system is great for puzzles because it allows for puzzles that are word based, rather than number based, but still eventually use a GPS. The website *what3words.com* can show you the words used for any particular grid square, as well as converting the words to standard GPS coordinates.

At *map.what3words.com* you can see a map with a red pin in the center. Drag the map to change the location. In the red bar at the bottom you can see the three words associated with the grid underneath the pin. Tap the red bar and choose "Share Pin Location," then "GPS" to get the coordinates.

The website *geocachingtoolbox.com* will also convert What 3 Words coordinates into standard GPS coordinates.

joined • transmitted • image

W3W style coordinates for the main branch of the Public Library in New York City, NY

Plus Codes

Recently, Google has gotten into the coordinate game and created a system that they call "Plus Codes." These codes combine the concept of Geohashes and What 3 Words. They consist of short string of random characters, up to 11 digits long. It includes a plus sign after the 8th character.

The first four characters are what they call the "area code," a square 100 Kilometers (about 62 miles) on each side.

The next six characters (four before the + sign, and two after), are the "local code," a square 14 meters on a side, (about 45 feet). They describe this area as being about half the size of a basketball court.

You can add one more character to get the area of the code down to 3 x 3 meters, the same area as What 3 Words.

Plus codes are, of course, easily recognizable by the plus sign that is incorporated into the coordinates. When you search a set of coordinates at Google the resulting map automatically displays the plus code for that location.

To convert a plus code to coords go to *plus.codes* and enter the plus code in the search bar (towards the bottom of the page.) On the resulting map you will see a small white bar at the bottom of the map with an UP arrow on the left side.

87C4VWQX+PWG

Plus Code style coordinates for the Lincoln Memorial in Washington, DC

Click that arrow and you will get a screen that looks like the image to the left here, which includes the coordinates in Decimal Degrees format.

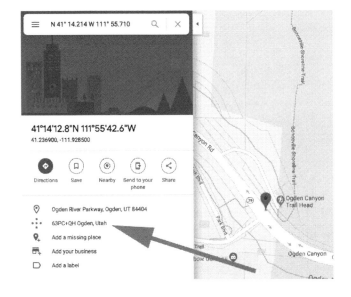

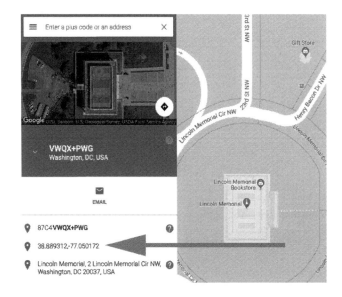

The 2 Mile Rule

Remember the 2 Mile Rule that we discussed earlier? The rule at *geocaching.com* that says that the final of a puzzle cache is usually within 2 miles (3.2 km) of the initial dummy coords? Knowing that the answer will most likely be coords also combines with the 2 Mile Rule to give you two more pieces of information about what you are solving for. As well as providing a lever for checking your final answer. How do those things combine? Well...

You are already probably familiar with your home coords, or the most frequently used coords in your area. If you are a cacher in Phoenix, Arizona, for instance, you will know that the north coords usually start with 33. The distance between two full degrees of latitude is approximately 69 miles (111 kilometers), well more than the 2 miles allowed. So unless the minutes in your dummy coords are either 59 or 00, your final degrees will be the same as your dummy coord degrees. In Phoenix, you automatically know that your answer will probably start with a 3, or a 33, or the words "three" or "thirty." Suddenly the image on the jigsaw puzzle box is a lot clearer!

The distance between minutes is just a touch more than a mile (just under two kilometers), so, if your dummy coords were 33 degrees 45 minutes, your final minutes would have to be somewhere between 43 and 47 minutes in order to stay within the 2 Mile Rule.

Like the north coords, the west coords of the final will look very similar to the dummy coords. Sticking with our example of Phoenix, Arizona, the west coords are very close to a line, and so they will start with either 111 or 112. But longitudinal lines differ from latitude, in that they are not parallel. The distance between them changes as you go north or south because they curve to meet at the poles. A degree of longitude is widest at the equator at approximately 69 miles (111 km) and gradually shrinks to zero at the poles. At 40° north or south, the distance between a degree of longitude is 53 miles (85 km). Again, unless the minutes in your dummy coords are either 59 or 00, it is unlikely that the degrees for your final will be different from the degrees in the dummy coords.

Your second advantage is knowing that the answer will be a certain length. In the western half of the United States, coordinates that are written in the standard format that *geocaching.com* uses (XX° XX.XXX') require 7 digits for the north and 8 digits for the west, 15 digits for an entire coordinate. In the eastern half of the US, the west coords will start with a zero. Some puzzles omit that zero, so you would only need 14 digits. If you are caching in Tennessee and the puzzle you are trying to solve includes 14 photographs, it is very reasonable to assume that each photograph will equal one digit of the coords, at least as a place to start!

But what if you don't see 14 or 15 things on a page?

50° 50.500

7 ITEMS
5 ITEMS
3 ITEMS
2 ITEMS

Don't get scared! COs know these tricks too, and they've come up with all sorts of ways to disguise those coords, and to make their caches a little bit trickier. The most obvious is that the coordinates are in a different notation style, using degrees, minutes and seconds, or decimal degrees rather than decimal minutes, or using UTM or British Grid or some other style.

If there is a place in the coordinates where a zero would be considered "obvious," such in the coordinates 41° 05.876 -111 55.600 a CO may omit those zeros and deliver those coordinates as 41° 5.876 -111 55.6. The zeros are not considered necessary for the coordinates as they can be easily guessed. Zeros are often difficult to include in a puzzle, which makes this a good shortcut for puzzle writers.

Another trick that COs might employ is to make the answer only part of the coordinates. As we discussed, the degree portion of the coordinates will probably be the same as the ones you are used to, so some COs will simply leave those out and only ask you to solve for the minutes and seconds. In that case you might be looking for 10 items on the page, rather than 14. Some COs will even warn you that they are doing this, telling you that you can "assume the degrees" or "assume the degrees and minutes."

Of course, the puzzle may not resolve to single digits. Rather than getting a 5 and a 0 you might instead get 50. Then you might get objects in a group of 6, or even 4. If you have groups of things on a cache page... photographs, icons, or words... consider how those groupings might be used to represent different coordinate notation styles.

The final thing that the 2 Mile Rule does for you is to help narrow down an answer. In solving some puzzles you might find yourself having solved everything except one or two numbers. If that's the case, start looking at the possible answers in a mapping program, preferably one with satellite view. If one possible combination lands you on the roof of a shopping center, you can most likely mark that off the list. Compare the possible locations with the hint as well. Does the hint mention a tree, but the coords land in the middle of a field? Probably not correct then. While this type of guessing is probably not what the CO was hoping for in terms of a solve, it can help you get past those really tricky nuts that just refuse to crack!

partial coords

The website *geocachingtoolbox. com* has a mapping tool that allows you to put in coordinates with up to three wildcards for unknown numbers. It will then show you a map of all the possible locations that would fit the coords!

One final note about the 2 Mile Rule: It wasn't always in place. Many older caches, especially those published prior to about 2007 or 2006 (depending on the whims of the local reviewer, of course), may not have been held to this rule, so if you are looking at an older cache and your coordinates are taking you more than 2 miles away... you may still have the right answer! Enforcement is also left to the discretion of the reviewer. Sometimes in a highly saturated area, or in special circumstances, reviewers might loosen the 2 mile radius a bit to help COs with placement. This is especially true in a piece of "geoart" where there may be high numbers of cache finals fighting for a placement.

Geocheckers

Many COs provide what are known as "geocheckers" on cache pages. Prior to 2017 COs had to use third party websites to provide Geocheckers, however *geocaching.com* now incorporates that option directly into their cache listings.

Geocheckers allow you to enter the answer to a puzzle, and find out immediately if it is correct or not. This way, you know for certain if you have the answer before you head out into the field.

Check your coordinates

(You have made 0 attempts in the last 10 minutes)

Cache Name: **GeoCheck Trial Cache**

GC Code: **GC0000**

Coordinate: ⦿N ○S [ ]° [ ]. [ ] ⦿W ○E [ ]° [ ]. [ ] [1 field]

Enter this code: 0 1 7 6 7 [ ] (5 numbers)

[Check]

If the CO has used a third party website there will be a link or a button that will take you to a webpage similar to the one above (from *geochecker.com*), where you enter the coordinates of your solution. If the CO has used the native checker at geocaching.com you will find a box similar to the one on the next page. The great thing about the built in solution

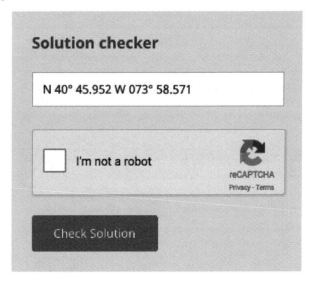

checker at geocaching.com is that when you get the solution correct it will automatically correct the coordinates for the cache and move the icon on the map both at the website and on the app. (For more about what that means see Chapter 18: After the Solve!)

One thing that COs may not realize is that the very presence of a geochecker provides you with a clue. The geochecker at *geocaching.com* can only accept coordinates as an answer; therefore, the answer to the puzzle must be in coordinates. However, some checkers, like Certitude, allow for an answer that is a word or phrase. If the puzzle has a checker on it, click to see what the checker is asking for in terms of the answer before you tackle the puzzle. No point in trying to get coordinates as an answer, if the correct answer is a phrase! If you see a third-party geochecker on a cache page it is advisable to click through first to see what form the answer should be in (numbers or a keyword) before you even start looking at a puzzle.

Another piece of info that the CO sometimes gives away with a geochecker is the relative difficulty. Some third-party checkers (such as the one from *certitudes.org* at left) show you how many people have checked their answers, and how many were right or wrong. Some even allow users to create accounts so that their name will appear in a list of correct answers on the checker page. With this information you can start to get a little information about the difficulty of the puzzle. If there are lots of wrong answers, and relatively few correct answers, the puzzle may be very difficult, or the answer may be ambiguous in some way, meaning that solvers have had to make several guesses before getting the correct answer. Which brings me to my next piece of advice...

If the CO has provided a geochecker, don't be shy about using it. If you are close, but you simply can't tease out those last numbers pound at the geochecker, and enter every possible combination. But be aware that some checkers will lock you out after a certain number of tries, or will make you wait a specific amount of time in between tries. The checker at *geocaching.com* for instance, allows you to try 10 sets of coordinates in 10 minutes before it locks you out for a while.

Geocheckers can also be set for "firm coords" or "soft coords." A firm coord solution will only accept the **exact** numbers that the CO initially entered. Soft coords allows a few feet of leeway, up to several yards. Puzzles that use math, or require you to base something off of a coordinate you measure yourself, will probably have soft coords to allow for variation in the answer. Note that the solution checker at *geocaching.com* does not currently allow for "soft" coords, so any answer you try there must be exact.

On third-party checkers, once you get a green light on the geochecker, don't just click away! Responses at most of the third-party geocheckers are customizable. Many COs put hints for the hide, spoiler photos, or exact coords in the responses, so be sure to read everything that comes back on the geochecker after you enter your coords. There could be valuable information on that screen! This option isn't available on *geocaching.com's* version.

CO's can also use checkers in tricky ways. They may write the puzzle to give you an answer that is on another continent, or in another state. This eliminates the advantage you have from knowing how local coords start. When you enter the false, faraway coordinates at the geochecker, you get the correct coordinates in the response. Again, this option isn't available on *geocaching.com's* version.

Links to third-party geocheckers are (usually) visible in the cache description on the app, but if the CO has used *geocaching.com's* native checker you will not know that unless you visit the webpage. Their checker is not visible within the app.

If you are new to puzzles I suggest making the first few you try ones that includes checkers. It will give you the certainty of knowing that you did the work correctly, and there is something satisfying about getting that "Success!" page to pop up!

Checksums

Some COs may provide an "old school" method of checking your answers which is known as a "checksum." Checksums are exactly what they sound like, a "sum" that "checks" the answers. The CO will provide you with a number. If you add the digits of your coords together and have the correct answer, they should equal that number. So, if your answer is 40° 38.667, you would add 4+0+3+8+6+6+7, or 34. Some COs will take it one step further and have you continue to add the digits of your answer until you arrive at a single digit. So in our example you would also add the 3 and 4 to get a final checksum of 7. This is called a "reduced checksum."

This process could also be called a "digital root," or a "digital sum."

Checksums can also be calculated using words. Using the A=1, B=2, C=3 etc substitution that I discussed earlier you can find the digital root of words. The website *geocachingtoolbox.com* has a tool in their "Text Functions" section that will do that work for you.

Solving it

Bringing together what you've learned.

Use this checklist to help you remember what items to examine when you first look at a puzzle. A simple, systematic approach, following the same steps every time you see a puzzle, will help you get over any anxiety you might feel about that "Big Blue Question Mark."

Checklist: GETTING STARTED

- [ ] Analyze the cache name.

- [ ] Check the Date Placed.

- [ ] Check the name in the "Placed By" section, including clicking through to see the profile.

- [ ] Check for Related Websites.

- [ ] Check the background image.

- [ ] Look at the Dummy Coords in "streetview."

- [ ] Examine the Additional Waypoints.

- [ ] Research any unfamiliar words or phrases in the description.

- [ ] Look at the Gallery.

- [ ] Examine the Trackables Inventory.

- [ ] Examine the Bookmark lists.

- [ ] Research the images on the page.

- [ ] Check for groups of things (14 photographs, 10 words, etc.).

- [ ] Click the geochecker to see what format the answer is in (coords or words).

 # alk-Through

Alrighty then! Time for some practice. As will be the pattern for the rest of the book, we'll start with a "walk-through." I'll show you a puzzle of the style discussed in the chapter, and then describe to you how to approach solving it. Remember, there is nothing at these locations. Here's the first one:

FIND A CACHE

 ## Fractional Advances

FC329MC

A cache by: DD MM.SS +/-   Hidden: 11/12/2018

Difficulty: ★★☆☆☆   Size: ▪■▪■■

Terrain: ★★★★★

N 37° 44.360 W 119° 32.421

In Yosemite, California, USA

🏅 **11 FAVORITES**

The cache is NOT at the listed coordinates.
You must determine the actual coordinates by solving the puzzle below.

Finding the coords for this cache should be fairly straight forward. I'll give you the exact instructions!

Step 1: Express the fraction as a decimal.

Step 2: Discard the whole digits, keep the ones after the decimal.

Step 3: Add what remains to the North coords.

Step 4: The subtract it from teh West coords.

Step 5: Go find teh cache!

Like I said, easy, right? Hmmmm... I feel like I've forgotten to tell you something...

Attributes:

 24/7

1   **Where to begin?** Examining the page we can see a couple things. The name of the cache is "Fractional Advances." Cache names aren't *always* a hint. COs might be making an inside joke, it might be a reference to the location, or it might just mean nothing at all. But let's hold onto that information for the moment.

2   **Now look at the rest of the info.** The "Hidden" date doesn't seem at all out of order. So probably nothing there. There is no "Related Web Page." The "Placed By" name might be a little fishy. DD MM.SSS is a reference to a method of writing coordinates, "Decimal Minutes," which is the method that *geocaching.com* uses on the cache pages. By itself it could be a name, but that "+/-" at the end seems off, I can't imagine many people using that in their name. So I'd click on that to see the cacher's profile. (A bit difficult to do in a book, but we'll pretend!) Aha! Turns out that the cache was actually placed by someone named *CacheMasterG*! So "DD MM.SSS +/-" becomes our first confirmed clue, and our second possible clue.

3   **The dummy coords are in the middle of a forest.** Probably no clues there. Nothing in the gallery, no TBs present. By selecting everything on the page I see that there is no hidden white text. (More on what I mean by that in Chapter 3!) That just leaves the description.

4   **The CO tells us in the description that the puzzle is straightforward.** He even gives us a list of instructions. The first item on the instruction list is to "Express the fraction as a decimal." Aha! Thinking back to the title, this confirms that the puzzle has *something* to do with fractions, so we now have two confirmed clues on the page.

5   **Let's examine the rest of the instructions.** Well, the CO told the truth. It does seem pretty straightforward. The problem is, he keeps referencing a fraction... and there is no fraction in the instructions! That's probably what he is referencing in the last sentence of the description when he says, "I feel like I've forgotten to tell you something..." He forgot to tell us the fraction!

6   **There has to be some extra information here somewhere.** This is the point where I'd usually look at the source code for the page, but there's nothing there that's out of the ordinary (More about that in Chapter 3). I suppose you could interpret the date as fractions, either 11/12 or 12/2011, but neither of those fractions reduce, so I couldn't follow the rest of the instructions. Then I spot it! The only attribute on the page is "24/7," meaning that the cache is available at any time of the day or night, every day. But 24/7 looks a lot like a fraction, doesn't it?

7   **Converting to a decimal.** Following the instructions we express 24/7 as a decimal and get 3.4285714. Step 3 says to discard the whole digits, that's 3, so we're left with .4285714. Then we're left with the math. This is where the hint from the cacher name comes in. As I've discussed there are several notation methods for coords, but the CO has been kind enough to give us confirmation that we should be using Decimal Minutes.

8   **A tiny bit of math later, and we have coords!** Adding to the north coords gives us 37° 44.7885714, and subtracting from the west leaves us with 119° 31.9924586. We can comfortably round those numbers off, which leaves us with N 37° 44.789, W 119° 31.992 as the final coords. Checking Google Maps shows us a thematically appropriate location for the final. [Remember, none of the cache locations in this book lead to real caches, but I have tried to choose interesting or thematic locations for each of the finals.]

Not bad, right? On the next page is another puzzle, for you to solve on your own this time. Good luck!

# olve It Yourself!

Here are some puzzle caches for you to solve on your own. Using the skills we learned in this chapter you should be able to solve these puzzles. Take careful note of the final coordinates that you get as a solution to these puzzles, and write them at the bottom of the page. If you need a reminder of how to use the puzzle stats or hints provided, please check page 11. Good luck!

Puzzle 1 Solution:

N __ __ ° __ __ . __ __ __ , W __ __ __ ° __ __ . __ __ __
As a secondary check you should be able to answer this question: *What equipment do you find at the final?*

Puzzle 2 Solution:

S __ __ ° __ __ . __ __ __ , E __ __ __ ° __ __ . __ __ __
As a secondary check you should be able to answer this question: *What animal do you find at the final?*

FIND A CACHE

 What a View!!

A cache by: kramerNY   Hidden: 11/11/2011

Difficulty:
Terrain:
Size:

FCF0CU5

LOG YOUR VISIT

- View Gallery
- Watch
- Bookmark
- Ignore

N 33° 59.568 W 118° 28.844
In Santa Monica, California, USA

12 FAVORITES

The cache is NOT at the listed coordinates.
You must determine the actual coordinates by solving the puzzle below.

Take your time and look around! The birds know what's up!

Cache can be found at 33° 59.ABC, -118° 28.DEF

Additional Waypoints

NAME	COORDINATE
A	N 53° 28.069 W 002 16.886
B	N 26° 06.275 W 080° 18.485
C	N 45° 01.234 W 093° 27.134
D	N 33° 50.994 W 084° 25.956
E	N 48° 13.026 E 011° 36.276
F	N 44° 57.468 W 093° 16.307

Attributes:

PUZZLE STATS

64 CHECKSUM   BEST VIEW

122   46   3

29   72

FIND A CACHE

What Wat Whut?

FCBRB4Y

A cache by: Olympia Mad   Hidden: 03/15/2017

Difficulty: ★★☆☆☆   Size: ■■■□□
Terrain: ★☆☆☆☆

S 06° 34.523 E 110° 37.699
In Central Java, Indonesia

18 FAVORITES

LOG YOUR VISIT

View Gallery
Watch
Bookmark
Ignore

The cache is NOT at the listed coordinates.
You must determine the actual coordinates by solving the puzzle below.

RISE &

_ _ _ _ _

Pulau Panjang

Attributes:

 **PUZZLE STATS**
47 CHECKSUM   BEST VIEW

 105   64   16
81   113

The Hidden World

So, we've learned how to look at a puzzle cache page, and we've learned some of the math and orienteering tricks that COs can use to create puzzles... now, let's start looking at some actual *puzzles,* shall we? One favorite puzzle type, and a very simple one once you know where to look, is the "Hidden Puzzle."

This puzzle type exists almost entirely in the description and is the equivalent of an "in plain sight" hide in traditionals. The puzzle solution is simply hidden somewhere within the cache description, like a game of "Hide and Seek."

Since 1844, when Edgar Allan Poe first published "The Purloined Letter," everyone has known that the best place to hide something is out in the open, right where everyone will already be looking. But since they won't anticipate that what they are looking for is right in front of their faces, most people simply... overlook it. This is especially true when you are concentrating on something else.

This chapter we'll look at ways that COs can hide puzzles "in plain sight" on the cache page, and ways for you to uncover those hidden puzzles.

You're looking right at it!

What does it mean when I say that the puzzle can be hidden in plain sight? Have a look at these sentences:

No orangutan reads the headlines. Chimpanzees open only respectable detective stories.

Notice anything? Look at it again, but pay attention to the first letters of the words:

No Orangutan Reads The Headlines. Chimpanzees Open Only Respectable Detective Stories.

N.O.R.T.H. C.O.O.R.D.S. Hidden right there in the words all along! This method of hiding the solution in plain sight can be accomplished in many ways. The first letter of each word is straightforward and can be spotted easily. But the CO can just as easily hide it using the second letter of each word, or the fifth. But in those cases there would probably be a clue somewhere else on the page that would tell you which letter to pay attention to.

the world's most famous acrostic

In Greek the fist letters of the acclamation "JESUS CHRIST, SON OF GOD, SAVIOUR" spell the word "ICHTHYS," which is Greek for fish.

This is why some Christians use a fish symbol to represent their faith. They are using an acrostic puzzle, and most probably don't even realize it!

This method of hiding information is called an "acrostic." The giveaway with acrostics is usually the awkward way that the sentence is written. It is actually quite difficult to construct sentences when the letters you can use limit your available words.

Let's look at another one:

Due to the hours of the park, please do not search for this cache after dark. East Avenue is the best way to enter the park.

120 acres of park land await your pleasure. Yards along the entrance drive are also stunning to view, with lots of great landscaping.

See it yet? At first that paragraph looks like a simple description of a park where the cache might be hidden, but look at the first word of each sentence. "Due East 120 Yards." This solution isn't coordinates, per se, but if you travel due east from the starting waypoints for 120 yards… I bet you'd find a cache. Note: The exact coordinates can be found using Waypoint Projection, which is discussed in detail in Chapter 5.

not spelling anything?

Rather than an acrostic word, you might be dealing with a substitution. If the first letter is an 'C', it might equal 3. See Chapter 6 for more info on that possibility!

There are many methods that could be used to hide solutions this way. Look at this one:

We the people *of* the United States, *in* order to form a more per*f*ect union, establish jus*t*ice, insure domestic tranquilit*y*, provide for the common defen*s*e, promote the general welfare, and secure the blessings of lib*e*rty to ourselves and our posterity, do ordain and *e*stablish this Constitutio*n* for the United States of America.

As you can see, any text can be used for this method of hiding a message. Have you spotted the one hidden here?

Look closely. You'll see that some letters are in a different font and are italicized. If you look over the whole text, using only the italicized letters, you'll find the words "Fifty seven." Italicized letters inside normal text, letters in slightly different fonts, or different colors could all be used in this way.

To go a little deeper it is even possible to hide, invisible to the cacher, a whole message on a cache page. With this method you could stare at the cache page for days and never see the message. How? By changing the font color to white! The text will be there, but invisible because the background is also white. One of the first things I do whenever I visit a puzzle cache page is to select all the text on the page. This can be done by clicking the mouse and dragging the cursor over the text, or by going to the Edit menu in the tool bar and choosing "Select All." Selecting all the text on the page puts a highlight over it and reveals every word, even that pesky invisible stuff. While it is selected there will be a colored bar over it, and suddenly that white text is no longer invisible. Another puzzle cache solved.

Thinking Outside The Cache Page

Just like the characters in the film *The Matrix*, when you look at a web page, you think you are looking at reality, but you are actually looking at something that is being created by your web browser reading a piece of computer programming. COs with the know-how can hide information inside that computer programming, information that your browser won't show you. But just like Neo, you have the ability to see the Matrix, and manipulate it!

The programming that tells your computer what to display on a website is called the "Source Code," and there are a couple ways to get a peek at it.

Go to your web browser (Firefox, Explorer, Safari, Chrome, etc.) and open a cache page. In most browsers, if you right click on a website, you get a menu that includes "View Source Code" or "Show Page Source." If you are using Safari and have never done this before, you will first need to activate the "Develop" menu. To do that, click on "Safari" in the top menu bar, then go to "Preferences." In that pop up menu, click the "Advanced" tab and then click the check box next to "Show Develop." Then you should be able to right click on a page and select "View Page Source."

All browsers allow you to view page sources, but each one handles it differently. Some give you that access through the tool bar menu, but choosing to view the page source will open a new window that shows you the website the way your browser sees it, rather than the translation that it creates for you to see.

If you don't know HTML, (the language that web pages are

another possibility
If you are seeing randomly italicized or bolded letters but they aren't adding up to words you might be dealing with a Baconian Cipher. Check Chapter 9 for help with dealing with that.

select all
You can also select all the text on a cache page by hitting "Command A" on a Mac or "Control A" on a PC.

Command is the key directly to the left of the space bar on a Mac. And Control is usually three keys to the left of the space bar on a PC.

These are called "keyboard shortcuts, and can come in very handy.

another shortcut
"Command U" on a Mac or "Control U" on a PC is the keyboard shortcut to view the page source.

written in) this will seem intimidating at first, but there are really just a few things that you are looking for.

In most browsers, you'll see numbers on the left. They'll start with 1 and going up to 2000 or so, depending on how much information is on the cache page. Pages with extra long descriptions, or lots of photos, will be longer. Those numbers are the "line numbers," and you can use them as a guide.

```
598        </div>
599
600        <br />
601        <div class="UserSuppliedContent">
602
603            <span id="ct100_ContentBody_LongDescription"><p><font color="#365F91">The
604 <p><font color="#76923C">This set of caches are maintained by the <a href="http://www
605 <p><font color="#E36C0A">About the art. This art has been placed in partnership with
606 <p><font color="#5F497A">Please be aware of your surroundings and take plenty of food
607
608        </div>
609
610        <p>
611
612
613        </p>
614        <p id="ct100_ContentBody_hints">
615            <strong>
```

3.1 An example of Source Code, from GC3FA3B

Line numbers will vary from browser to browser, but soon you'll learn which line numbers correspond to the area you need. In Firefox you'll want to scroll down to the 600's; in Safari, the 500's; in Chrome, the 600's; and in Explorer, the 550's. This isn't exact, and it will change depending on the cache page, but generally you'll want to start in that area. I'll warn you again that everything I am referring to here is only true at *geocaching.com*. Viewing the source code at other listing services will look different.

When you start looking at the source, you will notice lots of words, or letters in between carats, (this symbol: **<**) sometimes with slashes before them. They will look like this:

</body>

Those are called "HTML tags" and are the "bones" of the HTML language. In the same way that punctuation, and words or letters form sentences, tags come together to form the basic building blocks of HTML. Tags are the things that tell your browser what to do with the text that you enter when you create a cache page. For instance **<strong>** means that your browser should display the text in bold. A tag with no slash in it, like this **<i>** tells the browser to start doing something, in this case, to start displaying the text in italics. A tag with a slash in it tells the browser to *stop* doing that thing. **</i>** means to no longer display the text in italics.

So, start looking for a line that starts with this tag:

shortcut
For a faster and easier search open the page source and then use the "find" function of your web browser to look for the phrase "usersuppliedcontent." On most browsers you'll find the "find" command under the Edit tab, or use the keyboard shortcut CTRL-F on a PC, or Command-F on a Mac.

<div class="UserSuppliedContent">

Everything that follows that line, for the next little bit anyway, is what the CO typed in. In other words: the cache description. So, what are we looking for? Look around the description and see if you see anything written in green that looks like this:

<!-- There will be some kind of text here. -->

The tags at the beginning and end of that (**<!--** and **-->**) tell your browser, "Hey!

Ignore whatever is between here, it doesn't actually mean anything!" So, your browser doesn't display it on the regular cache page. That means that the CO can hide anything in there. A hint, part of the puzzle, or even the coords! The only way you'd ever see it is by viewing the page source. Web developers call these tags "comments."

When you see this tag:

</div>

That means that the user supplied content is over, and it goes back to the HTML that *geocaching.com* utilizes on all their cache pages. You will see those tags twice. **<div class="UserSuppliedContent">** and **</div>** appear around both the short description and the long description. Of course you will want to look at both.

Viewing the source info cannot be done through the geocaching app. The cache description must be accessed from the web. You can view the source on a tablet or phone if you use an app like "ViewSource" on an iPhone (.99¢ in the app store). If you are using Firefox on your tablet or phone you can view source code in the by prefixing the web page's URL with the following text: *view-source:* . For example, to view the HTML source for geocaching.com you'd submit the following text in the browser's address bar: *view-source:https://www.geocaching.com*

firefox

Typing the following text into Firefox's address bar, directly to the left of the page's URL, will cause the same source to show up in the current tab instead: **view-source:** (i.e., *view-source:https://www.geocaching.com*).

Keep Looking!

Even if there is no hidden text in the source code there are other things that you might be able to determine if you know just a couple other HTML tricks.

In my example (Figure 3.1) look at line 604 where it says the following:

<font color="#76923C">

hexadecimal

Learn more about Hexadecimal and other number formats in Chapter 11.

That tag is what tells the browser what color to display the text in. The numbers are a numerical system called "hexadecimal." If you see that command, but the hexadecimal numbers are **#FFFFFF**, the text that follows will display on the cache page as white. Another way to spot that pesky hidden text!

On line 613 of the example HTML I provided you'll see the tag **</p>**. That command tells the browser that it has come to the end of a paragraph, and should return to the left, just like hitting return on a keyboard. Some COs may also use **</br>**. Either command will accomplish the same thing.

Normally the text put in by the CO will simply display however it is interpreted by the browser, depending on how wide you have your window set, that sort of thing. A long sentence might be broken in only one place if you have a wide monitor, or if you have your browser window set very wide. But if you have a narrow browser window, or are looking at the text on a smartphone screen, it may break in multiple places. By using that tag the CO is enforcing where they want their breaks to be in the text, rather than allowing it to be controlled by the whims of how you have your browser set up.

I point this out because if you spot a lot of those **</p>** or **</br>** tags, the owner must have a very important reason for wanting the page to display a certain way, especially if the breaks are occurring in odd places like the middle of sentences, rather than actually at the ends of paragraphs. Perhaps there is an acrostic hidden in the text? By enforcing the page breaks, the CO could be ensuring that all the words in the acrostic line up along one side. Regardless, if you see a lot of those tags, look a bit harder because the CO is going out of the way to accomplish *something*.

unintentionally revealed

Some third party geocaching apps, like C:Geo, ignore the HTML commands regarding text color. That means that any text that the CO has colored white will be revealed in the app! So if you are using a third party app and you see coordinates in the middle of the description... that just might be your puzzle answer!"

The final thing to look for is a tag that contains **href** which is the tag that is used for creating a hyperlink to another website. Hyperlinks can be hidden on a cache page in many ways. A CO could make a single letter in the middle of a word, or a period at the end of a sentence into a hyperlink. If you only look at the cache page, the only way to discover that would be to slowly move your mouse around the screen until you happen upon the link, or to look for a tiny underlining under the letter or piece of punctuation. By viewing the page source you can see all the secrets that the CO has embedded into the description, with minimal effort. That **href** tag is much easier to spot than looking for underlining on a period, or random spots on a photograph.

You will also want to look at the source code for any webpage that the CO sends you to, either from a hyperlink on the page, or from the "Related Web Page" link. This is especially true of any page that they would seem to own, rather than, say, a link to Wikipedia.

Wonders of the Web

There are many other things that COs can do to webpages that would manipulate your experience. You are probably familiar with internet "cookies," tiny bits of code that are sent to your browser as you use that web, that do things like keep you logged into websites, even after you navigate away from the login page. A CO can drop a cookie into your browser that contains nothing but the coords!

Another manipulative file type is the "PHP" file, which is a type of web language similar to HTML. PHP can create all manner of interesting effects. There are puzzles out there where the puzzle coords are clearly displayed on the page... but only at certain times of day, or only if it is raining in the town where the cache is. PHP can also cause an image or page printed from the web to print completely differently than what you see on the screen!

Most of these things require a separate webpage, away from the regular *geocaching.com* listing, to host manipulated photos, or PHP scripts that would alter your web experience.

Solving it
Bringing together what you've learned.

Use this checklist to help you examine puzzle cache pages for hidden puzzles, hidden information, or unusually altered HTML that might contribute to a puzzle.

Checklist: HIDDEN PUZZLES

☐ Select all the type on the page to check for white text.

☐ Examine the first letters and first words to see if there are Acrostics on the page.

☐ Examine the text to see if there are letters or words in different fonts, or colors.

☐ Check the Page Source for hidden messages.

☐ Examine the Page Source for curiously placed line breaks or colored text.

☐ Examine the Page Source for hyperlinks to other webpages.

 # alk-Through

Time for our next walk-through. This is intended to show you one possible way to approach a cache puzzle, and help you see the steps involved in solving. Remember, there is nothing at these locations. Here's the puzzle:

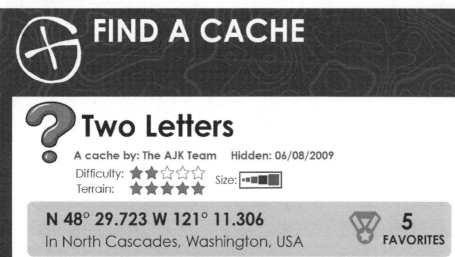

FIND A CACHE

? Two Letters

FCP22L3

A cache by: The AJK Team   Hidden: 06/08/2009

Difficulty: ★★☆☆☆   Size: ▪■■■□
Terrain: ★★★★★

N 48° 29.723 W 121° 11.306
In North Cascades, Washington, USA

5 FAVORITES

The cache is NOT at the listed coordinates.
You must determine the actual coordinates by solving the puzzle below.

A few weeks ago I got a very strange letter in my mailbox. It was weird... almost like a haiku or something. I shrugged it off and just shoved it into a drawer, but then last week I got another. Can you help me figure out what these letters are all about?

Here is the first letter:
The whales obey. No insects need elevators. Six eagles veered energetically nearby. The hedgehogs ran everywhere, escaping. This was outrageous.

And here is the second letter:
Corn snakes beckon. Foreign insects yell. Strong shrews greet ferrets tersely. Attacking, swooping normally. He will again challenge it.

I hope you can help me!

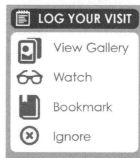

Attributes:

1 **Starting at the beginning.** I don't see anything out of the ordinary about the "Hidden" date, the "Placed By" name. Nothing in the gallery, no TBs present, no Related Webpage. By selecting everything on the page I see that there is no hidden white text. Probably nothing useful in any of those locations. The dummy coords are on top of a mountain, so there's probably no signs or anything to see on Google Maps. The cache name might be slightly interesting. I know that the alphabet is used in a lot of puzzles and it mentions letters, so I'll hang onto that piece of info.

2 **The attributes.** The attributes tell me that there is sightseeing nearby and that I will need a boat. Hmmm... well, it is listed as a five start terrain, which typically means that I'll need special equipment like a boat, so that checks out so far.

3 **Let's read the description.** Well... it seems pretty straightforward. She mentions receiving two letters and gives us the text of each. Two letters could mean one for the north and one for the west. The first letter has twenty words, and the second has nineteen for a total of thirty-nine. Neither of those is one of our geocaching "magic numbers," especially in Washington where the coords require fifteen digits. Each letter has five sentences, for a total of ten, which IS a number we can work with, if the puzzle only requires us to find the minutes. So, we have our second potential clue.

4 **What can we do with these ten sentences?** There are a couple ways that these six sentences could be used to hide coords. The most obvious would be the number of words in each sentence. Let's try that. The first letter would give us 3, 4, 5, 5 and 3. The second would give us 3, 3, 5, 3, and 5. That would give us 48° 34.553, -112° 33.535. Those are viable coords... but far too far away. Nearly 400 miles away, in Montana. Not good. So, what else can we do?

5 **Where does that leave us?** Let's go back to that idea of ten sentences and ten digits. If the first letter gives us the north and has five sentences, then each sentence would somehow be a single digit. The only other possible breadcrumb we've had is the word "letters" in the title, which is also repeated several times in the description. Can that add up to anything? The first sentence has thirteen letters, or, divided by word three, six, and four letters. Thirteen doesn't help us if we are looking for a single digit, neither does 364.

6 **Letters, letters, letters.** The word "letter" is mentioned 5 times. There has to be something there. Then I realize that she specifies "first letter." First letters could give us an acrostic, let's look at that. An acrostic of the first letters of each word from the first sentence of the first letter gives us T, W, O! The minutes for the local coords start with 29, so this is promising. An acrostic of the second sentence yields... N, I, N, E. Aha! We have it. So, the first letter gives us 29.732.

7 **The second letter.** Lets see what we can get from the second letter. An acrostic of the first sentence gives us C, S, B. Uhm... uh oh. Doesn't appear to be working. But this is the SECOND letter. Maybe that is a clue as well. In the first letter we looked at the first letters of each word, what if we looked at the second letter of each word in this example? Trying that the first word now gives us O, N, E. Much better! With all the sentences we have 11.328.

8 **We have coords!** Since we can assume the 48 and 121 for the north and west degrees, we add in the decimal minutes from the puzzle solution and get 48° 29.732, -121° 11.328, less than a mile away, and on water, just like the attributes suggest, so I think we have the answer. Remember, none of the cache locations in this book lead to real caches, but I have tried to choose interesting or thematic locations for each of the finals.

On the next page is another puzzle for you to solve on your own this time. Apply the lessons from this chapter, and you should make short work of it.

olve It Yourself!

Here are some puzzle caches for you to solve on your own. Using the skills we learned in this chapter you should be able to solve these puzzles. Take careful note of the final coordinates that you get as a solution to these puzzles, and write them at the bottom of the page. If you need a reminder of how to use the puzzle stats or hints provided, please check page 11. Good luck!

Puzzle 1 Solution:

N __ __ ° __ __ . __ __ __ , W __ __ __ ° __ __ . __ __ __

As a secondary check you should be able to answer this question: *What does the "sign" say?*

Puzzle 2 Solution:

N __ __ ° __ __ . __ __ __ , W __ __ __ ° __ __ . __ __ __

As a secondary check you should be able to answer this question: *What are these people doing?*

 # FIND A CACHE

 ## Type O

A cache by: Ithaca Scribble   Hidden: 06/18/2005

Difficulty: ★★⯪☆☆   Size: ▪▫■■□
Terrain: ★★☆☆☆

FCH31D1

LOG YOUR VISIT

View Gallery
Watch
Bookmark
Ignore

N 41° 39.470 W 086° 30.047
In South Bend, Indiana, USA

38 FAVORITES

The cache is NOT at the listed coordinates.
You must determine the actual coordinates by solving the puzzle below.

A little history about the area where the cache is hidden: The ather f the Stdebaker bothers, John Studebaker, lived near Gettysburg, Pennsylvania, where he wrked as a wago makr. ollwing the hge gowth on the horion nation he movd his family West in 1830 and settled nea the city f Suth Bend, Idiana.

Sons Hnry, and Clem, etablished ther shop fiing wagons. Ater success in the gld rsh their bothr J.M joned them manufacturin teir wagons. Wih their fourth brother Peter they oon establshed and epanded heir business.

ith the scond geeration the Sudebaker compan bega manufacturng their ifamous lectric car. J.M.'s son in law Frederick Fish helped the eforts to mve into manfactuing gasoline powered vehicles for the next ew decades. Fr years, nder the guidance of new geneations of Studebakers the compay enjoyed fame and fortune in the car manufacturg gam.

Attributes:

PUZZLE STATS

62 CHECKSUM   BEST VIEW

 117 8   40

 55   92

FIND A CACHE

The Space Between

FCL4DC4

A cache by: M0U53   Hidden: 06/18/2017

Difficulty: ★★★½☆   Size: ▪▫▪■■▫
Terrain: ★☆☆☆☆

N 40° 15.484 W 074° 42.771
In Trenton, New Jersey, USA

22 FAVORITES

LOG YOUR VISIT
 View Gallery
 Watch
 Bookmark
 Ignore

The cache is NOT at the listed coordinates.
You must determine the actual coordinates by solving the puzzle below.

When you first learn to dance, the most important thing to learn is that the space between the dancers is vital. Or... maybe it isn't. I was never that good a dancer anyway.

OXYGEN

ENGULF

ORMOLU

RODENT

HUNTER

ENGINE

TALLOW

OVERLEAF

ORMOLU

RIDDLE

ICEBERG

HONEST

40 15._ _ _   74 42._ _ _

Attributes:

PUZZLE STATS
49 CHECKSUM   BEST VIEW

 24    89   34

 12   120

Crossing Over

Sometimes when you look at a cache page it's instantly apparent what the puzzle is: a maze, a word scramble, a word search, a jumble, a crossword puzzle, a cryptogram, a Sudoku, a Ken Ken... the possibilities are numerous. But how do those familiar puzzle types turn into geocaching puzzles? Again, the possibilities are pretty varied, but in my experience, most of the time, when a CO uses a standard puzzle type, the solution that turns it into a geo-puzzle is usually fairly straight forward, but there are some tricky ones out there. We'll go over a few variations, and give you a few things to look out for.

This chapter is also intended to help you recognize a few puzzle types that, though common, you may not have been exposed to, and to show you some ways that familiar puzzles can be adjusted to create geo-puzzles.

See You In The Funny Papers

Americans have had a long love affair with puzzles, going back to the late 1800's. Word puzzles and games were very popular entertainment in the parlors and living rooms of Victorian America. A version of Crossword Puzzles started appearing in American newspapers in 1913, and since then we've had a puzzle of some sort in the papers almost daily. The recent preference is for Sudoku or Ken Ken style puzzles, but we still love our Crosswords, too.

Mazes

The simplest of childhood puzzles, one of the first ones we learn to do, is the Maze, comprised of a series of paths that hopefully lead us from the entrance to the exit. Like most things, it's all about the journey.

betamaze

Got a maze of black and white geometric shapes, but having trouble finding a path through? It might not be a maze at all! It might be words!

Go to *omniglot.com* and search "betamaze" to see examples, and how to read it. Below is the word "maze" written in the alphabet.

With puzzle caches there are only so many ways that a maze can come into play, but one of the simplest is for the correct path to cross the numbers you need for a coordinate. Here is a highly simplified version of that style of puzzle:

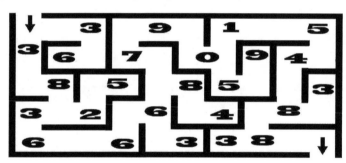

With a more complex maze you might want to look at the shapes that the correct path makes. With enough room in a maze, a CO might be able to make the shapes of letters or numbers that form the coordinates, or at least a clue as to what the next step is. This maze, when solved, forms the image of a watering can, for instance:

Word Searches

The next puzzle that we often learn as kids are word searches. A grid of letters that hides words or phrases that the puzzle solver finds and crosses off, or circles. Word searches are popular with teachers and grade school kids... and kids of all ages!

So... how do you turn it into a puzzle cache? There are a couple ways. First is the "left over letters" trick. Have a look at this word search:

Pretty standard stuff. 15x15 grid of letters, a list of 28 words to find. A straight forward puzzle that any geocacher would be happy to see on a cache page. I'll save you a few minutes and give you the solution:

```
K F N D L S M I L I E I
C A C H I N G I S R A N
O T C U A O S P A M R E
L W F N R O U W M R T H
D S A T T Z R O A I H C
N D N Y Z E C K L G C A
A O S L P A O L R O A C
K O E P N O E R O E C O
C W U F B T I R C K H E
O T T G A D D N K I E G
L F O S R S P G T H M A
E L G G U M U L T I E T
```

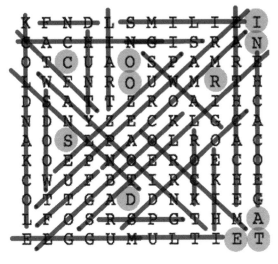

You'll see that after you complete the search, the remaining letters, the ones not used in puzzle words, give you exactly what you need to anagram "COORDINATES."

Just as we saw with mazes, you should also be on the lookout for any shapes created by the crossed out (or circled) words.

AMMOCAN	HUNT	SIGN
CACHING	LOCKANDLOCK	SMILIE
COORDS	LOGBOOK	SWAG
DNF	MICRO	TFTC
EARTHCACHE	MUGGLE	TNLNSL
FTF	MULTI	TRAIL
GEOCACHE	PUZZLE	TUPPERWARE
GPSR	ROCK	WAYPOINT
HIKE	SATELLITE	WOODS

Cryptograms

Another popular newspaper puzzle is the Cryptogram. Cryptograms are typically a quote that has been encoded using a Substitution Cipher. We cover substitution in detail in Chapter 6, but for now, all you need to know is that the alphabet has been mixed up in a random fashion and substituted for the regular alphabet. For instance, all the A's in a quote are replaced with P's, the B's with Z's, the C's with A's, etc. etc.

```
A B C D E F G H I J K L M N O P Q R S T U V W X Y Z
▽ ▽ ▽ ▽ ▽ ▽ ▽ ▽ ▽ ▽ ▽ ▽ ▽ ▽ ▽ ▽ ▽ ▽ ▽ ▽ ▽ ▽ ▽ ▽ ▽ ▽
P Z A Q V X R F S W M J U B G T N H Y C D E L O K I
```

Cryptograms are relatively easy to solve once you know the basic tricks. You start with what professional code breakers call "Letter Frequencies." The most frequently used letters in the English language are E, T, A, O and N, followed closely by R, I, S, H and D. In fact, 80% of the words in English are composed of combinations of just those 12 letters. That is a strong lever in solving standard Cryptograms.

The next step in standard Cryptograms would be looking for one letter words, or contractions, of which there are very few in English. But we aren't solving standard Cryptograms. Geocaching Cryptograms have a high probability of being about numbers, so let's look at how to deal with those.

All of the numbers, from 0 to 9, can be written out using just 15 letters of the alphabet: E, F, G, H, I, N, O, R, S, T, U, V, W, X and Z. And if we add A, B, D, L, M and Y to that we can spell every number in English, from 0 to as high as you care to count.

Without single letter words or contractions, what are your levers into a Geocaching Cryptogram? Well, the easiest is to look for the E's. A five letter word that ends in double letters is going to be THREE. That is the only number from 0 to 9 that has double letters. Above 9, only the teens have double letters. Also, look for a five letter word where the second and fourth letters are the same. That will be SEVEN. Those two words earn you the key to seven letters, almost half of the alphabet you need!

Or, if you simply want to get it solved and get out the door, there are a number of places online that will solve Cryptograms for you.

Crossword Puzzles

Crosswords have been one of the most popular puzzles for over a century. There are dozens of variations on them, different shapes, clue styles, or ways of determining what word goes in which boxes. But on average they all boil down to the same thing: words, arranged in horizontal and vertical lines, sharing letters where they cross. Most people know how to solve these, they are fairly straightforward, and beyond knowing certain frequently used words (like the famous piece of Olympic Equipment: the epee, or the alternate word for a veranda: lanai) there really isn't much in the way of strategy that comes in with solving them. So, let's focus on what you are looking for in terms of a geocaching crossword.

One frequent variation is to have colored squares spread through the puzzle (as I have done in the example). These squares might be the letters that you need to spell out the final coords, or they might use the letter to number conversion trick (A=1, B=2, C=3, etc. We discuss this more in the next chapter).

Another variation is to have the colored squares numbered 0 to 9. Then the cache page has coords with letters in them, like this: 39° AB.CDE, -094 FG.HKL. If an A lands in the square labeled 2 then A=2.

In a similar vein I have seen numbered squares that were intended to be put in alphabetical order based on the letter that appears there in the completed puzzle. So that if A landed in a box numbered 4, then 4 would be the first number of the coordinates.

Another possible variation would be to have the diagonals act as the true solution. You could also leave one of the long, unbroken lines, like 17 or 55 across in the example here, as the answer. With no other clue to what words should go there a puzzle solver would have to complete the full puzzle in order to fill out those lines.

Crosswords Variations

Since crosswords were invented, they have been modified, twisted, and reformed into dozens of varieties and variations. One of the most common variations is an "Acrostic Crossword," often simply called an "Acrostic." In this variation, you solve the words outside the grid, and then place them in the grid in a different order, giving you two levels of puzzling. Each square in the grid has both a number and a letter. The letter refers to the clue below, and the number refers to one of the letters within that word. You can solve each word and place the letters into the grid, or you can solve a word in the grid and use it as a hint to help you solve the word below. In the traditional version the grid will eventually form a phrase, quotation, or saying. In a geo-puzzle, the grid might form the coordinates.

Another variation is the "Cryptic Crossword," which is a much more difficult variation of the regular crossword. In

A. One way to get to the cache.
C A R
5 1 3

B. How a CITO leaves the area
T I D Y
2 9 10 7

C. Another way to get to the cache.
_ _ _ _
8 4 6 11

this style each clue is a mini word puzzle, usually a sort of text based riddle. For instance the clue may be "chaperon shredded corset." The answer would be "ESCORT," which is another word for chaperon, and is a rearrangement of the letters in "corset," thus making it "shredded." Like regular crosswords, cryptic crosswords have developed a language all their own, and certain clues turn up regularly. One example is having the word "unfinished" in a clue, indicating that the correct answer contains only part of a word; an "unfinished story" would be "TAL" instead of "TALE."

The "Enigmatic Variations" style of crossword is similar to a Cryptic Crossword, except the answer to be placed in the grid may not be an actual word, it may be an anagram of the word, the word with the vowels removed, or a portion of the word. For instance, the clue "talking, without the bean," would require the answer "SKING," which is the word "SPEAKING" with the letters spelling "PEA" removed.

Other variations include blackout crosswords, diagramless crosswords, tile crosswords, crushwords, shaped puzzles, or omni-directional puzzles. Blackout crosswords have no black squares, and require a letter in each square. This style has heavier bars on one side of the box to indicate where the ends of the words are. Diagramless crosswords also have no black squares, but add the wrinkle that the game grid is a shape other than square, and it may not even have numbers in the grid. Instead it is up to you to determine where the words go based on length. Tile crosswords have shapes other than square in the grid, though each shape still only contains one letter. A shape may be the width of one traditional grid square, but is three squares tall, or it could be three squares arranged to form a right angle. Crushwords go the opposite direction, and have more than one letter in a grid square. Rather than squares it uses a slightly stretched grid so that the squares become horizontal rectangles. Each rectangle may contain one, two, or three letters. Shaped puzzles may use a puzzle shape other than a grid: perhaps a spiral, or a snake shape. Finally, omni-directional puzzles are crosswords where the answer is not confined to straight lines. It may start on one line, then turn onto another line. It may form a square, it may wrap around other words... it could be anything. These tend to have names that help you understand how the words are to be shaped, like "Marching Bands," where the words form concentric squares.

Jumbles and Anagrams

Jumbles are word puzzles where the solver is presented with words that have been "jumbled," or randomly rearranged. Then they are asked to rearrange the letters back into the words and place them in a grid. Some of the grid spots are shaded or circled. The letters that fall into those spots are pulled out and then rearranged into a final word or phrase that solves a clue.

Anagrams are word puzzles that take words or phrases and rearrange the letters to create other words or phrases. Both of these can be solved using online anagram solvers that will show you all the possible combinations of those letters. The more letters you have, and the more common the letters, the more possible results you can get.

Personally, I am not a fan of anagrams for use in puzzles. I find that they can be very difficult to correctly solve because of all the possibilities. The word "geocaching" alone has 54 "phrases" that can be anagrammed from its letters. Most of them are nonsensical, (my favorite is 'gang choice') but it shows you the astounding variety of answers that can come from an anagram. Puzzle creators often think that anagrams are obvious... but then, they already know the answer! Anagrams can take effort to correctly deduce.

If you have a collection of unusual words ("Caging Echo," "Hang Ice Cog" or "Ha Conic Egg" in the case of "geocaching") try anagramming them to see what you might get. Cache names are frequently anagrammed hints or clues. For instance, a cache named "Nag A Ram" is probably about anagrams, as that phrase is an anagram of the word "anagram."

Sudoku

In the past decade Sudoku has almost caught up with Crosswords in terms of the number of newspapers that it appears in daily and its popularity.

5	3			7				
6			1	9	5			
	9	8					6	
8				6				3
4			8		3			1
7				2				6
	6					2	8	
			4	1	9			5
				8			7	9

Sudoku was invented in the late 1980's but started to become extremely popular in 2005. The objective is to fill a 9×9 grid with digits so that each column, each row, and each of the nine 3×3 sub-grids that compose the grid (also called boxes, blocks, regions, or sub-squares) contains all of the digits from 1 to 9. It is completed through simple logic.

In the sample puzzle for instance, a 5 already appears in the top left sub-grid, and in the top center sub grid, so only the top right sub-grid is missing its 5. The first horizontal row and the second horizontal row already have a 5 in place, so a 5 cannot appear in those lines of the top right sub-grid. So it must be in the bottom row. It can't be in the center; a 6 is already there. So it must be in the bottom left or bottom right of that sub-grid. Looking up and down those lines we discover that the far right line has a 5 in place, which eliminates that line in the top right sub-grid. Therefore the 5 MUST be placed in the lower left corner of that sub-grid. As you fill in more lines you get more and more information that helps you fill the entire puzzle.

There are many variations on Sudoku. "Mini-Sudoku" is basically the same, except it is a 6x6 grid, with 6 3x2 sub-grids. It only uses the numbers 1 to 6 in the solution. "Nonomino Sudoku," or "Jigsaw Sudoku," is a variant where the sub-grids are shapes other than square. Or "Greater Than Sudoku" where there are greater than and less than symbols in between each box which helps guide the placement of the numbers. There is also a variation called "Killer Sudoku" that uses math, and is similar to KenKen puzzles (see the next section). Killer Sudoku has shaded sections, or squares linked by dotted lines. These are called "cages." Inside those cages, there is a number that is the total of the digits that fill the cage. Cages may stretch across sub-grid borders, but the traditional rules requiring each sub-grid to contain only 1-9 remains in place.

Some Sudoku variations can have 16x16 grids, or 25x25, as long as it can be broken into evenly distributed sub-grids. There are also variations that link together several grids, so that one or more sub-grid is shared between two of the larger grids. Variations can also be done with letters, photos, or symbols rather than numbers. The only thing that matters is that there are nine unique items.

Looking for coordinates in a Sudoku is very similar to using a crossword. Colored squares can be placed in the puzzle, and yield numbers in the same way. Diagonals, chosen rows or columns might act as the answer, where the numbers directly become the coordinates, or they may be rearranged in some way described on the cache page. Numbering the sides and providing an X/Y coordinate for each number needed in the answer is also possible.

Some COs may use the numbers 0 through 8 rather than 1-9 to make it easier to deal with coordinates in areas where a 0 is required.

KenKen

KenKen puzzles are sometimes known as Calcudoku, or Mathdoku, because they are a variation on Sudoku style puzzles, except that they use math as a guiding principle for placing the numbers. Like in Sudoku, each row, horizontally and vertically, contain each number only once. However, the sub-grids in a KenKen are usually much smaller, and therefore do not have to contain all of the numbers.

In a KenKen puzzle, each sub-grid will have two things: a num-

11+	2÷		20×	6×	
	3-			3÷	
240×		6×			
		6×	7+	30×	
6×					9+
8+			2÷		

ber and a math operand, either +, -, ×, or ÷. The goal is to fill the puzzle with numbers, that when used with the math operand, equal the number given. So in this example, the upper left sub-grid is 11+, so that grid must contain two numbers that when added together equal 11. In this case, since the grid is 6x6, we only use 1 through 6. That upper right corner would, therefore, be filled with 5 and 6 since they are the only two numbers between 1 and 6 that yield 11 when added together. Some KenKen puzzles are larger and use more numbers, up to a 9x9 grid that uses 1 to 9.

Unlike Sudoku, KenKen puzzles usually do not come with some of the numbers previously positioned for you. It is up to you to find the clues you need from the math operands and the final products. Usually there are one or two that you can immediately identify, such as the 11+, which can only be 5+6. The order that they are placed in will require other clues, however. Whether the 5 goes in the upper or lower box in that subgrid will be determined by where else along that row a 5 appears.

More advanced Ken Ken puzzles will contain ONLY the solution, and not the operand. It will be up to you to discover what the operand for each sub-grid is.

Here again, the geocaching application could be composed of colored grid squares, or something even more straight forward. One row of the solved puzzle could represent north, and another row could represent west, or the diagonals could form the coords.

sudoku help
See Appendix 3 for some websites that will help you solve Sudoku puzzles.

Cross Sums

Similar to Ken Kens, Cross Sums, also called Cross Addition or Kakuro, are gridded puzzles that use math to determine number placement.

Cross Sums use only addition, and at the end of each row or column there is a number that is the sum of the numbers that are used to fill in the rows and columns, referred to as the "clue." The clue number is written in either the upper or lower half of a diagonally divided square. If it is in the upper half, then it refers to the horizontal line, and if in the bottom it refers to the vertical. For instance, in the example, at the upper left there is a 16, so the two numbers horizontally to the right will have to add up to 16. The clue 23 in the upper left refers to the vertical line of three boxes underneath it.

Cross Sums allow numbers 1 to 9, but unlike the puzzles that we have so far discussed, they can duplicate within a row or column. However, they *cannot* be duplicated within an answer. The answer to the clue 6 in the bottom row must be 1, 2 and 3, the only three digits between 1 and 9 that can add up to 6. That line is broken by a black square, which tells us that 1, 2, or 3 might also be used in the next solution on that row as well, and indeed we see that the only two digits that can add up to 3 are 1 and 2. Like KenKen you must use other lines to determine the order that those digits go into the grid.

The same (and by this time you're probably tired of me listing them) methods for hiding coords within this type of puzzle apply.

Paint By Numbers

Now for something a bit different! Paint By Numbers, also called Nonograms, Griddlers or Picross are a gridded puzzle that requires you to logically figure out which grids should be filled in, and which should be left blank.

The top and left of the grid is marked with a series of numbers that indicate the lengths of

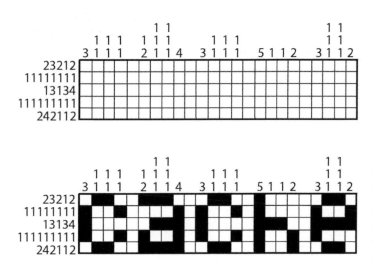

the shaded segments in each row (from left to right) and in each column (from top to bottom). There must be at least one unshaded square between each of the shaded segments. By determining which colors are shaded and which are not, you create a picture.

In my sample puzzle you would probably begin with that 5 in the top row. Since the grid is only 5 squares tall, the whole column would be filled in. Similarly, the columns that are marked with three 1s are easy to fill in as well. With only 5 possible squares to fill in, and knowing that one square must be blank in between each filled area... the only possible answer for that column is that every other space must be filled in. Once you have the simple ones out of the way, you can start filling in the more difficult ones, by comparing the numbers on the top and sides to see which should be filled. I'll provide you with the filled in version of this puzzle, so that you can see what it looks like.

Cache owners might spell out the entire coordinates using this method, or they might have numbers within the grid that get covered as the image is formed. The numbers that are left visible at the end are used to create the coordinates for the Final.

Islands in the Stream

"Islands in the Stream" is a puzzle that combines some of the aspects of Sudoku and Paint By Numbers. This puzzle could also be called Nurikabe, or Cell Structure. The puzzle is played on a the familiar grid of squares, which can be any size. At the start all, of the squares are white, but some of them contain numbers. The objective is to create a "stream" that flows through the puzzle. Within the stream are "islands," which are created by the squares with numbers in them. The number tells you how many squares make up the island. So, a square that says "4" must connect to 3 other squares to form an island that is 4 squares.

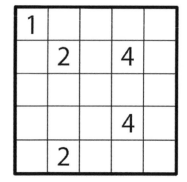 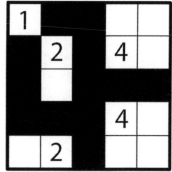

Two squares are considered "connected" if they are the same color and are adjacent vertically or horizontally--but not diagonally. Each island can only contain one number, and there must be only one stream, which is not allowed to contain "pools," meaning 2x2 areas of black squares. Islands can only touch diagonally. People who played Minesweeper will probably recognize some of these rules.

The caching application here may include streams that create the shape of numbers.

Still More Variations

There are dozens of logic puzzles of this variety. Simply google "Japanese logic puzzle," and you'll see many variations like Nurikabe, Hitori, Futoshiki, Kakurasu, and many many more. If there is a word or phrase on your cache page that seems like a hint, google it to see what turns up. The English names for some of these puzzles are things like "Skyscrapers," or "Neighbors," which seem like innocuous words, but might be just the hint you need to get the puzzle solved.

Stereograms

anagram solvers
See Appendix 3 for some websites that can help you solve anagrams, and jumble puzzles!

"It's a sailboat!" Sorry, just had to get that out of the way up front. Stereograms, sold under the brand name "Magic Eye," are images that take advantage of the human eye's ability to see in three dimensions, a process called "stereopsis." A lot of people lament these puzzles, saying that they can't do them, or can't see them. This image, for instance, contains the satellite to the right.

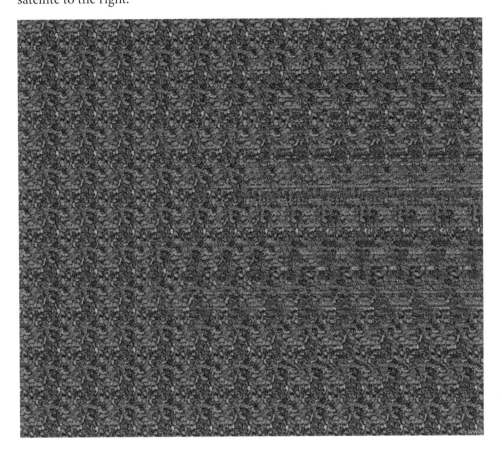

The good news is that if you are one of those people who simply *cannot* see the image hidden inside, there are websites that will break the image for you to allow you to see it. It makes it especially easy since the images for geocaching puzzles are stored online. *hidden-3d.com* or *magiceye.ecksdee.co.uk* can both accomplish this task for you. No more staring cross-eyed and lamenting your poor depth perception!

Keep in mind that stereograms do not always look like random static-y noise like the one above, or like a repeated pattern of rocks or flowers. There are stereograms that look like random computer printed text, or something else just as unassuming. If the image you are presented with in a puzzle seems to have large repeated areas, or repetitive elements, try treating it like a stereogram, just in case, whether that means using the web, or your own eyes.

Some puzzles use the techniques of stereograms, and the same quirk of the human eye in a very different way. Right are two similar blocks of text. They may not look like much, but treat them as you would a stereogram and you'll discover where you'd want to look for a cache.

If you look for a cache for too long the feeling that the cache is nowhere under the sun may rock your mind!	If you look for a cache for too long the feeling that the cache is nowhere under the sun may rock your mind!

Alphametics

An Alphametic, or a "cryptarithm," is puzzle type that combines words and numbers. In them a simple math equation is presented, using words instead of numbers. They are often a play on words, or a humorous combination of words. The first published example, presented by H. E. Dudeney, in 1924, was this:

$$\begin{array}{r} \text{SEND} \\ +\text{MORE} \\ \hline \text{MONEY} \end{array}$$

The idea is to replace the letters with numbers, on a one to one basis, one letter equals one number, throughout the puzzle, in such a way as to satisfy the equation represented by the puzzle. The only rule is that the leftmost letter in any line cannot represent a zero. In this case the answer was:

$$\begin{array}{r} 9567 \\ +1085 \\ \hline 10652 \end{array}$$

The numerical value of the letters are assigned and have nothing to do with the letter's place in the alphabet, or other values that letters may have. For the most part, alphametics are solved by hand with a combination of guessing and algebra, though there are alphametics solvers available online.

Ditloids

Ditloids are word puzzles that use a combination of numbers and initials to relay a fact, phrase or quotation. Solvers are given something like this:

52=C in a D

You have to use your knowledge to deduce what that may be referring to, and what the initials stand for. In this case: 52 = Cards in a Deck. As you can see, not all the words are reduced to initials: the', 'in', 'a', 'an', 'of', 'to', etc. are not normally abbreviated, though sometimes they are, which would make the puzzle slightly more difficult.

Ditloids may also be written without the equals signs. Like this:

SW and the 7 D

This ditloid solves to "Snow White and the 7 Dwarves," as you may have guessed.

Geocaching COs frequently use ditloids without the numbers in place, making the puzzles a bit more difficult. It is up to the solver to recognize the answers without the numbers and to solve both the word portion puzzle, and the number that corresponds. Can you solve this one?

Q in a G

Hopefully, you would eventually figure out that the answer to this one is "Quarts in a Gallon," or 4.

Some ditloids do not have a numerical answer, such as:

M + M + N H + V + C + RI = N E

The solution being "Maine + Massachusetts + New Hampshire + Vermont + Connecticut + Rhode Island = New England."

In a geocaching puzzle you may get the coordinates from the number, or if it is written like the last example, the number of letters in the correct answer, or an equation using ditloid answers, like this:

(O in a P) + (P in the SS)

Or "ounces in a pound + planets in the solar system," which would give you an answer of 24, (16+8).

What Else?

These are just a few of the common puzzle types that could be included. I could write several chapters covering just these types of puzzles. Pentominoes, Battle Ship, Waterfalls, Bridges, Star Battles, Sky Scrapers, Word Division, Fences... There are hundreds of variations on Crossword Puzzles alone. If you arrive at a cache page to see something that looks like one of these traditional puzzle types, examine that page looking for clues that will help you identify which one. Hopefully, if it is an unfamiliar type, the CO will have provided a couple clues to help you identify it.

One Last Thing

I'll toss out one last idea for you to consider... sometimes... *sometimes*... when you see a puzzle like this, something that looks like it might be a Crossover Puzzle, you might find that you solve the puzzle and are still left with no idea what to do. The CO simply hasn't provided a way to extract coordinates from the puzzle given to you. If you find yourself in this situation, there are a couple of things that you can consider.

First... you may just have to guess. There used to be a rather notorious Sudoku based puzzle in my area that you had to basically intuit the final coords based on the answers in the completed puzzle. It was always a struggle for solvers to laboriously enter all the possible answers into the geocheck before they hit the right one. There was a minor theme in the puzzle that helped, but it required some fairly intimate knowledge of the area of the final. I would not say that this was particularly good puzzle construction... but it was what it was.

The other possibility is that the puzzle may not *be* the puzzle. In the previous chapter we discussed the idea of the Hidden Puzzle: puzzles that are hidden in plain sight on a cache page. That concept can be layered on top of a Crossover Puzzle very easily. Almost all of the puzzle types that we have discussed here contain lots of numbers. A sneaky CO could very easily hide the Final Coords among those numbers, or have those numbers be the answer. What *looks* like a Sudoku may not actually be anything. The Final Coords could be simply found among the numbers that have been already placed on the puzzle.

If you think this might be the case, count the digits on the puzzle image. Are there 14? (or 15?) Those magic numbers might be a clue that the Sudoku is just a red herring! In the Sudoku at right, we should see almost immediately that the 8 in the lower right subgrid conflicts with two other 8s. That makes this unsolvable as a Sudoku, which means we'll probably have to look elsewhere for the puzzle. Simply being familiar with our local coords would help here because if we lived somewhere that the north coords started with 34, those two numbers are front and center, right at the top of the puzzle. After a

	3				4			
				1				
	1				8			
6		1						
	1					0		
						2		3
4								
				3				
				8	8			

little thought we'd probably be dancing a little jig, because simple reading each row left to right gets us 34 11.861, -102 34.388!

You will also want to consider the idea that what seems like a Crossover Puzzle is a whole *different type* of puzzle. For instance, an Acrostic (words formed by the first letters of other words) can be formed by the clues in a Crossword Puzzle. What might appear to be a Word Search could be a block of cipher text (See Chapter 10 for information on how to deal with Ciphers!). Or something that might look like a puzzle of one type may not be a traditional puzzle type at all.

red herring

A red herring is something that looks like a clue, but is actually meant to be misleading, or distracting from the actual clues.

One of my favorite cache puzzles in years past appeared to be a KenKen when you first looked at the page. However, after much work I realized that the KenKen was actually unsolvable, and that the puzzle had to be elsewhere. One afternoon in the shower (all my best ideas happen in the shower) it came to me! Even if the KenKen didn't actually work I still had some numbers and math operands on the page... so I simply arranged them left to right into an equation like this: 11 + 2 ÷ 20 x 6 x 3 - 3 + 240... etc. After doing the math... I had coords, with the top three rows forming the north, and the bottom three rows forming the west. The KenKen itself had never been the puzzle at all!

Finally... just because the cache page looks like it is a Crossover Puzzle, don't neglect the steps we talked about in Chapter 2, examining a cache page. Look at the placed-by name and date, look for hidden text, look at the source code... etc. The puzzle itself may be a total red herring, and not part of the actual geocaching puzzle at all.

Solving it
Bringing together what you've learned.

Use this checklist to help you examine Crossover Puzzle pages, and determine how to extract the coordinates that you need.

Checklist: CROSSOVER PUZZLES

☐ Identify the puzzle type and determine how to solve it.

☐ Examine the description to see if the CO provides a method for extracting coordinates.

☐ Examine the solved puzzle for coordinates.

☐ If there are no obvious coords, begin considering other ways that information might be hidden within the puzzle.

 # alk-Through

Our walk-through for this chapter is based on a classic game. This section is intended to show you one possible way to approach a cache puzzle, so that you see the steps an experienced person might use in solving the puzzle. Remember, there is nothing at these locations. Here's the puzzle:

1 **Off the top.** I always start with the basic elements, the "Hidden" date, the "Placed By" name. I check for Related Web Pages. This time there is nothing out of the ordinary there. The only thing in the gallery is the image for the puzzle, and there are no TBs present. No hidden white text. So there are no basic hints to be had in any of these areas. Checking the dummy coords finds me on the roof of the library. Cool, but I don't see a hint there.

2 **The description.** Wow... not a lot in the description at all. (This is typical of a lot of puzzle COs, especially those who do more graphic puzzles.) At least we know that we don't have to visit the library to make the find, not that I don't enjoy a good library.

3 **That graphic.** It seems like this whole puzzle is going to be contained in that graphic. Not a lot to go on, really... but let's examine it. Twenty-nine squares, some with letters some blank. They look kind of like Scrabble tiles, especially since they have a sort of woodgrain pattern on them, but they are missing the numbers that Scrabble tiles have. That number (29) isn't one of the magic caching numbers, and they are arranged into eight groupings, which also isn't an important number. It does look like it is broken into two subgroups, so maybe one for north, one for west? I'm not sure yet.

4 **What's the game?** The title of the cache asks if we "wanna play?" The tiles look kind of like Scrabble®. Maybe this has something to do with Scrabble®? Some of the eight groups spell out words, but two of them have blank tiles. Blank tiles are consistent with Scrabble® too, so at this point I'm pretty sure that Scrabble® is what's happening. It might be Words With Friends I suppose... but Scrabble® is more popular and well known, so I'm going to try that first.

5 **What can we do with that?** Okay. So... Scrabble®. How can you turn Scrabble® into a puzzle? We don't have a board, so we can't play the words we have. We could play it on a standard board. There's probably one in the closet we could pull out... but there's really no indication of where to play the words and that matters a lot when it comes to scoring in Scrabble®.

6 **Wait a minute...** Even if this puzzle was about playing the words and scoring them, I couldn't do that anyway because the numbers are missing from the tiles. Is that a clue? Turning to Google I see that there are websites that will tell me the number value of Scrabble® tiles. Let's look at the first word, "quizzed." A Q is 10 points, U is 1, I is 1, Z is 10, and we have two of those, E is 1, and D is 2. That gives us 10, 1, 1, 10, 10, 1, & 2. My first inclination is to add that up. 10+1+1+10+10+1+2=35. Hmmm... 35 is also the minutes of the dummy cache. Could be on to something here.

7 **The other words.** Blanks score zeros in Scrabble®, so the word with two blanks gives us 0. P=3, A=1, T=1, H=4, so 9 for "path." K=5, I=1, N=1, giving us 7 for "kin." Working the second set of words gives us 3 for "ton," 8 for "rake," 11 for "forty" and the last word is just BLANK-O... could be so, to, do, no... but it doesn't really matter since blanks are scored 0. And O=1, so I guess that word just earns 1 point. That gives is 3, 8, 11, & 1. Putting that in coord format gives us 38.111.

8 **We have an answer!** The north and west degrees for the area are 41° and 93°, so adding the partial coords we have to that we get 41° 35.097, -93° 38.111. I think we have the answer. [Remember, none of the cache locations in this book lead to real caches, but I have tried to choose interesting or thematic locations for each of the finals.]

On the next page is another puzzle, based on a variant of a crossword puzzle. It should be a simple solve if you can apply the material from this chapter.

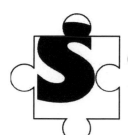olve It Yourself!

Here are some puzzle caches for you to solve on your own. Using the skills we learned in this chapter you should be able to solve these puzzles. Take careful note of the final coordinates that you get as a solution to these puzzles, and write them at the bottom of the page. If you need a reminder of how to use the puzzle stats or hints provided, please check page 11. Good luck!

Puzzle 1 Solution:

S __ __ ° __ __ . __ __ __ , E __ __ __ ° __ __ . __ __ __

As a secondary check you should be able to answer this question: *What Geocaching Tool Of The Trade do you find at the final?*

Puzzle 2 Solution:

N __ __ ° __ __ . __ __ __ , W __ __ __ ° __ __ . __ __ __

As a secondary check you should be able to answer this question: *What animal do you find at the final?*

FIND A CACHE

 ## Parchment

A cache by: CottiWompler   Hidden: 10/30/2016

Difficulty: ★★★☆☆   Size: ▪◼◻◻
Terrain: ★☆☆☆☆

S 39° 55.238 E 175° 03.127
In Wanganui, NZ

 **20 FAVORITES**

The cache is NOT at the listed coordinates.
You must determine the actual coordinates by solving the puzzle below.

FCN1CKC

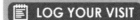 **LOG YOUR VISIT**

 View Gallery

 Watch

 Bookmark

 Ignore

P	A	R	A				T	
C	H	M	A	T		F	P	
E	N	T			P	A		B
		P	A	R	T			
T	G		C	H	M		D	A
A		C	E	N	T			P
	T				P	A	R	
		E	T			C	H	M
		A		P	H	E	N	T

S 39° AB.CDE
E 175° 0F.G0H

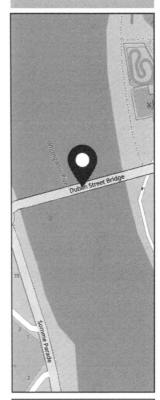

Attributes:

PUZZLE STATS

52 CHECKSUM   BEST VIEW

 👆 99   👢 111   🥊 60
💣 26   ☁ 5

FIND A CACHE

 ## No Left Turns

A cache by: *_Hotel_* **Hidden:** 12/30/2018

Difficulty: ★★★☆☆ Size:

Terrain: ★☆☆☆☆

FCQU4LY

📅 LOG YOUR VISIT

- 🖼 View Gallery
- 👓 Watch
- 🔖 Bookmark
- ⊗ Ignore

N 50° 42.308 W 003° 10.782
In Branscombe, Devon, UK

🏅 **13 FAVORITES**

The cache is NOT at the listed coordinates.
You must determine the actual coordinates by solving the puzzle below.

I once had a stubborn old mule that if I needed to get it from the barn to the field I had to take a strange route because it would only make right turns! Below is a map of my land. If you can follow my route you can discover the coords in the digits you pass.

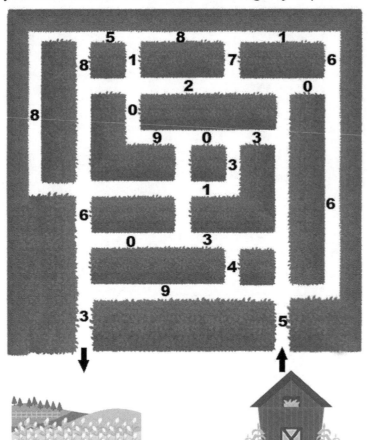

Attributes:

PUZZLE STATS

60 CHECKSUM | BEST VIEW

👆 **20** 👢 **115** 🥊 **62**

💣 **42** 🌳 **77**

Transforming and Orienteering

As we've mentioned, geocache puzzles most often resolve to coordinates and usually the coordinates of the final cache location, but that isn't always the case. There are many different things that can be done to transform a set of coordinates and give you a new destination. Most of them are based in a mathematical transformation or in using multiple waypoints cooperatively to find a different waypoint.

These methods often show up in geocaching puzzles and in multicaches, since some of them can be done in the field using a hand held GPS receiver. They take other factors into account-- distance, direction, or even the shape of the earth-- and change the original coordinates into something new. A lot of these are based on a game similar to geocaching that was played long before we had satellites in the sky: Orienteering. Orienteers navigate the forests and hills using nothing but maps, compasses and math to complete a predetermined course, moving from position to position to find "Control Points." It is a sport that existed at summer camps and Boy Scout Jamborees for decades before the GPS was even dreamed of. The methods used in orienteering can be applied to many puzzle applications, and they lie at the root of many geocaching puzzles.

In this chapter I'll you some of those methods, and how puzzle cache COs might apply them.

NOTE: From here on out, you can assume that if I say "minutes" or "seconds," I'm referring to degrees, not time. It just simplifies things.

o the Math

As you can probably guess, since Orienteering has been around for so long, there are many terms and definitions that have been created around it. Most of those cross over with math and geometry terms, and can be discussed in that way. For most geocachers, the math doesn't matter all that much. We just want to know where to go and look for the cache, right? Plus, our GPS receivers can do most of the heavy lifting with some of these, and for others, there are websites and apps that can complete the work for us. Not to mention the fact that geometric math over the surface of a sphere can get really complex. So, with that in mind, I'll be focusing on how to get results, not on teaching you how to do the math.

One small warning about mathematically manipulating waypoints: For all of these transformations there are different equations that can be used. Some take into account the curvature of the earth and some don't. Because of this, different websites and apps might give you slightly different results. So, when seeking a cache at a calculated waypoint, open your search radius a bit wider. The method you used may not match the method the CO used.

Using & Projecting Waypoints

A "waypoint" is, quite simply, where you are or where you want to go: a set of coordinates that describes a very specific place on Earth that you can travel from or towards. Think of it in terms of a hike. If you head down a trail looking for a particular waterfall, that waterfall is your "waypoint." If you know the coords of the falls and mark them in your GPS receiver the device will tell you the direction, and how far away you are.

A waypoint can also be your starting point. The set of coordinates given on a geocache page, where you can find the cache, the trailhead, or even parking, are waypoints.

Waypoints can be transformed in a couple ways. First is what we call "Projecting a Waypoint." When you get directions from someone, what do they typically tell you? Something like, "Take a left at Elm Street and drive for 3 miles." In the world of orienteering, what they are giving you is called "*distance and bearing.*"

Distance is easy; it can be measured in miles, feet, yards, meters, kilometers... any unit will do. Bearing is slightly different. A bearing is a fancy way of saying "direction." In our example, the direction was "left at Elm," but in most outdoor activities those types of directions don't make sense because you are standing in the middle of a field or forest. Instead, we use compass directions: north, east, west, and south.

When thinking about compass directions we can also think in terms of points along the edge of a circle. As we learned when we looked at latitude and longitude, circles can be divided evenly into 360 degrees. By thinking of it in this way, we could say that north would be at 360° (or 0°) or the top of the circle. Proceeding clockwise, south would be at 180°, or the bottom of the circle. East is exactly in between them, at 90°, and west is opposite that at 270°. To move towards one of these degree markings is called "bearing." Bearing can be expressed as any number between 0° and 360°, including decimal places such as 189.5° or 272.85°.

So, if we wanted to give someone directions where there were no landmarks or streets, we could say, "Travel for half a mile at a bearing of 135°." That would mean that they would be traveling in a straight line southeast for that distance. In geocaching and orienteering lingo, this is called "Projecting a Waypoint." Taking a known point and "projecting" it to a new location, which becomes our new destination.

Waypoints can be projected using almost any GPS receiver. Consult the instructions for your particular unit to find out how it handles this type of function. If you cache with an iPhone or an Android, you will need to use a web based calculator, or download an app that can do that. Currently the app provided by *geocaching.com* cannot project a waypoint.

As I mentioned, formulas for waypoint projection can vary. These differences in calculated results will be more apparent the further you are projecting. Projecting just a few hundred feet, or even a mile, is not really enough to make a difference, but if the CO has you project a waypoint from the equator to somewhere in Kentucky, or some other long distance, different methods can result in answers several miles apart, so check your results with the CO, or with a geochecker if one is provided.

True orienteers do their projections using compasses and maps, so they would need to understand how to work with the difference between "magnetic north," and "true north." True north is the point in the Arctic where all of the lines of longitude converge. Magnetic north is not a fixed point. The Earth's magnetic field is generated by the molten iron in the Earth's core, and that iron moves and flows, causing magnetic north to move. It is generally somewhere in the Arctic region of the Canadian wilderness, but it shifts subtly over time. Compasses point you toward magnetic north. The difference between true north and magnetic north is measured as an angle and is called the "magnetic declination." Most maps will have the declination marked on them. Navigating with a compass without accounting for the declination will leave you with an error. Over short distances, that error may only be a few dozen feet, but over long distances, the error compounds and you may be miles off by the end.

When projecting a waypoint using a GPS, most units default to true north, but some have settings that allow for magnetic north. Pay close attention to puzzle pages and watch for indications that the CO intends you to use a magnetic north, or compass based projection, rather than a GPS based, true north projection.

Centroids

The second way that a group of waypoints can be transformed is by finding what is known as the "Centroid." Imagine having 10 waypoints scattered around a city. A line could be drawn connecting those 10 waypoints into an irregular shape. The centroid is the geometric center of that shape, unlike a circle where the center point is equidistant from all points along the edge, or a square or rectangle where it is the intersection of two lines drawn from diagonally opposite corners, the center point of an irregular shape can be difficult to determine. But the good news is that finding the centroid of a shape determined by waypoints can really be quite easy. Since you know the latitude and longitude of the points along the edges, you already know the dimensions of the shape, much more definitively than you would with a random shape.

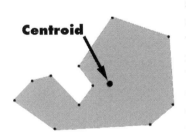

Centroid

Your first step is to convert the coords to Decimal Degrees (XX.XXXX°). Then you simply average the northing and average the easting. That averaged number is the centroid of your shape. (More on this in a few pages, but this method assumes a flat Earth and so might be off if the waypoints are very far apart.)

There are, of course, also websites and apps that will calculate that centroid for you. (See Appendix 2).

projecting on the web
See Appendix 2 for some websites that can project waypoints for you.

smartphone apps
See Chapter 18 to discover geocaching apps, and what they can do for you besides finding caches! See Appendix 6 for some non-geocaching apps that you may find very useful when puzzle solving.

america's centroid
The Army Corps of Engineers once determined the centroid of the continental United States by cutting an exact replica of the outline of the country from a steel sheet. Then they worked to find the point where it balanced perfectly on the point of a nail! That balance point, just outside Lebanon, Kansas was determined to be the centroid.

If you include Alaska and Hawaii, the US centroid is just outside Belle Fourche, South Dakota.

Interactions Between Lines

We were all taught in grade school geometry that a straight line can be drawn between any two points. We also learned that any line has a center point. This is sometimes used by COs as a puzzle point. If given two waypoints, you may find a cache at the center of the line connecting the two initial waypoints. Again, you can calculate this point by hand, but it would be faster and easier to use a web based calculator like *geomidpoint.com*. There you can enter two waypoints and it precisely calculates the center. It also allows you to calculate the centroid of several points, or the "center of gravity" for a group of points.

With two points you can draw a straight line... and with four? An 'X!' Imagine a cache where you are given four waypoints around your town, perhaps based on famous landmarks or four local benchmarks. Lines drawn between them will form an X on a map. The app "*GCTools*" handles this quite well, and will deliver you exact coords for the point where they cross. For a rough approximation simply drawing lines in Google Earth does almost as well.

Circles and Lines

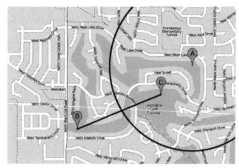

We talked earlier about drawing rings around waypoints to help determine proximity of caches for the 2 Mile Rule. In the same way that COs can use lines and their interactions to form puzzles, interaction between circles and lines could also be used. Again, think back to your geometry classes. In school we learned that a line from the center of a circle to the edge is called a radius, a line from edge to edge that crosses the center is called the diameter, a line from edge to edge that *doesn't* cross the center is called a chord, and the measure of the distance around a circle is called the circumference.

Imagine a cache where the CO tells you that the cache can be found 1000' from the 14th hole on a golf course, as well as along a line somewhere in between the 7th and 9th holes. With no waypoints given, you'd need to go and collect that information for yourself, or make a best guess from Google Earth, but with the waypoints in hand, you are ready to solve the puzzle.

benchmarks

Benchmarks are permanent features, or brass disks embedded in rocks or on buildings around the US. They were used by the US Geological Survey to create maps. Many geocachers also hunt these benchmarks, and you can look them up on *geocaching.com*.

A distance from a waypoint, without a bearing, basically describes a circle. To say only that a cache can be found 1000 feet from a waypoint leaves you not much further along because it could be in any direction away from that point. Drawing a circle around the waypoint with a radius matching the given distance gives you an idea of where it might be, which would be anywhere along that circle. Any point on the circle will fill the criteria of being 1000 feet from the waypoint. Mapping out the circle around the 14th hole leaves you with some info, but not enough.

A second piece of information is necessary to narrow down the placement, and that's where our line comes in. As we mentioned earlier, all you need to draw a line is two points. In this case, the line drawn between the two chosen golf holes will help. With that second piece of information we can see the intersection between the circle and the line and know where the cache should be.

You may also be given a line that forms a secant, crossing the circle in two places. In that case, the CO has given you a minor challenge because two waypoints satisfy the requirements of crossing the circle, so a guess on the geochecker (or in the field) will be called for.

Interactions Between Circles

In the same way that a line and a circle can interact, several circles could interact. Imagine a cache named "Olympic Rings" that offered a hide that was somewhere in the Centennial Olympic Park in Atlanta, GA. That park has a lot of landmarks: sculptures, flags, signs, and other things that can be used to describe very specific waypoints. Again, you would have to go and measure these waypoints, or try and pinpoint them on a map, but once you have the three waypoints, you can move forward with solving the puzzle.

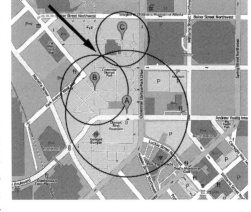

If the CO tells you that the cache is 1238' from the German flag on Centennial Plaza, 572' from the statue of Baron Pierre de Coubertin, and 361' from the Paralympic Legacy Statue, you once again have quite a few distances, but no bearings. We know that these three things are fairly close together, and that the CO has said that a cache can be found at the location that satisfies all three distances. We can assume that there is a point that *does* satisfy them all, found by drawing circles with the given radii, and seeing where they overlap. (Indicated by the arrow on the illustration.) You can see in the illustration that the circles overlap in several places, but that there's only one place where all three circles overlap. Three circles is the minimum number you would need to define a unique point, as two overlapping circles give you two different points, but three narrows down the choices.

This method is also referred to as "triangulation."

Circumscribed Triangles

Similarly, you only need three waypoints to describe the edges of a circle. Two waypoints could be a tangent that would cross the circle at any point, but three waypoints form a triangle and a circle can be drawn that would enclose a point. Any triangle can be enclosed by a circle that touches all three points of the triangle. This is called "circumscribing" a triangle. A CO could place a cache at the center point of the circle. Please note that the center of the circle may NOT be the centroid of the triangle, depending on how acute the triangle is. (Such as the one in the illustration here.)

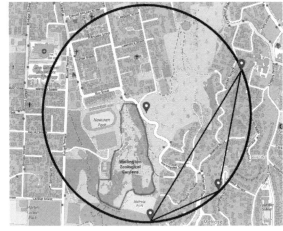

The iPhone app iGCT pro will calculate the center of the circle for you, but if you need to do it by hand you must first calculate the distance between the three waypoints giving you the lengths of the three sides of the triangle. Using those lengths calculate the radius of the circumscribed circle using the following formula:

Now, traditionally you would need to do a fair amount more math involving the perpendicular bisectors of the three sides, etc. etc But for our purpose you just need to calculate the overlap of three circles, with centers at our original waypoints, and radii that are equal to the radius we just calculated. The point where all three circles overlap will be the center of the circumscribed circle.

Resection

We've discussed what happens when you have a distance without a bearing... but what about the reverse? A CO could give you two or more directions to travel without telling you how *far* to travel knowing that somewhere these lines would eventually cross. The technical term for this is "resection." This technique is used by land surveyors as well as

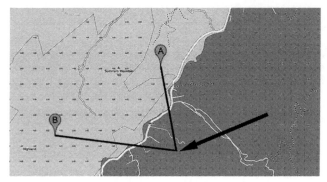

forest rangers to pinpoint locations. A forest ranger assigned to a fire tower would spot a fire and call in a bearing to the fire from his position, not knowing how far away it was. Another ranger, in a tower some distance away would then look for the fire and get another bearing. The firefighters, knowing the position of the fire towers, could then draw lines on a map, along those bearings, and head out to hopefully find the fire where the two lines intersected.

take a survey
Resection is one of the methods used by land surveyors to determine the edges of a piece of property.

In this cache, a CO would probably give you the position of the cache, rather than the landmarks. If a CO told you that there was a place where a fire tower was visible at a bearing of 277° and another at a bearing of 349°, how would you go about finding the cache? First you need to reverse the angles. Basically, move to the opposite point across a circle. If the angle in question is higher than 180° then you would subtract 180. If it is lower than 180° you would add 180. So, in this case 277°-180°=97° and 349°-180°=169°. Next we would need to determine the position of the landmarks, in this case fire towers, by looking on a map or going out into the field to measure with a GPS, and then finding the position on a map. Then you simply draw lines at 97° and 169°. The point at which they intersect will be where you will find the cache.

Antipodes

As kids we watched Bugs Bunny and various other cartoon characters do it. We heard about it, dreamed about it: digging a hole in our backyards so deep that we came out the other side in China. In reality... that just wouldn't work. Besides the burning magma and horrible pressure of being inside the Earth's core, China isn't actually *on* the other side of the Earth from most of the US. In order to dig through the Earth and end up in China, you'd have to live in South America. For those of us who live in the continental United States, if we dug through the Earth, we'd end up in the Indian Ocean. If you are lucky enough to live in Hawaii you'd come up on land... in Botswana.

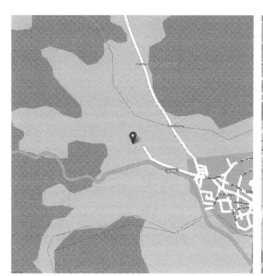

Outside El Burgo, Málaga, Spain
N 36° 47.544, W 004° 57.259

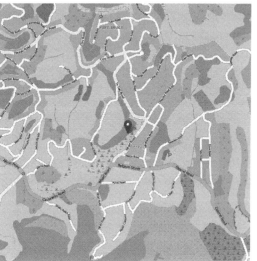

Outside Ostend, Auckland, New Zealand
S 36° 47.544, E 175° 02.740

This direct opposite point on a sphere is called the "antipode." Calculating your antipode is very simple. For the latitude (the north/south direction) it's as simple as adding a minus sign in front, or just changing the designation from 'N' to 'S.' As you can see in our example above, the north/south coordinates are numerically the same.

Longitude is a bit trickier but only requires *a little* math. First, convert your coordinates to decimal degrees (XXX.XXXX°) This simplifies the math, and you don't have to remember how to do Base 60 conversions in your head! Then take the coordinates of your starting point and subtract 180. Antipodes are always 180° of longitude apart. The example gives us W 004° 57.259 as the starting easting. Converted to decimal degrees we have W 4.95431900024.

Subtract that from 180, 180° - 4.954319 = 175.045681. Converted back to decimal minutes, the standard *geocaching.com* format, the numerical value is 175° 02.740. Change that direction designation of W to E and you have E 175° 02.740. If your CO is using the +/- modifier rather than the E/W designation, it would just be a matter of flipping the + and -. In this case we would have started with -004° 57.259, a negative, so the resultant coord would be a positive.

base 60

60 seconds plus 60 seconds isn't 1.2 minutes, as you might guess, but 2 minutes, because we use a Base 60 system for measuring degrees of latitude and longitude. Since we use base 10 for everything else, adding and subtracting minutes and seconds can get confusing!

Antipodes are a great way for COs to disguise coords and give an exciting and unexpected finish to a puzzle. They can be especially fun if you are lucky enough to live in an area that actually has something at your antipode!

Several websites will calculate antipodes for you. *Freemaptools.com* has what they call the "Map Tunneling Tool" that gives you two maps that you can click and drag. Each map shows the antipode of what is visible in the opposite map, and you can drag around either map individually.

ath Problems

A savvy cacher might start spotting a problem with all this. If the CO simply tells you to look 120' from a statue... well... do they mean the back of the statue? The front? One side? The top? Some sort of center point? What if the CO points you at something bigger like a building? A 10 or 15 foot difference, when it comes to geocaching, is going to be problematic. If you are presented with a cache that uses these methods, be prepared to expand your search area wider than normal, or hope that the CO will provide more precise coordinates as part of the geocheck.

oblate spheroid

Earth is slightly wider than it is tall, so it is a little bit smooshed in the north/south direction. This shape is called on oblate spheroid.

Different methods of converting coords also use different methods of rounding. A waypoint projection of .13 miles is less precise than a projection of 687', even though they are mathematically the same. The reason for this is in the way that different equations handle the rounding. Making a projection of .13 miles might put you out several feet. And if you are making multiple projections, from Point A to Point B, then again to Point C, then *again* to Point D... the rounding errors accumulate and you might end up several *yards* off by the time you get to D, especially if the CO doesn't give you objects along the way to correct your waypoints against.

This will be especially important if the distances you are working with are more than a few miles. All the examples that I've used in this chapter utilize short distances, and I have treated the math as if you were working with a flat surface, but, as we know, the Earth isn't a flat surface. In reality you are working across the surface of a sphere, so all of these lines are subtly curved to follow the curvature of the Earth. Look at this illustration. On a flat map, a line connecting two points seems very simple and straight forward. But if you connect those same two points on a globe, you appear to travel a very different path. Transferring that path back to the flat map gives you a much stronger idea of the actual projection.

When you are working with just a few hundred feet, as with most of my examples, that curvature isn't enough to matter. But if the CO asks you to project 4,000 miles from the equator, then you are in quite a different situation. At that distance, if you project in a straight line, you are actually projecting *through* the surface of the Earth, rather than across it. In order

to account for curvature at that distance make sure that the projection method you are using (be it app, website or pencil and paper) uses math that accounts for that.

"Great Circle" math is the most commonly referred to method. The problem is that it assumes that the projection is being done across the surface of a perfect sphere, which the Earth is not. A set of formulas called the "Vincenty Formulae," or Vincenty's Method, performs projections across the surface of an oblate spheroid. The computer program "FizzyCalc," which was designed for geocachers to aid in projections and conversions between coordinated formats, uses this method. (See Appendix 2 for information on downloading FizzyCalc.)

Long range projections will always be complicated and may require more than one attempt to get a correct answer. It is difficult to know if the CO used Great Circle math or Vincenty's Method to do the projection, or if they did the projection without considering the shape of the globe at all. So, if you are working on a cache that requires a long range projection, expect to need a little persistence in order to make the find. It may also be wise to contact the CO and ask them which website or app they used when they were designing the puzzle. If you use the same, you should get the same results.

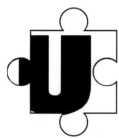

Units of Length

Most residents of the United States are still most familiar with the English Imperial System of measurement: inch, foot, mile, etc. However, we are at least aware that there is a second system in use in most of the world: the Metric system. We're familiar with the idea that distances can be converted between these two systems, that a meter is 1.0936 yards or 39.370 inches, and that a kilometer is .621 miles. But there are dozens of other units of measure, both real and fictional, ancient and modern, that a puzzle CO might employ when creating a puzzle.

Imperial

Even though Americans are most comfortable with the Imperial System, there are aspects of it that have fallen out of use, or were specialized and so didn't get taught to the average person. We all know inches, feet, yards, and miles, but there are several other units that we aren't commonly taught.

A *thou*, or a *mil*, is 1/1000th of an inch. This is most commonly used in manufacturing, and most often refers to the thickness of plastic or glass. For instance, the average credit card is 30 mil thick.

A *chain* started as a length of distance for surveying and equals 66 feet. It doesn't really exist as a standard unit today unless you work on the British Railway, or are laying out Cricket fields. Surveyors in historic Texas used a different length of chain called a *Texas Chain*. It was measured in a length called a *vara*, which was a Spanish unit of measure. A Texas Chain is about 55 and a half feet.

Unit	Relative to Previous	Feet	Notes
Thou		0.000083	Also referred to as a mil.
Inch	1000 thou	0.083	
Foot	12 Inches	1	
Yard	3 Feet	3	Defined as 0.9144 meters in 1959
Chain	22 Yards	66	The distance between two wickets on a Cricket field.
Furlong	10 Chains	660	220 Yards
Mile	8 Furlongs	5280	1760 Yards
League	3 Miles	15,840	No longer officially used
Maritime Units			
Fathom	about 2 Yards	6.08 or 6	
Cable	100 Fathoms	608	One tenth of a nautical mile
Nautical Mile	10 Cables	6,080	Used for measuring distances at sea. Currently defined as 1,852 meters.
Gunter's Survey Units			
Link	7.92 Inches	0.66	1/100th of a chain.
Rod	25 Links	16.5	Also called a pole, or a perch. Equal to 5.5 yards.
Chain	4 Rods	66	100 links, or 1/10th of a furlong.

The *furlong* was originally named after the length of a "furrow" on one side of a plowed acre of land. A furlong is 10 chains long. If you ever visit Myanmar, they still use furlongs on their road signs instead of fractions of miles.

Another unit that is now rarely seen outside fairy tales and fantasy novels is the *league*. A league in the standard English meaning was three miles; however, the term has been used by hundreds of civilizations from the Romans forward.

The problem is that every civilization defined it differently. The distance of a league ranged from the Roman definition of 1,482 meters, to the Norwegian definition of 11, 299 meters. You can probably start with 3 miles as the beginning point, though.

At sea, Imperial units of measure add the *fathom, cable* and *nautical mile.*

A *fathom* is precisely measured as 1/1000th of a nautical mile, which is 6.08 feet. In practice most people simply rounded the unit to 6 feet, which was referred to as a *"warship fathom."* Fathoms were used to measure the depth of water above 30'. If the water was less that 30' deep, charts indicate the distance in feet.

A *cable*, or a *cable length* is 100 fathoms, or 608 feet. The US Navy measures a cable as 120 fathoms long, or 720 feet.

A *nautical mile* is the distance spanned by one minute of latitude or one minute of longitude at the equator: 6,080 feet, or 1852 meters.

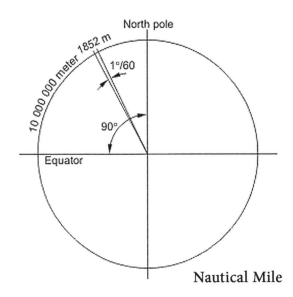

Nautical Mile

In modern times land surveyors use fractional units to describe the areas of land that they survey. But in the 1600's, before the sophisticated tools we use today, surveyors used physical measurements and had specialized units because of them. It started in 1620 with Edmund Gunter, who proposed a piece of chain that was 100 links long, as a standard length of measure. Why a chain? Well, rope stretches but metal will retain it's shape when pulled taut. This came to be known as *"Gunter's Chain."* Each link of the chain was 7.92 inches long, which seems like a strange length to choose until you consider that a square link is 1/100,000th of an acre. 10 links equals 6 feet 8 inches, and 25 links equals one *rod.* Four rods, made up a *chain.*

Metric

International use of the Metric system began in earnest in the early 1800's, under Napoleon's reign, although the system itself is much older. The metric system was designed to accomplish two things: first to standardize measures so that a meter in England would equal a meter in France, and anywhere else in the world, and second to simplify fractional measurements buy using tenths rather than eighths as the standard division.

acres

An acre was originally defined as being the area of land that could be plowed by one man, with one ox, in one day.

The metric system works by establishing a base unit of measure, the meter for distance, and then using prefixes to describe larger or smaller units of that measure.

The meter was originally intended to be one ten-millionth of the distance from the Earth's equator to the North Pole (at sea level), starting at the Equator and passing through Paris. From 1889 to 1960, there was a bar of platinum and iridium that stood as the official object against which the meter could be measured. As science progressed and we came to refine our knowledge of the shape of the Earth, it was redefined. In 1960 the official length of a meter was defined as being "equal to 1,650,763.73 wavelengths of the orange-red emission line in the electromagnetic spectrum of the krypton-86 atom in a vacuum." This was apparently still a bit imprecise for some people, and so in 1983 we got the current definition of a meter as "the length of the path traveled by light in

1 yottameter	=1,000,000,000,000,000,000,000,000 meters
1 zettameter	=1,000,000,000,000,000,000,000 meters
1 exameter	=1,000,000,000,000,000,000 meters
1 pentameter	=1,000,000,000,000,000 meters
1 terameter	=1,000,000,000,000 meters
1 gigameter	=1,000,000,000 meters
1 megameter	=1,000,000 meters
1 kilometer	=1,000 meters
1 hectometer	=100 meters
1 decameter	=10 meters
1 meter	
1 decimeter	=0.1 meters
1 centimeter	=0.01 meters
1 millimeter	=0.001 meters
1 micrometer	=0.000 001 meters
1 nanometer	=0,000 000 001 meters
1 picometer	=0.000 000 000 001 meters
1 femtometer	=0.000 000 000 000 001 meters
1 attometer	=0.000 000 000 000 000 001 meters
1 zeptometer	=0.000 000 000 000 000 000 0001 meters
1 yoctometer	=0.000 000 000 000 000 000 000 0001 meters

vacuum during a time interval of 1/299,792,458th of a second." Glad they cleared *that* up.

Converting between units within metric is as simple as moving the decimal point. Converting into imperial units can get trickier, but there are plenty of resources that will do that for you.

UTM coordinate notation is based on meters, so a puzzle that uses one may also involve the other.

Ancient Units

Another area to consider when looking at puzzles are ancient units of measure. We've been measuring things for quite a long time, and archaeologists and historians have worked out the modern equivalent of a lot of these measures.

The Egyptians tended to use measurements based on the arms and hands: finger, palm, hand, fist, and span, as well as the cubit. A finger is essentially 3/4 of an inch (.74 inches, or 1.88 cm). Four of those make a palm (2.95 inches ,or 7.5 cm). Five fingers is a hand (3.69 inches, or 9.38 cm). And six fingers is a fist (4.23 inches, or 10.75 cm.) A span is 3 palms and 12 fingers (8.85 inches, or 22.5 cm.) A cubit was about 18 inches (17.7 to be exact, or 45 cm.) For long distances, the Egyptians used *khet*, or rods, which were 100 cubits long, and *iteru*, which were 20,000 cubits.

UNIT	COUNTRY	IN KM	IN MILES
Arab Mile	Ancient Syria	1.925	1.196
Austrian Mile	Austria	7.586	4.71
Croation Milja	Croatia	11.13	6.91
Danish Mil	Denmark	7.532	4.68
German Meile	Germany	7.532	4.68
Hungarian Mile	Hungaria	8.3536	5.19
Irish Mile	Ireland	2.048	1.273
Portuguese Mile	Portugal	2.0873	1.2786
Russian Mile	Russia	7.468	4.64
Scots Mile	Scotland	1.81	1.12
Statute Mile	Britain and Ireland	1.524	0.9488
Swedish Mile	Sweden and Norway	10	6.21

The Romans also used measures based on the hand, but they added measures based on the foot. The Roman foot was approximately 11.65 inches (29.59 cm) and, in Latin, was referred to as a *pes*. Their version of the *cubit* was 1 and 1/4 *pedes* (the plural of pes.) Two and a half pedes was known as a *step* or a *pace*. 5 pedes was the *double pace*. The units that you are most likely to encounter is a *stadium*, a *mile*, or the *Roman league*. A stadium was 625 pedes (607.14 feet, or 190.5 meters) and became the furlong in the imperial system. The Roman mile was 5000 pedes, and is 4,854 modern feet, about 91.9 percent of the modern mile. The Roman league was 7,500 pedes, 7,281 modern feet, and 1.379 miles.

Every country and civilization seemed to have its own variation on the mile, either longer or shorter than the modern mile. An engineering puzzle CO could combine any of the methods I've discussed here with a variation on the mile, for an added twist.

Unusual Units

Over the years there have been hundreds of official measurements, but there have been just as many units of measure that were created as jokes or to make a point.

One of the most famous of these is *The Smoot*. The Smoot was created in 1958 by the MIT fraternity Lambda Chi Alpha. It was created as part of an effort to measure a bridge on campus using a frat pledge by the name of Oliver Smoot. Mr. Smoot was 5'7" (1.7 m) when the measurement was taken, and so that became the official length of a Smoot. The length of the bridge was determined to be "364 Smoot, plus or minus one ear." And so, the ear became the smaller unit of the Smoot, the foot to the Smoot's yard as it were. This measurement is so popular that Google Earth includes it in their list of units that can be used with the ruler tool in the program.

Another humorous unit is the *Sheppey*. The Sheppey was defined by British authors Douglas Adams and John Lloyd as the "distance at which a sheep remains picturesque." It is reckoned to be 7/8 of a mile.

A *parsec* is a distance used in astronomy to measure interstellar distances. A parsec is approximately 3.26 light-years or about 1.917×1013 mi (3.085×1016 m). Not many people can imagine that distance or work with it. But if you combine it with the metric prefix of "atto," which means a factor of 10^{-18} or 0.000000000000000001, it becomes a reasonable distance. An attoparsec is 1.215 inches, or 3.085 centimeters.

Google's built in calculator can do conversions between many unusual units of measurement and miles simply by typing the number and the units as follows: 100 Smoot to miles into the google search window. Google can also handle these units:

If you see an unusual word attached to some numbers, don't hesitate to do some research. There might be a unit of measure that you are unfamiliar with associated with the word.

Doing Conversions

Google's built in calculator can do conversions between many unusual units of measurement and miles simply by typing the number and the units as follows: 100 Smoot to miles into the Google search window.

Google can also handle these units: ångström, Astronomical Units, ATA picas, ATA points, chains, Ciceros, cubits, Didot points, english ells, fathoms, feet and inches, flemish ells, football fields, football pitches, french ells, furlongs, Half Ironman Triathlon bikes, Half Ironman Triathlon runs, Half Ironman Triathlon swims, Half Ironman Triathlons, hands, imerial cables, IN picas, IN Points, inches, indoor track lengths, international cables, Ironman Triathlon bikes, Ironman Triathlon runs, Ironman Triathlon swims, Ironman Triathlons, itinerary stadion, kilometers, Kpc, length of a cricket pitch, light days, light hours, light minutes, light seconds, light years, marathons, meters, metres, metres, microns, miles, Mpc, nails, nautical leagues, nautical miles, Olympic Pools, Olympic stadion, Olympic Triathlon bikes, Olympic Triathlon runs, Olympic Triathlon swims, Olympic Triathlons, outdoor track lengths, Parsecs, Planck Lengths, PostScript picas, PostScript points, Rack units, rods, scottish ells, Short Course Pools, Short Course Pools, smoots, spans, Sprint Triathlon bikes, Sprint Triathlon runs, Sprint Triathlon swims, Sprint Triathlons, TeX picas, TeX points, thou, Truchet picas, Truchet points, US cables, yards

ngular Units

I've previously discussed degrees, minutes and seconds, and how they function, but, like units of length, there are several alternate units that could be used in place of degrees that you might need to be aware of when solving puzzle caches. Some of these are used by the military, some are used mathematicians, but they could all be potentially used by puzzle makers.

Radians

Perhaps the most common form of angular measurement after degrees is the radian. The radian is an angle that marks off a portion of the circumference of a circle that is equal in length to the radius of that circle. One complete radian is 57.3 degrees, and so it takes slightly more than 6 radians to make up a full circle. 6 times 57.3 equals 343.8 degrees. Smaller portions of radians are measured in decimals. To convert from radians to degrees, multiply the measurement in radians by $180/\pi$. To convert from degrees to radians, multiply the measurement in degrees by $\pi/180$.

Angular Mils

An *angular mil*, sometimes just referred to as a *mil*, should not be confused with the unit of length that shares the name "mil." The word mil comes from *milliradian*. A milliradian is mathematically $2\pi \times 1000$, so there are roughly 6283.185 milliradians in a circle, making a mil 1/6283rd of a circle. This is known as a *trigonometric mil*.

1/6283 is kind of a clunky number to use in math or in the field, however, so some countries and agencies have redefined

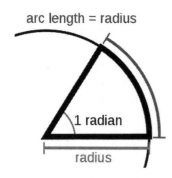

arc length = radius

1 radian

radius

the mil to make it easier to use. This redefined mil is known as an *angular mil*. The Russian Military have reckoned an angular mil at 1/6000th of a circle. The American Military went the other direction and reckoned it at 1/6400th. The Swedes use 1/6300th. I'll be talking mainly about American Mils (which is the most common definition, also used by NATO), but some COs may use other definitions, if it fits the theme of their puzzles better.

Mils divide the circle into 6,400 subsections, making 1 mil 1/6,400th of a circle, or .05625 degrees. A full degree contains 17.77777 mils. Compasses are usually marked in 10 or 20 mil increments to allow for more precise measurement of direction than the standard compass points. It is more precise than even degrees since most compasses are marked in only 5 or 10 degree increments and estimating smaller increments of degrees can be difficult.

To convert mils to degrees, multiply the number of mils x .05625. To convert degrees to mils, multiply the number of degrees x 17.77777.

If you are a person who is familiar with good quality compasses, or with some gun scopes, you may have already seen mils without knowing what they were.

Turns

As you can probably guess from the name, a *turn* is one full revolution of a circle, or 360°. A full circle isn't really useful for measuring parts of circles though, so the circle is broken down into *centiturns*, which is 1/100th of a turn, equal to 3.6°, or further broken down into *milliturns*, which are 1/1000th of a turn, or 1/10th of a centiturn, or 0.36°.

Gradians

Gradians, sometimes called *grads*, are a unit of angular measure used by surveyors and civil engineers. They were created as a way of simplifying measurements by rounding off the numbers. Rather than the unwieldy 360 degrees, gradians divide a circle into 400 units, or 1/400th of a turn. That means that a quarter of a circle will be an even 100 gradians, instead of 90°. Having nice round numbers to work with often simplifies equations and makes conversions simpler. A single gradian equals .9 degrees, and a single degree equals 1.11 gradians.

Because of some confusion between the words grad and grade, (as in "centigrade," a dated way of referring to Celsius temperatures) a new unit was needed to refer to the units in this measure. It was decided that this unit would be called a *gon*, and would be represented by a superscript lowercase g, like this: 50^g. In surveying, where tiny subdivisions are necessary, fractions of gradian can be referred to as c (1 c = 0.01 grad) and cc's (1 cc = 0.0001 grad).

Quadrants, Sextants, and Octants

Quadrants, sextants and *octants* are all units of measure named for 18th century tools for ocean navigation. A quadrant covers 90° of a circle, a sextant 60°, and an octant 45°. Smaller segments are measured as decimal portions of the whole, so 90° equals 1 quadrant, and 45° equals 0.5 quadrants. 1 Sextants is 60° and 30° is 0.5 sextants. A single octant is 45° and 0.5 octants are 22.5°.

A circle divided into octants corresponds to the eight primary directions (N, NE, E, SE, S, SW, W, & NW) and so sailors will sometimes record or report wind direction in terms of the number of octants matching the direction of the wind.

Others

There are a few other units of angular measure that you might stumble across: *pechus*, which were an ancient Babylonian unit; *hexacontades*, which were ancient Greek units; *Signs*; *Angle Hours*; or *Points*. Keep an eye out for unusual words and research any unknown word to see if there is a unit of measure associated it.

Solving it
Bringing together what you've learned.

Use this checklist to help you examine puzzle cache pages for words or clues that the puzzle might be based on an orienteering or transforming problem.

Checklist: ORIENTEERING

- ☐ Check for words related to Waypoint Projection, like project, bearing, distance, or waypoint.

- ☐ Check for words related to lines, like midpoint, intersection, cross, or centroid.

- ☐ Check for words related to circles, like radius, circumference, diameter, tangent, area, or proximity.

- ☐ Check for words related to resection, like intersection, survey, projection, landmark, view, or bearing.

- ☐ Look for alternate units of measure for either length or angle.

 # alk-Through

Ready to see how you might tackle a puzzle of this type? This is intended to show you one possible way to approach a cache puzzle, and the steps involved in solving. Remember, there is nothing at these locations. Here's the puzzle:

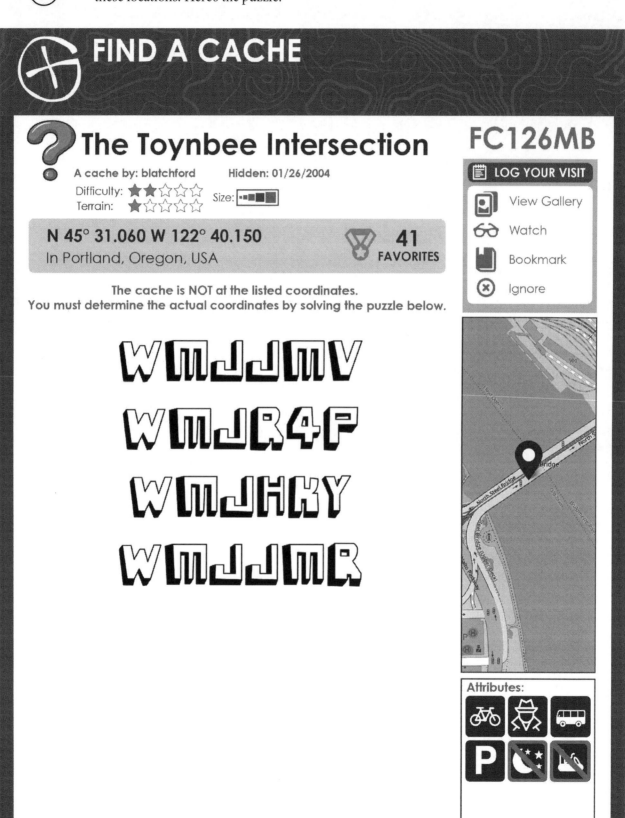

FIND A CACHE

The Toynbee Intersection

FC126MB

A cache by: blatchford   Hidden: 01/26/2004

Difficulty: ★★☆☆☆   Size: ■□□□
Terrain: ★☆☆☆☆

N 45° 31.060 W 122° 40.150
In Portland, Oregon, USA

41 FAVORITES

LOG YOUR VISIT

View Gallery
Watch
Bookmark
Ignore

The cache is NOT at the listed coordinates.
You must determine the actual coordinates by solving the puzzle below.

WMJJMV
WMJR4P
WMJHKY
WMJJMR

Attributes:

1 **Getting started.** Placed by, date, and the gallery look normal. There are no TBs present. No Related Web Page links. Attributes seem like they are pretty standard for an urban cache. By selecting everything on the page, I see that there is no hidden white text. The cache name mentions an intersection, but the dummy coords are in the middle of a bridge. That might be something.

2 **Toynbee street?** I open up Google Maps and plug in "Toynbee Street, Portland," just to see if there is an actual "Toynbee intersection." There is no street by that name, so it isn't about a real place. The name is interesting though. I set that aside for further consideration.

3 **The description is minimal.** There isn't really a description. Just those four codes, or whatever they are. All four start with "WMJ." That's interesting, but doesn't really ring any bells. They look almost like GC codes, but there is no code on *geocaching.com* that starts with either WM or WMJ. I try to Rot-13 the codes to see if WM might actually be GC in a Caesar cipher, but it isn't.

4 **Time for some research!** Not much to go on here, but I have a few ideas. First up is "Toynbee." Google gets me a couple references to "Arnold Toynbee," a British economic historian, I'm not seeing a connection. The fourth return is a Wikipedia entry for something called "Toynbee Tiles." Looking at those, they seem to be mysterious "tiles" that have been implanted into streets around the US. No one knows where they are coming from or what they mean exactly, but they have appeared in dozens of cities, for over 30 years. The lettering looks kind of like the "code" lettering on the cache page. That could be something.

5 **What is this code?** I try a quick google of the codes. The first one, "WMJJMV" turns up a page titled "SW Broadway and Yamhill Toynbee Tile" on *waymarking.com*! Now we're onto something. Waymarking, is an off-shoot of geocaching, also owned by Groundspeak, and involves sort of "virtual geocaching," finding objects or locations, but no physical caches. Like caches each waymark has a code assigned to it, that starts with "WM." I look up the other three codes and find that all four lead to the location of Toynbee Tiles in Portland. I make note of the coordinates of each of the waymarks.

6 **Now what?** Okay! I have four locations and a definite theme going here, but I still lack any sense of coordinates where I might find a cache. Where can I get those from? I have four sets of coords... I plug the four coords into Google Earth and drop pins at each location. I make a geometric shape that turns out to be kind of a lopsided box with a low side to the west. Not helpful. Maybe a centroid of the four points? That might be the answer, but then I remember the title: the Toynbee INTERSECTION.

7 **At the Intersection.** Based on the reference to an "intersection" I think we have an "X marks the spot" kind of thing going on here. I can make a rough approximation from Google Earth by drawing lines between my four pins. It looks like it falls roughly at the corner of 2nd Ave. and Morrison St. If there is a good enough hint for the hide on the cache page that might be enough. But can we get precise coords? For this I turn to one of my favorite tools: a smartphone app called GCTools. Within the app, I choose "Line Intersections" and enter the four sets of coords. The tool calculates the intersection and returns the coords, 45° 31.063, -122° 40.459, right at the street corner I saw in Google Earth! (Remember, none of the cache locations in this book lead to real caches.)

There are other online tools that could be used besides the one I chose. Have a look at Appendix 2 to see what those might be, but *geomidpoint.com* would probably be my go-to. But please note that different tools may provide slightly different answers. This is the kind of cache where you have to hope that the CO provides a "soft" or "fuzzy" geochecker, one that will give you the green light if you enter any coords within a certain distance of the correct ones, usually 30 feet.

On the next page is another puzzle, for you to solve by yourself. With everything you've learned in this chapter, hopefully you will find it easy.

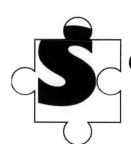olve It Yourself!

Here are some puzzle caches for you to solve on your own. Using the skills we learned in this chapter you should be able to solve these puzzles. Take careful note of the final coordinates that you get as a solution to these puzzles, and write them at the bottom of the page. If you need a reminder of how to use the puzzle stats or hints provided, please check page 11. Good luck!

Puzzle 1 Solution:

N __ __ ° __ __ . __ __ __ , W __ __ __ ° __ __ . __ __ __

As a secondary check you should be able to answer this question: *What animal do you find at the final?*

Puzzle 2 Solution:

N __ __ ° __ __ . __ __ __ , W __ __ __ ° __ __ . __ __ __

As a secondary check you should be able to answer this question: *What image do you find at the final?*

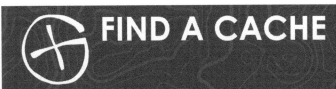 # FIND A CACHE

 ## Secret Fishin' Hole

A cache by: Longi.dude   Hidden: 12/13/2011

Difficulty: ★★★☆☆
Terrain: ★☆☆☆☆   Size:

FCJJAWX

LOG YOUR VISIT

- View Gallery
- Watch
- Bookmark
- Ignore

N 46° 00.465 W 091° 27.998
In Hayward, Wisconsin, USA

41 FAVORITES

The cache is NOT at the listed coordinates.
You must determine the actual coordinates by solving the puzzle below.

Years and years ago, my great grandpappy found this fishin' hole with the biggest fish he'd ever seen. He fished there and brought home record holding fish what seemed like every time.

When great grandpappy passed on he whispered the secret of his fishin' hole to my gramps. Even though my Daddy begged to know where it was Gramps kept that secret until he was 'bout ready to kick the bucket and he finally told my daddy.

Daddy didn't want to torture me by keeping the secret for so long, but he wanted to make me work for it, so he told me this.

"If you take a fly rod, with EXACTLY 864.512 ells of line, and you cast ALL that line at 4892.0889 mils, where the lure lands will be the biggest fish you ever seen."

I didn't want to tell my daddy, but I have no idea what he's talking about! Do you?

Attributes:

PUZZLE STATS

52 CHECKSUM   BEST VIEW

15   107   71

31   85

FIND A CACHE

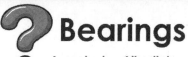 **Bearings**

A cache by: Albertials   Hidden: 08/08/2008

Difficulty: ★★★⯪☆   Size: ▪▪■■▫

Terrain: ★☆☆☆☆

FC85TAW

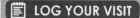 **LOG YOUR VISIT**

 View Gallery

 Watch

 Bookmark

 Ignore

N 39° 47.183 W 104° 32.145

In Watkins, Colorado, USA

🏅 **51 FAVORITES**

The cache is NOT at the listed coordinates.
You must determine the actual coordinates by solving the puzzle below.

Given 2 coordinates and bearings find the final.

First bearing North 39° 46.985' West 104° 34.256'
Bearing from cache 236.31°

Second bearing North 39° 47.183' West 104° 32.145'
Bearing from cache 112.53°

Good luck out there!

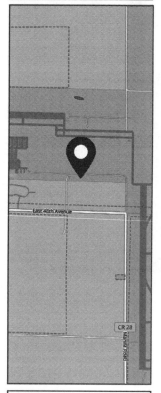

Attributes:

PUZZLE STATS

53 CHECKSUM   BEST VIEW

👆 **95**   👢 **37**   🧤 **11**

💣 **109**   ☢ **68**

Substitution

One of the most classic geocaching hide techniques is the cache container that looks like one thing but is actually a cache. That bolt, log, rock, pine cone, cactus, or even that soda can you see might be a cache container. The same thing can be said about things you might find in a geocaching puzzle.

Anything you find on a cache page might be something in disguise. A phrase, a word, or even a letter that, if you turn it on its side, is actually something else, like coded information, or hidden information. A thing that is standing in for something else, just like the cache that is pretending to be a bolt.

The easiest way to create this style of puzzle is to find something that our mind associates with a number or a letter; something that, at first glance, is exactly what it appears to be, but with a little thought, we can find correlates to something else, and then substitute that thing for the number. We do this very easily with shapes: a triangle can be substituted for the number 3, a square for 4, a pentagon for 5, etc.

In this chapter we'll explore some of the more esoteric ways that puzzle cache COs can use this idea to create puzzles.

hings That Aren't Numbers... But Then Again Are

With a little thought you can probably come up with several things that directly represent a number, a letter, a word, or even an idea. A photo of a hand with the fingers spread can represent the number 5. A red circle with a slash through it means that something is not allowed. A red octagon is all you need to think of the word "stop." Culturally we have come to agree that certain things are inexorably linked to words or numerical concepts, and when we see them, we immediately know the meaning. They have become so accepted that we don't even have to think about their meanings anymore.

Caching puzzles can be built using these items that have multiple meanings, and can be substituted for one another. The idea of replacing one thing with another to slightly obscure the real meaning is a rich source of material for puzzle making, though most times the replacement won't be as obvious as a hand equaling five. You may have to do a little thinking and research to see how the items relate to another idea.

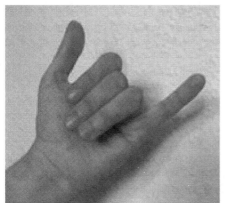

consider other cultures

While it's somewhat meaningless in the West, this hand sign would mean "6" to someone who grew up in China. If it isn't familiar to you look for hints on the page that might point to another language or culture!

The simplest, and one of the most common substitutes of all, is a letter for number swap. Numbers have a proscribed order based on their value: 0, 1, 2, 3, 4, etc. Letters also have a prescribed order, A to Z. They also have an ordinal order. The first letter is A, the second letter is B, the third letter is C. In other words A=1, B=2, C=3, etc. until you reach Z=26. This is one of the first codes that little kids often learn. And of course you can use this in reverse 1=A, 2=B... and so forth. Very experienced puzzle solvers often have this type of substitution memorized because it shows up a LOT.

1	2	3	4	5	6	7	8	9	10	11	12	13	14	15	16	17	18	19	20	21	22	23	24	25	26
A	B	C	D	E	F	G	H	I	J	K	L	M	N	O	P	Q	R	S	T	U	V	W	X	Y	Z

Some COs may continue the alphabet substitution using lowercase letters. In that case they pick up at 27, and so 27=a, 28 =b, etc.

27	28	29	30	31	32	33	34	35	36	37	38	39	40	41	42	43	44	45	46	47	48	49	50	51	52
a	b	c	d	e	f	g	h	i	j	k	l	m	n	o	p	q	r	s	t	u	v	w	x	y	z

A full alphabet would look like this:

1	2	3	4	5	6	7	8	9	10	11	12	13	14	15	16	17	18	19	20	21	22	23	24	25	26
a	b	c	d	e	f	g	h	i	j	k	l	m	n	o	p	q	r	s	t	u	v	w	x	y	z

27	28	29	30	31	32	33	34	35	36	37	38	39	40	41	42	43	44	45	46	47	48	49	50	51	52
A	B	C	D	E	F	G	H	I	J	K	L	M	N	O	P	Q	R	S	T	U	V	W	X	Y	Z

Or possibly this:

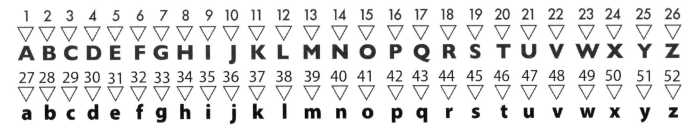

The lowercase letters may start at 1 and the uppercase start at 27 or vice versa. This doesn't particularly matter if the information being encoded is text, after all it will still be readable even if you reverse the upper and lower cases. But if the letters are being used to encode numbers you will want to try it both ways until you get the answer you are looking for.

Let's look at something a little more advanced, starting with numbers. There are many things in the world that can be associated with a number. Have a look at this list:

Zinc

Silicon

Potassium

Oxygen

Neptunium

Titanium

Gadolinium

Beryllium

There's nothing that immediately springs to mind that would give us a set of coordinates based on this list… a little research is what's called for next.

A web search on these words will turn up several bits of information. First, that they are all elements. But what can you do with that? Here's where a little bit of esoteric knowledge might come in. Someone familiar with chemistry will know the answer right away, someone who isn't might take a little more research, but eventually you'll discover that elements are assigned numbers. Once you have that knowledge you will see that Zinc = 30, Silicon = 14, etc. and you soon you have the numbers 30, 14, 19, 8, 93, 22, 64 and 4. A slight rearrangement of these numbers to fit the standard coordinate formats and soon you'll know that there is a cache to be found at N 30° 14.198, W 93° 22.644.

So, in this case, the replacement puzzle would work like this: the necessary numerical digits are replaced by an element that is associated with that number. While it is not as obvious as a hand equaling 5, just a little digging and research turns up the association that we are looking for.

This type of conversion to numbers or substitution with numbers happens all over the place, once you start looking for it. Think about all the things in your day to day world that could be represented by just a number:

- Race cars or drivers
- Sports figures' jersey numbers
- Bus or train lines
- Sizes

alternate starts

In the standard alphabet A equals 1, B equals 2, etc. but some CO's will get sneaky and start with a letter other than A. For instance N may equal 1, O equals 2, etc.

step by step

Remember the steps we covered in Chapter 2 for approaching an unknown puzzle type. Count the items in the puzzle, and research!

magic numbers

Coordinates can be written in different ways, but will often use 6, 10, 14 or 15 digits, so those are magic numbers for geocache puzzle solving.

- Sports positions
- Issue numbers
- States
- Presidents
- B Vitamins
- TV channels
- Interstates or roads
- Grocery store produce numbers
- Playing Cards
- Symphonies
- Pool balls

This list is by no means comprehensive, but any of those things could be turned into a cache puzzle. So when you see a collection of things on a page (Remember! Look for groups of 6, 10, 14 or 15!), consider how those things might relate to a number.

There are also some obscure ones that you may not consider at first, but a little research will turn up an answer. Try this one:

> If thou survive my well-contented day,
> Devouring Time, blunt thou the lion's paws,
> Full many a glorious morning have I seen
> What's in the brain that ink may character
> If the dull substance of my flesh were thought,
> Devouring Time, blunt thou the lion's paws

Perhaps at first you'd think, "Nice poem, but what the heck does it have to do with geocaching?!" We are certainly going to have to look a little closer at this. We can see right away that, again, there are 6 lines in the poem; groups of 6 are important, right? Then... research mode kicks on. (Repeat after me: "Google is your friend!") But what would you research in this case? With a search like this you want to find the right balance. Searching the whole poem will tell you that this has *something* to do with Shakespeare's Sonnets, and that's an awesome start, but it may not give you exactly what you need to know.

However, we know that six is a magic number here, and we have six lines. So, let's try one line at a time. A search of the first line of the poem should connect you to a specific sonnet. You might even notice right away that about half of the search results have a "32" in them. We've uncovered a number! And if you lived in the southern half of the United States you'd know that 32 is a common number for the north degrees. Let's search another one... the second line returns Sonnet 19. Again, we know that 32° 19' is in the southern US. And it should all roll down-hill from there. Because Shakespearean Sonnets have no titles, they are traditionally assigned numbers. Those six numbers taken together will give you 32, 19, 33, 108, 44 and 19. If you format those numbers as coords, you might try 32° 19' 33", -108° 44' 19" or 32° 19.330, -108° 44.190, or 32° 19.033, -108° 44.019, all of which are viable coordinates that you might want to run through a geochecker if one is available. The first set, 32° 19' 33", -108° 44' 19", happens to take you to a ghost town in New Mexico named "Shakespeare."

Another way to approach this replacement idea is referencing the numerical order of things. Things that have a set and unchanging order, like the planets or chapters in a book, easily relate back to a number. Mercury is the first planet from the sun, so Mercury equals 1, Venus equals 2, Earth equals 3, etc.

Here's another puzzle to try:

Where would you start if you saw these images on a cache page? What would you do?

If this *was* on a cache page, you could start right away by doing a reverse image search. But since that isn't an option here, where do you start? Some people might recognize these men immediately... for others it would take a bit of research. But there's at least one here that most anyone should recognize fairly quickly: Barack Obama. Thinking of presidents, a couple of these guys look "presidential." So presidents are probably a good enough place as any to start. Just searching presidents turns up some lists, some history... but unless you are a presidential scholar, you probably can't connect more than one or two of these gentlemen to a name. So, turn to image searching. An image search of the word presidents shows you several interesting things, including a couple charts of images. From there you can start matching these guys up. Pretty quickly you can be sure that you're dealing with presidents, and you can start matching up names. In short order you can build a list.

TOP ROW (L to R)	BOTTOM ROW (L to R)
Dwight Eisenhower	William Henry Harrison
Barack Obama	John Adams
Andrew Jackson	James Buchanan
Martin Van Buren	James Monroe
John Quincy Adams	Jimmy Carter

Now what? Given what we've been discussing in this chapter I bet you can guess the next step pretty easily, but without that information, what would your next step be? The only answer is more research. Remember, in a geocaching puzzle your goal is probably a number. So, how can you get numbers from presidents? Several ways came to mind: election years, years in office, or presidential order. Election years are tricky... Jackson, for instance, was elected in 1828, but inaugurated in 1829. You may also consider birth years. (We know death years won't work since two of them are still living). Either way, the whole year is too long... 4 digits times 10 Presidents would give us 40 digits to work with... far too much. Just using '29 might work, but there again you end up with 20 digits. You might reduce it to just the last digit, or 9. For years in office, most of them would be variations on 4 or 8... that won't get us very far. You could try the letters to numbers trick, and convert the first letter of their last name to a number. Eisenhower would be an E, or 5. Presidential

image searches
Remember that Google Images or *TinEye.com* can search the internet based on images rather than words. See Chapter 2 for a full explanation.

order might be interesting. Dwight Eisenhower was the 34th president, Barack Obama was the 44th, etc. In the end, if we follow that pattern, we have 10 numbers: 34, 44, 7, 8, 6, 9, 2, 15, 5 and 39. Together that's 14 digits, another one of those magic geocaching numbers. If we put in the appropriate breaks we get 34° 44.786, -92° 15.539. A worthy set of coordinates to try! And if that doesn't work, you could also try a different format, like 34.44786°, -92.15539°.

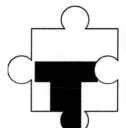

hings That Aren't Letters, But... You Know The Rest

Just as you can represent a number with a thing that isn't actually a number, you can represent a letter with something that isn't actually a letter.

Looking back at our initial example of the Periodic Table, let's look at a different list of elements:

Tungsten, Einsteinium, Tellurium, Radon

Tungsten is 74 on the Periodic Table, Einsteinium is 99... those numbers don't really get us anywhere. So we go back to the research phase on this one... what other things can we learn about the elements? Some further research should bring you to the discovery that Tungsten is represented by 'W,' Einsteinium by 'Es,' etc. After researching all the elements we have W Es Te Rn, or 'Western.' This isn't a complete puzzle, but it should show you a way to think about this puzzle type.

Letter only substitutions are less frequent than numerical ones, but you could build a puzzle around US State abbreviations, airport codes, or just about anything you could abbreviate.

There are a few things around that aren't abbreviations that can still bring you to a letter based solution. Imagine being presented with a puzzle that looks like a page from a telephone book. If one of the numbers was 1-893-689-3687, what could you do with that? Anyone old enough to remember that phone numbers used to have letters in them, or just old enough to remember texting before the advent of the smartphone, will probably immediately have a place to start: numbers on phones have corresponding letters.

1-893-689-3687 starts with 8 (since 1 doesn't correspond to any letters), which could correspond to T, U or V. 9 could correspond to W, X, Y or Z. That U or V doesn't mesh well with any of those letters, but T... well... a T could go with a W as a way to begin spelling two, twelve, or twenty. Going through the whole telephone number shows us that 1-893-689-3687 spells out "twenty-four." More telephone numbers from the puzzle would get you complete coordinates. That also works in reverse; COs can give you letters and you find the phone numbers.

Some telephone codes will tell you which letter by using a slash, or a line. A back slash and a 2 (like this: \2) indicates the first of the three letters associated with that number, or 'A.' A straight line (|2) is the center letter, or 'B,' and a forward slash is the third letter, 'C' (/2). Texting also used this method in the past. Before phones had full typewriter-like keyboards you would press a number on your phone pad to get letters. Pressing 2 once would get you and A, 22 for B, and 222 for C. 3 brings up D, 33 E, and 333 F, etc. This type of notation was known as "T9," "Vanity Code" or "Predictive Text."

Some telephone codes will vary on how they handle Q and Z which were not originally on old school rotary phones. Q might be represented by 7, and Z by 9, or Q and Z may be assigned to the 1.

A similar example of this would be the Dvorak computer keyboard. The familiar keyboard that most of us use is called the "QWERTY Keyboard," after the first six letters on the upper row. What you might not realize is that there are other ways to lay out a keyboard. The Dvorak is one of those, an alternate system for laying out computer or typewriter keys. The physical layout of the actual keys is very similar to a regular keyboard, but the letters are all in different places. A 'Y' on a standard QWERTY keyboard is in the same position as the 'F' on a Dvorak Keyboard, and so an 'F' could be substituted for a 'Y'. Here is the Dvorak keyboard layout:

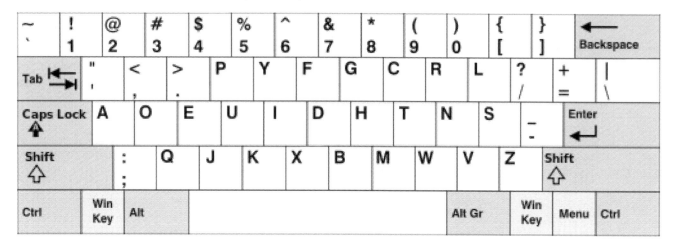

One giveaway to look out for is that text typed on a QWERTY board, meant to be converted to Dvorak, will have no "Es" (or the 'E' will always be at the ends of sentences) as the position of the 'E' on a QWERTY board is the period on a Dvorak.

swapping keyboards
See Appendix 5 for some websites that convert QWERTY text to Dvorak, and vice versa.

Similarly, there are alternate keyboard layouts that will yield symbols other than letters when you press the keys. In 1992 Microsoft introduced one of the most familiar of these: Wingdings. Wingdings are a 4 collections of symbols and images known as "Printer's ornaments." When printers used to set type by hand, they would use these ornaments to fill empty spaces, or to mark the ends of paragraphs or articles. Now they can be typed from most computers by changing the font. Windings, Windings 2, Wingdings 3, Webdings, Zapf Dingbats, and Monotype Sorts all have this sort of image, and come pre-installed as a standard font on most computers, especially those that use Windows. Puzzle COs can type anything and convert the text to one of these fonts to obscure the meaning. Once you recognize it for what it is, solving is pretty easy. You can simply copy and paste the symbols into a word processing program and change the font. If the CO has converted it to an image, you can just match the characters against a chart like those that we provide in Appendix 8.

WingDings 2

A	B	C	D	E	F	G	H	I	J	K	L	M	N	O	P	Q	R	S

T	U	V	W	X	Y	Z	a	b	c	d	e	f	g	h	i	j	k	l

m	n	o	p	q	r	s	t	u	v	w	x	y	z	0	1	2	3	4

5	6	7	8	9	!	"	#	$	%	&	'	(	)	=	~			-	^

¥	`	{	@	[	+	*	}	;	:	]	<	>	?			,	.	/

Look for these images, not just in groups but spread out throughout the page. As we discussed in the chapter on hidden puzzles, these symbols could be interspersed through a standard paragraph of text, or as the bullet points, or line marks on a list. At first, a puzzle designed in this way would seem to be about the list, but in reality would be about those marks!

appendix
See Appendix 8 for dozens of substitution based codes from pop culture, video games, literature, comic books, and more!

Find that font!

There are a hundreds of thousands of fonts available online. If you are given a puzzle that you suspect might be a type of font there are a few things you can do. Look for identical shapes within the text. Remember, there are repeated Es in the word 'three,' and several numbers start with F and S so compare the beginnings and ends of words to see if there are identical shapes. If there are that's a good indication you are dealing with a font.

The next step is to search for the font on Google. If, for instance the puzzle is a series of ballerinas you might search "ballerina font," or "ballet font." Search those two phrases on Google and look at the images. You'll see several curlyque script fonts, but you'll also see fonts that are made up of silhouettes of ballerinas. Most times you can click through and see a character map that will help you identify which dancer is associated with which letter.

I'll cover this more in Chapter 9: Codes and Ciphers, but pay close attention to the description for hints. Even though the shapes on the page might look like just squiggles and curls it could be a font associated with a video game, comic book, or other pop culture property. There may be a hint on the page that will narrow it down. For instance if the name of the cache is "Good News Everyone!" you might be able to identify that as a Futurama quote, which would help you know that you might be dealing with the Futurama Alphabet.

reaking Through

Okay... but what if you just don't know, and can't find through research what substitution is being used? What then?

There's one trick you can try. If there is a large amount of things on the page, 30, 40, 50 characters worth, you can probably assume that the substitution is being made for letters rather than numbers. We know that geocaching numbers usually appear in groups of 6, 10, 14 or 15, but spelling something out takes a lot more characters. If you simply can't find what substitution is being made, or what font was used... make it up. Working with a guess is better than having no direction at all to go in, right? What if you were presented with this puzzle?

Animals have no inherent connection with numbers. These all seem to be mammal tracks, so it can't be about the number of legs they have, since it would all be 4, even if you could identify exactly which animal each one represented. It doesn't seem to be about toes... that would just be a bunch of 2s and 4s. There are 64 prints here. That would be more than enough letters to spell out a set of coords. But we're still left with the dilemma about which paw print represents which letter. The easiest step would just be to make arbitrary choices. If a one to one substitution is what the CO has done, we can do that to. We'll just start at the beginning: the first print can be A, the second print can be B, the third track can be C, etc.

🖐 = A 🐾 = B 🐾 = C 🐾 = D etc.

And then you begin substituting those for the tracks in the puzzle.

Keep working that way until you have substituted all of the paw prints (or whatever your CO has given you) for letters. Then you'll end up with something like this:

ABCDAE FGHD FGDAE IJKJL
AMG FGHD JCNBAE AMG
FCFAE FCKJ LCLJ GLJ

And *that*, we know how to deal with, right? It's just a Cryptogram, as we discussed in Chapter 4. Break it by hand, or run it through a Cryptogram solver online (like *quipquip.com*) and soon enough you'll have a cache to find. The CO may have *intended* for you to learn an alien language or discover something new about animal prints.... but you have a solution and that's what matters.

Obfuscations

There are a few tricks that COs might use to make it harder for you to solve this kind of thing. Online Cryptogram solvers often have trouble if there are non-English words or misspelled words mixed in. The text may also be backwards, or have the spaces taken out so that you can't see the word lengths. You might have to track down the original source font or solve it by hand.

If you must solve by hand one trick to look for is double letters. There are very few English words that begin with double letters, and so if you have words with double letters at the beginning that might be an indication that your text is backwards.

We have an added benefit in our puzzle solving that there's a large possibility that any text we've been given will probably contain numbers, so we can use that as a lever to solve a cryptogram. The most frequent letters in English are E, T, A, I, O and N in descending order of frequency. However, when you consider only number words, that frequency changes to E, T, N, O, I and S. So there is a high likelihood that the letter that appears the most will be E.

Also, consider how your local coords start. If your local coords start with 4 you might try making the first letter and F, or N for North.

Solving it

Bringing together what you've learned.

Use this checklist to help you apply what you've learned in this chapter, and uncover items that could be substituted for numbers or letters.

Checklist: SUBSTITUTION

☐ Look for items on the page in groups of the "magic geocaching numbers" 6, 10, 14 or 15.

☐ Research!

☐ Consider ways that the items on the page might relate to numbers, either directly or indirectly.

☐ Consider ways that the items on the page might relate to letters, either directly or indirectly.

☐ If you have a code you can't identify try using substitution and the cryptogram method.

 # alk-Through

For the walk-through on this puzzle I'm going to try something a little different and show you multiple ways that the puzzle can be approached. First, take a look at the puzzle and see if you can imagine a few approaches that you might take. Here's the puzzle:

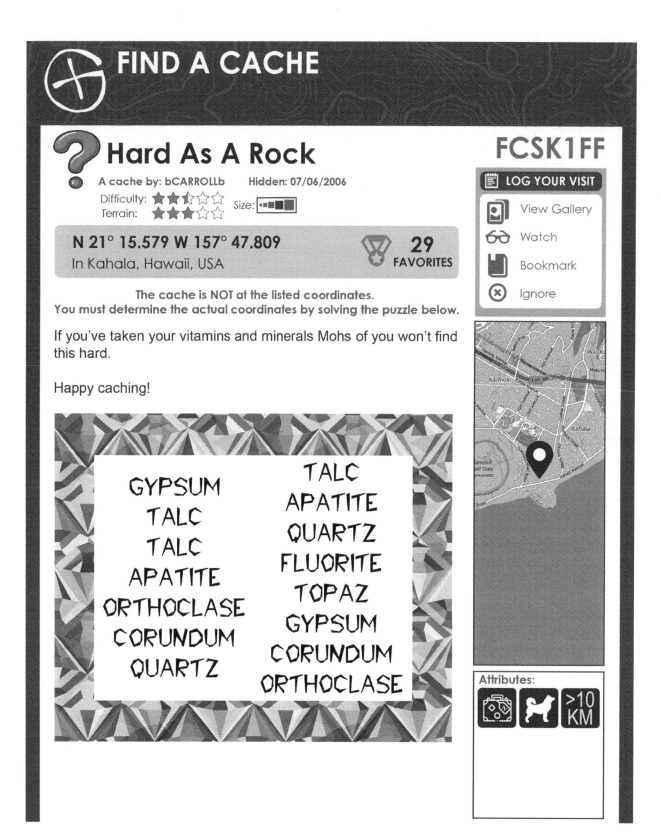

1 **The front door method.** As I said, I believe there are multiple methods that I could use to approach this puzzle, so I will show you three different avenues of attack. As usual I start with the basic information, but find nothing useful immediately. Reading the description gives me a couple things... the CO repeats the word "hard" that is also in the title, makes a somewhat awkward reference to "vitamins and minerals" and misspells the word "most" as "Mohs," including a capital letter. I'd count that as three big clues. My first thought would be to google "Mohs" to see what I get. That doesn't turn up anything useful so far, just a bunch of references to a skin cancer surgery. Let's try again with some added words, and google "Mohs hard." Right away that helps. I get a bunch of returns about something called the "Mohs Mineral Hardness Scale," which loops in the CO's third hint with the addition of a reference to minerals. Clicking on any of those links gives us a 10 point scale that rates the hardness of a mineral from 1 (talc) to 10 (diamond). All of the minerals in the puzzle are referenced on the chart. The first column starts with Gypsum, which is a 2 on the scale, followed by talc, which, as we've said, is a 1, so our coords start with "21." Going down the whole column we get 2, 1, 1, 5, 6, 9, 7 or 21° 15.697!

2 **The second victory.** Let's pretend for our second method that the written portion of the description didn't exist. Without the words "Mohs, "hard" or "mineral," could we still get an answer? Well... I've already spoiled that answer for you, but yes, there are other methods to finding an answer here. With just the image of the mineral names to go on, what would you do first? The first thing I'd notice would be how many names there are. In the far western state of Hawaii it would take fifteen digits to render the local coords, and there happen to be fifteen names in this list, so it will likely be that one name equals one digit. The next obvious step for me would be to google the minerals listed. Doing them one at a time would just return quite a bit of information about each mineral, so we need to narrow the search. The easiest way to do that is to google them together. I'd do at least three of the minerals, but you can do all the ones named if you like. If you google "gypsum, talc, apatite, orthoclase" the Mohs scale turns up in all of the top ten results. Seeing that many returns of the same thing I'd definitely look closer at it. By comparing the second column to our chart we get 1, 5, 7, 4, 8, 2, 9, 6. We can quickly arrange that into the coords -157° 48.296.

3 **The back door method.** The last method I'll show you involves no research, no googling, just solving through logic and hard work. We start here again with the fact that we have fifteen minerals listed, and we need fifteen digits to make the coords. It takes seven digits to write the north coords in Hawaii, and eight digits for the west. Since the CO was kind enough to divide the columns into one group of seven names and one group of eight, we can guess which column corresponds to which direction. With that knowledge we can start making some educated guesses about what each mineral means. The local north coords begin with 21°. So we can guess that "gypsum" will represent 2, and "talc" will represent 1, since the column with seven names starts with those two words. That is confirmed by the fact that the second column also starts with "talc," and since the local west coords start with 1, we'd expect to see talc there. The west also tells us that "apatite" represents 5, and "quartz" is 7. With those five digits figured out we can spread out to the other times that those words appear in the puzzle, which gives us nine of the fifteen digits. With just that we already have 21° 15.XX7, -157° XX.2XX.

So, how do we get the other six digits? More educated guessing. We can start with the west minutes. The dummy coords have 47 in that position, but we know it can't be 7, since we know that quartz is 7, and the puzzle says "topaz" there. The dummy coords are close to the 47/48 line, so let's just make a guess here that it is 48. It could just as easily be 45 or 49 and still be inside the 2 Mile Rule, but 45 lands in the ocean, and as for 49, remember... we're just guessing. That gives us 21° 15.XX7, -157° 48.2XX, still four digits away. At this point we've used 1, 2, 4, 5, 7, and 8, so those four digits could only come from 0, 3, 6, or 9. Our biggest clue to figure them out is that they repeat: north has "orthoclase," then "corundum," while the west has "corundum," then "orthoclase." It could be 21° 15.037, -157° 48.230, or 21° 15.307, -157° 48.203, or 21° 15.067, -157° 48.260, etc. If we are right about the 48 guess we'd only have twelve combinations to try, and if it is 49, not 48, that's twelve more. If the CO left a geochecker you can try combinations until you get a confirmed answer. If not you would have to look at the coords on maps, measure it against the 2 Mile Rule, look at where the coords land geographically, etc. Possibly more work than actually solving it, but a workable method.

On the next page is another puzzle for you to solve on your own. Apply the lessons from this chapter, and it should be a simple solve.

olve It Yourself!

Here are some puzzle caches for you to solve on your own. Using the skills we learned in this chapter you should be able to solve these puzzles. Take careful note of the final coordinates that you get as a solution to these puzzles, and write them at the bottom of the page. If you need a reminder of how to use the puzzle stats or hints provided, please check page 11. Good luck!

Puzzle 1 Solution:

N __ __ ° __ __ . __ __ __ , W __ __ __ ° __ __ . __ __ __

As a secondary check you should be able to answer this question: *What word describes what you find at the final?*

Puzzle 2 Solution:

S __ __ ° __ __ . __ __ __ , E __ __ __ ° __ __ . __ __ __

As a secondary check you should be able to answer this question: *What food do you find at the final?*

FIND A CACHE

 New phone. Hodag? **FC290EB**

A cache by: TourOfTikis   Hidden: 10/16/2016

Difficulty: ★★⯪☆☆   Size: ▪▪■□□
Terrain: ★☆☆☆☆

N 45° 38.271 W 089° 24.968
In Rhinelander, Wisconsin, USA

51 FAVORITES

LOG YOUR VISIT
- View Gallery
- Watch
- Bookmark
- Ignore

The cache is NOT at the listed coordinates.
You must determine the actual coordinates by solving the puzzle below.

I was out the other daylooking for a spot to place a cache, when all of a sudden... I heard some REALLY weird noises. I dropped the cache and ran!

I am not sure I ever want to go back and find that cache... but I have transcribed to the best of my ability the sounds I hear, maybe yuo can use that and find the cache yourself?

SKiE!

hiyLa!

Hope you don't run into anything spooky!

Attributes:

PUZZLE STATS
68 CHECKSUM   BEST VIEW

 13    87    118
 50   1

FIND A CACHE

? Castaway

A cache by: AintBillyBob   Hidden: 02/07/2014

Difficulty: ★★☆☆☆   Size: ▪▪□□□
Terrain: ★☆☆☆☆

FCS727M

S 45° 02.508 E 169° 11.828
In Cromwell, NZ

28 FAVORITES

The cache is NOT at the listed coordinates.
You must determine the actual coordinates by solving the puzzle below.

Ain't it always the way? All you want are a few easy caches, something to get your numbers up, maybe shift your mood with a little outdoor therapy, but you just can't get the satellites or spot the cache? Sigh... hope you have better luck with this one.

Attributes:

PUZZLE STATS
53 CHECKSUM   BEST VIEW

 6
 66
 106
 23
 96

 # Indexing Puzzles

In the previous chapter I talked about the idea of substitution as a puzzle method -- finding something that appears or happens in a particular order and then substituting numbers for the items. For instance, a puzzle that involves the names of the planets and substitutes numbers for the order in which they orbit, starting from Mercury, closest to the sun, and then working our way outwards. Mercury would therefore represent 1; Venus would be 2, Earth as 3, and so forth.

But what if the items that you are given don't appear to have a natural order, but instead seem like a random collection of words, phrases or items? The puzzle would then be to determine what order to put the items in, for them to make sense. This type of puzzle is called an "Indexing Puzzle" and is a favorite among many puzzle creators.

In this chapter I'll give you a full explanation of indexing, and show you how puzzle COs may use it.

lace Your Order!

An index, at its most basic, is a way of ordering things. The most common way that we have of doing that is by placing things in alphabetical order. Most indexes that we interact with in our lives will be alphabetical. The idea, however, can be stretched and distorted into many other shapes. The creation of an index is just the invention or discovery of a way to order things.

Humans are really good at indexing. If you have children, you will probably have noticed this behavior. Kids often "index" their toys by sorting them based on color, size, or even something as esoteric as which ones they like best. The systems they use may not be immediately apparent to outside eyes, and they may not even make sense if asked to explain, but it will make sense to the child.

So how does a system of indexing work in a puzzle? In the introduction I mentioned an index of the planets in our solar system based on their position from the sun.

Imagine you live near the 35th parallel and find a puzzle cache with the following in the description: "NASA sure has been busy lately! They've been sending out new probes like crazy to all the planets from smallest to largest. In just the past year, they sent three probes to both Neptune and Mercury, two to Uranus, one to mars, four to Saturn, and a whopping five to Venus! Unfortunately for fans of Jupiter, they haven't sent any probes there this year."

Immediately we can see that the description mentions seven planets, which we know is one of the geocaching magic numbers. Each planet has a number of probes associated with it: Neptune and Mercury = 3, Uranus = 2, Mars = 1, Saturn = 4, and Venus = 5. The description says that Jupiter got no probes, so maybe that is a 0. So, we have seven numbers, but the order that they are given in, 3321450 doesn't make sense for the local coords. How do we know what order to put them in? We need... an index!

The easiest and most obvious way to order the planets would be by the order of orbit around the sun, as we mentioned. By arranging the numbers in that way we get 3510423. Being near the 35th parallel I imagine you'd be pretty happy to see that 35! We can break those numbers up in typical coordinate style and have a pretty good northing: 35° 10.423'.

But what if we live near the 31st parallel, not the 35th? That's a different kettle of fish. Arranging by orbital order would yield an incorrect answer. We need a different way of indexing. What other methods can we use to order the planets? Several possibilities come to mind: by size, by relative temperature, by the number of moons, by the order of discovery...

With so many possible ways to index, we can only hope that the CO left us a clue, so we go back to the description and notice that the CO used the phrase "from smallest to largest." If we rearrange the planets in the order, from smallest to largest, the list goes: Mercury, Mars, Venus, Earth, Neptune, Uranus, Saturn, and Jupiter. Placing our numbers in order by the size of the planet they are associated with gives us the number sequence 3153240, or 31° 53.240'. That's a better set of numbers for the 31st parallel.

Anything that can be associated with an order can be used in this way. Consider all the ways that things can be placed in a specific order, including chronological. Some things, like the Stations of the Cross (a 12 image series of traditional paintings that depict the path Jesus took with the cross) have both a chronology and numbers associated with each image. Other things, like the events of the story of Goldilocks, have a clear chronology but not a defined number of steps. You can divide the story in steps in several different ways. For instance, is Goldilocks finding the beds and breaking them one item in the index? Or two? If you count each bed and break as one, that's just 3 items, but separately it could be as many as 7 or 8!

Order Up!

An indexing puzzle works by giving you a group of items or objects and asks you to place them in order by some unknown index. It can also work in the reverse. You may be given a series of objects that have already been indexed, and your job as the puzzle solver is to figure out *how* they were indexed.

Imagine a puzzle that presents you with a series of stills from episodes of Star Trek, like Captain Kirk with the Gorn, or Spock mind-melding with the Horta. There are no obvious numbers associated with these, and no reason to change the order that they are presented in. So, what can we do?

Well, these things already exist in all sorts of indexes. *Star Trek* episodes are ordered by season, by episode number, by the date and year that they actually aired, numerical order of airing, by production code, and even by internal logic like the "stardate" of the story (Star Trek talk for the date). In this particular case, the episode that the Gorn appeared in, entitled "Arena," was Season 1, Episode 18, had a production code of 019, originally aired on January 19, 1967, and the stardate in the episode was 3045.6. The episode with the Horta was entitled "Devil in the Dark," and was Season 1, Episode 25, with a production code of 026, originally aired on March 9, 1967, and the stardate in the episode was 3196.1. Depending on how many episodes are arranged on the page, and what your local coords look like, any of these numbers might be helpful.

Double Indexing

Don't overlook the possibility that a puzzle may require you to index its pieces in multiple ways. A series of car photographs could be indexed against the year in which they were released, but still not yield usable coords unless you realize that they must be separated into 2 door cars and 4 door cars, and then those two subgroups must be indexed by year. A group of photos of baseball players may require you to divide them into the American League players and the National League players before indexing them against a second theme, like their jersey numbers.

Leading Indexes

Whether you are looking to place your information into some semblance of order, or you are seeking to discover what order your information may already be in, there are many ways that information can be ordered. Here's a list of just a few possible ways of indexing you may want to consider.

PEOPLE
Year of birth
Year of death
Age at death
Height
Number of awards won

SPORTS
Uniform number
Car number
Number of years playing
Yearly records
Lifetime records
Awards won
Rankings in a particular year

COLORS
Rainbow order (Roy G Biv)
Billiard ball order
Monopoly spaces order
Resistor code colors

WORDS
Alphabetical
Number of letters
Numerology value
Root word
Language of origin

CARS
Make, or model
Year produced
Doors
Horsepower
Gas mileage
Engine size

PRODUCTS
Date they were invented
Model number
Patent number

CHARACTERS
Book, issue or episode number they
debuted (or died) in.

FOOD
Serving size
Cost
Package size or weight
Calories per serving

U.S. STATES
Land area
Year founded
Order of acceptance into the union
Number of stars on their flag
Number of the most prominent inter-
state highway through the state
Ordered by zip code
Ordered by area code
Ordered east to west (or N to S)
Population
Number of counties
Number of border states

BOOKS
Alphabetical by title
Alphabetical by author
Order in which they were written
Dewey Decimal order
Library of Congress number
Publication dates
Number of chapters
Number in a series
ISBN Number

CHEMICALS
Melting point
Boiling point
Freezing point
Burning point
Number of atoms in one molecule
Molecular weight
Acid/base status
Solubility

BUILDINGS
Alphabetical by name of building
Alphabetical by architect
Year constructed
Number of floors
Height
Street address

PLANTS AND ANIMALS
Color
Alphabetically by species, genus,
family, etc.
Number of limbs
Number of petals on flower
Geographically by habitat E to W
or N to S

MOVIES
Release year
Awards won
Run time
DVD Region codes
By director's name

MUSIC
Key
Tempo
Name of composer
Number of movements
Opus number
Year composed

SONGS
Length
Album order
Album track number
Billboard position
Release date
Number of weeks on the chart

ELEMENTS
Atomic number
Atomic Weight
Alphabetical by name
Alphabetical by atomic symbol
Number of electrons
Type of element (Metal, gas, etc.)
Period, block, or group on the elemental table
Year of discovery

CITIES
Land area
Year incorporated
Population nationally
Population within a state
Order in which a specific highway passes
through them
Sports teams records

U.S. PRESIDENTS
Presidential number
Number of terms served
Presidential term
Age at election
Height
State of origin
Age at death

As you can see, almost anything can be indexed! It's just a matter of finding the order and finding what the order means to the puzzle.

Solving it

Bringing together what you've learned.

Use this checklist to help you apply what you've learned in this chapter, and determine if you need an index or order of items to help solve the puzzle.

Checklist: INDEXES

☐ Look for groupings of items in the geocaching "magic numbers," 14, 15, 10, or 6.

☐ Consider ways that those groupings can be ordered against an existing index.

☐ If no pre-existing index can be found, consider ways that you might be able to create an index of the items in the groupings.

☐ Consider dual indexing, separating the items by one index, and then ordering them by a second index.

alk-Through

Are you ready for our next walk-through? This exercise is intended to show you one possible way to approach a cache puzzle, and help you see the steps involved in solving. Remember, there is no actual geocache at these locations. Here's the puzzle:

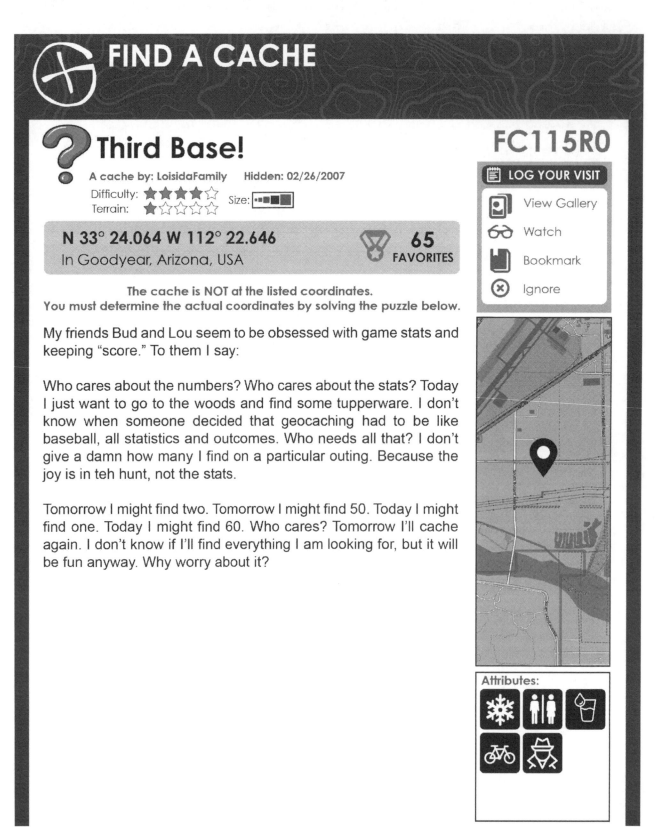

FIND A CACHE

? Third Base!

A cache by: LoisidaFamily   Hidden: 02/26/2007

Difficulty: ★★★★☆   Size: ▪▪■■□
Terrain: ★☆☆☆☆

N 33° 24.064 W 112° 22.646
In Goodyear, Arizona, USA

65 FAVORITES

FC115R0

📋 LOG YOUR VISIT

- View Gallery
- Watch
- Bookmark
- Ignore

The cache is NOT at the listed coordinates.
You must determine the actual coordinates by solving the puzzle below.

My friends Bud and Lou seem to be obsessed with game stats and keeping "score." To them I say:

Who cares about the numbers? Who cares about the stats? Today I just want to go to the woods and find some tupperware. I don't know when someone decided that geocaching had to be like baseball, all statistics and outcomes. Who needs all that? I don't give a damn how many I find on a particular outing. Because the joy is in teh hunt, not the stats.

Tomorrow I might find two. Tomorrow I might find 50. Today I might find one. Today I might find 60. Who cares? Tomorrow I'll cache again. I don't know if I'll find everything I am looking for, but it will be fun anyway. Why worry about it?

Attributes:

1 **First looks.** Alright, nothing in the basic areas of date, name, gallery or TB inventory. The attributes all seem to check out. No Related Web Page links. There's no hidden white text and nothing unusual in the source code... so all the bases are covered. We'll have to look deeper.

2 **What's in a name?** The title mentions a baseball concept, which is also mentioned in the description when the CO compares geocaching to baseball. Two mentions of something is usually enough for me to check it off as a potential theme. So, we have our first clue!

3 **Let's read the description more closely.** The description mentions baseball, as we noted. It also mentions the concept of statistics and keeping score several times. Could be another clue. There are several repeated words. "*Today,*" "*Tomorrow,*" and "*Who*" are in the description several times. Repetition also sets off bells for me in puzzle solving, so I'll take note of these words as well.

4 **The first Google.** Time for a little research. Plugging my three words (today, tomorrow and who) into Google gets me nothing. It's too broad. Is there anything else from the description that could be used to narrow it down? Most of the words in the description are pretty common, it would be hard to use them. The CO mentions two specific names, "Bud" and "Lou." Maybe that will help? Adding Bud and Lou to the previous three words gets a couple interesting hits. The first four returns mention the Abbot and Costello routine "Who's on First?" And, hey! Turns out Abbot and Costello's first names were Bud and Lou! I think we're onto something!

5 **On the team.** Alright, let's read the script for this routine. "*Who*" is mentioned a lot, of course. Not far into the script we find "*Today*" and "*Tomorrow,*" as well as several other phrases from the description: *Who, Today, Tomorrow, I don't know, I don't give a darn, Because,* and *Why* all appear in the script as the names of players. The phrase "*Third base!*" from the title, is also in the routine. We've definitely found a big piece of the puzzle. But how do we get numbers from this information?

6 **Playing the game.** Looking closely I see that there are 7 sentences in the second paragraph, and eight in the second. That probably means that one paragraph is for North, and one for West, and one sentences equals one digit. Each sentence also starts with the name of a player, so it is most likely the names that will get us the numbers. What we need here is an index. It could be the order that the players are mentioned in the routine. "*Who*" is mentioned first, so he could be 1, but "*Who*" is also the first player mentioned here, and the North co-ords should start with 3, not 1. Maybe the first paragraph is for West? That should start with 1. But we need eight digits for West, not seven, so that can't be it. There are no jersey numbers listed in the routine. It could be the base that they play, but we have two problems: "*Who*" is on first, so that would still give us a 1, which we already discounted, and there are only three bases, so how would we get a number higher than 3?

7 **The second Google.** Time for more research. Back to Google! But what to search? Here's where the real leap in logic takes place in this puzzle. We have players names and their positions on the field. What we need is numbers... let's try Baseball Position Numbers. Right off, we have a hit! Wikipedia tells me that for scoring and statistics (there are those words again!) each position on the field is assigned a number. The pitcher is 1, the catcher is 2, etc. "*Who*" was on first base, which is assigned a 3 in this indexing scheme. So our first two sentences both start with "*Who*" which would give us 33, just as we would expect! From there we can compare each player's name with their position and the position number to get coords.

8 **We have an answer!** Going through the entire description that way, we end up with 3, 3, 2, 5, 3, 6, 8 from the first paragraph, or 33° 25.368. The second paragraph gives us 1, 1, 2, 2, 3, 1, 5, 7, or 112° 23.157. So our coords are 33° 25.368, -112° 23.157. (Remember, none of the cache locations in this book lead to real caches, but I have tried to choose interesting or thematic locations for each of the finals.)

On the next page is another puzzle for you to solve. Apply the lessons from this chapter, and it should be a simple solve.

Based on a puzzle concept by cacher EastVillageFamily. Thanks for letting me use it Mark!

olve It Yourself!

Here are some puzzle caches for you to solve on your own. Using the skills we learned in this chapter you should be able to solve these puzzles. Take careful note of the final coordinates that you get as a solution to these puzzles, and write them at the bottom of the page. If you need a reminder of how to use the puzzle stats or hints provided, please check page 11. Good luck!

Puzzle 1 Solution:

N __ __ ° __ __ . __ __ __ , W __ __ __ ° __ __ . __ __ __

As a secondary check you should be able to answer this question: *What instrument do you find at the final?*

Puzzle 2 Solution:

N __ __ ° __ __ . __ __ __ , W __ __ __ ° __ __ . __ __ __

As a secondary check you should be able to answer this question: *What old school medium is in the fountain at the final?*

FIND A CACHE

 ## Caching Soundtrack

A cache by: 52farmallcubs   Hidden: 04/17/2009

Difficulty: ★★★½☆   Size: ▪▪■■▫
Terrain: ★☆☆☆☆

N 28° 19.867 W 081° 34.369
In Orlando, Florida, USA

22 FAVORITES

FCDGL12

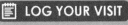

The cache is NOT at the listed coordinates.
You must determine the actual coordinates by solving the puzzle below.

Your answer for this puzzle will be in decimal degree format. Happy hunting!

cachewell   POSITION
TYPE I • NORMAL

 GEO MIX TAPE

(A) DATE . .   N.R.   ○YES ○NO

1. Looking for Satellites- David Bowie 2. Searching- George Jones 3. Hunting High and Low- AHA 4. I've Found a Hiding Place- Charlie Daniels 5. Sign Your Name- Terrence Trent D'Arby 6. Satellite- Elton John 7. Half set of Co-Ordinates- Out of Phase

(B) DATE . .   N.R.   ○YES ○NO

1. Another Day In The Park- The Strolling Scones 2. Multi-String Theory 3. The Missing Coordinates- Scar Symmetry 4. Out In The Woods- Susan James 5. We Didn't Find Anything- Peter Broderick 6. Under The Lamppost- Jennifer Bresnahan 7. TFTC- The Travelbugs

Attributes:

PUZZLE STATS
51 CHECKSUM   BEST VIEW

 6   66    106
23   96

FIND A CACHE

 ## Quite A Collection

FC35MM

A cache by: M0n3yp1tt

Hidden: 12/02/2004

Difficulty: ★★★☆☆   Size:

Terrain: ★☆☆☆☆

N 34° 00.645 W 118° 22.798
In Culver City, CA, United States

29 FAVORITES

LOG YOUR VISIT

- View Gallery
- Watch
- Bookmark
- Ignore

The cache is NOT at the listed coordinates.
You must determine the actual coordinates by solving the puzzle below.

Attributes:

PUZZLE STATS

 **50** CHECKSUM   BEST VIEW

 98   **44**   **125**

141   **132**

Tell Me A Story

You arrive at the cache page and find... a story. No pictures, no images, nothing. Just a rambling story. The only way you know that this cache is a puzzle at all is that it has the blue question mark at the top. What do you do?

Of all the cache types this is the one that I get the most questions about, and the one that people seem to find the most frustrating. I think the problem with them is that they are vague and there are just too many possible ways to solve them. Oh, you say you can't even think of one way to solve them? Well... read on!

I discussed a few possibilities in the previous chapter, using acrostics, first words, or first letters, or having text hidden within the story using italics or different fonts, but let's look at a few other possibilities.

eading Comprehension

Well, perhaps it seems like an obvious place to start, but when you are confronted with a story puzzle the first step... is to read the story.

Read through it once for "pleasure." Even if you know that text contains information it can often be difficult to see that information on the first reading. The human brain is wired for storytelling, and so we are often distracted by a narrative. Reading through once gets that out of the way, so that you can focus on the detail for a second reading. Think about reading the directions for something. Do you ever understand everything about it on the first reading? I know I don't. It usually takes a second reading to start to get the details.

What are you reading for? That depends a lot on the puzzle, but the general advice is: anything weird. Is there anything that stands out about the story? Does it have a lot of Zs? Are the sentences unusual lengths? Is there anything repetitive about the story? Do any of the sentences seem awkwardly constructed? Any of those things could be hints to the solve method.

ake your story count

My first piece of advice when faced with a story puzzle is to count things. Recall from the second chapter the discussion of geocaching "magic numbers." These are the number of digits required to create coordinates, so 14 (or 15) for a full set of coordinates, 10 for just the minutes and seconds, or 6 for just the seconds. Look carefully at the story. Are there 14 sentences? If so, each sentence could represent a single digit of the coordinates somehow. This would be especially true if there are two paragraphs of seven sentences each. The first paragraph could represent to north, and the second the west.

So how do the sentences represent numbers? There are several ways. The following paragraph contains the first seven digits of a set of coords:

> Yesterday I went caching. I didn't find anything. Not one thing. In fact I failed at every cache. Couldn't find the big ones, or the small ones. Geez! I suck at geocaching.

Do you see them? Start with the fact that there are seven sentences. Each sentence therefore might represent one digit. Counting the number of words in each sentence will help you see that the coords are 44° 37.914. One giveaway that this was the case is the one word sentence, "Geez!" If your story contains multiple one word sentences you may be looking at something similar.

Let's try another. This story also contains the first seven digits of a set of coords:

The cache I found was painted blue.

Knowing that you are looking for seven digits makes this one pretty obvious since there are seven words. Each word must represent a digit in the coords. By counting the number of letters you would get the coords 35° 15.374.

Here's a more difficult one. Again, you are looking for seven digits:

Teepees unexpectedly made everyone's evening more serene.

Counting individual letters can't be the answer since "unexpectedly" has twelve letters. What other possibilities are there? You may notice that there are is an uncommonly high number of occurrences of the Letter E in this sentence. If you count the individual Es you'll find the coordinates 43° 13.213. Packing all of the digits into one sentence is an extreme example, and makes the answer pretty obvious, but imagine having 14 sentences and counting the number of occurrences of a single letter in each sentence, whether it is E, or some other letter.

You can count letters, either by occurrence, or by the over all number of letters, or count punctuation, sentences, or words. Any of those could be used to create a puzzle.

Counting Concepts

Besides the concrete examples from the previous section there are some less straightforward ways that counting could come into play in a story based puzzle. Consider this story, once again containing seven digits:

> This morning was my annual meeting with Mike, Dan, Joan and Angie. Mike and Dan were on time, but Joan was late as usual. When Angie showed up she also had Karl, Phil, Carol, and Jacqui with her, which I hadn't been expecting at all! So there I was, with Mike, Dan, Angie, Joan, Karl, Phil, Carol and Jacqui when Diane called in and asked to be put on speaker so that she could listen in! Jacqui and Carol got the conference call set up. While they were doing that Mike, Dan and Phil went and got coffee for us all. Once everyone was finally there and settled in Dan and Angie gave a great presentation.

So? What do you see? There are no obvious repeated letters, several of the sentences are too long for it to be words (because there are more than 9 words). What else can you count?

In this instance you would count what I call "concepts." The repeated concept in this story

is people or names. So if you count the number of names in each sentence you would get coords of 43° 59.232.

This type of counting could be applied to any concept: birds, animals, caching words, almost anything that can be repeated in a story.

Start with the basic approach to a cache page, examining the cache name, cacher name, date, attributes, etc to see if there is a theme and then look for repetitions of the theme within the text of the description. For instance if the cache is named "Ships Ahoy," and has a "Boat Required" attribute, perhaps the story mentions the names of famous ships or types of boat?

The techniques of counting and the idea of concepts can be combined. If each sentence in your story mentions a species of snake, but only one per sentence, it can't be like the names in the story above, but perhaps it is about identifying the conceptual idea, and then counting something else, perhaps letters? So in our snake example, an "asp" would equal 3, and a "cobra" would equal 5, etc. Or it could be a letter to number transformation, in which case our asp would equal 1, because A=1, and our cobra would be 3 because C=3.

idden Stories

The "Story Puzzle" can also be used in combination with previously discussed methods to hide the relevant information within the cache page, in the source code, or in plain sight.

Hidden Figures

One favorite technique of geocache COs is hiding numbers among the words of a story. It can be as simple as having the numbers right there in the story. Go through your story and look for number words. If there are 15, 14, 10, or 6 number words those could be your coordinates in the order that they are given in the story. Remember to look for homophones like two/to/to, four/for/fore, and eight/ate.

Another method is to hide the number words in the story. Think of it as a Word Search puzzle, except instead of scrambled letters with hidden words, its a story.

Have a look at this sentence. It contains three numbers:

> The rhino never swam with reef fish because of his weight.

Can you spot them? Look again. The numbers are 1, 3 and 8. Can you find them now?

The rhinO NEver swam wiTH REEf fish because of his wEIGHT.

Some of the hidden numbers may spread across words (as in "one" and "three" above), or hidden within other words (as in the "eight" in "weight.")

The weakness of this type of puzzle are the unusual letters that are in many number words, specifically V, X and Z from five and seven, six, and zero. Another weakness is the word "eight," because the "gh" combination is relatively uncommon, and the double E in "three," which stands out.

The following story contains a complete set of coords:

> North of here is a fort you see on every brochure. This fort yonder, if I've never mentioned, is eventually going fall, stone by stone.
>
> West of there is even land that women of our family love and men of our tribe want worked. With reeds and willows they expect this event.

What do you notice right away about this story? For me it would be the words "North" and "West" which gives me a clue that each paragraph will represent one direction. Of course, not all COs will be this obvious about things. Those words may even be hidden in the same way as the numbers, or ignored all together. In that case you will have to remember the geocaching "magic numbers" (15, 14, 10, & 6) to help you know how many numbers you are looking for.

The second thing I would notice is the repetition of the word "fort," especially since both are followed by a word that begins with a Y, making "forty." Another obvious repetition is the word "stone," which of course contains "one."

Next, the phrase "with reeds and willows" is kind of awkward, and doesn't really make sense, which makes it an obvious hiding spot. Consider that kind of awkward phrasing the text equivalent of the "unnatural pile of sticks" that often hides a cache.

Finally, the combination "even" occurs twice, which is likely going to point at the number "seven."

> **NORTH** of here is a **FORT Y**ou see **ON E**very brochure. This **FORT Y**onder, i**F I'VE** never mentioned, i**S EVEN**tually going fall, st**ONE** by st**ONE**.
>
> **WEST** of there i**S EVEN** land tha**T WO**men o**F OUR** family love and men o**F OUR** tribe wan**T WO**rked. Wi**TH REE**ds and willows they expect thi**S EVEN**t.

So you end up with N 41° 45.711', W 72° 44.237'. Notice that in the North, 41 is represented by the word "forty" followed by "one," but in the West, 44 is represented by the words "four" followed by "four." This kind of change makes it easier for the CO to hide the necessary words within the text.

If you think you might be faced with this kind of puzzle, start with the number at the beginning of your local coords and see if you can find that number near the beginning, or the end of the story. Why the end? Because some tricky COs will give you the numbers in reverse!

Hidden Text

Using white text (as I previously discussed in Chapter 3) on cache pages to hide coordinates is common. That idea can be used in conjunction with story puzzles by hiding the white text between paragraphs, or single letters of white between words rather than the standard spaces. You can see this hidden text by selecting all the text on a cache page by hitting "Command A" on a Mac or "Control A" on a PC, or by selecting the text using the cursor as you would if you intended to copy the text. Either of those will highlight the text in color, revealing the hidden white text.

Hidden Links

Another proper method is hiding a weblink within the story, usually making a period or some other piece of punctuation the link because it is so small that it will be difficult to see. The easiest way to see hidden weblinks is to look at the source code.

In most browsers, if you right click on a website, you get a menu that includes "View Source

Code" or "Show Page Source." If you are using Safari and have never done this before, you will first need to activate the "Develop" menu. To do that, click on "Safari" in the top menu bar, then go to "Preferences." In that pop up menu, click the "Advanced" tab and then click the check box next to "Show Develop." Then you should be able to right click on a page and select "View Page Source."

Remember, viewing the source info cannot be done through the geocaching app. The cache description must be accessed from the web. You can view the source on a tablet or phone if you use an app like "ViewSource" on an iPhone (.99¢ in the app store). If you are using Firefox on your tablet or phone you can view source code in the by prefixing the web page's URL with the following text: *view-source: .*
For example, to view the HTML source for geocaching.com you'd submit the following text in the browser's address bar: *view-source:https://www.geocaching.com*

Once you are in the source code the thing to look for is a tag that contains **href** which is the tag that is used for creating a hyperlink to another website. You can also use this method to look for the white text I previously mentioned.

 # ndexed Stories

The "Story Puzzle" can also be used in combination with previously discussed methods to hide the coordinates using the "indexing" method I discussed last chapter. Have a look at this story:

I started my caching career in Colorado. Later I found a cache in my second state, Louisiana. It took a long time but then I added Virginia and Massachusetts. Soon after I found a cache in Delaware then in New York. I was privileged to find one of the best caches in Hawaii on a trip there. The last two states I've found caches in are Utah and Pennsylvania.

You probably notice right away that there is a "concept" around states. Counting doesn't work, as most sentences have either one or two states. Counting letters in the individual state names doesn't get very far as you get 8 (Colorado), 9 (Louisiana), 8 (Virginia), 12 (Massachusetts), 8 (Deleware), 7 (New York) 6 (Hawaii), 4 (Utah) and 12 (Pennsylvania). So, 89812876412. That's 11 digits, and not really easily divided into coords. Plus 89° and 81' doesn't exist as minutes can't go higher than 59'.

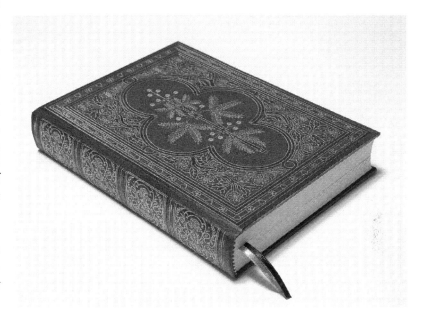

It could be initial letters of each state C, L, V, M, D, N (or maybe NY since it is two words), H, U and P. That could be 3,12, 22, 13, 4, 14, 8, 21, 16. That gives us 15 digits which could divide as 31° 22.213, -41° 48.2116. Which... if you lived in the North Atlantic you'd probably be pretty happy with.

But let's say that we are caching in southern Utah where the coords should be in the neighborhood of N 38°, W 111°. Can we find a way of getting similar numbers from those states?

There are several ways that sates can be indexed. The population, the number of counties, the most prominent area code, the code for the largest airport... How do we narrow it down besides just guessing?

If I know that the coordinates will probably start with 38 I would try googling "Colorado 38" to see if there is an association between the state and the number. The first few returns are about "Title 38," which is a law within the state. Not helpful... but down around the fifth return I see "Colorado was the 38th state to join the union." Oooo! Now that I can work with! If I look up each state I get you get 38 (Colorado), 19 (Louisiana), 10 (Virginia), 6 (Massachusetts), 1 (Deleware), 11 (New York) 50 (Hawaii), 45 (Utah) and 2 (Pennsylvania). So, 381910611150452, which can be divided into 38° 19.106, -111 50.452. That puts me firmly in the area I need to be in!

Indexing Layers

The above method could have an extra layer of difficulty. Imagine the same story as above, but instead of each state being listed in the story the CO listed the capitals of each state, leaving it up to you to determine which state they were referring to.

By layering two concepts like that a CO provides a much more challenging puzzle, because the method for solving it is obfuscated. If you think you have spotted a concept (like capital cities) but can't find a way of indexing the information to get coordinates, try moving up the conceptual ladder a bit and looking for another layer. that could provide a different way of indexing the information.

he Story Doesn't Matter

Another thing to look for is stories that are presented as images rather than as text on the page. If the story was typed up on a different system, like Photoshop, or is a screenshot from Word or something like that, it opens up the possibility that the content of the story doesn't even matter.

Images can be used to hide a lot of information (see the upcoming chapters on Steganography and Computer Software for more about how this might be done.) It could have something to do with the file itself, the space around the words, and many other things.

Another use for a story image is that there is information hidden within the story somewhere. I once did a non-geocaching story puzzle (in an escape room) where we were presented with a sheet of printed out text. We noticed right away that the text contained quite a few Xs, but counting them, or the words containing them were getting us nowhere. I circled all the appearances of X on the page as part of my solve process, but it was a friend who noticed that all the instances of the letter form a sort of grid. Using other clues in the story we determined that the Xs represented dots in Braille, and spelled out the word we needed to move on in the puzzle.

If the CO went to the trouble of creating an image rather than typing the information into the cache page that tells you something. There is likely something about the puzzle that relies on the positioning of the words, or some aspect of the image, or the file itself.

Solving it
Bringing together what you've learned.

Use this checklist to help you apply what you've learned in this chapter, and determine what information the story puzzle might contain.

Checklist: STORIES

- ☐ Look for groupings of items in the geocaching "magic numbers," 14, 15, 10, or 6.

- ☐ Examine the story for numbers or numerical homophones.

- ☐ Look for white text or hidden links.

- ☐ Look for concepts within the story.

- ☐ Look for things that you could count, like words, letters, punctuation or concepts.

- ☐ Look for acrostics, or hidden numbers.

- ☐ Consider a letter to number conversion of the first letters, letters from conceptual words or other sources.

- ☐ Look for indexes that you could apply to the concept of the puzzle.

- ☐ If the story is an image look for other methods of hiding information.

 # alk-Through

Are you ready for our next walk-through? This exercise is intended to show you one possible way to approach a cache puzzle, and help you see the steps involved in solving. Remember, there is no actual geocache at these locations. Here's the puzzle:

FIND A CACHE

? I Been Everywhere

A cache by: mAlTm   Hidden: 04/11/2017

Difficulty: ★★☆☆☆   Size: ▪▫■■■
Terrain: ★☆☆☆☆

FCSUB4R

LOG YOUR VISIT
- View Gallery
- Watch
- Bookmark
- Ignore

N 35° 38.534 E 139° 44.068
In Tokyo, Japan

36 FAVORITES

The cache is NOT at the listed coordinates.
You must determine the actual coordinates by solving the puzzle below.

I been everywhere, man, I been everywhere. I been from Santa Fe to Seattle, from Auckland, to Woollongong, fromToronto to Guadalajara, from Paris to Peru. I been from Beijing and Prague to Cairo.

I been from San Francisco to Chicago, from Melbourne to Kuaii, from Kabul to Buenos Aires. I been from Moscow to Madrid, from London to Hanoi, from Orlando to Montevideo. I been from Tipei to Riga, from Pyongyang to Nairobi, from Bogata to Kathmandu and from Seoul to Kingston.

I really wish I had started caching before I did all that travelling...

Attributes:

1 **First looks.** Okay, I don't see anything in in the basic areas of date, name, gallery or TB inventory. The attributes are pretty basic. No Related Web Page links. There's no hidden white text and nothing unusual in the source code... time to read the description.

2 **Long description.** Reading through the description I immediately see that there are a lot of cities mentioned. I also see a repetition f the phrase "I been everywhere." That is two concepts that I can look into.

3 **Sing along!** A quick google shows me that "I been everywhere," is the title of a song originally written about Australian towns, but rewritten several times for different countries, including America. The description lists songs from a dozen different countries, so possibly unrelated to real versions of the songs.

4 **Deeper look at the songs.** Time for a little research. Wikipedia has a great list of every city mentioned in every version of the song. A few of the cities here are in various versions, but most of them have never been in any version of the song. I'm going to rule out the song as part of the puzzle for now.

All those cities. Well, if it is unrelated to the song maybe it has to do with the city names. The cities are from a large variety of countries, some repeat, but most don't. I notice that some of the cities are capitals, but many aren't. I don't immediately see anything that connects them.

5 **Time to count.** At this point I'd start counting things, looking for those magic numbers. There are 31 total cities mentioned, too many for the geocaching numbers. I see 7 sentences, but all the city names appear within the first two paragraphs. Those paragraphs contain 6 sentences (magic number!) divided into 3 sentences each (another magic number!) 6 sentences could mean the last three digits of North and East. One paragraph for North, and one for East, 3 digits each?

6 **Other things.** In my counting I notice two other things, first that each of the 6 sentences in the first two paragraphs begin with "I been everywhere." The last paragraph doesn't contain that phrase at all. The second thing I noticed is that the first sentence has no city names in it.

7 **Counting.** Counting city name occurrences per sentence I end up with 0, 8, 3, 6, 6, 8 and 0. I'm going to guess that since that one lonely sentence doesn't contain the phrase "I been everywhere" I can ignore it. That gives me 0, 8, 3, 6, 6 and 8, which I can put into the standard coords for this area and end up with 35° 38.083, 139° 44.668, which seem like good coords to me!

On the next page is another puzzle for you to solve. Apply the lessons from this chapter, and it should be a simple solve.

olve It Yourself!

Here are some puzzle caches for you to solve on your own. Using the skills we learned in this chapter you should be able to solve these puzzles. Take careful note of the final coordinates that you get as a solution to these puzzles, and write them at the bottom of the page. If you need a reminder of how to use the puzzle stats or hints provided, please check page 11. Good luck!

Puzzle   1
Solution:

N __ __ ° __ __ . __ __ __ , W __ __ __ ° __ __ . __ __ __

As a secondary check you should be able to answer this question: *What toy do you find at the final?*

Puzzle 2 Solution:

S __ __ ° __ __ . __ __ __ , E __ __ __ ° __ __ . __ __ __

As a secondary check you should be able to answer this question: *What unusual color is the item visible at the final?*

FIND A CACHE

Geocaching Planning

A cache by: Izella Grizella **Hidden: 02/26/2007**

Difficulty:
Terrain:

Size:

N 41° 54.835 W 087° 46.723
In Galewood, Illinois, USA

65 FAVORITES

FCAK0PI

📋 **LOG YOUR VISIT**

📷 View Gallery
👓 Watch
📖 Bookmark
⊗ Ignore

The cache is NOT at the listed coordinates.
You must determine the actual coordinates by solving the puzzle below.

Ever tried to get a bunch of cachers together? It's like herding cats! Some want a long hike, some want a numbers run, some want puzzles, some want Earthcaches. After consulting all my friends before a recent outing here is the list of everything they wanted in a cache:

 A hike shorter than 1 km
 Campfires allowed
 A scenic view
 Boats required
 Take less than an hour
 A picnic table nearby
 Dogs allowed

I couldn't find a cache that fit all the requirements that the team wanted, so I decided to place a puzzle that would satisfy them all!

Attributes:

PUZZLE STATS
64 CHECKSUM BEST VIEW

👆 **83**   👟 **150**   🥊 **130**
💣 **38**   ☁ **76**

FIND A CACHE

...connected to the...

A cache by: Lynnguistics   **Hidden:** 07/22/2018

Difficulty: ★★★☆☆   Size: ▪▫◼◼◻
Terrain: ★☆☆☆☆

FCM3X1C

LOG YOUR VISIT

📷 View Gallery
👓 Watch
🔖 Bookmark
ⓧ Ignore

S 37° 42.476 E 144° 59.872
In Melbourne, Australia

🏅 **32 FAVORITES**

The cache is NOT at the listed coordinates.
You must determine the actual coordinates by solving the puzzle below.

I keep injuring myself when I am out caching! It started two years ago when I tried to get that Eclipse tin out from under a boardwalk, then I tumbled backwards and broke my coccyx!

I was barely recovered from that when I slipped off a sidewalk trying to find myself on a webcam and fractured my calcaneus. That one really hurt!

I broke my clavicle trying to climb a tree for the final of a puzzle cache.

Last summer it was my left tibia after sliding on some wet leaves.

Just a few days later I was crossing a stream on a log, and some old rotten bark peeled away. I slipped, and ended up in the drink, soaking wet... and a shattered ulna on my right.

Here I sit, with my most recent injury, a cracked trapezium. In the meantime I guess I'll solve solme puzzle caches and hope for the days when I can finally get out there and collect some smilies again.

Attributes:

☠

PUZZLE STATS

80 CHECKSUM   BEST VIEW

👆 91   👢 142   🥊 36

💣 136   🌲 100

Codes and Ciphers

Codes and ciphers. The very idea strikes fear into the heart of many puzzle solvers. Part of the problem is that we don't really properly make a distinction between the two... we often use the word code when we mean cipher, and vice versa. One of the most popular "codes" in the world, Morse Code, isn't even actually a code -- it's a cipher. I'll try and make a distinction, but as you'll see, the line gets a bit blurry.

Puzzle cache owners love codes and ciphers! I think the geeky nature of them appeals to the same sweet spot as geocaching, and there is a long association between secret codes and science fiction or fantasy writing which also taps into our geeky nature. It crosses into the geocaching sweet-spot, that desire to know secret things, seek out secret places, and discover what someone else has created something for you to find.

But here's the good news: you already know how to handle codes. At its most basic level the idea of substitution that we discussed in the previous chapter is a code. A code is defined as "a system of words, letters, figures, or other symbols used to represent words or phrases," and that's substitution. The trick with codes is learning to recognize them. Recognizing a code is the biggest step towards being able to decode it. Hopefully after this chapter you'll be able to recognize several on sight.

Ciphers are a bit trickier since they don't rely on words, but on steps or systems. They can range from very simple to exceedingly complex, but most involve aspects of letter substitution and/or rearrangement of the letters, using a given set of rules, to disguise the content of the message.

This chapter will cover some of the simpler codes and ciphers, and then, in the next chapter, we'll move to more advanced types.

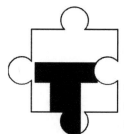he Code Blues

Codes, started as a way to communicate secretly. In order to send a message to your troops in battle or your spies in the field you needed to be able to do it in a way that the enemy couldn't read. Many other uses for codes have come up over the years, but the idea remains the same.

The definition of a code bears repeating: a word, a symbol, or a series of letters or numbers are chosen to represent a word or a phrase. This can be as broad or as narrow as the situation requires. A single word is all it really takes. Think of a spy, waiting to find out the parameters of a mission. He is told by his handlers to check the window of a pet shop. If he sees a green bird, he knows that he has been given the go ahead. That one image represents the entirety of the code.

Of course it can get much more advanced. If he sees a red bird, then he knows the mission has been aborted. A blue bird means then the mission has changed. If there is a yellow bird then the spy's cover is blown, and he must run. The list could go on and on.

When talking about codes and ciphers the message that you are trying to convey is known as the "plaintext," or "cleartext." The encoded message is called the "ciphertext." Very rarely it may also be called "codetext." These words will help you as we move forward.

Telegraph Codes

When sending messages by telegraph was the norm, companies used to send dozens and dozens of telegrams a day, to their agents in the field, to other branches of their company, to their suppliers, shippers, and buyers... it all added up. At ¢25 a word, sending a long telegram could get cost prohibitive quickly. Western Union, Marconi, or any of the dozens of other companies that sent telegrams were aware of this, and developed code systems to help. These codes served two purposes: first to make the messages being sent shorter, and second to establish customer loyalty. After all, if you own a copy of the Marconi Code, you'd be much more likely to use the Marconi Company to send it. How did these codes work? It was actually quite ingenious. The code books would list thousands of 5 letter words. Each word would correspond to a sentence or phrase. So, instead of saying, "If the price is low, purchase 10 tons of raw iron ore." You could instead send

20160	VYFMA	Sugar.
20161	VYGAB	beet sugar.
20162	VYGEC	cane sugar.
20163	VYGID	Suggest(s).
20164	VYGME	suggest that.
20165	VYGOF	can they suggest ?
20166	VYGUG	can you suggest ?
20167	VYGWI	do not suggest.
20168	VYGYK	if they suggest (that).
20169	VYHAL	if you suggest (that).
20170	VYHBA	we cannot suggest.
20171	VYHEB	what do they suggest ?
20172	VYHIC	what do you suggest ?

A sample from the Marconi Telegraphic Code Book.

a telegram saying, "Apple victor casks." By looking up the words in another copy of the code book the recipient would find that "Apple" meant "If the price is low," "victor" meant "purchase 10 tons," and "casks" meant "raw iron ore." Three words were far less expensive to send than original 12 word message. Other companies used 5 letter codes that may not have actually been words, or 5 number codes.

To understand these codes, you would have to know which code book was being used. As I said, dozens of companies set up these types of codes. The books also changed from year to year. If the cache page mentions telegrams and has a series of 5 letter words, or 5 letter codes, try to determine what telegraph company code book might be being used. Many of them are now available online at Google Books, or *Archive.org*.

The Problem

Knowing which book you might need to decode a telegram brings up the real problem with codes: needing to have a codebook at all. If one person uses a code system at one end to encode a message, the person at the other end must have the exact same book in order to decode the message. That wasn't a problem with Telegraph Codes, where the telegraph office probably had copies, and the code was public knowledge. To be truly secret and secure, the codebooks had to also be secret, perhaps only one or two existed, and if the enemy could get a copy, then the code was useless, and a new code had to be created. Naval codebooks were historically bound in lead sheets so that if the ship were to fall under siege, the Captain could throw the codebook overboard and the weight of the lead would pull the book to the bottom, keeping it out of enemy hands.

Book Code

One way around the problem of lost codebooks is to use a book that anyone can find or buy. This method is called a "Book Cipher" or an "Ottendorf Cipher," even though it's actually a code. (See what I meant about those two definitions getting mixed up?)

In a Book Cipher, the plaintext is encoded by finding the word that you want to use inside a book. What you send to the other party is the information on how to find that word. Pretty simple, right? The trick is making sure that, like a traditional codebook, the person receiving the message has the exact same book. Simply saying the title, however, is not enough. I could say that a code was based on *The Life of Pi*, which is a very popular book that a lot of people own copies of. But there have been over 25 editions of that book! Some paperback, some hardback, some illustrated, some not, different page counts, different print sizes.... the list goes on and on. In order to use that book for this type of code, you would have to be very specific. So, if a cache page makes reference to a very specific book, say, the 1974 edition of the *Riverside Shakespeare,* then you can be pretty sure that it is an important book.

Now that we know how to narrow down the book, the next thing we need is to know where the word is. This is usually done using a series of three numbers that correspond to the page, the paragraph, line or sentence, and the word. It would look something like this: 219-4-102. If I know that my book is the 1974 edition of the *Riverside Shakespeare,* then I can see that if I go to page 219, count down to paragraph 4, and then count to word 102 I would find the word "three."

There are many variations on the Ottendorf: page, paragraph, word, or page, line, word, or page, sentence, word. Some people who use this type of code might use four numbers to indicate what they want you to find, perhaps using page, paragraph, sentence and word. The more specific you can be the less the puzzle solver has to count to find what they are looking for.

But what if there's no book on the cache page? Well... don't worry, this code could be used on a plaque, a historical marker, a statue, a sign -- anything that has text. Remember on our checklist from Chapter 2, I suggested looking at all the waypoints on a cache page. If you see something that looks like it could be a Book Cipher, for instance lots of numbers grouped in threes, and you see a historical marker at the waypoint, try using the marker as your code book.

I hear you asking out there, "Can I use a Book Cipher to point to single letters on a page instead of words?" Well, sure! In that case, the Book Cipher becomes a true cipher and is no longer a code. Codes work on the level of words or phrases, but never make use of the alphabet, or text at the level of letters. Once you get down to manipulating letters, you are beginning to use Ciphers.

national treasure

The movie *National Treasure* used an Ottendorf Cipher as part of the plot. The code was based on the "Silence Dogood" letters in the National Archives.

beale cipher

One variation on a book cipher, known as the "Beale Cipher," uses only letters from a single document. The most famous use, and where the cipher gained its name, was in the Beale Pamphlet, which purported to be a map to a multi-million dollar treasure. It used the Declaration of Independence as its source text.

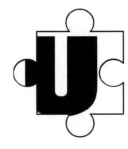 **tility Codes**

We are surrounded by codes. Area codes, zip codes, bar codes... there are a million and one ways that manufacturers and businesses use codes in their every day work. Attaching a code to something makes it easier to track and easier to refer to. Calling something "CO38797" is a lot easier than calling it a "KOOL VUE 1000 SERIES DIRECT FIT COLD AIR INTAKE WITH TUBE." Product numbers, parts numbers, etc. are all open to puzzle makers.

These codes work similarly to the telegraph code. If you don't know what the codes mean it will simply seem like a string of numbers, but looking them up in an index, a book or a database will give you the knowledge to know what that string of numbers is standing in for.

Books

Earlier I mentioned to you the possibility of using Dewey Decimal numbers to structure a puzzle, but books have a

myriad of referencing numbers that could be used. Besides Dewey, there is the Library Of Congress System, another way of marking shelf tags and book spines. The Library of Congress also uses an in-house system called the "Library of Congress Control Number," or an LCCN. There is also the ISBN, or "International Standard Book Number." This is a number assigned to all books sold on the mass market, through bookstores and the like. It is a 9, 10, or 13 digit number that relays information on the publisher, where the book was published, and the title. All of these variations can be looked up on the web, at various book sellers or at library websites like *worldcat.org,* which is a website that searches library catalogs around the world. LCCNs can be retrieved at *loc.gov,* the Library of Congress website.

Your Calls & Letters

Two of the most well known public databases of utility codes are area codes and zip codes. With zip codes we have numbers that represent specific areas covered by a post office. A zip code might represent a broad area, like 89049 which represents the area around Tonopah, Nevada. 89049 is over 10,000 square miles. Larger than the state of Maryland! It might also represent a very tiny area, like 11109 in Queens, New York. 11109 represents just 2 square blocks!

Telephone area codes are more layered. While older area codes were assigned to specific states, and some to very populous and specific cities, the newer area codes that have been added to accommodate the proliferation of cell phones now spread across state lines and might cover much broader areas.

Model Numbers

Parts numbers, product numbers, model numbers, or item numbers are another very versatile way that this type of puzzle can be utilized.

Let's consider for a second the website for Wal-Mart. As many commercial websites do, *walmart.com* basically acts as a giant database where information can be looked up. You can look things up in a variety of ways, such as by the exact name, by product type, by keyword, by manufacturer, or by item number.

At *walmart.com,* search "Bondhus FELO 6 Piece Ergonic Screwdriver Set." That's a precise search, and returns exactly that product. But you could also get to the same product by searching keywords "6 piece screwdriver," and looking through the results. The most powerful and direct search is by the model number, which is "53167." Where the other searches, even the full name of the item, will return extra items that use the same words, the item number returns *only* that precise item. Some websites will also use both the manufacturer's model number, as well as their own, internal, numbering system.

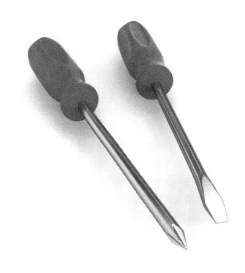

Flow of Information

The great thing about using this type of information as the basis for a puzzle is that information flows in several directions. Sticking with the example of *walmart.com*, let's look at three different paths towards coordinates that a puzzle maker could take.

The first would be to use the Item Number as the coordinates. Imagine a cache where the initial coords land in the parking lot of a Wal-Mart. Something in the description hints you to look for an item online, and gives you two specific items to shop for. One of them is the screwdriver set we've already mentioned, the Bondhus FELO 6 Piece Ergonic Screwdriver Set, the other is the Great Neck Saw 4 Piece Pliers Set. If you go to *walmart.com* and look up the screwdrivers, you will find the Model Number, 53167. For the pliers you will find the Model Number 58526. Those are 5 digit numbers, and with both codes together we'd have 10 digits. 10 digits is one of those magic geocaching numbers, right? You can plug it directly into coords, like this:

$$\text{N } 39° \text{ XX.XXX} \rightarrow \text{N } 39° \text{ 53.167}$$
$$\text{W } 82° \text{ XX.XXX} \rightarrow \text{W } 82° \text{ 58.526}$$

Coming at it from the other side, a puzzle CO could give you the Model Numbers first. With the two model numbers we've already given you (58526, and 53167) you may have noticed that the product they reference contains a number, a 6 piece screwdriver set, and a 4 piece pliers set. If a CO gave you 14 (or 15) product numbers that each contain a number within the product name, then you would have the digits you need for a set of coordinates.

Finally, you could encounter a puzzle that combines puzzle ideas. Imagine getting the following 6 Item Numbers on a cache page:

$$1620814978 \quad 004768409 \quad 550277453$$
$$004623652 \quad 551743016 \quad 001154211$$

When you look up these items at *walmart.com*, you will find a variety of things from jewelry to a bathroom rack. The first item, 1620814978, is a book about zirconium, the second is a titanium ring, and the third is a hair product that uses silicon. Nothing obviously numeric or useful there, until you realize that each of those things, zirconium, titanium, and silicon, are elements. Using their atomic numbers, a(s we discussed in the previous chapter), will get you the following coords, in D°M'S" format:

$$40° \text{ 22' 14"}$$

The second set of item numbers will get you a similar set of coords for the west, usingthe atomic numbers of gold, iron and nickel, which are mentioned in the other three product names. Hopefully the CO has built the puzzle with enough hints and nudges to help you move between these steps,\ and make the necessary leaps in logic to solve the puzzle.

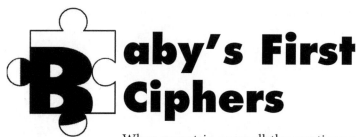

aby's First Ciphers

omniglot

The website *omniglot.com* can help you determine which alphabet you might be looking at and show you how to transform them into something you can read.

alphabets

See Appendix 8 for complete charts of several popular pop culture alphabets!

When you strip away all the mystique and mystery that are built up around them, a cipher is really just a fancy way of saying an alphabet, and any one can invent an alphabet. That was basically what I did with the paw print alphabet in the previous chapter; I invented the "Paw Print Cipher." It probably won't be useful for much, but it could be used as an alphabet. In the language of cryptography, invented alphabets that simply replace one character with another character are known as "monoalphabetic substitution ciphers." In Chapter 10 we'll get into Polyalphabetic Ciphers, where more than one alphabet is used in the encoding system.

There are dozens of alternative alphabets in the world associated with other languages, and other ways of writing. Simply substituting one of those alphabets for the standard Latin Alphabet that we use in English would act as a cipher. For someone who doesn't speak Russian, seeing a Cyrillic Alphabet would stop them just as cold as any other cipher you might imagine.

The Interlac Alphabet

Besides the alphabets of the world, there the alphabets of *other worlds*. Some simple research online will find alphabets like Klingon, Vulcan, Gallifreyan, Na'Vi, Sindarin, Atlantean.... the list goes on and on, and I can tell you that all of them have ended up on a cache page at some point or another! Especially the more pop culture oriented ones.

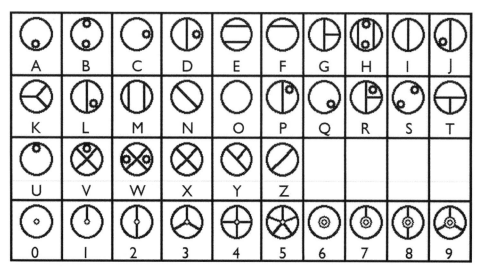

The Bionicle Alphabet

Any boy who grew up reading comic books in the 60's and 70's will tell you that it was an ultimate mark of comic book knowledge to be able to read "Interlac." Interlac was the language spoken by the Legion of Superheroes, a group of young superheroes in the 30th century. Rather than bearing an 'S' on their chests to represent themselves, like Superman, The Legion featured the first letters of their names in Interlac prominently on their costumes. Since it was just a substitution cipher, and most of the letters were similar to their English counterparts, it was pretty easy to learn.

Another pop culture/kid oriented alphabet that has taken a solid root in the geocaching world is the *Matoran* alphabet from the Lego game *Bionicle*. Even though Bionicle itself isn't as much of a household name as some other Lego sets, this alphabet is inexplicably popular among cachers and has shown up in dozens of caches. The alphabet itself is simply based on a geometric series of circles and lines. Much like Interlac you might be able to guess which symbols correspond to the standard alphabet with a little educated guessing.

The big-daddy of pop culture alphabets, though, are the alphabets of JRR Tolkein's novels. Besides being a novelist, Tolkein was a linguist and created not only alphabets but entire languages for his novels. Tolkein created 9 different alphabets and over a dozen different languages for his *Lord Of The Rings* series, including cursive and script variations.

Each of these alphabets has been studied, modified and adapted to be used for not only the different languages that Tolkein created, but for different Earthly languages. People have devoted themselves to learning these languages and alphabets.

in English   in Tengwar   in Serati   in Cirth

Alternative alphabets are the most basic ciphers, but admittedly the ones I've discussed so far are not the most *useful* ones. Since the inception of the written word people have worked to modify alphabets to make them more useful. Most frequently they are used as a way to shorten messages, or to make messages readable over long distances, through fog, or by someone with a disability that prevents them from seeing or writing text properly.

Let's take a look at some alternative alphabets that were created with specific and useful purposes in mind.

Morse Code

Invented in 1844 by Samuel Morse, Alfred Vail and Joseph Henry, Morse Code was the system used to send information across telegraph lines, the precursor to telephones. As I mentioned before, it isn't a true code, even though we call it one, but is instead a cipher.

These days Morse isn't used for much, but it's a favorite among the types who are attracted to codes and ciphers because it is a simple one, and one that a lot of us learn to use as kids in Boy or Girl Scouts. And of course, who hasn't heard of "SOS," which is a common idiom that comes from Morse Code.

Morse was composed of what is referred to as "dots and dashes." On a telegraph, a "dot" was a quick beep, and a "dash" was a longer beep, the length of three dots. In between dots and dashes, there was a pause that was the length of a dot, and in between letters there was a pause that was the length of a dash. Dots and dashes may also be referred to as "dit" and "dah." "Dit" meaning dot, and "dah" meaning the dash.

Some geocaches use audio files where you listen to Morse Code exactly the way that a telegraph operator would have done. (See GC2E17K for a great example of this!) In those cases you will have to quickly write down the dots and dashes so that you can translate them. I'll be honest, it isn't the easiest thing to do. But if you search YouTube, there are videos there that flash visual representations of dots and dashes on screen at the same time you hear the sounds. Those will help you get used to hearing Morse and translating it. There are many geocaches out there that require decoding Morse in the field, after finding a radio station, or a device that plays the sound file, so practice is useful!

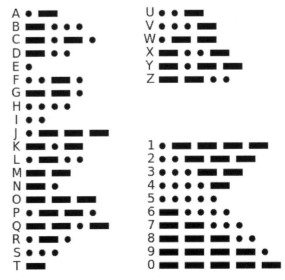

Morse Code will also often be represented visually on a cache page. The dots and dashes are written out, just as we have done on this chart.

As a kid you might have learned to use Morse Code visually with a flashlight, alternating short flashes and long flashes the way that the long and short sounds are used in classic telegraphy. Morse uses what we called a "binary system," meaning that there are two elements that make up all the letters, a dot and a dash, or a short and a long. That means, in terms of puzzle making, that almost any two things could be substituted for that short and long in order to make up a message encoded in Morse. Take a look at the puzzle at left.

On its own, you may not be able to get very far, but if the cache was named "Birds on a Telegraph Wire," you might be clued in that Morse Code was involved. In this case it looks like you have two types of bird, a thin one and a fat one. We could try to see if the thin bird might represent a dot and the fat one might represent a dash. When we consult the chart we quickly see that "dot, dash, dash, dash" is J, but "dash, dash" is M. No English words start with JM. So, let's try it the other way around. "Dash, dot, dot, dot" is a B, and "dot, dot" is an I. Now we're getting somewhere! After we decode it all, we can see that these birds (oddly enough) spell out 'BIRD' in Morse Code.

Keep your eye out for words like dot, dash, telegraph, telegram, cable, wire, Vail, Western Union, or stop. These might indicate that you're dealing with a Morse based puzzle.

A	⠁	M	⠍	Y	⠽		
B	⠃	N	⠝	Z	⠵		
C	⠉	O	⠕	1			
D	⠙	P	⠏	2			
E	⠑	Q	⠟	3			
F	⠋	R	⠗	4			
G	⠛	S	⠎	5			
H	⠓	T	⠞	6			
I	⠊	U	⠥	7			
J	⠚	V	⠧	8			
K	⠅	W	⠺	9			
L	⠇	X	⠭	0			

Braille

Another of these invented alphabets is Braille, created by Louise Braille in 1824, at the age of 15. Braille is a system of writing that allows the blind to read by feel. The letter forms are made by raised bumps in a 2x3 grid. Sometimes when it is written or drawn on a cache page, the "empty dots" or the flat areas of the letter, will be blank, and other times they will be represented by empty circles, or a smaller dot. (It depends on the CO and what source they used to create their puzzle.) Try your hand at this one:

Were you able to decode the word used there? One thing you might have noticed was that the first letter could be decoded as either an 'A' or a '1.' In professional Braille a number would be preceded by a Braille symbol to let you know that the next symbol was encoding a number. It looks like a backwards version of the symbol for 'V' seen in this chart. Some COs skip this step, so beware. If you aren't getting what you need by decoding letters, try numbers.

If you suspect Braille is being used, be on the lookout for things arranged in a 2x3 grid. Sometimes, if only numbers are used in the puzzle, a CO might arrange things in a 2x2 grid because, as you can see from the chart here, the bottom 2 dots are always flat (empty)when numbers are being encoded.

Much like Morse, Braille is essentially an arrangement of binary elements. Raised or not raised, high or low, bumpy or flat, full or empty. Now... Let's look at a puzzle!

Again... there might not be much in this image to connect you immediately to Braille, but imagine arriving on a cache page named "Blind Drunk," and finding this image. It might take you a little while to make the connections, but the word "blind" might be an immediate clue that Braille is possibly being used. One problem... there's nothing in the image that looks like Braille dots, is there?

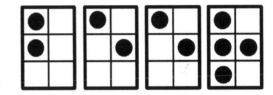

Then, it hits you. There are 6 bottles in a 6-pack. And they are arranged in the carrying case in a grid of 2x3. Does that sound familiar? Then you notice that these carriers aren't full. There are slots with bottles, and slots without... empty, and full... we might be able to use that to form Braille after all. Mentally rotate these carriers in your mind and look at them from above. They would look like this:

Once you see the carriers from that perspective you can easily see the Braille influence, and determine that those carriers spell "BEER." You could do similar puzzles with muffins in a tin arranged in a 2x3 grid, or chocolates in a box with a 2x3 grid.

The Moon Alphabet was a forerunner of Braille. It was also designed for use by blind readers. It used raised lines and shapes rather than dots. See Appendix 8 to see the Moon Alphabet.

Watch for words like blind, fingertips, feel, reading or unseen that might hint that you are dealing with a Braille puzzle.

Optical Telegraphs

In an era before telegraph wires and the ability to send information electronically, how were generals supposed to get information to and from their troops in the field? Horses can only run so fast... and so they were left with a quandary. Enter French engineer Claude Chappe. In 1792, Chappe introduced a system that became known as the "Semaphore Telegraph," or "Optical Telegraph." This was the first use of the word semaphore, it would later come to mean a different style of code, but this is the root.

Chappe proposed large windmill like structures, usually positioned on hills, that had a central pole and a beam across the top that had two arms at either end. By manipulating a series of handles and cranks inside the building the arms could be swung around into 192 different positions, depending on the angles of the arms and the beam. Towers would be positioned within sight of each other through the countryside. One tower would send a message, and in the next tower down the line, someone would watch the message, relay it to the operator there, who would send it again to the next tower, etc. Eventually the message would arrive at a tower near the destination, and it would be relayed to the troops in the field. The message of relaying information became wildly popular during Napoleon's reign. A message could get from Paris to any of the borders of France in less than an hour

134

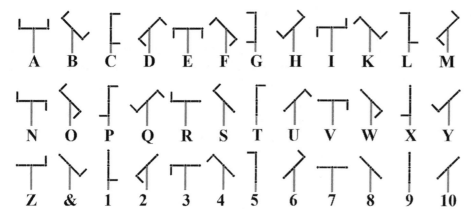

Chappe Code

using this system, which would be the equivalent of instantaneous in that era!

Chappe's code can be expressed today using a simple line drawing. You'll note that there is no 'J' in Chappe Code. Use the 'I' to represent both I and J.

As you can imagine , this system quickly became the envy of most of Europe, and several different countries established their own versions of it. In England, a differing system was designed by Lord George Murray, who proposed a wooden framework with six metal shutters mounted inside. The shutters had two positions, controlled by military personnel inside a shed. In one position, the shutter was closed and filled the square of the framework. It was painted with a white circle to make it more easily visible from a distance. The other position was open, so that from a distance the viewer would be looking at the edge of the shutter. The various shutter positions represented different letters and phrases. A message could get from London to any of the borders of England in 60 seconds or less. This system was in use throughout the Napoleonic Wars, but was retired in 1816.

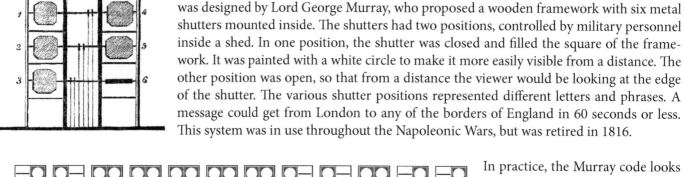

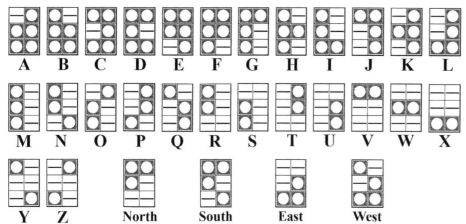

Murray's Shutter Code

In practice, the Murray code looks somewhat similar to Braille.

The Prussian Military adopted a system of six arms on a pole. Each arm had three positions, allowing for up to 729 different combinations. Their version of the telegraph lasted a bit longer than other nations, being used specifically for coded governmental messages well into the 19th century.

There are many variations on the optical telegraph, proposed by various people, or used by other countries. Some variations to look out for include: Hooke, Gamble, Pasley, Garnet, French Tuileries, Edgeworth, Popham or Holyhead-Liverpool.

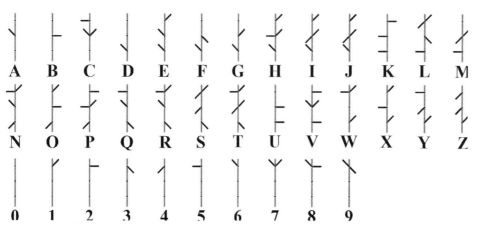

Prussian Telegraph Code

Semaphore

Optical telegraphs helped the army, but the navy also needed a way to communicate with each other over long distances. The idea of arms on a pole that can be seen at a distance was transformed, and modern semaphore was born. Semaphore is made up of two flags, held in the left and right hands of a sailor on the deck of a ship. By positioning the flags in one of 5 positions on each side, the sailor can convey his message in a way that can be seen from the deck of another ship.

This is another code that shows up in Boy Scout manuals and in children's mystery novels. Semaphore uses some of the same hand positions to convey either letters or numbers. When it is being done in the real world, the sailor will tell the person he is sending the message to whether he is transmitting numbers or letters by showing the appropriate sign

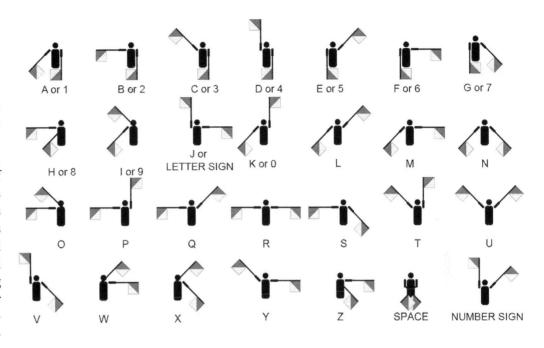

at the beginning of the message, but be warned, some COs skip this step, or don't even realize that it is supposed to happen, so be careful about how you start translating. Here's a test word for you to translate:

It is slightly more difficult to create alternate variations of Semaphore like we did with Braille or Morse. Because this alphabet is not composed of binary parts, it is much more difficult to use in puzzles. It takes quite a bit of information to convey the two hand positions, but it has been done. One very famous example of this is in one of Alfred Hitchcock's "Three Investigators" books. In that story the investigators found clocks stopped at various times. Eventually they discovered that the position of the clock hands corresponded to the hand positions in Semaphore and used that information to solve the mystery. This method could be done with sticks, twigs, or lines. Anything that can be arranged in angles to show the hand positions. Here's a puzzle I call "Dinner on the Titanic."

Naming the puzzle after a famous ship should hopefully link you mentally to a nautical way of thinking, and hopefully that will get you to Semaphore. Can you decipher it?

Maritime Flags

Similar to Semaphore, Maritime Flags are used by sailors for communication. Here, a collection of 26 colorful square flags with high contrast patterns make up the alphabet. For instance, a red diamond on a white field represents F, or a small white square in the center of a blue flag represents P. Here is a black and white representation of the system, but I encourage you to look for maritime flags online, as the color representations are very important. Once you see them, you will know them when you see them on a cache page. This alphabet is VERY difficult to represent in any way other than what it actually is, due to the high variety of colors and patterns that make up the flags.

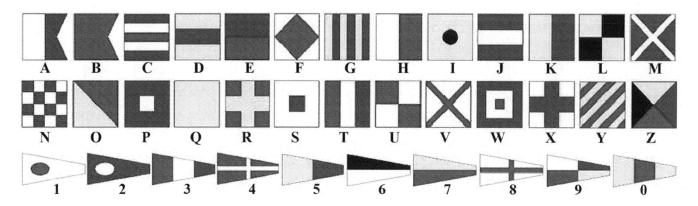

Ciphers: The Next Step

Ciphers have staggering variety. There have been centuries of opportunity for people to create codes for every purpose imaginable. The ones we've focused on so far have been very simple Monoalphabetic Substitution Ciphers, created to either aid people in a specific application or to add flavor to stories.

Just as many ciphers have been created for less altruistic reasons: namely, to *hide* information. Secret organizations, spy rings, and criminals have all created alternate alphabets to cover their tracks. The problem is that Monoalphabetic Ciphers are pretty easy to crack. As we discussed at the end of Chapter 6, when we talked about Cryptograms, it is fairly easy to look at letter frequencies and consider what the content of the message might be, and figure out what the message actually *is*. To combat that, cipher creators had to begin creating new wrinkles in their ciphers, beyond simply substituting a letter or a symbol for another.

Take "The Adventure of the Dancing Men," a Sherlock Holmes story where a young man comes to Holmes complaining that his new wife has been receiving mysterious messages composed of stick figures in various poses.

Holmes quickly figures out that the messages are a cipher, wherein each different figure represents a different

6.15 The Dancing Men Cipher

letter, a simple substitution cipher. Holmes breaks the cipher exactly the way that we discussed: by looking at letter frequency. He easily identifies which stick figure represents "E," because it is the one that showed up most often in the text. The interesting twist in this cipher was that it did not use spaces. Holmes had to discern that if the figure had a flag in its hand,it meant that it was the last letter of a word. This allowed him to break the text into proper spacing. (Not that this slowed Holmes down very much.)

Pigpen Cipher

The Pigpen Cipher is another childhood favorite. It dates back to at least the 18th century, and variations of it were used by both the Rosicrucians and the Masons, leading some to refer to it as the Rosicrucian Cipher, or the Freemason's Cipher. It was also rumored to have been used by prisoners of war on both sides during the Civil War.

The Pigpen is what is known as a "positional cipher." It starts by drawing two X's and two tic-tac-toe grids. The second set has dots placed in it. The next step is to place letters into the grids.

From there, it becomes a simple substitution cipher. The shapes from the grids stand in for the letters. Can you decipher the following?

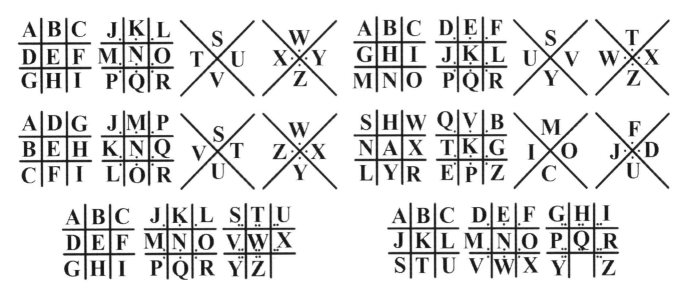

This cipher is just barely a step above a simple substitution. What makes it more complex is that the letters can be arranged in almost any fashion. Here are some variants:

When the alphabet can be rearranged like this, it requires the person receiving the message to know what order to place the letters in. This is what's called a "keyed cipher." Both the sender and the receiver must know the key: the order that the letters appear in. This flexibility makes the Pigpen a sort of a cross between a substitution cipher and a keyed cipher. If you are sure you have a Pigpen cipher, but aren't getting the results you want, the CO may have used a non-standard letter arrangement. Remember, you can always use the substitution trick I taught you at the end of the last chapter (with the paw print alphabet) and treat the result as a cryptogram.

Caesar's Cipher

According to the historian Suetonius, when Caesar wanted to send an encrypted message he would simply replaced each letter in the message with a letter shifted three letters down the alphabet. So, an "A" would become a 'D," a "B" would become an "E," etc.

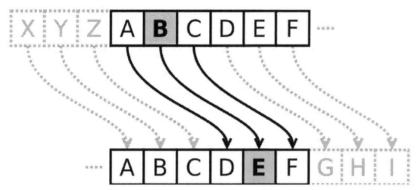

Because of his use of it, this type of cipher has become known as a Caesar Shift. Geocachers are, of course, familiar with this cipher as the "ROT-N Cipher." The "ROT" is short for "rotational," referring to the fact that the letters in the alphabet have been "rotated" a specific distance. A Caesar Shift cipher can shift 1 time, or 26 times and achieve a different alphabet. *Geocaching.com* uses a rotation of 13 (ROT-13) to encode the hints on the cache pages. In fact, some very experienced geocachers know ROT-13 so well that they can read the hints without even decoding them!

Here are a few samples to try:

Can you decode this word coded in ROT-16? **HECQD** Using the chart, just go to the 16th line, and move over to the first letter (the H), and then follow that column up to the standard alphabet to see what letter it represents. In ROT-16, H=R.

What about these in ROT-8? **IVBWVG IVL KTMWXIBZI**

Or this phrase in ROT-22? **E YKIA PK XQNU YWAOWN JKP PK LNWEOA DEI**

All of these examples, and my chart, are based on a forward rotation, but you might want to be aware that some COs

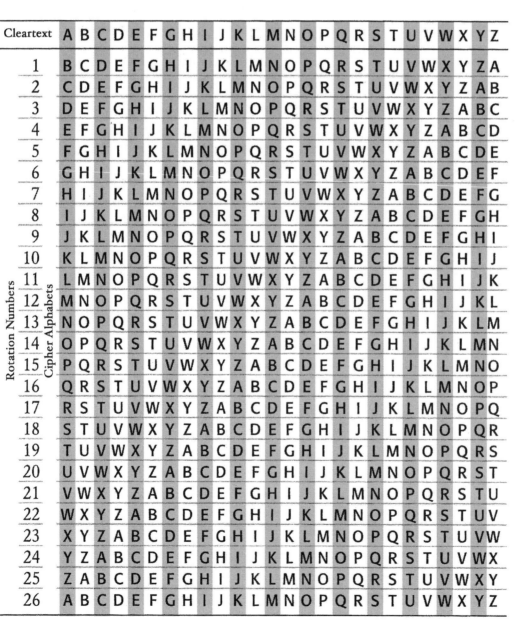

Cleartext	A	B	C	D	E	F	G	H	I	J	K	L	M	N	O	P	Q	R	S	T	U	V	W	X	Y	Z
1	B	C	D	E	F	G	H	I	J	K	L	M	N	O	P	Q	R	S	T	U	V	W	X	Y	Z	A
2	C	D	E	F	G	H	I	J	K	L	M	N	O	P	Q	R	S	T	U	V	W	X	Y	Z	A	B
3	D	E	F	G	H	I	J	K	L	M	N	O	P	Q	R	S	T	U	V	W	X	Y	Z	A	B	C
4	E	F	G	H	I	J	K	L	M	N	O	P	Q	R	S	T	U	V	W	X	Y	Z	A	B	C	D
5	F	G	H	I	J	K	L	M	N	O	P	Q	R	S	T	U	V	W	X	Y	Z	A	B	C	D	E
6	G	H	I	J	K	L	M	N	O	P	Q	R	S	T	U	V	W	X	Y	Z	A	B	C	D	E	F
7	H	I	J	K	L	M	N	O	P	Q	R	S	T	U	V	W	X	Y	Z	A	B	C	D	E	F	G
8	I	J	K	L	M	N	O	P	Q	R	S	T	U	V	W	X	Y	Z	A	B	C	D	E	F	G	H
9	J	K	L	M	N	O	P	Q	R	S	T	U	V	W	X	Y	Z	A	B	C	D	E	F	G	H	I
10	K	L	M	N	O	P	Q	R	S	T	U	V	W	X	Y	Z	A	B	C	D	E	F	G	H	I	J
11	L	M	N	O	P	Q	R	S	T	U	V	W	X	Y	Z	A	B	C	D	E	F	G	H	I	J	K
12	M	N	O	P	Q	R	S	T	U	V	W	X	Y	Z	A	B	C	D	E	F	G	H	I	J	K	L
13	N	O	P	Q	R	S	T	U	V	W	X	Y	Z	A	B	C	D	E	F	G	H	I	J	K	L	M
14	O	P	Q	R	S	T	U	V	W	X	Y	Z	A	B	C	D	E	F	G	H	I	J	K	L	M	N
15	P	Q	R	S	T	U	V	W	X	Y	Z	A	B	C	D	E	F	G	H	I	J	K	L	M	N	O
16	Q	R	S	T	U	V	W	X	Y	Z	A	B	C	D	E	F	G	H	I	J	K	L	M	N	O	P
17	R	S	T	U	V	W	X	Y	Z	A	B	C	D	E	F	G	H	I	J	K	L	M	N	O	P	Q
18	S	T	U	V	W	X	Y	Z	A	B	C	D	E	F	G	H	I	J	K	L	M	N	O	P	Q	R
19	T	U	V	W	X	Y	Z	A	B	C	D	E	F	G	H	I	J	K	L	M	N	O	P	Q	R	S
20	U	V	W	X	Y	Z	A	B	C	D	E	F	G	H	I	J	K	L	M	N	O	P	Q	R	S	T
21	V	W	X	Y	Z	A	B	C	D	E	F	G	H	I	J	K	L	M	N	O	P	Q	R	S	T	U
22	W	X	Y	Z	A	B	C	D	E	F	G	H	I	J	K	L	M	N	O	P	Q	R	S	T	U	V
23	X	Y	Z	A	B	C	D	E	F	G	H	I	J	K	L	M	N	O	P	Q	R	S	T	U	V	W
24	Y	Z	A	B	C	D	E	F	G	H	I	J	K	L	M	N	O	P	Q	R	S	T	U	V	W	X
25	Z	A	B	C	D	E	F	G	H	I	J	K	L	M	N	O	P	Q	R	S	T	U	V	W	X	Y
26	A	B	C	D	E	F	G	H	I	J	K	L	M	N	O	P	Q	R	S	T	U	V	W	X	Y	Z

Rotation Numbers — Cipher Alphabets

use a backward rotation, so that rather than "A" clicking forward to become "B," as I show, it would click "backward" to become "Z." If you aren't getting the results you want, you may want to try that.

in pop culture

The pigpen cipher has been used in many pieces of popular culture, like Dan Brown's novel *The Lost Symbol*, the video game *Assassin's Creed II* and the book series *39 Clues*.

As you can probably guess, Caesar shifted codes are very easy to break, since they are essentially cryptograms, made even easier because the alphabet remains in order rather than being randomly ordered. The only real "key" is knowing how many spaces the alphabet was rotated. Many websites are capable of showing you all 26 possible rotations as one result, so that you can simply scan for readable text. This is sometimes called "ROT-Everything" and is a very handy first step for almost any unknown cipher type.

One way to make a Caesar slightly more difficult is to apply a key. This is known as a "Keyed Caesar." With a Keyed Caesar, you replace the first few letters of the alphabet with a key word. The rest of the alphabet stays in order. For instance a keyword of "PUZZLE" would have a cipher alphabet that looked like this:

A	B	C	D	E	F	G	H	I	J	K	L	M	etc.
↓	↓	↓	↓	↓	↓	↓	↓	↓	↓	↓	↓	↓	
P	U	Z	L	E	A	B	C	D	F	G	H	I	etc.

As you can see, the repeated letter "Z" from "PUZZLE" is only used once. The P, U, Z, L, and E become the first letters of the cipher alphabet, and the remaining letters follow in alphabetical order. Again, this doesn't provide much of a challenge, but it does provide *some*. It still doesn't prevent a frequency attack or simply treating the text as a cryptogram, however.

The Atbash

Similar to the Caesar shift is the Atbash Cipher. Atbash was originally a Hebrew cipher ori- and was named for letters of the Hebrew alphabet. The idea is that you reverse the alphabet for the cipher text, so that the first letter is substituted for the last, the second letter for the next to last, etc.

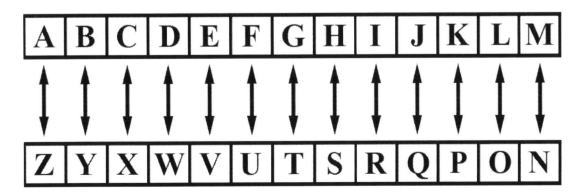

A	B	C	D	E	F	G	H	I	J	K	L	M
↕	↕	↕	↕	↕	↕	↕	↕	↕	↕	↕	↕	↕
Z	Y	X	W	V	U	T	S	R	Q	P	O	N

Aleph, the first Hebrew letter, was substituted for *tav*, the last letter in the Hebrew alphabet. The second letter, *beth* was substituted for *shin*, the next to last. If you combine the sounds of those letters you get something like Atbash.

The Vatsyayana

The last variant on the Caesar Cipher that we'll look at is the Vatsyayana, sometimes called the Kama-Sutra Cipher. This cipher was described in the 45th chapter of the Kama-Sutra, but it also gets its name from the fact that it "pairs" random letters. Rather than an orderly pairing of letters, like the Caesar or the Atbash, the Vatsyayana scrambles the alphabet and then arranges it in pairs like lovers. If the "A" is paired with the "K" then one letter will stand in place for the other, throughout the cipher text. In that way it is similar to a cryptogram puzzle, except cryptograms aren't mirrored. In a Cryptogram, if A=K, K does not necessarily =A, whereas in The Vatsyayana code A=K, and K=A.

Here is a sample Vatsyayana Alphabet:

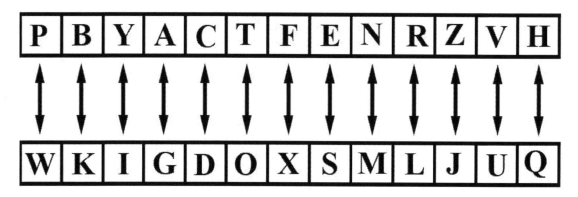

Keep in mind, though, that the letter pairs can be arranged in any fashion. It is up to the whims of the person who created the puzzle!

ayered Ciphers

I'll close out this chapter on basic ciphers by discussing a common trick that COs use to make caches slightly more difficult: Layered Ciphers. This might also be called Double Encryption. The idea here is that the cipher text has been run through two (or more!) cipher types. For instance, you may get a series of Semaphore flags that look like this:

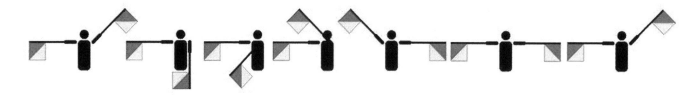

Decoding that is a fairly straightforward experience, except... you end up with gibberish! **QBHOYRQ** is not a word. What would be your next step with this puzzle? Knowing that Semaphore can also be used to encode numbers, I would look at that first; however, Q, O, Y and R don't stand for numbers, so that isn't the answer. Next I'd search the word at Google to see if it turned up anything but in this case, it doesn't. Finally I'd start looking at other ciphers (hopefully the CO will have left a clue or two to help me figure out which one!) This is difficult with short words like the one I've presented here because you can't see patterns very well, but I usually start with a Caesar Shift.

By running a ROT-Everything on the text I quickly see that ROT-13 returns the answer "DOUBLED."

Layered ciphers can be a little bit off putting because you begin decoding what seems like the obvious answer and hit what looks like a brick wall at first. For instance, a puzzle that is very obviously Morse Code, but returns gibberish might seem like a dead end. If you are positive that you have identified the initial cipher correctly, keep at it. That gibberish may be hiding a second cipher. I have seen caches out there that have cipher layers that are 3 or 4 levels deep!

Simple Substitutions

Remember my advice from the end of the substitution chapter (Chapter 6). If you are faced with a large block of strangely encoded text and you can't track down what code or alphabet might be in use, try substituting letters for the symbols and running the result through a cryptogram solver. For instance, if you have a bunch of differently shaped leaves, go through the text and assign the letter "A" to all the oak leaves, and "B" to the maple leaves, etc. until you have gone through the entire cipher text. The resulting text should solve as a cryptogram. (See Chapter 6 for a more involved explanation of this concept.)

frequency analysis

Frequency analysis, a method of breaking ciphers by looking at which letters are most often repeated, and what letters most frequently occur in the written language, was first employed by an Arabic scholar named Al-Kindi in the 9th century!

cipher websites

See Appendix 4 for websites that encode and decode ciphers for you.

Solving it

Bringing together what you've learned.

Use this checklist to help you apply what you've learned in this chapter and determine which cipher you might be working with.

Checklist: BASIC CIPHERS

- [ ] Try to identify the cipher or substitution alphabet you are working with.

- [ ] If you have only letters, try a "ROT-Everything" approach.

- [ ] Look for keywords that might help you determine which cipher you are looking at. For instance "blind" for Braille.

- [ ] Look for "binaries" like off/on, black/white, thick/thin, high/low, etc. that could form Morse or Braille.

- [ ] Try substitution and solving as a cryptogram

- [ ] If the results of a cipher don't look like what you expected, consider that the text might have been double encrypted.

alk-Through

It's time for another walk-through to show you how I might approach solving a puzzle of the type covered in this chapter. Remember, there is no actual geocache at these locations. Here's the puzzle:

FIND A CACHE

? The King's Forest

A cache by: Team Podcaster Hidden: 07/10/2005

Difficulty: ★★☆☆☆ Size: ▪▪▪▫▫

Terrain: ★☆☆☆☆

N 40° 05.344 W 075° 23.147

In Valley Forge, Pennsylvania, USA

28 FAVORITES

The cache is NOT at the listed coordinates.
You must determine the actual coordinates by solving the puzzle below.

We have lots of beautiful forests in the area, not exactly at the area where the dummy coords are... but, hey, they are out there. At least not all of the trees in the area have been chopped down to make telegraph poles.

Maybe once you figure out this code you'll find a nice forest.

FC555SD

📋 LOG YOUR VISIT

🖼 View Gallery

👓 Watch

📖 Bookmark

ⓧ Ignore

Attributes:
🚲 🚐 🏕

1 **The beginning.** I start where I always do: date, name, gallery, Related Web Page, TB inventory, double check for white hidden text, and in the source code. Nothing there. So we have to look elsewhere to find the puzzle. Looking at the dummy coords, I see that they land in the parking lot of the "King of Prussia Mall." The puzzle's name references a king as well. Okay, maybe a clue there, maybe just a play on the location.

2 **The description.** The description is short and sweet, a couple of references to trees, and we see some cartoony looking trees in the image as well, so we might have a tree theme going. One thing that stands out immediately is the word "telegraph." It's a very old fashioned word and most people usually refer to those as "telephone poles" or "power" or "electric poles." Not sure what to do with that quite yet, though.

3 **The image.** Let's look a bit more closely at the image. There are two rows of trees, with 17 trees in each row. You only need 14 characters to represent the coords in this area, 16 if you include the "N" & "W," so too many for that. I doubt one number is represented by one tree. 34 trees might be enough to spell the coords. The description specifically mentions a code. The trees have to be the source for it, as there isn't anything else on the page that could represent a code.

4 **The code.** It seems like the key to this puzzle is going to be identifying the code. My first impulse would be "tree code," or something like that. Some googling for "tree code" brings up a lot of computer science stuff that looks like flow charts, so I don't think that's it. I happen to know that there is an ancient alphabet called "Ogham" that used trees as a basis, but this doesn't look like that either. Looking back at the other clues that we found I remember the reference to "telegraphs." Maybe "telegraph code?" Googling that yields a lot of references to Morse, which also doesn't look like this.

5 **The research.** There has to be something else here that I am overlooking. Read the description again. They reference the area of the dummy coords, the King of Prussia Mall. Is that meant as a clue? They also specifically reference "trunks" being "turned into telegraph poles." The trunks are the most prominent thing about the trees in the image. Let's try variations on those things. Back to Google. "Trunk code" brings me information about telephone systems, but I don't see anything useful. "King code" is mostly about legal stuff. "Prussian code" has a lot of information about how to render the color Prussian blue in HTML code... but in the image search for that term, I spot something that looks familiar -- an image of something that looks kind of like the tree trunks in the puzzle image. Let's investigate that.

6 **The key.** Clicking through to the image search shows me the image, which certainly looks like the tree trunks. It comes from a Wikipedia entry on "Prussian Optical Telegraph Code." Aha! Both the telegraph clue and the Prussian clue pay off! Googling that phrase gets me a Wikipedia page with a key for this Prussian code. By comparing the first tree trunk to that key I see that it would represent "F." A good start! The local coords start with 40, so "F" is good. The next tree represents "I." Hmm... not the "O" I was expecting, but that's okay, the minutes on the dummy coords are 5, so we might still be on track. And, yes, the next tree represents "V."

7 **The answer.** From there it's like rolling down hill. The first row of trees spell out F, I, V, E, Z, E, R, O, Z, E, R, O, S, E, V, E, N: 5.007, making our north coords 40° 05.007 since we can assume that the 40° stays the same. The second row of trees gives us T, W, O, T, W, O, F, I, V, E, T, W, O, F, O, U, R: 22.524. Now we have complete coords: 40° 05.007, -75° 22.524! We're ready to go out and make the find! (Remember, none of the cache locations in this book lead to real caches, but I have tried to choose interesting or thematic locations for each of the finals.)

You could also solve these one using the "cryptogram" backdoor, assigning a letter to each tree shape, then treating the result as a cryptogram.

On the next page there is another puzzle for you to solve without my help. Apply the lessons from this chapter, and you should make short work of it.

Solve It Yourself!

Here are some puzzle caches for you to solve on your own. Using the skills we learned in this chapter you should be able to solve these puzzles. Take careful note of the final coordinates that you get as a solution to these puzzles, and write them at the bottom of the page. If you need a reminder of how to use the puzzle stats or hints provided, please check page 11. Good luck!

Puzzle 1 Solution:

S __ __ ° __ __ . __ __ __ , E __ __ __ ° __ __ . __ __ __

As a secondary check you should be able to answer this question: *What animal is unusual about the wall at the final?*

Puzzle 2 Solution:

N __ __ ° __ __ . __ __ __ , W __ __ __ ° __ __ . __ __ __

As a secondary check you should be able to answer this question: *What animal is on the wall at the final?*

FIND A CACHE

? Knot Knots

A cache by: braddison   **Hidden: 04/23/2004**

Difficulty:    Size:
Terrain:

S 34° 04.053 E 150° 45.490

In Campbeltown, AU

20 FAVORITES

FCCBAT1

LOG YOUR VISIT

- View Gallery
- Watch
- Bookmark
- Ignore

The cache is NOT at the listed coordinates.
You must determine the actual coordinates by solving the puzzle below.

Often in geocaching you will come across a need for a few basic knots. Here are a couple knots that have come in handy when I've been on the trail, look closely, maybe they'll help you find this cache and sign the log!

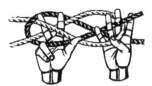 

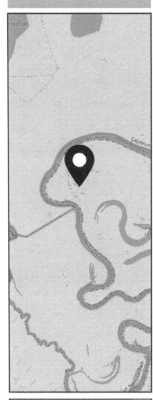

Attributes:

PUZZLE STATS

61 CHECKSUM   **BEST VIEW**

 2    53   149

126   25

FIND A CACHE

 ## Caching In The Dark

A cache by: Lewis Carroll　　**Hidden: 04/18/2019**

Difficulty: ★★★☆☆　　Size: ▪▫▪■■▫

Terrain: ★☆☆☆☆

FCAL1C3

LOG YOUR VISIT

 View Gallery

 Watch

 Bookmark

 Ignore

N 38° 15.512 W 085° 45.920

In Louiseville, Kentucky, USA

10 FAVORITES

The cache is NOT at the listed coordinates.
You must determine the actual coordinates by solving the puzzle below.

Ever wish you could see in the dark so you could just keep caching forever? Learning this alphabet might help!

Attributes:

 48

 147　127

 78　 41

Advanced Ciphers

So far I have only talked about the most basic ciphers. In this next chapter, I'll show you some of the most common examples of advanced cipher systems; ciphers that use multiple steps or transformations to hide their content and keep their mysteries hidden.

With the proliferation of cipher and code websites to be found online it has become less important for puzzle solvers to know how to decode cipher text by hand. While that is an awesome advancement for puzzlers, it does make recognizing the ciphers more difficult because we are less familiar with what the result looks like. With this chapter I hope to familiarize you with the basics of several cipher types, at least enough so that you can start to recognize what cipher you might be dealing with.

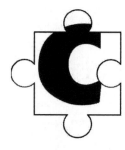

Ciphers: Learning to Run

All of the ciphers discussed in the previous chapter were either "open ciphers" like Morse and Braille, whose solutions are well known public knowledge, or simple substitution ciphers that will pretty easily fall to a simple Cryptogram solver. We should never forget, though, that ciphers were originally created to be secretive. Even something as simple as the Caesar Shift, which today is used for kid's toys, was enough to hide secrets when it was created.

Every time a cipher is introduced, there is always another side, be it enemy or just curiosity, out to find out how to break it. So, over time, ciphers have gotten more and more difficult, with additional layers and steps that one must go through in order to solve them.

Since we've been building off the Caesar Shift, let's stay along that line and look at...

The Affine

The Affine Cipher seems complex at first, but it will start to give you a flavor of what types of transformations cipher creators will send text through in order to hide the secrets they want to keep. Here's how an Affine works: First you transform the letters of the alphabet into their corresponding numbers, starting with 0 for the first letter, like so:

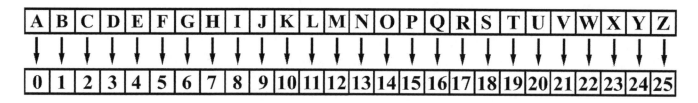

A	B	C	D	E	F	G	H	I	J	K	L	M	N	O	P	Q	R	S	T	U	V	W	X	Y	Z
0	1	2	3	4	5	6	7	8	9	10	11	12	13	14	15	16	17	18	19	20	21	22	23	24	25

Next you have to choose two numbers. Now... I won't get into the cryptologist speak here, but for complex mathematical reasons, the first number can only be 1, 3, 5, 7, 9, 11, 15, 17, 19, 21, 23, or 25 because it must be less than 26 and not divisible by any of the same integers as 26, except 1. Let's choose 5. We'll choose 8 for the second number.

To encode a letter, you then multiply the corresponding number by your first choice, then add your second choice to the result. For "C" the process would be 2 x 5=10, 10 + 8=18.

Next we have another really "math-y" step. We have to convert the result, in this case 18, by an operation known as Mod 26.

"Mod," which is short for "modulo," has to do with the remainder of a number following division. For example, "5 Mod 3=2" means that 5, after being divided by 3, has a remainder of 2. I know it seems confusing, but, in fact, you already know how to do modular math because we use it for analog clocks. Think of it this way: if it's 7:00 now (am/pm doesn't matter), where will the hour hand be in 7 hours?

7 + 7 = 14, but we can't show "14:00" on a standard clock. It would be 2. Because we are familiar with it, we do this math with very little thought, but in math terms, you are actually saying 7 + 7 = 14, and 14 Mod 12 = 2 Mod 12 (2 is the remainder when 14 is divided by 12).

The equation "14 mod 12 = 2 mod 12" is a math-y way of saying, "14 o'clock and 2 o'clock look the same on a clock." You use Mod 12 math everyday without realizing it!

Because our alphabet is 26 letters, we are working with Mod 26. In our example of encrypting the letter "C" we had made it up to the point of having the number 18. Converting that to Mod 26 is easy because it isn't higher than 26, so 18 in Mod 26 is simply 18! If we look back at our original chart where we converted letters to numbers, we see that 18 is an "S," so our "C" would be encoded as "S."

A higher number provides a bigger challenge. "R" equals 17 in our chart. 5 x 17 = 85, and 85 + 8 = 93. In order to find the Mod 26 for 93 you divide 93 by 26 and check the remainder. In this case, you'd end up with 15. 15 = P on the chart, so "R" encodes as "P."

Now... we've taken all these steps, learned all these new things, but in the end we still have a monoalphabetic cipher. Once you've chosen your numbers however you encode your text, a letter will always equal the *SAME* letter throughout the cipher text. And we know what that means it's vulnerable to being able to be solved with a simple Cryptogram Solver. In other words, it isn't very secure.

mod design
For other uses of the Mod function see Chapter 14, the Math chapter!

Polyalphabetic Ciphers

If a Monoalphabetic Cipher is vulnerable to a Cryptogram Solver because it uses the same alphabet throughout the cipher... what is the logical step to prevent that? Using *more than one* alphabet in the cipher. By using different alphabets, you force the person trying to break your code to change their methods every line, every word... or even every letter.

What do I mean by different alphabets? Are you going to have to learn Cyrillic and Kanji in order to use these ciphers? No, by a different alphabet I mean the traditional English alphabet in different orders. Think about it this way... If I gave you a cryptogram that had three lines of encoded text that used a Monoalphabetic Cipher, you would assume that is J=R in the first line, it would continue to do so through the next two lines as well. But with a Polyalphabetic Cipher, that would not necessarily be the case. J may equal R in line one, but in line two, J=K, and in line 3, J=M. Leon Battista Alberti invented this concept in 1467. The Alberti Cipher was pretty simple. He would start off with one Caesar Shifted alphabet, say 13, and continue along for a while. Then he would simply shift to a new alphabet, perhaps Caesar Shift 8, and then continue. He signaled to the recipient that he was changing ciphers in the text by capitalizing a letter.

Homophonic Ciphers

One of the earliest known polyalphabetic ciphers is the "homophonic" cipher. The first example we have of its use is from a letter written in 1401! As we have seen, one of the simplest way to crack a monoalphabetic cipher is to do a frequency analysis, checking how frequently certain letters appear and then testing those against the letters that appear most frequently in standard text. If your cipher text has a high frequency of "Ks" it might very well be standing in for "E," because "E" is the most commonly used letter in English. How do you get around that? The simplest way is to even out the frequency. You would do that using more than one character as your stand in for "E." In English, E occurs with a frequency of 17%, meaning that a letter has a 17% chance of being an "E." To even out the frequency, we would use 17 different characters to stand in for E. The letter "N," at a frequency of 10% gets 10 different stand-ins. If you do that for all the letters in the alphabet, then your frequency analysis would so show a 1% frequency for every character, giving you no clue as to which letter the character may be standing in for.

One popular cipher that uses this method is known as the "Mexican Army Cipher." This cipher uses a code wheel with 5 rings. Rather than having an alphabet on all of the wheels, the alphabet only appears on the outer wheel. The four wheels in the middle contain numbers, 1 to 26 on the first, 27 to 52 on the second, 53 to 78 on the third and 79 to 100, as well as 4 blanks spaces on the last. Each of the four number wheels are turned and aligned.

To encode a word, you would find the letter on the outer ring, and then randomly choose one of the 4 possible two digit numbers aligned with that letter on the four inner rings. It takes two characters (the two digits of the number) to encode each letter.

Besides the cipher text a message encoded using the Mexican Army Cipher must also tell you how to align the rings. This is normally done by telling you which numbers align with the "A."

code wheels

Code wheels are two or more circles of paper with the alphabet printed around the edges. Just like a Caesar cipher you turn one wheel and substitute the letter in your message with the letter it is aligned with on the second wheel. Chapter 9 has a photo of a code wheel using numbers rather than letters on the first page!

The Vigenère

The first true polyalphabetic cipher that most people learn is the Vigenère. The Vigenère is also enormously popular among geocache puzzle makers. Like a lot of the ciphers we've discussed, the Vigenère builds off of the Caesar Shift. But where our examples above shifted every line or every few words, the Vigenère shifts after every *letter*. A Vigenère begins with what is known as a "tabula recta," which is a table with all of the Caesar Shift alphabets listed on it.

The next step is something new to our discussion of ciphers: choosing a keyword, sometimes also known as a passphrase. For the Vigenère the letters in the keyword are what tell you which alphabet you should use to encode. For our example let's choose the word "GEOCACHE." You begin by writing out what you wish to encode (remember this is called the clear text, or plaintext) and then write your passphrase over and over beneath it, until it is as long as your clear text. We'll use "NORTH CO-ORDS" as the plaintext.

To accomplish the encoding you would move down the column on the far left side until you arrive at the first letter of your alphabet key, in this case "G." Then you would find the first letter of the clear text, which is "N," on the alphabet at the top of the tabula recta. The letter at that intersection of that row and column is the encoded letter.

Using the passphrase "GEOCACHE" the first letter would encode as "T."

What makes this cipher so secure is that encoded letters don't tend to repeat. In our clear text of "NORTH COORDS," there are two "Rs," but the first "R" encodes as "F," and the second encodes as "X."

	A	B	C	D	E	F	G	H	I	J	K	L	M	N	O	P	Q	R	S	T	U	V	W	X	Y	Z
A	A	B	C	D	E	F	G	H	I	J	K	L	M	N	O	P	Q	R	S	T	U	V	W	X	Y	Z
B	B	C	D	E	F	G	H	I	J	K	L	M	N	O	P	Q	R	S	T	U	V	W	X	Y	Z	A
C	C	D	E	F	G	H	I	J	K	L	M	N	O	P	Q	R	S	T	U	V	W	X	Y	Z	A	B
D	D	E	F	G	H	I	J	K	L	M	N	O	P	Q	R	S	T	U	V	W	X	Y	Z	A	B	C
E	E	F	G	H	I	J	K	L	M	N	O	P	Q	R	S	T	U	V	W	X	Y	Z	A	B	C	D
F	F	G	H	I	J	K	L	M	N	O	P	Q	R	S	T	U	V	W	X	Y	Z	A	B	C	D	E
G	G	H	I	J	K	L	M	N	O	P	Q	R	S	T	U	V	W	X	Y	Z	A	B	C	D	E	F
H	H	I	J	K	L	M	N	O	P	Q	R	S	T	U	V	W	X	Y	Z	A	B	C	D	E	F	G
I	I	J	K	L	M	N	O	P	Q	R	S	T	U	V	W	X	Y	Z	A	B	C	D	E	F	G	H
J	J	K	L	M	N	O	P	Q	R	S	T	U	V	W	X	Y	Z	A	B	C	D	E	F	G	H	I
K	K	L	M	N	O	P	Q	R	S	T	U	V	W	X	Y	Z	A	B	C	D	E	F	G	H	I	J
L	L	M	N	O	P	Q	R	S	T	U	V	W	X	Y	Z	A	B	C	D	E	F	G	H	I	J	K
M	M	N	O	P	Q	R	S	T	U	V	W	X	Y	Z	A	B	C	D	E	F	G	H	I	J	K	L
N	N	O	P	Q	R	S	T	U	V	W	X	Y	Z	A	B	C	D	E	F	G	H	I	J	K	L	M
O	O	P	Q	R	S	T	U	V	W	X	Y	Z	A	B	C	D	E	F	G	H	I	J	K	L	M	N
P	P	Q	R	S	T	U	V	W	X	Y	Z	A	B	C	D	E	F	G	H	I	J	K	L	M	N	O
Q	Q	R	S	T	U	V	W	X	Y	Z	A	B	C	D	E	F	G	H	I	J	K	L	M	N	O	P
R	R	S	T	U	V	W	X	Y	Z	A	B	C	D	E	F	G	H	I	J	K	L	M	N	O	P	Q
S	S	T	U	V	W	X	Y	Z	A	B	C	D	E	F	G	H	I	J	K	L	M	N	O	P	Q	R
T	T	U	V	W	X	Y	Z	A	B	C	D	E	F	G	H	I	J	K	L	M	N	O	P	Q	R	S
U	U	V	W	X	Y	Z	A	B	C	D	E	F	G	H	I	J	K	L	M	N	O	P	Q	R	S	T
V	V	W	X	Y	Z	A	B	C	D	E	F	G	H	I	J	K	L	M	N	O	P	Q	R	S	T	U
W	W	X	Y	Z	A	B	C	D	E	F	G	H	I	J	K	L	M	N	O	P	Q	R	S	T	U	V
X	X	Y	Z	A	B	C	D	E	F	G	H	I	J	K	L	M	N	O	P	Q	R	S	T	U	V	W
Y	Y	Z	A	B	C	D	E	F	G	H	I	J	K	L	M	N	O	P	Q	R	S	T	U	V	W	X
Z	Z	A	B	C	D	E	F	G	H	I	J	K	L	M	N	O	P	Q	R	S	T	U	V	W	X	Y

N	O	R	T	H	C	O	O	R	D	S

↓ ↓ ↓ ↓ ↓ ↓ ↓ ↓ ↓ ↓ ↓

G	E	O	C	A	C	H	E	G	E	O

rows and columns

Generally the horizontal lines of letters in a grid are referred to as a "row," and the vertical line is referred to as a "column," just like the columns on the front of a building.

Most people will use an online cipher tool to decode a Vigenère cipher, but in case you are interested in doing it by hand, I'll show you how.

The steps to decode are simply the reverse of the encoding process. First you will need to determine the passphrase. To simplify matters, we'll use "GEOCACHE" as our passphrase. Our cipher text for this example will be "CIGVCQVVJW." Our first step is to write our passphrase beneath the cipher text, just as we did with our clear text the first time.

C	I	G	V	C	Q	V	V	J	W

↓ ↓ ↓ ↓ ↓ ↓ ↓ ↓ ↓ ↓

G	E	O	C	A	C	H	E	G	E

We begin with the first letter of our passphrase and find that letter in the left-most column. In this cache it is "G." Move out across the "G row" until you have arrived at the first letter of the cipher text, in this case "C." Follow that column upward to the uppermost row. The letter that appears at the intersection of the column and uppermost row is the deciphered letter. Here it would be "W." You would continue in that manner until you have deciphered the entire message.

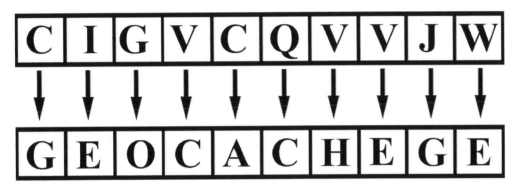

Vigenère Ciphers are still vulnerable to decryption attacks, but it takes a LOT more work, and certainly more than running it through a Cryptogram Solver.

There are a couple of ways to make Vigenères even more secure. One is to add the numbers 0-9 to your tabula recta. (This is a wrinkle that not a lot of geocachers are aware of.) The second is to add a key.

trithemius

Vigenère Ciphers are sometimes referred to as Trithemius Ciphers. Trithemius invented a very similar cipher using a tabula recta, but his cipher used no keywords. Instead the first letter of the clear text is found in the left hand column. You then move right until you are underneath the 'A.' The letter at that intersection is the first letter of the cipher text. The second clear text letter goes beneath the 'B,' the third beneath 'C,' etc.

The Keyed Vigenère

I can hear you out there saying, "Wait... Vigenères already have a key!" This is true, but you can add a second key, making it even more secure. The first variation I will describe of a Keyed Vigenère is the most common. In it, rather than using the standard alphabet across the top of your tabula recta, you add a keyword called an "alphabet key," similar to what we did with a Keyed Caesar. If your alphabet key was "PLATYPUS," rather than having ABCDEFGHIJKLMNOPQRSTUVWXYZ as the top index for the columns, you would have PLATYUSBCDEFGHIJKMNOQRVWXZ, (the repeating "P" gets dropped, just like in a Keyed Caesar.)

And finally we come to the Autokey Vigenère. Autokeys are the most secure form of a Vigenère because the answer itself becomes part of the key. Starting with our previous examples, we'll use "GEOCACHE" as our passphrase, and "PLATYPUS" as our alphabet key.

Encoding a set of coords like "North thirty one fifty seven five ninety two, west eight eight twenty two three thirty six," using an autokeyed Vigenère cipher results in a cipher text of "Ytifj fpxhvz vuh xassc zasrs vmpk aeaain zbf, faks imdsp qqjwm jehamk kpv pwhhi sebxkz kxl."

If you run that through a standard Keyed Vigenère Decoder you will get a partial result, like this: "North thilgs itu fnqvj mpxcv ebbc pajnac szd, tjsq yxlyn bethx bcujby sbi xjpta vmzvcg sgm." As you can see... things start off well, but then fall apart.

In an Autokey Cipher, rather than simply using the same passphrase over and over like we did above, your passphrase is the passphrase *plus* the clear text. So, in this case, the passphrase becomes GEOCACHENORTHTHIRTYONE... etc. Once you decode a portion of the cipher text, it becomes an extension of the passphrase in order to complete the decoding.

The Beaufort

The Beaufort Cipher is sort of a backwards version of the Vigenère. Rather than finding the intersection of 2 letters from the row and column, you start at the top and find the first letter of your passphrase. Let's use the same information we used on our example Vigenère. The passphrase would be "GEOCACHE." Then you move down the column until you find the letter you wish to encode, in this case that's "N," the first letter of "NORTH COORDS." You then move to the left until you reach the outside alphabet that governs the rows. That letter is your cipher text letter, so, in this case "H."

The Gronsfeld

Another variation of the Vigenère is the Gronsfeld Cipher. Rather than using letters on both sides of the tabula recta, the Gronsfeld uses numbers on one side and the alphabet on the other. This, of course, means that your alphabet key will be numbers rather than letters, but otherwise it encodes just the same. You write your alphabet key under your clear text, just as before:

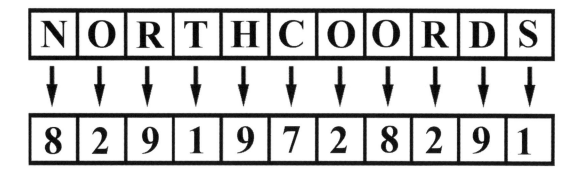

Then you find the number on the tabula recta, and move across the row to the right until you are underneath the letter that you want to encode. The letter in your column is the cipher text letter.

In this case you find the 8, then move right along that row until you are under the "N." At the intersection you find "V," so the cipher text for "N" in this case is "V." The Gronsfeld is slightly less secure than the Vigenère, simply because there are less possible combinations, but it still takes more effort to crack.

miniaturization
Over the years pre-printed One Time Pads got smaller and smaller, to make hiding them easier. One famous spy carried his inside a hollowed out nickel!

The One Time Pad

The final example of a Polyalphabetic Cipher that I'll discuss is the One Time Pad. One Time Pads are, if treated properly, the single most secure cipher that can be created. What makes it so secure? Well, first it is created on the principles of randomness. There is no alphabet, or even series of alphabets, that are used in the encoding. It is encoded using a string of random letters. But most importantly each cipher gets used only *one time*. That isn't really practical for a geocaching puzzle of course. Not many COs would be willing to redo a cipher each time it was found, but the method of encoding could certainly be used.

To begin, you need a long string of random letters to create a cipher alphabet. The cipher alphabet must be as long or longer than the message that you want to encode. There are many methods that have been created to generate these letters: rolling dice, shuffling playing cards, flipping coins, etc. However you get your random alphabet, for ease of use, most One Time Pads arrange them in groups of 5, like this:

one name pad
One time pads gained their name from military and spy use. Spies would be given pads of paper with cipher alphabets preprinted on them. One duplicate of the pad existed with the agency. The spy and the agency would agree on a sheet to use from the pad, which would then be destroyed later, ensuring that each cipher alphabet was only used once!

GHPLQ	BHPAX	VBNLE	XHWSD	ACVJW	ZNKGU	ADLPE
HCNIQ	WNMIL	AOIUE	LXDGH	SDFMO	WHUST	WSBNL
MNBSL	MSNBC	KWSLF	XCVAL	AHCPE	AMSJF	ANSGF
KWJPC	HATBC	DUGBQ	WHCKD	SKIZT	OSTNT	AISTH

The next step is to convert your clear text to numbers. To do this you, use the same method that we used for the Affine Cipher at the beginning of the chapter. Let's encode the word "TRAVELBUG."

Now... One Time Pads don't necessarily have to start at the beginning of the pad. They could start anywhere. The first five letters in something encoded with a One Time Pad usually tells you where to start. For this, we'll start with HCNIQ, in the second line.

For ease of explanation, we'll keep the regular alignment of the alphabet and the numbers, but it is possibly to do a Caesar shift style shift with these so that A = 5 instead of 1. But for now, let's stick to A = 1.

1	2	3	4	5	6	7	8	9	10	11	12	13	14	15	16	17	18	19	20	21	22	23	24	25	26
A	B	C	D	E	F	G	H	I	J	K	L	M	N	O	P	Q	R	S	T	U	V	W	X	Y	Z

To encode "TRAVELBUG," I would start with "T." T = 20. The first letter of our cipher alphabet is "W," as we are starting with the first block of letters following HCNIQ. W = 23.

Next we add the two numbers together: 20 + 23 = 43. Finally, we need to convert that 41 back to a letter. 41 obviously doesn't correspond to a letter, so what do you do? The simplest way to consider it is just subtract 26, (another use of Mod 26 math). 43 - 26 = 17.

With our final result of 17, we look at the chart and see that 17 = Q. So "T" encodes as "Q." You move through the entirety of the clear text in that fashion until you have the whole message encoded.

Decoding is simply the reverse. If you begin with "F" you convert that to a number, in this case 6. Starting in the same place on our One Time Pad as before, the second letter in the cipher alphabet is "N." N = 14, so 6 - 14 = -8. In this case we end up with a negative number. To get our clear text, we would need to add 26 this time. -8 + 26 = 18, and 18 = R. "R" is the second letter of our decoded text.

There are variations to this method. As I mentioned the alphabet might be Caesar shifted, or A may be made to equal zero rather than one. The math may also be altered. Rather than going directly from the result of our simple math outlined above, the encoding may add a secondary step, such as adding or subtracting 1. In my first example above, by encoding the "T" in "TRAVELBUG," I ended up with 17 = Q. But if there was a secondary step to the math, such as adding 1, I would have arrived at 18 = R.

The strength here is that there is no pattern. You won't be able to assume that the most frequently seen letter will probably equal "E" as you can in Cryptograms or Caesar Shifts. A five letter word like "BNOJP" has just as much chance to decode to "NORTH" as it does to "SOUTH," there is no way of knowing. The weakness of this cipher is also in the randomness. In order to break a One Time Pad, you MUST know what the cipher alphabet was. If your One Time Pad was misplaced, or destroyed, you could not decode messages.

One way around this is to use familiar text as the Cipher Alphabet, combining the idea of an Ottendorf Cipher and a One Time Pad. This wouldn't be strong enough for real world espionage or secrecy because the letters aren't random, but for geocaching, it would work just fine. If the description on the page was "This cache was placed in honor of my grandfather, who was a World War Two veteran." You could break that text into groups of 5, and use it as your one time pad:

THISC ACHEW ASPLA CEDIN HONOR OFMYG RANDF
ATHER WHOWA SAWOR LDWAR TWOVE TERAN

Or you can use any piece of text that you like, really:

TOBEO RNOTT OBETH ATIST HEQUE STION WHETH
ERTIS NOBLE RINTH EMIND TOSUF FERTH ESLIN
GSAND ARROW SOFOU TRAGE OUSFO RTUNE
ORBYO PPOSI NGEND THEMX

There are other variations on the One Time Pad, including a Numeric Pad, which takes the step of converting the clear text to numbers using a method known as a "straddling checkerboard." Then the text is enciphered using a One Time Pad made of numbers, rather than letters. A full explanation of this method can be found online.

Polygraphic Ciphers

Polyalphabetic Ciphers substitute letters from the clear text for letters from the cipher text, one for one. Polygraphic Ciphers, on the other hand, substitute two or more letters of cipher text for each single letter of clear text, or substitute two cipher text letters for two clear text letters. These letter groups are known as digraphs or trigraphs.

puzzles within puzzles

Starting in 1930, a British magazine called *The Listener* featured crossword puzzles that contained a Playfair Cipher in the central squares of the puzzle. This style of puzzle still appears in the weekend edition of the *London Times*.

The Playfair Cipher

In the previous section we discussed several ciphers that built off of the concept of the tabula recta, a table with all of the Caesar Shift alphabets listed on it. The Playfair Cipher, and most of the others that we will discuss in this section, build off of something called a Polybius Square. A Polybius Square is simply the alphabet arranged in a 5 by 5 grid. Because the English alphabet has 26 letters, one letter has to be left out or combined with another. This is usually "Q" or "J." "J" is usually combined with "I," and it is up to the decoder to decide if an "I" or a "J" is the appropriate letter for that spot. (This is what I've done in my example). If "Q" is taken out, it is usually just skipped.

Some sneaky COs will use a non-standard Polybius, arranging the letters randomly or in columns rather than rows. It could even be arranged as a spiral, starting with A at the center and spiraling outward.

A	B	C	D	E
F	G	H	I	K
L	M	N	O	P
Q	R	S	T	U
V	W	X	Y	Z

The Playfair Cipher uses an alphabet key like other ciphers that we've discussed. The Polybius Square is arranged using that key. Here is an example using the alphabet key "SATELLITE."

S	A	T	E	L
I	B	C	D	F
G	H	K	M	N
O	P	Q	R	U
V	W	X	Y	Z

The first step in encoding is to break the word into digraphs (letter pairs). If there is an odd number of letters you add an "X." If a letter doubles, you insert an "X" between them. So, the word "LETTER" would be broken up as LE TX TE RX.

Let's encode the word "TICKS." Broken up it would be TI CK SX.

The next step is to locate the letter pairs on the Polybius Square and follow three simple rules:

1. If the letters appear on the same row of your Polybius Square, replace them with the letters to their immediate right (wrapping around to the left side of the row if a letter in the original pair was at the end of the row).

2. If the letters appear on the same column of your Polybius Square, replace them with the letters immediately below (wrapping around to the top side of the column if a letter in the original pair was on the bottom side of the column).

keywords

Look for variations on the name of this cipher, such as the phrase "fair play" or a suggestion by the CO that you "follow the rules."

tap code

Also known as "Smitty Code," "Knock Code," or "Jail Code," Tap Code combines elements of Morse code with a numbered Polybius Square. It works by "tapping" or "knocking" two numbers -- first the horizontal number, and then the vertical -- to represent the letter at that intersection. Two taps, a pause, and then one tap would equal B. It is sometimes written using periods, and spaces. A single space represents the pause between the two digits, and double spaces represent the longer pause between letters. The pause between words is represented by a slash, like this, which says "Tap code:"

····· ·· ···· ··· / ··· · ··· ·· ··· · ·····

fair play?

Even though the Playfair Cipher was created by a man named Charles Wheatstone, in 1854, it is called the Playfair Cipher after Lord Lyon Playfair who tried to get the British government to use it.

so easy a kid can do it?

When Lord Playfair submitted the Playfair Cipher to the British Government, they rejected it because they thought it was too complex. Lord Playfair argued that he could teach it to a school boy in less than 15 minutes, but they replied, "That is very possible, but you could never teach it to a government worker."

3. If the letters are not on the same row or column, replace them with the letters on the same row but at the other pair of corners of the rectangle defined by the original pair. The order is important: the first letter of the encrypted pair is the one that lies on the same row as the first letter of the plain text pair.

Our first digraph is "TI." "T" and "I" form the corners of a rectangle, so we would use Rule 3.

The opposite corners of the rectangle are "S" and "C." "T" comes first, so we encode it first. 'S' appears on the same row as 'T,' so T = S. And therefore I = C in the cipher text. So the first digraph in our cipher text is 'SC.'

The next digraph is "CK." "C" and "K" are in the same column, so we need to use Rule 2.

Rule 2 tells us that if the letters are in the same column we use the letters immediately below them to encode. Below the "C" is "K," so C = K. And below the "K" is "Q." K = Q. The second digraph in our cipher text is therefore "KQ."

Finally, the digraph "SX." These two letters form a rectangle again, so we use Rule 3 again.

"S" is on the same row as "T" at the opposite corner, so S = T, and at the other end "X" is opposite "V." Meaning X = V. That leaves us with the digraph "TV" as our final pair.

The final cipher text is: SC KQ TV.

When you are presented with cipher text that is broken into pairs, the Playfair is your first go-to cipher to try and decode it.

Decoding simply takes the encoding steps backwards. Let's decode the cipher CL CZ. The first digraph, "CL" forms a rectangle. The opposing corners of the triangle are "FT" (following the rules laid out in Rule 3 of the cipher to order the letters.)

The second digraph, "CX," also forms a rectangle, with the opposing corners being "FX." Together, removing the space, we have FTFX. The final "X" is just padding, to make the cipher text have an even number of letters, so we can remove it, leaving us with FTF as the decoded answer.

The Bifid Cipher

The Bifid Cipher expands on the Polybius Square idea by adding numbers to the edges of the square, 1 through 5. We start at the top left corner and work down the left side, and across the top.

	1	2	3	4	5
1	A	B	C	D	E
2	F	G	H	I	K
3	L	M	N	O	P
4	Q	R	S	T	U
5	V	W	X	Y	Z

This creates a grid system, whereby you can locate a number within the square by referring to its position within the grid. This is done with a pair of numbers, the first referring to the row number, counting down from the top. The second refer to the column numbers, counting left to right.

The letter "A" is found at the coordinates 1,1. To encode something using the Bifid system, you have to find the column and row numbers for each letter, and then write them down with the row above column. Encoding the word "MICRO" looks like this:

Next you rewrite the numbers, reading left to right, and breaking them into pairs: 32 14 32 43 24. Then you take those number pairs and find the letter that corresponds to them. Row 3, column 2 is "M." Row 1, column 4 is "D." Etc. In the end, your encoded message is "MDMSI."

M	I	C	R	O
3	2	1	4	3
2	4	3	2	4

A short message like I've done here can be written as a single string of text. A longer message, like a whole set of coordinates may be broken into segments. For instance the clear text could be broken into segments of five letters, not regarding the normal word breaks. For instance, the phrase "WEST COORDINATES" may be broken into WESTC OORDI NATES. The number of letters that the text is broken into is known as its "period."

Just like a Playfair, Bifids can also use alphabet keys to reorder the alphabet. Or the order of the alphabet could be mixed or arranged in columns rather than rows.

The Trifid Cipher

Bifid Ciphers introduced a coordinate system to the ciphers we've learned, but it only worked in two dimensions, columns and rows, and we live in a three dimensional world, which also includes a third dimension. The Trifid Cipher brings that third dimension into play. Instead of a 5 by 5 Polybius Square, the Trifid uses a 3 by 3 *Polybius Cube*. Three 3 x3 Polybius Squares on three layers of a cube.

Encoding a letter now requires three numbers, a row, a column and a layer.

Encoding our previous example of "MICRO" now looks like this:

Layer 1			Layer 2			Layer 3		
1	2	3	1	2	3	1	2	3
1 A	B	C	1 J	K	L	1 S	T	U
2 D	E	F	2 M	N	O	2 V	W	X
3 G	H	I	3 P	Q	R	3 Y	Z	

M	I	C	R	O
2	3	1	3	2
1	3	3	3	3
2	1	1	2	2

From there forward, it works exactly like the Bifid Cipher, reading the rows from left to right, breaking the new numbers into 3's, and finding the corresponding letter to encode.

triffids

The Trifid Cipher should not be confused with the novel, or movies "Day of the Triffids" and "Night of the Triffids," though I have seen those movies used as hints towards the cipher.

The Four-square Cipher

Using a Polybius Cube might seem fancy, but the Four-square Cipher sees your cube and raises you *FOUR* Polybius Squares. Generally, to help distinguish them, two of the squares are written as lower case Polybius Squares, and two use upper case.

Encoding using Four-square starts in a way similar to the Playfair, by splitting the clear text into pairs. Sticking with our example of "MICRO," we get MI CR OX as our pairs.

The first pair is "MI," so we locate the 'm' in the upper left Polybius Square (the lower case square), and the 'i' in the lower right one. Just like Rule 3 in the Playfair we then look for the opposite corners of the rectangle. For "m" that would be "O" and for "i" it would be "G," so MI = OG.

Like all the other ciphers in this section Four-square can use an alphabet key or mixed alphabets.

a	b	c	d	e	A	B	C	D	E
f	g	h	i	k	F	G	H	I	K
l	m	n	o	p	L	M	N	O	P
q	r	s	t	u	Q	R	S	T	U
v	w	x	y	z	V	W	X	Y	Z
A	B	C	D	E	a	b	c	d	e
F	G	H	I	K	f	g	h	i	k
L	M	N	O	P	l	m	n	o	p
Q	R	S	T	U	q	r	s	t	u
V	W	X	Y	Z	v	w	x	y	z

The Nihilist Cipher

In the 1880's a group of anti-Czarists rose in Russia in an attempt to overthrow the Russian monarchy. They called themselves the "Nihilists." Like all good secret organizations, the Nihilists needed a secret code to pass messages between themselves and so was born... the Nihilist Cipher.

The Nihilist Cipher uses a numbered Polybius Square, just like the Bifid Cipher, but adds a keyword and an extra step in the transformation.

	1	2	3	4	5
1	A	B	C	D	E
2	F	G	H	I	K
3	L	M	N	O	P
4	Q	R	S	T	U
5	V	W	X	Y	Z

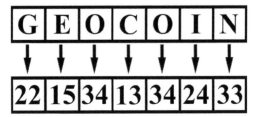

Let's encode the word "GEOCOIN." First you would convert the word to its Polybius Square numbers: the number of the row first, then the number of the column.

Next you write your keyword beneath those numbers, and convert your keyword into Polybius Square numbers as well. Let's use "GPS" as our keyword. Since it is shorter than the clear text, we just repeat it until we have the same number of letters.

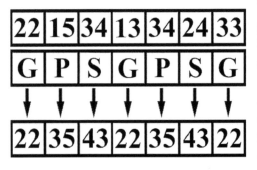

The final step is to add together our Polybius Numbers from both the clear text and the keyword.

And there you have it! Your cipher text in this case is the final sum of those numbers: 44 50 77 35 69 67 55.

22	15	34	13	34	24	33
+	+	+	+	+	+	+
22	35	43	22	35	43	22
=	=	=	=	=	=	=
44	50	77	35	69	67	55

Nihilist Ciphers can become a keyed cipher if you use an alphabet key to change the order of the alphabet. You can also use a Polybius with a mixed alphabet to make the encryption stronger.

keywords
Like other Polybius Square based ciphers, the Four-square can use alphabet keys or mixed alphabets. In this case, there would be two alphabet keys, one for each of the cipher alphabets, which are the capitalized alphabets in our example chart.

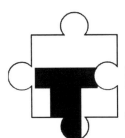# Transpositions

One of the common features among the ciphers we've looked at so far is that the cipher text remains in the same order as the original clear text, but that doesn't always have to be the case. Transposition ciphers encode the text by taking it and rearranging it into a new pattern.

Imagine having a jigsaw puzzle with letters printed on each piece. When the puzzle is assembled, the words would be easily readable. But if you break the puzzle up and shuffle the pieces, you end up with gibberish. This is how a transposition cipher works. No letters change, just the order that the letters are presented in. In order to decode the text, you need to know how to reorder the text into it's proper pattern. The "rule" that governs the order is how the jigsaw goes back together.

The Rail Fence

The simplest form of Transposition Cipher is the Rail Fence. Imagine an old picket fence with the zig-zag top. Now imagine the text of your cipher written along the edge of that zig-zag, moving up and down. You would end up with something like this:

The secret message here is "COORDS ARE IN THE SOURCE CODES." But if this was all there was to the code, it wouldn't be much of a code! To encode take that text and arrange it as if you were reading left to right, not following the zig-zags. The final cipher text here would read:

```
C       A       H       C       S
  O   S R     T E     R E     E
    O D     E N     S U     C D
      R       I       O       O
```

CAHCS OSRTEREE ODENSUCD RIOO

In order to decipher the text, we would need to know how "tall" the peaks and valleys are supposed to be. In the example, I used a cipher that was 4 letters tall. But it could have been any number, and decoding the message would be quite different.

One thing to look out for here is that some people who use this cipher break the cipher text into blocks of 5 letters. This serves two purposes: one, it disguises how tall the fence is, which you could figure out by knowing how many letters wide it is. And it also makes the text easier to recite. A group of 5 letters is easier to rewrite with no mistakes than a group of 8.

Route Ciphers

Route Ciphers at first may appear to be simply a block of letters. I can be confused with other cipher types or even a word search! Route Ciphers combine the idea of rearranging text with a maze of sorts. Rather than reading left to right, the person decoding the text would need to know a pattern to follow in order to properly read the message.

Here is the alphabet, A through Y, arranged as a Route Cipher:

K	S	T	X	Y
J	L	R	U	W
D	I	M	Q	V
C	E	H	N	P
A	B	F	G	O

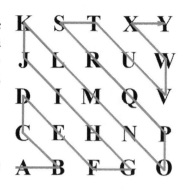

Knowing what the clear text is makes this a pretty simple message to decode, especially since the alphabet has a very familiar order. Traditionally, to decode a route cipher, you would need to know what "route" to follow, since you won't have alphabetical order to guide you.

Simply follow the arrow to decode this text.

There are hundreds of ways that Route Ciphers can be arranged. Here is another possibility:

U	V	W	X	Y
T	G	H	I	J
S	F	A	B	K
R	E	D	C	L
Q	P	O	N	M

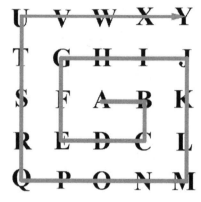

Route Ciphers are also sometimes presented as standard Cipher Text, not in a grid like the ones presented here. In that case, it would be up to you, as the decoder, to not only figure out what the route is, but to figure out how to arrange the text.

Columnar Transposition Ciphers

One way to convey the "rules" for reordering cipher text is to do it by keyword. The Columnar Transposition Cipher does just that. In Columnar Transposition, you must first choose a keyword. Let's use "BENCHMARK" as ours. Next you would build a table, similar to a Polybius Square. Rather than being a set 5x5 table, this table will have a row length that is the same length as your keyword -- in our case 9 letters. It will have as many letters in the columns as are necessary to completely fill in the text. Let's use coordinates as our clear text: 43° 52.746, -103° 27.544.

B	E	N	C	H	M	A	R	K
N	F	O	R	T	Y	T	H	R
E	E	F	I	F	T	Y	T	W
O	S	E	V	E	N	F	O	U
R	S	I	X	W	O	N	E	H
U	N	D	R	E	D	T	H	R
E	E	T	W	E	N	T	Y	S
E	V	E	N	F	I	V	E	F
O	R	T	Y	F	O	U	R	X

You'll notice that there is an extra "X" at the end to make things a nice even rectangle. This is done with a "Regular" Columnar Transposition. It can be left out though, which is called an "Irregular" Columnar Transposition.

The next step is to rearrange the columns by alphabetizing the letters in the keyword.

Then the cipher text is transcribed down the columns (ignoring the keyword, of course): TYF-NTTVUNEIORUEEORIVXRWNY etc. The cipher text that results can be handled in a number of ways. A nice CO might leave the text in an ordered grid, as you see here in the encoding steps, in which case it is up to you to determine how to change the order and decode. Or it could simply be left as text, and it would be up to the solver to

A	B	C	E	H	K	M	N	R
T	N	R	F	T	R	Y	O	H
Y	E	I	E	F	W	T	F	T
F	O	V	S	E	U	N	E	O
N	R	X	S	W	H	O	I	E
T	U	R	N	E	R	D	D	H
T	E	W	E	E	S	N	T	Y
V	E	N	V	F	I	I	E	E
U	O	Y	R	F	X	O	T	R

determine the dimensions of the original table. This is where the difference between the Regular and Irregular types comes in. If you have 45 letters of text, you can guess various table sizes: 3x15, 5x9, 9x5, 15x3, etc. But the original table may also have been 6x8, with three empty spaces at the end!

Columnar Transposition can also be double encoded, running the clear text through a Caesar shift or some other cipher, before placing it in the table. This would prevent puzzle solvers from being able to make educated guesses about the proper order of the columns. The sample coordinates here are in South Dakota. As a cacher living in South Dakota, you could probably guess that the first two words of the cipher are going to end up being "North Forty" or "Forty Three." Knowing that would make putting the columns back in order pretty easy, even without the keyword.

Columnar Transpositions, since they are not dependent on any sort of transformation of the letters, could also include numbers in the clear text, or use numbers to pad the text.

One last thing... I've solved a couple Columnar Transposition Cipher caches, and I've noticed a trend. I'm not sure if it is something that COs do to make the puzzles look more intimidating, or to make them look more like Word Searches, or what, but a lot of COs put the coordinates into their clear text twice. I've solved no less than three Columnar Transposition puzzles that included the phrase, "We're so nice we've given you the coords twice!" So if you see that in a description... try this first!

nihilism survives

The Nihilists may not have risen to power during the Russian Revolution, but their cipher survived and was later adopted by the government. During WWII, Russian spies used variations on the Nihilist Cipher to communicate with Moscow.

kryptos

The third cipher of the Kryptos statue outside the CIA Headquarters was solved using a Transposition Cipher.

The fourth cipher remains unsolved after more than two decades.

The ADFGVX Cipher

In 1918, the German government sponsored a conference among its cryptology community to try and find a new cipher for military use. The ADFGVX Cipher was one of the ones chosen. ADFGVX has two common variations: ADFGX, which uses the standard 5x5 Polybius Square that we have used so far, and ADFVGX which uses a 6x6 Polybius Square that uses all 26 letters of the alphabet, as well the numbers 0-9. Both traditionally use a randomly arranged alphabet, although a regular alphabetical order alphabet could be used, or an alphabet key as we have in previous ciphers. Both variations of the cipher combine the Polybius Square and columnar transposition into a new cipher. For the example, we'll use the large Polybius Square with both letters and numbers.

	A	D	F	G	V	X
A	Y	E	X	2	L	I
D	U	G	Q	W	K	1
F	S	0	R	O	P	A
G	7	4	3	T	Z	6
V	V	8	F	N	J	H
X	C	B	M	D	9	5

You would encode your clear text using this square. For this example, let's use the phrase "LOCK AND LOCK." You locate the letter within the Polybius Square and note its coordinates on the grid, row first, then column. So "L" would encode to "AV." The entire cipher text would be AV FG XA DV FX VG XG AV FG XA DV.

L	O	C	K	A	N	D	L	O	C	K
↓	↓	↓	↓	↓	↓	↓	↓	↓	↓	↓
AV	FG	XA	DV	FX	VG	XG	AV	FG	XA	DV

The next steps are handled as a Columnar Transposition. You choose a keyword or a keyphrase. Let's use "FIND." Perform the steps of creating columns of text under the keyword, and then reorder the columns by alphabetizing the keyword. Our example has two "Xs" at the end to pad it.

F	I	N	D		D	F	I	N
A	V	F	G		G	A	V	F
X	A	D	V		V	X	A	D
F	X	V	G		G	F	X	V
X	G	A	V		V	X	G	A
F	G	X	A		A	F	G	X
D	V	X	X		X	D	V	X

Finally, transcribe the columns: GVGVAX AXFXFD VAXGGV FDVAXX is the final cipher text.

The Enigma Machine

Between the two World Wars, cryptography took some great leaps forward, primarily driven by mechanical methods of encoding text. These machines, and the machines built to crack the resulting ciphers, were the forerunners of early computing and have been incredibly important to the history of computers.

One of the most famous of these was the Enigma machine. The Enigma was designed as a machine for encoding and decoding only, it wasn't capable of transmitting or receiving messages. There were several settings and pieces that could be swapped out, or have their order changed,which would change how messages were encoded. Each day Enigma operators were given a list of settings and swaps to perform on their machine for that day. The cipher could not be performed, or cracked by hand. It could only be done by another Enigma Machine.

The history of the Enigma and how the Allies came to crack the cipher is a fascinating story. I encourage you, if you are at all interested, to read up on it. But for our discussion here, it is only important that you be aware that the Enigma exists. Cracking an Enigma cipher will take more than just a simple password. There are rotor orders, rotor settings, ring settings, plug-board settings... it is a complex operation.

If you are looking at a cache page that includes a cipher, keep an eye out for the word Enigma, or words like rotor, plug, plug-board, Bletchley Park, ring, lampboard, stecker, wheel, or German. They might indicate that you are dealing with an Enigma Cipher.

Enigma encoded text might maintain the regular word lengths and spacing, but it is often presented broken into groups of 5 letters.

One last thing... there are any number of Enigma simulators online, but they are not all created equal. Some assume certain settings, other are modeled after earlier or later models and some may not have a plug-board, or may use 4 rotors instead of 3, etc. If you are convinced that you are dealing with an Enigma Cipher but you aren't getting good results, try another simulator, or ask the CO what simulator they would recommend.

Cryptographic Hash

A "hash function" is a mathematical algorithm that maps data of a variable length to a hash of a set length. That's a lot of words, I know... but basically it means this: If you encode one sentence with 5 words, and one sentence with 25 words, using the same hash function, the result will be the same length in both.

What a hash returns is not technically a block of ciphertext: it is called a "digest." Depending on the type of hash being used a digest will always return a block of a certain size, but the thing that makes a hash so secure is that the smallest change in the input will alter the digest dramatically. Compare these two nearly identical sentences:

This is a very small file with a few characters

this is a very small file with a few characters

| **Digest of sentence 1:** | 75cdbfeb70a06d42210938da88c42991 |
| **Digest of sentence 2:** | 6fbe37f1eea0f802bd792ea885cd03e2 |

Simply changing the first letter from a capital to a lower case completely changes the digest.

Like the Enigma Machine, hashes can't really be decoded by hand, but you should be aware of their existence. Different hash algorithms have different names, but here are some of the more popular ones that you should be on the watch for: **AP, BKDR, BP, DEK, DJB, ELF, FNV, JS, MD** (there are several variations of MD: they are usually followed by a number to differentiate them), **PJW, RIPEMD** (usually followed by a number), **RS, SDBM, SHA** (usually followed by a number), Tiger, and Whirlpool. If you google the specific name of the hash that you think you might need, you will find websites for each type that will expand the digests for you!

Public Key Encryption

All of the encryption methods we have discussed so far have been what are known as "symmetric-key encryptions," meaning that the key to encrypt it is the same as the key to decrypt. This means that if your key is discovered or broken, not only could someone decipher your messages, but they could send you back messages using the encryption key and possibly convince you that the intended recipient of your messages is still in place.

Public key encryption solves that problem by making the keys asymmetric. The key used to encrypt is not the same as the key used to decrypt. In this scheme, you have a private key that decrypts any message that was encoded using a different key, a public key that is published and well known. The most popular public key algorithm is one created by three mathematicians named Ron Rivest, Adi Shamir and Leonard Adleman. The algorithm is known as the RSA Algorithm, using each of the initials of their last names.

Again, this is a system that can't be done by hand, you need a computer program to encode and decode messages using this system. The public key alone can be up to 528 characters long.

Cribs

Some COs may be kind enough to provide you with something known as a "crib" when they present you with cipher text. Simply put, a crib is a word in the clear text.

Going into most geocaching ciphers, we can be reasonably assured that the clear text will contain numbers or the word "north" or "west." A crib is confirmation from the CO that a certain word actually does appear. This is especially useful if you are dealing with a route cipher, a rail cipher, or a columnar transposition. Particularly in those ciphers the cipher text is the same letters as the clear text, simply rearranged. Being aware of a crib would help you determine how to rearrange the letters in order to get clear text.

Some COs may also refer to this as a "probable word."

Final Cipher Advice

I've introduced you to maybe 2% of the ciphers in the world. People have been formulating methods to keep information secret for centuries, and as computers became more and more sophisticated and able to do calculations at much faster rates, the complexity of ciphers increased. Breaking a cipher is mostly about figuring out which one it is. To help with that, at least to some extent, I've created a flow chart in Appendix 7 that gives

166

dot dot dash

The letters A, D, F, G, V & X were chosen because they are all very different in Morse Code, making transcription errors, and therefore mistakes in the decoding, less likely.

missing keys

Need a keyword but can't find one on the page? Try the name of the cache, the cacher's name, or the GC code.

you starting points to tackle a cipher-based puzzle. It won't solve the more advanced ciphers, but it will help you identify the more common ones.

In all honesty, when I arrive on a cache page and find a cipher, if the cipher text still has the spaces and word lengths of regular text, I automatically run it through a Cryptogram Solver first. There are several ciphers that are vulnerable to this and some COs get caught up in the cute name (like the Kama Sutra Cipher) or the history and don't realize that the cipher is that easy to unravel.

If that doesn't work my next step is trying it against all of the Caesar shifts. This is a really common cipher type. If *that* doesn't work... **then** I start looking for exotic ciphers.

Wikipedia has an incredible ciphers section. Look up any of the ciphers that we've discussed in this book, and then look at the bottom of the Wikipedia page for a link to their Cryptography Portal. There you'll find more in depth discussion of all of these ciphers, including variations that I did not cover, as well as dozens of other cipher types. Just reading the list of names so that you are familiar with them might be all you need to help you crack a puzzle cache that has plagued you for years!

There are lots of good books about ciphers, and about the history of the interplay between cipher makers, and the people dedicated to breaking them. Simon Singh's "*The Code Book,*" is an especially good, and very readable example. Reading about ciphers will help you in identifying them, and give you some knowledge that might be useful in identifying hints, clues, or breadcrumbs that COs may have left on their pages.

If you are a PC user (sorry Mac users, I feel your pain) and you just want to cut to the chase you might be interested in a program called CryptoCrack. CryptoCrack is a very powerful code breaking that can not only identify ciphers, but break them, even if the keyword is unknown.

Solving it
Bringing together what you've learned.

Use this checklist to help you apply what you've learned in this chapter and determine which cipher you might be working with.

Checklist: ADVANCED CIPHERS

- [ ] Identify the cipher you are working with.

- [ ] Look for hints to keywords or alphabet keys that you might need to decode certain ciphers. If the CO hasn't provided one, try the cache title, the CO's name or the GC code.

- [ ] Compare your cipher to the information on the cipher flow chart in Appendix 7.

- [ ] If the results of a cipher don't look like what you expected but you are sure of the type, consider that the text might have been double encrypted.

168

 **alk-Through**

We've learned a good deal about ciphers at this point, so it's time to apply it to a couple puzzles. Here's one that I'll solve, and you can follow along. On the next page is one for you to solve on your own. Remember, there is no actual geocache at these locations. Here's the puzzle:

FIND A CACHE

 **Netwon's Prism**

A cache by: k1d_fl4sh   Hidden: 08/09/2010
Difficulty: ★★★★☆   Size: ▪▪■■□
Terrain: ★☆☆☆☆

N 44° 32.118 W 110° 49.063
In Yellowstone, Wyoming, USA

32 FAVORITES

The cache is NOT at the listed coordinates.
You must determine the actual coordinates by solving the puzzle below.

Right away you'll notice that this puzzle is a cipher. Only there isn't a password or a keyword given. You'll have to find that on your own. Good luck with that. But you won't have to look very far. It's right here on the page. Very prominently.

Pcs'rm nder rnf kvtvc gu njihwlpcm kvgxug jes dowm uvfm lpcm fbc nvvyisb zfv aztre uej ewlkug jes.

FC47KLS

LOG YOUR VISIT

View Gallery
Watch
Bookmark
Ignore

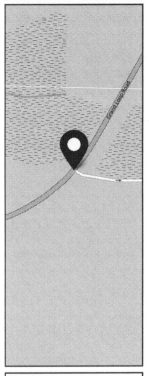

Attributes:

1 **Start at the very beginning.** I start with the basics: date, name, gallery, related web pages, TB inventory, double check for white hidden text, and in the source code. Most of it comes up with nothing, but hidden just below the cipher text in the description is some white text that says "There's nothing here but I like the way you think!" (Hard to show that in a book, but trust me...)

2 **Cache description.** Well, the description lays it all out there, reveals that it is a cipher, and tells us that we'll need a keyword. It could be a Keyed Caesar, a Keyed Vigenère, or a couple other cipher types. Caesar and Vigenères are probably the two most common cipher types used in geocaching, but Keyed Caesars are less common that Vigenères and far less common than standard Caesar shift type ciphers, so I'd probably start with Vigenère, just based on experience. Naturally that won't always be the answer, but just like I always start with the basics on a cache page, it is usually the first cipher I try as well.

3 **A Vigenère.** There are many Vigenère solvers available online. I am partial to the one found at *rumkin.com/ tools/ciphers/*. In the menu on the right, I choose "Keyed Vigenère," and have a look at the page. They have a drop down menu to choose whether you want to encrypt or decrypt a message. In this case we want to decrypt. There is an input for an "Alphabet Key," a password, which they call "Passphrase," and a spot to put your cipher text. What they are calling an alphabet key is there in case you want your tabula recta to start with an arrangement of the alphabet that is not the standard A to Z. There is no indication that our CO has done that, so we can simply leave that blank. We can cut and paste the cipher text from the cache page and put it into the box labeled "Your Message." In some cases COs will put a jpeg of text rather than text that you can cut and paste, which means you will have to type the text in by hand. If that is the case, be very careful, making sure that you copy everything correctly. With some ciphers, a single letter in the wrong spot will mean that the rest of the message won't decrypt properly.

4 **Where is the password?** Since the CO was kind enough to tell us we'd need a password I have to assume that it is something I can find. They even tell me that it's on the page somewhere. In this case my first thoughts are always the GC number, and the cacher's name. In this case both of those contain numbers, which is possible in a Vigenère if there were numbers in the original tabula recta, but there are no numbers in the cipher text given by the CO, so I doubt that's going to be it. I try them just in case, but still have gibberish. My next go-to solution is the title, but that doesn't work out either in this case. It has to be hidden in the description somewhere. It could be a pun. The sixth sentence in the description says, "It's right here on the page." I've done many puzzles where the description says something along the lines of "The password is easy to find," and sure enough... the password was literally the phrase "easy to find." So I try, "right here on the page," "right here," and "right," and several other variations, but nothing works out.

5 **Aha? Aha!** There isn't a lot left in this description to work with, but the CO promises the password is very prominent. What is prominent on the page? The title is naturally the most prominent thing, but we tried that. Is the title a clue? A prism is a piece of crystal that splits white light into rainbow colored light. I don't immediately see anything about rainbows or light on the page. The next most prominent thing is the ciphertext, but a cipher can't be its own keyword. Capital letters are more prominent than lowercase... maybe the capital letters? Looking at all the caps in the description I see R, O, Y, G, B, I and V.... oh! Not just caps! An acrostic! ROYGBIV, the memory mnemonic that kids learned to remember the seven rainbow colors, Red, Orange, Yellow, Green, Blue, Indigo and Violet.

6 **The answer.** Using 'ROYGBIV' as my password, I quickly get a short message that includes final coords 44° 31.504, -110° 50.291, and an appropriately thematic final location.

On the next page is another puzzle, for you to solve on your own this time. Apply the lessons from this chapter, and you should be able to solve it.

olve It Yourself!

Here are some puzzle caches for you to solve on your own. Using the skills we learned in this chapter you should be able to solve these puzzles. Take careful note of the final coordinates that you get as a solution to these puzzles, and write them at the bottom of the page. If you need a reminder of how to use the puzzle stats or hints provided, please check page 11. Good luck!

Puzzle 1 Solution:

S __ __ ° __ __ . __ __ __ , E __ __ __ ° __ __ . __ __ __

As a secondary check you should be able to answer this question: *What equipment do you find at the final?*

Puzzle 2 Solution:

N __ __ ° __ __ . __ __ __ , W __ __ __ ° __ __ . __ __ __

As a secondary check you should be able to answer this question: *What equipment do you find at the final?*

FIND A CACHE

Transformation

FCK4RT3

A cache by: X-Cutioner   Hidden: 07/10/2005

Difficulty: ★★★☆☆   Size: ▪▫◼◼◻

Terrain: ★☆☆☆☆

📋 **LOG YOUR VISIT**

📇 View Gallery

👓 Watch

📑 Bookmark

⊗ Ignore

S 20° 22.795 E 118° 35.828

In Port Hedland, Australia

39 FAVORITES

The cache is NOT at the listed coordinates.
You must determine the actual coordinates by solving the puzzle below.

Below are all the digits and characters you'd need to locate this cache. (Plus one extra.) However, they are in the wrong order. To find the proper order you may need these clues:

A groundhog burrows.

Americans refer to a lorry as an 18-wheeler.

Scaling is a form of transformation.

They may seem like the last thing you need, but trust me, they will help in the end.

2E1S028839251275|8

Oh, and that symbol before the 8? It's on your keyboard above the return key.

Attributes:

PUZZLE STATS

63 CHECKSUM   BEST VIEW

👆 9   👢 116   🥊 138

💣 63   ☁ 128

FIND A CACHE

 ## Fair Play

A cache by: MarilynMac   Hidden: 10/06/2005

Difficulty: ★★⯪☆☆
Terrain: ★☆☆☆☆   Size: ▪▪▪■▫

FCS4K1M

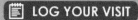 **LOG YOUR VISIT**

 View Gallery

 Watch

 Bookmark

 Ignore

N 47° 27.868 W 092° 32.107

In Durham, North Carolina, USA

42 FAVORITES

The cache is NOT at the listed coordinates.
You must determine the actual coordinates by solving the puzzle below.

You know those teams? The ones that can't seem to win, but you still root for them? It's about the love of the sport, no matter what the sport is. The keyword is sportsmanship. The attitude is fairplay. It's why we love them. Get out there, and play your game!

DT	QT	RB	YB	IO
XP	RB	YB	MO	NZ
RB	YB	MO	BY	DH
HM	HD	PZ	RS	EH
UU	PZ	TD	TL	TY
QH	TD	MZ	DY	RR

Attributes:

 **PUZZLE STATS**
65 CHECKSUM   BEST VIEW

👆 82   👟 140   🥊 45
💣 57   💥 14

Alternate Numerical Systems and Computers

I've talked quite a bit about alphabets and alternate ways to write words. There are just as many ways to write numbers. I'm not talking about cryptology or ciphers. These are mathematical ways of looking at numbers that differ from the everyday 0 through 9 that we all deal with.

A lot of these numerical systems are used by computer scientists, and so they appeal to the geeky core of a lot of geocachers. The good part of this is that they are fairly easy to identify.

In this chapter I'll show you several of these numerical systems as well as some basic computer information that frequently shows up in caches.

ll Your Base...

Humans have 10 fingers, and we've all learned to count that way, using our fingers to keep track of numbers as we move forward. This is one of the reasons that cultural anthropologists think that we settled on a base 10 numbering system, almost world wide. But what does "base 10" mean?

In order to understand bases there are just a few components that you need learn. First is that the number in the phrase "Base X," where "X" is a number, tells you how many single digit numerals are used in that system. Base 10 uses 10 numerals: 0 through 9. Base 2 uses 2 numerals: 0 and 1. Base 16 uses 16 numerals: 0 through 9 and the letters A through F.

decimal

Base 10 is also known as the "decimal" system. The prefix "deci-" means "ten."

Second, we have to understand where our counting "ticks over." Think about an odometer in a car. In a brand new car with absolutely no mileage on it, you'd start at 0. When you start driving around, that little wheel that keeps track of your mileage starts to turn... 1... 2.... 3... etc. until you reach 9. In base 10 you only have the numerals 0 through 9 to express your numbers, so what happens when you count something higher than 9? On our odometer, when we reach 9, something interesting starts to happen: the wheel to the left starts to move. As the wheel with the 9 starts to show a 0 again, we begin to see a 1 on the next wheel. That second wheel represents the 10's place, the next is the hundreds place, etc.

0 1 2 3 4 5 6 7 8 9 10 11 12 13 14 15 ... etc.

Binary Numbers

The same concepts apply to base 2. In base 2 we only have two numerals: 0 and 1. So if our car had a base 2 odometer, we'd get something that looked familiar for the first mile, but in the second mile our first wheel would begin showing 0 again. Our "ticking over" happens much earlier, at the second mile, which is expressed as "10." Counting in base 2 (also known as "binary") looks like this:

0 1 10 11 100 101 110 111 1000 1001 ... etc.

So if you are working in a binary system, 100 does not equal 10 times 10! The binary number 100 is the equivalent of 4 in the decimal system.

a quick joke

There are 10 types of people in the world. Ones who understand binary, and ones who don't. I've often seen this joke used as a hint on cache pages.

Binary number systems are popular with puzzle makers because you can use any opposing set of things to represent it. We mentioned this back in the first chapter on ciphers when we discussed Morse Code, and the same idea applies here. Any combination of two items can be used to represent binary numbers. This is why binary was instrumental in the creation of computers, because numbers could be represented by a circuit within the computer being either off or on. In puzzle terms almost anything can represent these two states. A series of photos of cats and dogs for instance might have the cat representing zero and the dog representing 1. Have a look at the puzzle on the next page. See if you can discover how it uses binary to encode the coordinates.

The first thing you should notice right away is that there are 6 rows of cubicles. 6 is one of the magical geocaching numbers. Each row had 4 cubicles in it... that's 24 cubicles, not a number that we can work with yet, but let's keep looking. The next thing you should notice is that there are two types of cubicle: ones with occupants and ones without. In the world of binary that's all we need, we just have to determine which type of cubicle represents 0 and which represents 1. All of the binary numbers between 0 and 9 have 4 or less digits, so each row of cubicles could represent one number. Only one of the rows has a person in the first cubicle, reading left to right. Logically, an empty cubicle could represent 0 and an occupied cubicle could be 1. In the first row on the left we have empty, full, full, empty, or 0110. We can drop the first zero which gives us 110. Looking at a binary chart, we discover that 110 = 6 in decimal. Good start! The next row yields 11, or 3 in decimal. The last row gives us 100, or 4 in decimal. So the northing is going to end in 634.

If we were wrong about our assumption that empty equals 0, we could test it here. If empty equals 1 then the first row would give us 9, but the next row would be 10. If we think that the CO has only given us single digit numbers, to tell us the last three digits in the northing and the easting, then that 10 won't get us very far because we'd end up with four digits rather than three. So our initial assumption was probably right.

Octal Numbers

The next most commonly used numerical base is base 8, or octal. The base 8 system uses only the numerals 0 to 7, so counting with it would look like this:

$$0\ 1\ 2\ 3\ 4\ 5\ 6\ 7\ 10\ 11\ 12\ 13\ 14\ 15\ 16\ 17\ 20\ ...\ \text{etc.}$$

After 7 comes 10, which is where the "octal odometer" ticks over, and we start again.

Octal is another important numbering system in computer languages and has shown up in pop culture quite a few times. The Na'vi from the movie *Avatar*, and the Ancients from the television series *Stargate* both used an octal system.

Be on the lookout for groupings of numbers that are missing the numerals 8 and 9, which might indicate that you are looking at an octal based cache puzzle.

Duodecimal Numbers

dozenal society

The Dozenal Society of America is an organization that advocates switching over to base 12 numbers for every day use. They claim that the duodecimal system is easier to use, and faster to learn.

So far we've talked about numbering systems that use less numerals than our own. Duodecimal numbers, also known as dozenal, are a base 12 system. That brings us to a peculiar problem. In all of the previous bases that we've discussed, the numerals used are the ones we are familiar with because the base requires less numbers than decimal. Base 12 would require new numerals since it goes beyond the digit 9 before you have numbers in the "tens" place. Base 12 isn't widely used so there isn't a consensus on how these extra numerals are written. Some people use "A," "T," or "X" for the tenth number, and "B" or "E" for the eleventh number. Others use a rotated number 2 for the tenth number, and a backwards 3 for the eleventh number. The word for 10 in duodecimal is "dek," 11 is "el," and 12 is "doh."

The base 12 equivalent of 10

The base 12 equivalent of 11

saturday morning

The educational cartoon series "Schoolhouse Rock" episode "Little Twelve Toes" dealt with the duodecimal system, and multiplication by 12.

Counting in base 12 would look like this:

$$0 \ 1 \ 2 \ 3 \ 4 \ 5 \ 6 \ 7 \ 8 \ 9 \ Ɫ \ Ɛ \ 10 \ ... \ etc.$$

Hexadecimal Numbers

The next most commonly referred to base is Hexadecimal, or base 16. Hexadecimal, (sometimes just referred to as "hex"), is another numbering system that is very useful in computers because a hex number represents half a byte, the standard unit of measure in computer storage.

Like duodecimal, hex requires extra numerals in order to be written. The standard way to do this is by using the traditional numbers 0 through 9 and adding the letters A through F.

$$0 \ 1 \ 2 \ 3 \ 4 \ 5 \ 6 \ 7 \ 8 \ 9 \ A \ B \ C \ D \ E \ F \ 10 \ 11$$
$$12 \ 13 \ 14 \ 15 \ 16 \ 17 \ 18 \ 19 \ 1A \ 1B \ 1C \ ... \ etc.$$

"A" in hex is equivalent to "10" in decimal, and "10" in hex is equivalent to "16" in decimal.

Base 31

One base that is not widely used in the rest of math, but is of particular interest to geocachers, is Base 31. Have you ever wondered how the unique GC number that *geocaching.com* assigns to caches are calculated? They are in Base 31. *Geocaching.com*'s version of Base 31 (slightly modified from the standard) uses the numbers 0 through 9, as well as the letters ABCDEFGHJKMNPQRTVWXY and Z. You'll note that I, L, O, S and U are omitted.

In the beginning GC numbers were assigned kind of randomly, which is why two of the two oldest existing caches, GC28 and GC30, GC30 is paradoxically the older cache. Later, the GC codes were assigned in hexadecimal. It was the letters 'GC' with a four digit hex number following. That is until, in April 2003, they reached GCFFFF, which was the highest possible hexadecimal number that they could assign with 4 digits. So, after the 65,535th cache, (that's FFFF in hex) something had to change. Their solution was to shift to a Base 31 system, starting with GCG0000 or GC number 65,536.

That worked fine for a while, until December 2006 when they reached GCZZZZ. ZZZZ is 512,400 in decimal, the highest number you can write in Base 31. The decision was made then to shift to 7 digits instead of 6. The next cache would be GC10000. That cache still exists as of this writing and is a memorial to the rollover into 7 digits. The addition of that 7th digit will allow GC numbers to continue to build until the 28,218,031st cache, which will be GCZZZZZZZ. With the 2 millionth cache being placed in 2013, we are certainly on our way, but it will be a while before we reach 28 million and need to add an 8th digit to GC numbers.

Base 31 is not a common base, but getting a peak at the decimal conversion is actually pretty simple. On any cache page, hover your cursor over the "Watch" link on the right. A web address will pop up that ends in "w=" and a number. That number is the decimal conversion of the GC number. You can also use *geocachingtoolbox.com* (See Appendix 2).

You may be able to see the potential for geocache puzzles here. By simply referencing a GC number, either for an existing cache, or for a cache that may not yet exist, a CO can reference a set of numbers that will be completely hidden in plain sight. Converting the GC code to decimal numbers could give you some, or all of the numbers that you need to find the final location.

fractions

Keep in mind that fractions, and decimals can also be converted to alternate bases, though it becomes more difficult to do by hand. Online converters are the way to go if you have a decimal in a different base.

negative base

It is also possible to convert numbers to negative bases, though it doesn't have a lot of practical use.

ncient Numbers

Base system numbers use what is known as the "positional" system. We know that the numeral "2" alone means something different than the numeral "2" when it is followed by a "0" because of the position it's in. "2" followed by "0" has the "2" in the "tens" place, so we know that it means 2x10.

Other systems use what is known as "tallying." The most familiar of these is the Roman system. Roman numerals use the alphabet to signify value, but position doesn't matter. A single "I" means the same thing as the "I" in "IV." Numbers to the left are subtracted from the larger number to the right. Numbers to the right are added to the larger number.

Tallying number systems require a little math to decipher. In Roman numerals, it's just addition and subtraction, but others might require multiplication or division.

Maya Numerals

The ancient Maya of Pre-Columbian Central America used a vegisimal system, or Base 20.

Roman Numerals

SYMBOL	VALUE
I	1
V	5
X	10
L	50
C	100
D	500
M	1,000

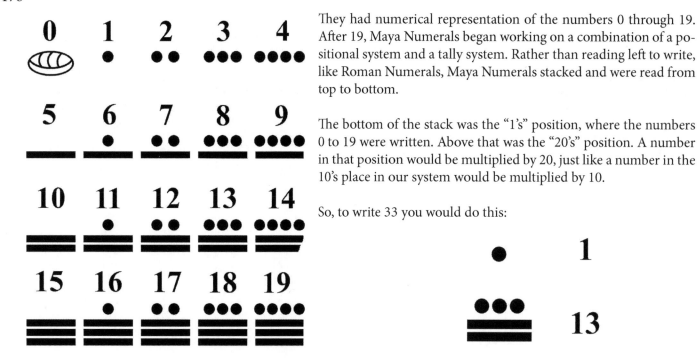

They had numerical representation of the numbers 0 through 19. After 19, Maya Numerals began working on a combination of a positional system and a tally system. Rather than reading left to write, like Roman Numerals, Maya Numerals stacked and were read from top to bottom.

The bottom of the stack was the "1's" position, where the numbers 0 to 19 were written. Above that was the "20's" position. A number in that position would be multiplied by 20, just like a number in the 10's place in our system would be multiplied by 10.

So, to write 33 you would do this:

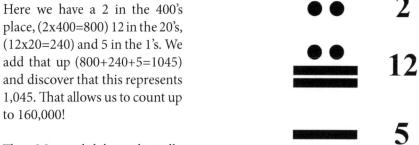

1x20 is 20, and 20 added to the 13 in the 1's position gives us 33. This was good up until 399, which would be expressed with the numeral for 19 in the 20's position (19x20=380) and also in the 1's position. (380+19=399.) To count higher you needed to add a number into the next highest position, the 400's place.

Here we have a 2 in the 400's place, (2x400=800) 12 in the 20's, (12x20=240) and 5 in the 1's. We add that up (800+240+5=1045) and discover that this represents 1,045. That allows us to count up to 160,000!

The Maya didn't technically have a concept of zero as we use it, but if there was not a number in a specific place, for instance if the 5 was not in the 1's place in the previous example, then they placed a white shell in that spot, or later a shape that represented the shell.

Cuneiform Numerals

Several ancient civilizations used a Cuneiform writing system for numbers, including the Sumerians and Babylonians. Cuneiform is a sexagesimal system, or base 60, although it doesn't use 60 distinct numerals. Instead it uses two numerical symbols: an upright wedge shape (often noted as 'Y') and a sideways wedge shape (often noted as '<'.)

The Y shape was used as a hash mark, essentially. A single Y represented 1, YY represented 2, etc. up to 9. After 9 you see that they switched to the < symbol for 10. It too worked as a hash mark, << representing 20, <<< for 30, etc.

After 59, our odometer clicks over, and we start having numbers in the "60's" place. Because the Sumerians didn't have a concept of zero the representation for 1 and for 60 are actually the same: Y. It was up to the person reading the numbers to know in context which was being referred to. After 60 it became easier. With a Y in the 60's place we begin counting again, with a small space between the first Y and the second: Y Y.

Cuneiform uses both the tally system, and positional system. The first 60's place is based on the tally system, so Y <<YYY represents 60+23, or 83. But if we put something in the next spot to the left, like so: Y Y <<YYY, then the first digit must multiply by 60. So, 60x60=3600. 3600+60+23=3683.

1	11	21	31	41	51
2	12	22	32	42	52
3	13	23	33	43	53
4	14	24	34	44	54
5	15	25	35	45	55
6	16	26	36	46	56
7	17	27	37	47	57
8	18	28	38	48	58
9	19	29	39	49	59
10	20	30	40	50	

You may notice something familiar about using a base 60 system. Our understanding of circles and the math involving them, for instance the idea that there are 360 degrees in a circle, was based on Sumerian math. That is the reason that degrees are subdivided into 60 minutes, and minutes are subdivided into 60 seconds. The Sumerian Base 60 math counts up to 59, and then the "odometer" clicks over, and we have a digit in the next highest place.

That math still influences us today in the way we write times, and latitude and longitude coordinates, because both are based on the Sumerian base 60 math.

gaming

A puzzle in the popular game *Assassin's Creed 2*, called 'Synapses,' used a base 60 system as part of the solve method.

Egyptian Hieroglyphic Numerals

Egyptian, compared to some of the other ancient numbering systems, is really straightforward. It employs 7 symbols: a rod, an ox yoke, a coil of rope, a lily, a crooked finger, a frog (or a tadpole,) and a man with his arms up. Each represents a place, and to express multiples, you simply repeat the symbol. So 9 is a row of nine rods, 60 is six ox yokes. 300 is three ropes, etc.

Egyptians did not have a concept of the number zero,

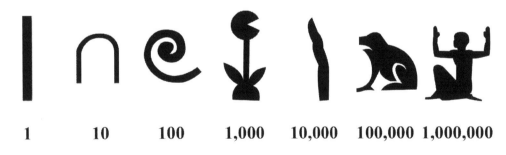

| 1 | 10 | 100 | 1,000 | 10,000 | 100,000 | 1,000,000 |

but because each of their numeral places was marked by a different symbol, if that symbol isn't present then you know that it isn't needed. For instance, a representation of 101 would not need a symbol for the ox yoke because there are no 10's.

The representations of the Egyptian symbols that I have presented here are somewhat simplified and stylized. They can be represented in a number of ways, some looking much more colorful and "drawn," and some looking like simple outlines. Watch for general shapes, or keywords that suggest that you should be looking at Egyptian as a possible solution method. Also, we should note that Egypt went through three major periods of history, each about 500 to 600 years long. As you can imagine the way that numbers were written drifted a little during those periods, but they remained generally the same.

Egyptian Hieratic Numerals

Hieroglyphics were used primarily by the Egyptians as part of stone carvings and adornments on physical objects. Later in their history, they also developed papyrus, a form of paper, and began writing on it. That writing was different than the hieroglyphic style, and is known as Hieratic. The Hieratic system is different in that each number has a unique symbol, rather than repeating the same symbol as hieroglyphics did. In hieroglyphics, in order to write the number 9,999, thirty-six glyphs would have to be carved: nine rods, nine yokes, nine ropes and nine lilies. Hieratic used just 4 symbols, one for 9, one for 90, one for 900, and one for 9,000.

1	2	3	4	5	6	7	8	9
10	20	30	40	50	60	70	80	90
100	200	300	400	500	600	700	800	900
1000	2000	3000	4000	5000	6000	7000	8000	9000

Hieratic numbers can be written and read either left to right, or right to left, and, like hieroglyphs, do not use a zero. If there is no representative number needed in a certain place, that place is simply ignored.

Again, the Egyptian civilization lasted for thousands of years, and hieratic numbers changed over the centuries. The 10's numbers, for instance, rotated to the left and became more of a triangular shape over time.

I	Π	Δ	⌐Δ	H	⌐H	X	⌐X	M
1	5	10	50	100	500	1,000	5,000	10,000

Greek Numerals

Like the Egyptians, the Greeks used several different numbering systems through their history. One of their early systems was the "Acrophonic" or "Attic system." It worked in the same way that Roman numerals did, using different symbols.

Later the Greeks adopted what is known as the "Alphabetic System," or the "Ionic System." This system used the lowercase version of their alphabet. An accent was placed to the right of the letter. If it was in the 1's, 10's, or 100's place, the accent was towards the top of the letter. In the 1000's place the accent was placed towards the bottom. The 100's place, duplicated the numbers from the 1's place, relying on the accent to differentiate between them.

α′ 1	β′ 2	γ′ 3	δ′ 4	ε′ 5	F or ϛ′ 6	ζ′ 7	η′ 8	θ′ 9
ι′ 10	κ′ 20	λ′ 30	μ′ 40	ν′ 50	ξ′ 60	ο′ 70	π′ 80	ϟ′ 90
ρ′ 100	σ′ 200	τ′ 300	υ′ 400	φ′ 500	χ′ 600	ψ′ 700	ω′ 800	ϡ′ 900
α, 1000	β, 2000	γ, 3000	δ, 4000	ε, 5000	F or ϛ, 6000	ζ, 7000	η, 8000	θ, 9000

Hebrew Numerals

Writing numbers in Hebrew is a combination of systems. Like the Egyptians they did not have a concept of zero. Letters from the Hebrew alphabet stand in for the numerals. Each number, 1 to 9, is assigned a letter, and each tens place, 10 through 90, is assigned a letter. In the hundreds place, only 100 through 500 get individual letters, whereas 600 through 900 are created one of two ways. The first option is by using combinations of previous letters. 600 for instance would be the letters for 100 and 500 written together. The second option is using an alternate form of the corresponding 10's place letter. In Hebrew, when a letter appears as the last letter of a word, it is written in a form called "sofit." The sofit form signifies that you have reached the end of a word. The letter for 90 is called "tsade," but 900 can be written using the sofit form of tsade. (I use the sofit forms in the chart.)

א 1	ב 2	ג 3	ד 4	ה 5	ו 6	ז 7	ח 8	ט 9
י 10	כ 20	ל 30	מ 40	נ 50	ס 60	ע 70	פ 80	צ 90
ק 100	ר 200	ש 300	ת 400	ך 500	ם 600	ן 700	ף 800	ץ 900

The fact that Hebrew letters have a use both in language and math is one of the reasons that some people suspect that there might be a hidden code in parts of the Bible. Adding together the values of the letters in certain words give you a new number, which in turn can point back to a letter. Successive words can therefore be said to form new words.

There is also mystical or magical importance placed on certain Hebrew letters or words in a system called "Gematria." In Gematria the numeric values of letters are added up. If two words have the same value, they are said to be related in some way. Some also believe that the numbers, and therefore words, that correspond to your birth date or age are important for you in some way.

Chinese & Japanese

Though they use different spoken words Chinese, (both Mandarin and Cantonese), and Japanese use the same characters to represent their numbers. Unlike the previous languages we've discussed they do have the concept of zero, and represent it with either of these characters:

零 or ○

The rest of the Chinese and Japanese numerals act basically as a decimal system, except that they have individual characters for each place, and so those numbers are represented by "Number/Place Marker," kind of like the zero in the western system.

一 1	二 2	三 3	四 4	五 5	六 6	七 7	八 8	九 9
十 10	二十 20	三十 30	四十 40	五十 50	六十 60	七十 70	八十 80	九十 90
百 100	二百 200	三百 300	四百 400	五百 500	六百 600	七百 700	八百 800	九百 900

The Abacus

It's not a numeral system per se, but the abacus is another ancient math method that shows up frequently in puzzles. There are dozens of variations on abacuses found around the world, but they all have the basic form of a series of beads on rods or wires inside a wooden frame. Some use 10 beads on each wire, some use more or less, but I am going to focus on the Chinese variation.

Chinese abacuses have two rows of beads separated by a wooden slat. The two areas created by the division are called "decks." Each wire in the bottom deck has five "earth beads" and two "heaven beads" in the upper deck. Each of the earth beads has a value of 1, and each of the heaven beads has a value of 5. The beads are only counted if they have been pushed against the divider.

To begin, all the beads in the upper deck are pushed to the top, and the lower deck is pushed to the bottom. In this position, everything has a value of 0.

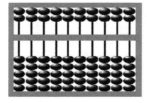

Because it can be used for both whole numbers and decimal numbers, abacuses do not have a set position for numerical places. The first wire of beads on the right could be the 1's place, or you could decide that the 4th wire from the right is the 1's place, which would allow for three places of decimals. (Some abacuses will have a vertical divider that predetermines where the decimal places are.)

If you move a bead from the lower deck up to the divider, then you have 1 in that place, if you move a bead down from the top, then you have 5 in that place. Simply add those numbers to get the value of the abacus. This abacus has a value of 6:

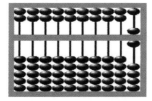

Assuming that the far right wire represents the 1's place, this abacus has a value of 7,218. If I shift the 1's place to the fourth wire from the right, this abacus has a value of 45.097.

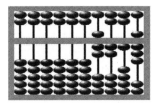

As you can see, if there is a zero in a specific place, as in the decimal 10's place here, both beads are in their neutral zero positions.

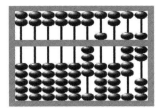

Other variations of the abacus use 10 beads on each wire, instead of beads with a value of 5, each bead has a value of only one, and there is no bar in the center dividing the decks. The Japanese variation uses one heaven bead and four earth beads.

Abacuses can be used to perform all of the major math functions: addition, subtraction, multiplication and division.

Computers and Numbers

Throughout the section on base number systems, I have mentioned their importance to computing and computer languages. Generally the numbers are used in the same way, but they may have slightly different meanings or representations when used in this manner rather than in math.

Baudot or Murray Code

In the early days of computers, methods of input and output were not regulated and different computer creators used different methods. A lot of these were left over from the closest analogs of computers at the time: teletype and telex machines. These machines were the ancestors of telegraphs, but rather than having an operator who would sit and note the messages as they came across the wire ,these machines would receive the message and print it out without the intervention of a person.

In 1870 Émile Baudot invented a five bit code to be used with early versions of these types of machines. Baudot's code was a variation on Morse, but rather than using two distinct tones, a dot and a dash, like Morse, Baudot used the concept that would eventually turn into Binary computer codes: off and on. In Baudot's case, he invented a keyboard with five

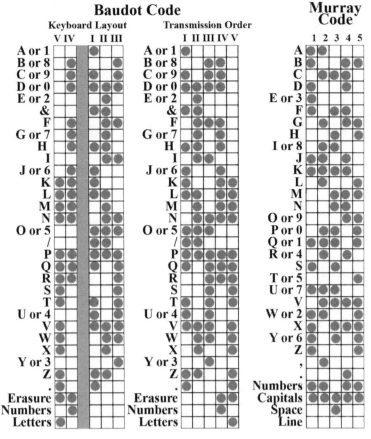

keys that looked similar to a piano keyboard. The operator would press certain keys simultaneously, and the keys that had been pressed would be transmitted to a receiver. Baudot Code can be visually represented both in the way it is sent, the keyboard layout, and the way it is received. As with Semaphore the same arrangement of components can represent both a letter or a number, so there is a character that tells you when you have switched between.

In 1901 Donald Murray transformed Baudot's idea by creating a machine at the other end to receive the message. That machine had a ribbon of paper tape that would have holes punched in it corresponding to the keys that had been pressed at the other end. Murray further transformed the method by altering the keyboard where the message would be input, so that they looked like the keyboards we are familiar with today. Finally, he altered Baudot's original code so that the machinery punching the holes would be less likely to jam. For instance he changed the codes for the most frequently used letters to make sure that they used the least holes.

Murray's version of what is still known as "Baudot Code" is the most popular version. Similar to Binary and Morse, it can be used in a puzzle using any two objects or states, to create the punched or not punched (off/on) state of the paper. Some puzzle COs will present the punch holes down the center of the encoding; others won't. But even if it has the strip it could be either Murray or Baudot. In Murray the strip would fall between 2 and 3.

Punched Cards

Another technology that influenced early computing was the "punched card." The punched card was one of the earliest means of storing and retrieving information, long before anyone thought of calling something a "computer." Punched cards have been used to store information for use by such diverse machines as player pianos and automated knitting looms.

In computing they came to be known as "Hollerith cards" or "IBM cards." Driven by IBM use from the 1900's through the 1950's, punched cards were the primary medium for storing information. By some estimates, at the height of punch-card computing American companies were using more than 10 million of them a day.

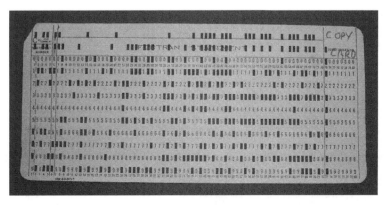

The cards perfected by IBM were a bit bigger than 7"x 3" and were printed with 80 columns of the numbers 0 through 9. Information was stored on them through a series of square holes that were punched out of the card, removing numbers from the columns. So, the question for puzzle solvers is: How do you read them?

The important step in reading punchcards is to divide the card. Imagine four "zones" at the top of the card. The first three are blank, but the fourth coin-

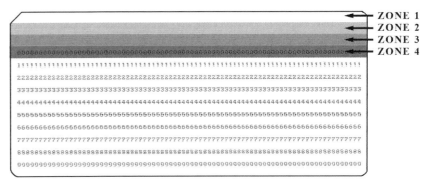

cides with the row of zeros. Below that are the characters 1 to 9 in columns. It takes (at least) two holes to encode a character on a punch card: one in one of the 4 zones at the top, and one that removes a number from the column directly below the first hole.

If there is a hole in Zone 1, the number removed equals itself. 1=1, 2=2, etc. In the example to the left, the first column encodes the number 2.

If there is a hole in Zone 2, a letter from A to I is being encoded. The number punched corresponds to the position of the letter in that sequence. So 1=A, 2=B, 3=C, etc. In the example the second column is encoding "D." If there is a hole in Zone 3, a letter from J to R is being encoded. The example encodes "P."

Zone 4 gets a bit tricky. The first 18 letters of the alphabet are encoded in the previous two zones, leaving only 8 letters (S to Z) to be encoded here, but 9 possible positions. Some iterations of the punchcards leave the 9 as a null, or an unused character, meaning that 1=S, 2=T, etc., but some iterations leave the 1 as the null character meaning that 2=S, 3=T, etc. Which character you need will depend on which encoding scheme the CO used.

cold play

The album "X&Y" by the band Cold Play uses a version of Baudot code to encode the name of the album on the album cover. The cover features six strips of broken color bars. Reading top to bottom, two blocks of color represent a 1, and two empty blocks represent a 0.

You'll notice that I said that it takes at least two holes to encode a character. Non-alphanumeric characters, like periods, commas, or math operands, can also be encoded on punch cards but they typically require two numbers to be punched out. A period would have a hole in Zone 2, and a 3, and an 8 punched from the column below. Other non-alphanumeric characters varied by card type and encoding scheme.

ASCII

ASCII in an acronym, standing for the *American Standard Code for Information Interchange*, and it is pronounced *ASS-kee*. In the 1900's, a group called the "American National Standards Institute" formed to create a standard set of definitions and sizes for industries. What is the actual size of a two by four, what size bolts are manufactured, that sort of thing. They insure that if you buy a light bulb, it is going to fit the light sockets in your home, even if the two were manufactured by different companies. In the 1960's, with the rise of computing the ANSI came together to create a standard set of definitions for computer programming, specifically around how letters and numbers are represented.

Since computers use numbers to represent everything, the ANSI methodically assigned numbers to each letter, character, space, and action like "Return" or "Shift." The goal was to make sure that these numbers were consistently applied, not just across companies, but across numbering systems. That a capital "M" would be represented by the equivalent of the decimal "77," whether it was in binary, octal, decimal or hexadecimal. The complete ASCII set includes 127 characters, and the Extended ASCII set adds 128 more.

punch out

Until well into the 60's nearly 30% of IBM's profits came from the sale of equipment related to punch cards.

As you can see, this sets up several different scenarios that puzzle writers might employ. A hexadecimal number might represent, on the one hand, a number, such that converting to

Character	Decimal	Hexadecimal	Octal	Binary
A	65	41	101	0100 0001
B	66	42	102	0100 0010
C	67	43	103	0100 0011
D	68	44	104	0100 0100
E	69	45	105	0100 0101
F	70	46	106	0100 0110
G	71	47	107	0100 0111
H	72	48	110	0100 1000
I	73	49	111	0100 1001
J	74	4A	112	0100 1010
K	75	4B	113	0100 1011
L	76	4C	114	0100 1100
M	77	4D	15	0100 1101
N	78	4E	116	0100 1110
O	79	4F	117	0100 1111
P	80	50	120	0101 0000
Q	81	51	121	0101 0001
R	82	52	122	0101 0010
S	83	53	123	0101 0011
T	84	54	124	0101 0100
U	85	55	125	0101 0101
V	86	56	126	0101 0110
W	87	57	127	0101 0111
X	88	58	130	0101 1000
Y	89	59	131	0101 1001
Z	90	5A	132	0101 1010

decimal would give us the information that we needed, or on the other hand, it might represent an ASCII character, a letter, a symbol, or a number.

Of course, the reverse is also true. By presenting us with a few letters or characters, the CO might be asking us to convert those characters to their decimal equivalents in ASCII. A set of coordinates like 38° 37.480, -90° 11.085 could be written as:

& % 0 Z n U

The decimal equivalents of those letters and symbols would yield us the numbers that we need when we look at an ASCII table.

You'll notice that the Binary on the chart is written in groups of 8 characters, even though the leading 0 isn't strictly necessary. This is done because of the way that computers store information. A single binary digit is known as a "bit," and 8 of those together are a "byte." So if you are working with binary and find 8 digit blocks, it is quite possible that they are encoding ASCII as a final result, and not just numbers.

Rot47: ASCII Meets Caesar

Earlier we talked about the Caesar Cipher, or ROT-N Cipher. Caesar Ciphers work by essentially folding the alphabet back on itself and aligning the two halves; the letters substitute for each other. (Look back at Chapter 9 if you need a refresher on Caesar's Cipher.)

By adding some of the characters from the ASCII set, we can get a larger collection of characters and make a cipher that looks less like English, though it does make it look even more like ciphered text. This method uses both the upper and lowercase alphabet, plus the symbols !"#$%&'()*+,-./:;<>+?@[\]^_`{} and |, for a total of 94 characters. The cipher itself is referred to as "Rot 47."

Using Rot 47, the phrase "The quick brown fox jumps over the lazy dog" enciphers to %96 "F:4< qC@H? u@I yF>AD ~G6C %96 {2KJ s@8].

Rot 47 has a couple benefits. Though it can be solved by hand like a cryptogram, it is much harder because of the extra characters. It can be made even more difficult by mixing upper and lowercase in the clear text. Take the word "cache," if the clear text is all in uppercase, it would encode as "rprwt." All in lowercase would encode as "42496." If you mix cases, like this "cAcHe," you get "4p4w6." Let's say your local coords start with 33° 33'. That's a lot of threes, and would be easily seen in most simple codes. But if you mix the cases differently each time they appear (tHreE, ThrEe, THrEE, etc.) it makes them harder to identify.

ASCII Art

In the early days of computers and the Internet, before the high speed data lines that we have available today, people still wanted the ability to send and receive images, no matter how crude. The Bulletin Board and BBS users of the 70's and 80's created what came to be known as "ASCII Art," to solve this problem.

ASCII art combines the 96 printable characters from the ASCII and Extended ASCII character sets and arranges them in art that ranges from photographic in detail, to simplistic. It does this by assigning relative values of shading to the characters. For instance a 'B' or a '#' would be a dark character, the equivalent of a black pixel in the art, because they both fill their available space. A '/' or a 'I' would be a middle gray because they fill about half of their space, and a '.' or a '`' would be used in the light areas because they fill almost none of their space.

In geocaching puzzles, a CO might create a piece of ASCII art to represent either the coordinates or a clue, but present it in a way that renders it at first unrecognizable. For instance, if you were presented with the following on a cache page, you might think that it was a cipher of some sort:

```
           . _ " " " " _ .
          /              \
       . - .         |               |          . - .
      (_.  '._       |  |_\ /_| |       _.'  ._)
       '-._'-.(_     A     _).-'_.-'
        '-._|  ____   |_.-'
     _.-'_\`" " " " "`/_'-._
   .-._.'_.-'     `_____'    '-._'-._.
  (,_.'`                              `'._,)
```

But if you were to copy and paste that collection of symbols and letters into a word processing program and change it from left justification to center justification, *this* magically appears:

```
              . _ " " " " _ .
             /              \
          . - .      |          |       . - .
         (_.  '._    |  |_\ /_| |     _.'  ._)
          '-._'-.(_     A     _).-'_.-'
           '-._|  ____   |_.-'
        _.-'_\`" " " " "`/_'-._
      .-._.'_.-'  `_____'  '-._'-._.
     (,_.'`                      `'._,)
```

188

ASCII art might be disguised simply by changing the font, the size of the letters or the width of the page. If you think that you might be working with a puzzle that uses ASCII art but you don't immediately see the picture, try taking it into TextEdit (on a Mac) or Notepad (on a PC). Those programs allow you to make the window wider or more narrow independently of the size of a printed page. You can simply drag the edge to open up more space, like you do on a web browser. A window that is narrower than the width of the art will cause it to have line breaks in unintended places and will therefore not show the image properly.

You can also try changing the justification (center, left or right) or changing the font. A good deal of ASCII art was created to display properly in the font Courier.

Unicode

With all the computers in the world and all the different alphabets, number systems and symbols programmers needed a way to stay consistent across many different devices, programs and uses. In 1988 representatives from Xerox, Apple and a few other companies came together to create the "Unified Character Code," which assigned a unique hexadecimal number to every character in every major language in use around the world, plus numbers punctuation marks, diacritics, mathematical symbols, technical symbols, arrows, dingbats, emoji, etc. etc. The assigned numbers might be 8, 16 or 32 digits depending on how the symbol is being used and by what type of device.

π Я 音 æ ∞

The upside is that when you press the 'T' on your keyboard, the keyboard translates that to Unicode U+0054 in this case, which is sent to your monitor, which knows the U+0054 means 'T' and displays that shape, no matter if the monitor and keyboard were manufactured by two different companies, continents apart.

As I discussed back in the section about Utility Codes (page 100) this type of code can flow several directions. I could give the code, for example U+004E, which would be a capital N. That N could be the beginning of a set of coords if I gave you 15 more Unicode Codes. From the other direction I could give you the letter, such as 'Q,' which you would need to look up on a Unicode table to determine is U+0052. That 52 might be the beginning of coords.

Another possibility would be to give you the symbol itself, which you would have to locate on the table. That's a daunting task but there are websites like *shapecatcher.com* that allow to you draw the character using your mouse and it will identify it for you. From that you will learn the hexadecimal number that is assigned to the character. If you convert that hex to decimal you may get coords, for instance A2D3 in hex is 41683 in decimal, or 41.683 in coord format.

Finally, the CO may give you the name of the character, for instance "Tifinagh Letter Yar," which looks like a circle, but has the hex code U+2D54 assigned to it. 2D54 is 11604 in decimal.

Base64

When you send an image or another file type in an email, it goes without saying that what you are sending is a stream of binary code, not the actual image. We also know that computers themselves use binary for their inner workings. So what happens when something within the binary code that creates an image just happens to match up with a bit of binary code that might tell your modem to shut down, for instance? To get around this potential problem ,image files are encoded using a file type called "Base64." Besides the advantages of not confusing your networks, Base64 is used because it encodes quite a bit of information in a tiny package.

As with the other numerical bases we've discussed, Base64 uses 64 different characters to count: 0 to 9, A to Z in capital letters, a to z in lower case letters, as well as the symbols +, /, and =.

mime

Base64 (without a space in between) is sometimes called "MIME encoding," and should not be confused with Base 64 (with a space) which is a mathematic base using 64 digits.

Besides images, text can also be converted to Base64. For instance, the phrase "The flag of Luxembourg" would look like this in Base64:

VGhlIGZsYWcgb2YgTHV4ZW1ib3VyZw==

An actual *IMAGE* of the flag of Luxembourg would look like this in Base64:

```
/9j/4AAQSkZJRgABAgAAZABkAAD/7AARHVja3kAAQAEAAAAZAAA/+4ADkFkb2JlAGTA
AAAAf/bAIQAAQEBAQEBAQEBAQEBAQEBAQEBAQEBAQEBAQEBAQEBAQEBAQI
CAgICAgICAwMDAwMDAwEBAQEBAQECAQECAgIBAgIDAwMDAwMDAwMDAwMDAw
MDAwMDAwMDAwMDAwMDAwMDAwMDAwMDAwMD/8AAEQgAFAAhAwERAAIRAQMRAf/
EAKIAAAEEAwAAAAAAAAAAAAAABAwYKAgQFAQEAAAYDAAAAAAAAAAAAAAAAAQID
BAYJBQgKEAAAAgUHCQkBAAAAAAAAAAgADBAcIERLUJWWWGCFTFKQVBtZYGTFRUhM
01aXVFgkRAAACAwkOAgsAAAAAAAAAAABEQIGogNjJJRlBwgYUdESUpLSE9ME1BV
VF1Y1GUFyk6MUNFRkhAUJ/9oADAMBAAIRAxEAPwB5qgHj2M1NJiQuv6MQy9cJDBuO2C
BiisMJRAdMygIJ0rWYttMI0frttQnEO+PUK81nqsJPKhLNozBLYJJjCtz1Br4Bo+OVt/
d2mumJDottOXbbkHffS0/Vg70ZiUK5gMA0fHK2/u7TXTEdFtpy7bcg74Wn6sHejMShXMBgG-
j45W393aa6YjottOXbbkHfC0/Vg70ZiUK5gnmBGOflmfr7A3U1L3o1sOX7ZknfGNWmKtneL-
Ne3UzBZYWf2eg3VLDqzEe3OVnMQ0m4bMITiGEoyD+hyhKCbXlaqVKiypLFwxBl9QeqHi6W/
oLQCosah8bSRo+Ue/R+QMetDBtm3uXDZuIkjZQpVmyULaoS+YPQBPcke94BloYNs29y4bNx-
EiyhSrNkoW1QeYPQBPcke94BloYNs29y4bNxEiyhSrNkoW1QeYPQBPcke94HW6w8IXgetcZn+/S1suUnzb-
KD1Yvre9BE9SV73gVPmrYektM7a87SF0vou3zDd2RNlb38Zo1UaJGCWNcGjV/wCG6ZdOnTh-
HiXQxUNr6mk8cgnQpeGw7kFQ2vqaI5BOg8Nh3ISorW1NEcgnQeGw7kTuqrY+OThYx-
BOhk0Q+492P/2Q==
```

What You're Looking For

As with ciphers and codes, the key to getting past numerical bases and these computer encoding systems is really figuring out what you're looking at. Here the easiest way to determine that is to examine the text and find the highest number it contains. That number plus 1 is your base.

In Binary, for instance, the highest number you see is "1." 1 + 1=2, letting you know that you are working in Base 2. This isn't fool proof, of course. You may be working in base 9 and be unlucky enough to just not have an "8" (the highest number in Base 9) in the puzzle, which might lead you to believe you are working with Base 8, but in general you want to start with the assumed base, (the highest number you see, plus 1) and work with that until it stops making sense.

If you see letters mixed with numbers, you know you are working with something higher than Base 10. Remember that Base 12 can use "A, T, X, B" or "E," or the inverted "2" and "3" to represent the numbers higher than 9. If you see letters up to "F," you are dealing with Hexadecimal. Upper case, lower case letters and a few symbols? That's would be Base 64.

Your next step is determining whether you are dealing with the numbers purely as numbers, or as part of a computer encoding scheme. They key here is probably volume. If the CO is only asking for you to convert numbers between bases, you probably will only have a few numbers. Encoding something more advanced, like text or an image, requires a much larger collection of characters.

If you try a Base 64 decoder and you still end up with gibberish, especially if it includes characters that you don't recognize, you probably have an image on your hands, not actual text. Open *Notepad* or *TextEdit* and paste it into a document. Save the document, and then change the file name, adding ".jpg" at the end. Then you can reopen the file as an image. If there are other files types that could be presented in this way, see Chapter 12 and 13 for much more about this, including how to determine which file type you might be working with.

Solving it

Bringing together what you've learned.

Use this checklist to help you apply what you've learned in this chapter and determine which cipher you might be working with.

Checklist: NUMBERS AND ENCODING

☐ Examine the puzzle for ancient number or math systems that might be in use.

☐ Identify the numerical base you are working with.

☐ Convert the numerals to Base 10 (decimal) to see if it makes sense.

☐ Run the text through an ASCII decoder to see if it is encoded text.

alk-Through

Time for some practice! Here's a puzzle that uses the themes and techniques we've covered in this chapter (combined with techniques from previous chapters.) On the right is a walk-through of how I'd go about solving this puzzle, so that you can see the techniques at work.

FIND A CACHE

Just TRY to Get Home

FCJB611

A cache by: erawluob   Hidden: 07/06/2009

Difficulty: ★★⯪☆☆   Size: ▪▪■■▫
Terrain: ★☆☆☆☆

N 40° 42.266 W 074° 08.449
In Newark, New Jersey, USA

🏅 **23** FAVORITES

LOG YOUR VISIT

🖼 View Gallery
👓 Watch
📑 Bookmark
⊗ Ignore

The cache is NOT at the listed coordinates.
You must determine the actual coordinates by solving the puzzle below.

I don't know about you, but it seems like at least three times a week I end up sitting in traffic, trying to get home after work. It used to be I could leave the office just a little early and not have a problem, but lately the roads seem to fill up by 3 o'clock. Maybe I need to switch to third shift.

Well, I can't fix the traffic problems... but maybe I can give you something to think about while you're sitting there.

Attributes:
🚌 P 🚐

1 **Getting started.** Like all caches we start with examining the basic things that the cache owner can change. The cacher's name hasn't been altered, the placement date seems good, there is no Related Web Page, the initial co-ords provide no hints... The word "TRY" in the title is in all caps, but seems like it is just a way of emphasizing the word. Difficulty and terrain are listed as a 3/3, and we have attributes that reference a parking area nearby and public transportation. Nothing stands out as being a huge hint.

2 **Let's read the description.** A fairly straightforward description... a couple of jokes about traffic, maybe that's why the CO chose the attributes of parking and public transportation, they're just a joke on the idea of traffic jams. Nothing really stands out as a hint yet, so we still don't have a direction.

3 **The image.** After the description, we have an image. This is most likely where the puzzle is going to be. It seems like a basic image, continuing the theme of traffic and cars. We have four rows of vehicles. 26 cars in total. Nothing there that sets off the "magic numbers" alarm bells.

4 **What else is there?** Besides the cars, there are buildings, road lines, stars, craters on the moon... I'm not seeing anything there that's helpful. All of the pieces we've examined so far have had something to do with cars or traffic, so it probably isn't something about the buildings or stars, unless the CO is just throwing us a huge red herring.

5 **Looking closer at the cars.** Okay... so, let's examine those cars. Looking closely we notice that there are really only three types, that just repeat. We have the convertible, the pick-up and the sedan, arranged in different groupings. Wait... three car types. Hmmm....

6 **Could that be it?** Noticing that there are three car types sets off a minor alarm bell. This cache is also rated a 3/3, and I seem to remember something else as well... looking back at the description, I see that the CO mentions being in traffic for "three weeks," leaving work at "3 o'clock," and working "third shift." That's a lot of threes. I bet three is going to be the key here! Then it hits me, the "TRY" in the name. Could that be a pun on "tri?" As in "trinary?"

7 **"Tri"-ing to solve it.** So we have two major themes: the cars, and the threes. They have to combine, and I think it might be trinary numbers. We have three car types... what if each type represents a number in a substitution code? If we're talking trinary that means only three possible values we'd have a 0, 1, and a 2 (The highest value used is always one less than the name of the base, for example base 10 uses the numbers 0 through 9). So which car represents which one?

8 **Making assignments.** Looking at the cars again we have three types, the convertible, the pick-up and the sedan... and... wait a minute! The windows! On the sedan we can see two windows; in the pick-up we see one; and the convertible has no visible windows... that's the 0, 1, 2 I've been looking for! Let's try that. Starting at the top left we have two pick-ups, a 1 and a 1, then a space before the next car. So... 11? Then a new number? Hey, if I do that, I have 14 groupings of cars! And 14 IS a magic geocaching number.

9 **Final steps.** In the end we have 11, 0, 11, 2, 12, 22, 11, 21, 11, 0, 100, 20, 2, & 12 according to the car groupings. Consulting a trinary chart, I see that 11 is converted to 4 in base 10. That's promising, since the dummy coords start with 4 as well. Going down the line and converting from trinary to base 10, we have 4, 0, 4, 2, 5, 8, 4, 7, 4, 0, 9, 6, 2, 5. If we break those numbers into standard coordinate notation, we end up with 40° 42.584, 74° 09.625! Those look like good coords! (Definitely not a spot you can actually visit, but that's okay since there is no actual cache anyway, but thematically appropriate!)

On the next page is another puzzle for you to solve on your own this time. Apply the lessons from this chapter, and you should make short work of it.

olve It Yourself!

Here are some puzzle caches for you to solve on your own. Using the skills we learned in this chapter you should be able to solve these puzzles. Take careful note of the final coordinates that you get as a solution to these puzzles, and write them at the bottom of the page. If you need a reminder of how to use the puzzle stats or hints provided, please check page 11. Good luck!

Puzzle 1 Solution:

N __ __ ° __ __ . __ __ __ , W __ __ __ ° __ __ . __ __ __

As a secondary check you should be able to answer this question: *What animal do you find at the final?*

Puzzle 2 Solution:

N __ __ ° __ __ . __ __ __ , W __ __ __ ° __ __ . __ __ __

As a secondary check you should be able to answer this question: *What character do you find at the final?*

FIND A CACHE

Egypticus Hieraticus

FCK4N3T

A cache by: Tommy Kane   Hidden: 05/06/2007

Difficulty: ★★⯪☆☆   Size: ▪▪▪◼◻

Terrain: ★☆☆☆☆

N 51° 27.644 W 112° 42.641

In Drumheller, Alberta, Canada

38 FAVORITES

LOG YOUR VISIT

- View Gallery
- Watch
- Bookmark
- Ignore

The cache is NOT at the listed coordinates.
You must determine the actual coordinates by solving the puzzle below.

Add your solution to the following:
N 51° 2_ . _ _ _ W 112° 4_ . _ _ _
to get coords.

Attributes:

PUZZLE STATS
42 CHECKSUM   BEST VIEW

 4    84   124

 144   54

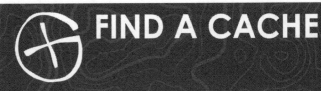 **FIND A CACHE**

 Character Study

A cache by: AaronDawg   Hidden: 02/14/2019

Difficulty: ★★★☆☆   Size: ▪▫■■□

Terrain: ★☆☆☆☆

FCFB1BY

N 43° 38.540 W 094° 05.890

In Blue Earth, Minnesota, USA

🏅 **16 FAVORITES**

The cache is NOT at the listed coordinates.
You must determine the actual coordinates by solving the puzzle below.

74	68	69	72	74
79	6E	69	6E	65
7A	65	72	6F	74
68	72	65	65	65
69	67	68	74	66
69	76	65	73	65
76	65	6E	66	6F
75	72	6F	6E	65

Attributes:

 **PUZZLE STATS**

60 CHECKSUM | 🧍 BEST VIEW

 👆 134   👟 21   🥊 110

💣 51   💥 101

Steganography

Steganography is the other side of the coin from cryptography. In cryptography the goal is security, sending a message in the most secure method possible. Steganography is not about security, but secrecy. With cryptography, if an unintended person finds the message, they may not be able to read it, but they know that they have *something*, a message or a secret of some sort, if they can just figure out how to read it. With steganography you achieve secrecy as well as security: no one will know that you sent a message at all.

Think of steganography as an "in plain sight" hide. Hundreds of people look at that type of cache every day without realizing there is anything special about that rock, brick, or reflector, but if you know what to look for, a whole new world can be revealed. You may have an image, a block of text, or a physical object of some type that is, in reality, your message. If you've ever spent a summer-camp night writing messages in lemon juice and then holding the page over a flame until the message appeared, you've practiced a form of steganography.

Steganography has a long history and comes in many forms. In the age of computers, steganography has grown more and more complex, while conversely becoming simpler to handle.

I'll show you some of the basic forms of steganography, and describe some of the more advanced versions. Hopefully you'll gain an understanding of what might be going on in these types of caches.

ld School

The history of steganography goes back to the ancient Greeks. The historian Herodotus tells the story of Histaeus, the ruler of Miletus, who wanted to send a message to another nearby king, in order to convince him that they should come together and attack the Persians. To keep his message secret, Histaeus shaved the head of his most trusted slave and tattooed a message on the slave's bare scalp. After the hair grew back, the slave was sent with the message safely hidden.

Later Herodotus tells the story of Demaratus, an exiled Greek sailor, who sent a message to the Spartans, warning them that the Persians were about to attack. In those days, there were reusable writing tablets made of thin sheets of wood with wax spread on them. Letters could be pressed into the wax. When it was time for a new message, they could strip the wax off the board and put on a fresh coat. To hide his message, Demeratus wrote directly on the wood backing of the tablet, and then hid the message underneath wax. He hid the tablet with the message in a shipment of wax tablets, and so it went through the Persians' naval blockades completely unsuspected.

Scytale

A scytale (pronounced like "sky-tally") is a Roman invention that combined the idea of steganography and a transposition cipher. To create a scytale, a length of some material,

like a ribbon or a leather strap, was wrapped around a rod. The message was then written on the ribbon, down the length of the rod, rotating and returning to the beginning when necessary. When the ribbon was unfurled, the text would be enciphered, just like a transposition cipher. In order to read the text, the person at the other end had to know what diameter of rod to wrap the ribbon around. Without that knowledge, the message was just a jumble of letters.

The steganography came in with the hiding of the messages. The strips of material were often used as horse reins or as closures on clothing.

we are spartans
The Spartans of ancient Greece used scytales as their primary form of coded communication.

In modern terms, a scytale can be created using ribbon or paper, and the puzzle is in knowing the size of the object to wrap it around. A ribbon with letters on it could be left in a container in the field and will reveal it's contents when wrapped around a soda can or an item found inside another stage of the cache. A block of text from a cache page may need to be printed, cut into strips and wrapped around a standard household pencil or other standardly sized object.

Grilles

In 1550, Girolamo Cardano described a method of passing a message in plain sight by using what he called a "grille," a piece of paper with holes cut in it. Using his technique, any piece of text, a letter, a book, anything, could be converted to hide a message. By placing the paper with the holes over the piece of text, all of the unimportant parts would be hidden and the true message contained within would be visible through the holes of the paper.

The text in our example would seem like a note between farmers. But after the grille is placed, a set of coordinates are revealed. Holes in the grille can be cut to reveal full words, parts of words, or even single letters, making the system very versatile.

As you can see, this type of message is very secure because you might look at the original text and suspect that there is a message, but there are several places where you could go wrong. For instance at the end of the first line you find "six types." You might assume that the 'ty' from types could combine with the 'six' to form "sixty," but when we look at the actual grille we see that 'sixty' isn't actually used. In line two the complete word "forty" appears, but it also isn't used in the actual message.

Another useful quirk of the Cardan Grille is that each grille can have multiple positions. A rectangular grille, such as the one used in the example, can have four positions: the position shown is the first, but it could also be rotated 180° and still fit the size and shape of the original page. The grille can also be flipped over to the back and placed in two positions.

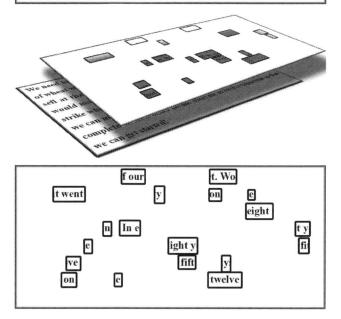

We need to take half of our corn to market. Word is that six types of wheat went higher than forty dollars a ton last week. If we could sell at that price, especially at the current low freight prices, we would make a killing! In extreme conditions like this is is best you strike while the iron is hot! We might yet be able to turn a profit if we can move very quickly. We have fifteen days until the harvest is complete on most other farms. Meet me at twelve tomorrow so that we can get started!

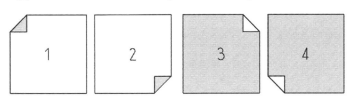

Cardan Grilles become even more flexible if the original text is evenly spaced in a grid rather than disguised as a letter or other regular text. With an evenly spaced text and a grille that focuses on single letters a new world of possibilities opens. At right is a sample text.

A grille like the one I described would show you that the word "GEOCACHE" was hidden inside the text. But if you rotate the same grille 180° you will also find the phrase "AMMO CANS" hidden within the same text.

This arrangement would allow for 8 different grille positions: the initial position, plus three 90° turns on each side of the card. (I marked on corner in the illustration to make it easier to see.)

B	A	H	M	G	K
D	P	E	Q	M	2
O	3	O	N	9	C
C	E	O	A	I	A
V	C	A	N	7	T
O	S	H	6	E	L

The trick with a Cardan Grille is transmitting to the puzzle solvers both the text and the grille. Be on the lookout for images with regular shapes that could be laid over a block of text to reveal its secrets: a crossword puzzle grid with the black squares cut out, or a photo with square objects that can be cut out are popular methods.

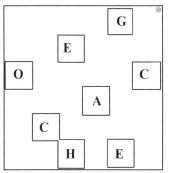

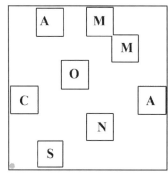

# ext Within Text

In Chapter 3, we discussed acrostics and text hidden within other text by italicizing letters or changing letters to fonts that were different than the rest of the text. Those are all methods that would fall under the umbrella of steganography. Let's look at a few other ways that text can be hidden within text.

The Baconian Cipher

In 1605, the English philosopher and scientist Sir Francis Bacon devised a method of hiding a message within regular text that involved both steganography and a code. First, let's look at the code. Each letter is replaced with a five bit code consisting of "As" and "Bs." The letters "I" and "J," and "U" and "V" are usually combined.

A	AAAAA	G	AABBA	N	ABBAA	T	BAABA
B	AAAAB	H	AABBB	O	ABBAB	U-V	BAABB
C	AAABA	I-J	ABAAA	P	ABBBA	W	BABAA
D	AAABB	K	ABAAB	Q	ABBBB	X	BABAB
E	AABAA	L	ABABA	R	BAAAA	Y	BABBA
F	AABAB	M	ABABB	S	BAAAB	Z	BABBB

For this example, let's encode the phrase "EARTH CACHE." Starting with E=AABAA, etc.

EARTH CACHE

E   A   R   T   H
AABAA AAAAA BAAAA BAABA AABBB

C   A   C   H   E
AAABA AAAAA AAABA AABBB AABAA

Note that a lot of puzzle COs stop here. Since the Baconian Cipher is a Binary Cipher (as we've discussed with Morse, Binary, and Baudot), you can create a puzzle using any two words, objects, or states (loud or soft, high or low, etc.) to encode the information.

BUT! At this point we've only covered the cryptography side of the Bacon. Now we have to look at the steganography side. The strength of Bacon's cipher is that he devised several ways to hide his messages inside text. The most popular is through the use of italic or bold letters.

Your first step is to choose the text that you'll be hiding your message inside. This is called the "cover text." I'll be encoding this message inside a typical log. The first step is to divide the log into five letter segments.

TOOK NOTHING LEFT NOTHING, SIGNED LOG, THANKS FOR A COOL CACHE.

TOOKN   OTHIN   GLEFT   NOTHI   NGSIG

NEDLO   GTHAN   KSFOR   ACOOL   CACHE

Those five letter segments are then laid over the five letter A/B codes.

TOOKN   OTHIN   GLEFT   NOTHI NGSIG
AABAA   AAAAA   BAAAA   BAABA AABBB

NEDLO   GTHAN   KSFOR   ACOOL   CACHE
AAABA   AAAAA   AAABA   AAAAA   AABAA

Each letter in your text now relates to a letter in the code, either an "A" or a "B." The letter "T" to "A," "O" to "A," the next "O" to "B," etc.

The final step is to rewrite the text with the proper word length and spaces. The wrinkle is that when you rewrite it, the letters that had been over "Bs" should be altered in some way, either italicized, bolded, or rendered in a different font.

TO*O*K NOTHIN*G* LEFT *N*OT*H*ING, *S*IG*N*ED *L*OG. THANKS
F*O*R A COOL CACHE.

This can be as obvious or as subtle as a CO chooses. It should be noted that if the CO uses this method in the description, it will be visible by looking at the source code. If a letter has been italicized, it will be surrounded by the tags **`<i>`** and **`</i>`**. If it has been bolded it will have **`<b>`** and **`</b>`** around it, or something similar there are a few ways to do that using HTML. Some COs will get around this by rendering the description as an image rather than through the standard method.

There are other methods that are completely invisible, however. One is to divide the alphabet into sections, all of the letters from "A" to "M" equal "As", and all of the letters from "N" to "Z" are "Bs." Rather than every letter in the cover text being used, as in the previous method, only the first letters of each word are used, creating an acrostic. I'll use a typical cache log to hide this one as well Here is the text:

A NICE LONG WALK TO FIND CACHE. TOOK THE TRAVEL BUG.
WILL DROP IT SOON.

The acrostic from this log is: **ANLWTFCTTTBWDIS**

We divide that into five letter segments: **ANLWT   FCTTT   BWDIS**

And replace each letter with "A" or "B" depending on which half of the alphabet it is in. "A" appears in the first half, so it is replaced by an "A," "N" appears in the second half so it is replaced by a "B," etc.:

ABABB   AABBB   ABAAB

Then it's just a matter of checking the code table, where see that ABABB=M, AABBB=H, and ABAAB=K, or MHK, which as most cachers know is geocaching shorthand for "Magnetic Hide-a-Key."

William Friedman, a US Army Cryptographer, wrote a treatise on Bacon's Cipher that he titled "How to Make Anything Signify Anything," trying to convince the Army that Bacon's cipher could be used during war time. He created examples of encoded messages in sheet music (the A's were standard notes, and the B's had tiny gaps printed in their stems) and in a drawing of a daisy (the A's were petals with pointed ends, and the B's had rounded ends). There's no evidence that the Army ever used any of his ideas, but he proved that anything with a binary state could be used to encode this cipher. He would have make a heck of a puzzle CO!

ew School

The introduction of computers to the world opened up a whole new wave of steganographic possibilities. Digital image files contain a lot of what is known as "white noise." White noise in a sound recording is the hiss of a record or tape playing. This noise is purely random and contains no information. In digital images, there is a certain amount of white noise created by the way in which the files are created or saved. This randomness means nothing to you as a viewer. Steganography can exploit this white noise by replacing it with information.

Text in an Image?

In previous chapters we've talked about hiding text inside the hidden language of a webpage. A similar method can be used to hide text in an image. When a computer opens an image file, there is a collection of characters and commands that explain to the computer what to display (more on that in the next section). I previously showed you HTML tags that tell a web browser, "Pay attention to what happens between these two tags." In the same way image files have indicators that tell the computer which parts of the file are actually meaningful. That allows a puzzle CO to add extra information to the file. If the computer reaches the point where the file says, "Stop paying attention now," there can still be information in the file, but the computer will simply ignore it. Try this yourself. Open TextEdit (on a Mac) or Notepad (on a PC) and use it to open any image file, like a JPEG or a GIF. Note that this will not work with Microsoft Word. Word is a smart program and will simply open the image. But if you use a text editor, rather than an image you will get a bunch of text that looks like this:

```
´¿yù´fä  1±r4q≤ë-í3s√ÑEUT"!QÇ2¡RÇC1që·a"#˜/
?˚‚øk˚.üé{ëúáÏˉÙGœ-◊ÌÅ"ÒœqÂ≥Á-?G_µˉ6O«=«îœüD|ˉ~◊.]?ˉP{>}ÛÙu'_ˉt.s<yAÏˉÙGœ-◊ÌÅ"ÒœqÂ≥Á-?
G_µˉ6O«=«îœüD|ˉ~◊.]?ˉP{>}ÛÙu'_ˉt.s<yAÏˉÙGœ-◊ÌÅ"ÒœqÂ≥Á-?G_µˉ6O«=«îœüD|ˉ~◊.]?ˉP{>}
ÛÙu'_ˉt.s<yAÏˉÙGœ-◊ÌÅ"ÒœqÂ≥Á-?G_µˉ6O«=«îœüD|ˉ~◊.]?ˉP{>}ÛÙu'_ˉt.s<yAÏˉÙGœ-◊ÌÅ"ÒœqÂ≥Á-?
G_µˉ6O«=«îœüD|ˉ~◊.]?ˉP{>}ÛÙu'_ˉt.s<yAÏˉÙGœ-◊ÌÅ"ÒœqÂ≥Á-?G_µˉ6O«=«îœüD|ˉ~◊.]?ˉP{>}
ÛÙu'_ˉt.s<yAÏˉÙGœ-◊ÌÅ"ÒœqÂ≥Á-?G_µˉ6O«=«îœüD|ˉ~◊.]?ˉP{>}ÛÙu'_ˉt.s<yAÏˉÙGœ-◊ÌÅ"ÒœqÂ≥Á-?
G_µˉ6O«=«îœüD|ˉ~◊.]?ˉP{>}ÛÙu'_ˉt.s<yAÏˉÙGœ-◊ÌÅ"ÒœqÂ≥Á-?G_µˉ6O«=«îœüD|ˉ~◊.]?ˉP{>}
ÛÙu'_ˉt.s<yAÏˉÙGœ-◊ÌÅ"ÒœqÂ≥Á-?G_µˉ6O«=«îœüD|ˉ~◊.]?ˉP{>}ÛÙu'_ˉt.s<yAÏˉÙGœ-◊ÌÅ"ÒœqÂ≥Á-?
G_µˉ6O«=«îœüD|ˉ~◊.]?ˉP{>}ÛÙu'_ˉt.s<yAÏˉÙGœ-◊ÌÅ"ÒœqÂ≥Á-?G_µˉ6O«=«îœüD|ˉ~◊.]?ˉP{>}
ÛÙÏÕ>ˉÔˉÄ¡‚±.˚◊=œ<†˚|ˉ|ˉ#ÁÈsP©ˉvÕ:úÁˉˉ<1ã„Ín√.ˉc˚ˉ=ëGWˉ∫XÒføÒÔâûfsœÚ?©eèÏˉ è˚f÷√è‚H¨¶f-
ˉÍ«+õˉ£ôüÂâ¢è‚8.TÁS'$v°ˉI"ˉ#£Q'ÍfL„ß<Nì#£Q'ÍfL„ß<Nì#£Q'ÍfL„ß<Nì#£Q'ÍfL„ß<Nì◉
```

It's meaningless text when you look at it that way, but if you scroll all the way to the end of the file (it will be pretty big if it's a JPEG), you might find text that is readable -- if a CO has placed it there, that is. Similar to the methods of hiding text inside the source code of websites, an image file has characters that tell the computer where to stop and start an image. Any text placed outside these characters is simply ignored by the computer, but is there for you to read!

An Image in an Image!

Let's look a little closer at how digital images are made. You may be aware that digital images are composed of pixels, tiny colored squares that our eyes blend into images. Each pixel is defined by three numbers, each of which is a value between 1 and 256, that sets a level of level of red, green or blue (this is where we get the term RGB display). This provides us with over 16 million color combinations at our disposal (256 * 256 * 256 combinations of R, G and B).

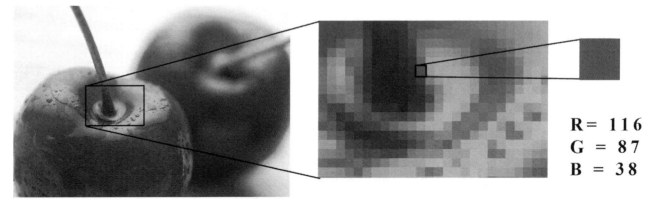

R = 116
G = 87
B = 38

However, much of this is completely lost on us. The color palette available on our computers is much richer than what we can detect at a glance with our eyes. You can usually shift any pixel in an image file several spots up or down the Red, Green or Blue scales without being able to tell anything has changed. That's the key to hiding information inside an image.

Computers read those RGB values as binary. Let's take the color yellow, which would be made up of the maximum amount of Red, the maximum amount of Green, and zero Blue, so Red 256, Green 256, Blue 0. In binary that would be: Red 11111111, Green 11111111, Blue 00000000. In the image above I have highlighted a single pixel, and given you the RGB breakdown for that pixel (if it were in color, of course).

Most of the information that tells the computer how much red to put into a red pixel (or green, or blue) is contained in the first few bits. Although the first four bits take up as much memory space as the last four bits, they actually tell almost 95% of the story. (Think of it this way, if you have $867,530.90 in your checking account, for all intents and purposes that's about the same as $867,500.00.) So what we can do is take a few of the relatively meaningless bits at the end, chop them off and use that space to hide totally unrelated information. The resulting very small differences in color caused by the alteration of the last couple of bits will be imperceptible to the naked eye.

For another analogy, imagine a book where you would read one story if read all the evenly numbered pages, and a completely different story if you read the odd numbered pages. This is what this form of steganography allows to happen.

The classic example of photographic steganography is the tree, which hides a cat. The two images below can actually be found in the same file, using the method I outlined above. By removing the "least significant bits" from the colors of the tree image, the cat is revealed.

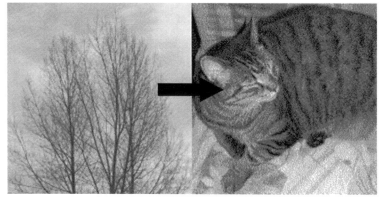

So, how do you see these extra images? The methods aren't overly simple, and they depend greatly on the method that was used to combine the images. There are several programs that have been created to combine images, and of course, separate them again. The bad news is that if those programs were used, pretty much the only way to untangle the two files is using the same (or a similar) program. This is especially unfortunate for Mac users as the great majority of these have been written for PCs only. (See Appendix 5 for a list of some of these programs.) Some of these programs also lock the steganographic images behind a password that will be needed to unlock the second image.

There are methods that use photo editing software like Photoshop, GIMP, or the website *pixlr.com* but, again, unless you know how the image was constructed, you won't be able to reverse the process. If you have reason to believe that image steganography is being used in a puzzle, don't hesitate to contact your CO and ask their suggestion as to which program to use.

An Image... in a Song?!

Finally, let's look at a relatively new and exciting way of hiding an image: Spectrograms. Spectrographs are scientific tools that have been created to visualize sounds. Spectrographs take a sound and build a sort of chart from them, mapping the sound over the axes of time and frequency, with an added representation of the amplitude of the sound, represented by the darkness of the color. The term spectrograph refers both to the machine that creates the image, and to the image that is created. The images are sometimes also called "spectral waterfalls" or "voiceprints." To the right is

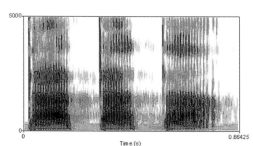

a typical spectrograph. It represents someone speaking the syllables "ta-ta-ta."

The amazing thing about spectrographs, however, is that they can also work backwards: taking an image and converting it to sound. These image-to-sound files are called "Spectrograms." A musician, or someone talented in sound mixing can take one of these audio files and place it seamlessly into a song or other audio file, essentially hiding an image within the song.

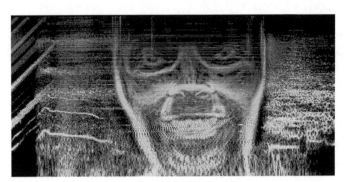

By using a spectrograph program to analyze the song or audio file, users can see the images that have been hidden inside the audio. These can be quite sophisticated images. Below is a photograph of the musician Richard D. James that was hidden in a song he released under his alias, "Aphex Twin."

As you can probably imagine, things hidden in this manner don't sound particularly... melodic. For the most part, they sound like static, or a series of overlaid tones, not exactly a "song" you'd want to listen to on a road-trip. The images they produce also aren't always crystal clear (though some are), so it is difficult to hide things like small text, but larger, blockier text can be easily hidden.

In order to see the spectrographic representation of an audio file you'll need sound editing software like *Audacity* (a free download).

Solving it

Bringing together what you've learned.

Use this checklist to help you apply what you've learned in this chapter, and determine which cipher you might be working with.

Checklist: STEGANOGRAPHY

- [ ] Carefully examine the text on the page for different fonts, italicized letters, or bolded letters

- [ ] Look for images or objects that can be cut to create a Cardan Grille.

- [ ] If you have an image, download it and try opening it in a text editor.

- [ ] Look for hints or instructions that might indicate that you are dealing with an image that is hidden steganographically.

# **alk-Through**

This is a difficult puzzle type for some people, so let's look at how you might approach one with this type of theme. At right is a walk-through of how I'd go about solving this puzzle, so that you can see the techniques at work.

FIND A CACHE

 ### Note The Score on a Pad

FC34GLE

A cache by: BirdTraxx   Hidden: 07/15/2011

Difficulty: ★★★½☆   Size: ▪■■□□
Terrain: ★☆☆☆☆

N 39° 02.486 W 094° 35.253
In Kansas City, Missouri, USA

16 FAVORITES

📋 **LOG YOUR VISIT**

- View Gallery
- Watch
- Bookmark
- Ignore

The cache is NOT at the listed coordinates.
You must determine the actual coordinates by solving the puzzle below.

Attributes:

1 **Had to happen sooner or later.** Well... sooner or later we had to run into a puzzle that wasn't entirely obvious from looking at the cache page. This is a common puzzle type, where there is nothing on the page but an image. They can be a challenge to tackle because there are dozens of possible approaches. But, as always, let's start at the beginning. Besides the standard checks of name, date, gallery, Related Web page, and inventory, which turn up nothing, let's check the dummy coords. They land on a tennis court, so thematically similar to the image. The name mentions "scoring" so another thematic link... but none of this gives me a lever to solve the puzzle.

2 **What to do without a description?** There's no description, so there's really nothing to go on. So, what do you do? My first step is to add a few steps to the initial check sequence: looking for white text and checking the source code, which turn up nothing. Finally, I'd also check to see if there is a "background image" on the page. Even though it looks just like a normal cache page, some COs can cleverly hide images in the background, "underneath" the regular page. Right clicking in the area of the background would give me a new menu with the choice to "View Background Image" if there was one. In this case it is grayed out, so it's just the standard page background. The name mentions scoring, so it could have to do with the score of a badminton game, but with nothing in the description that would help with that process... I'm not sure where to go.

3 **The image.** That just leaves the image. It is stored at *geocaching.com*, so the name has been stripped and replaced with a series of numbers, so there's nothing there. First step for me is always an EXIF viewer. (More on that in the next chapter.) I right click on the image and choose "View Image" from the menu that pops up. I copy the URL from the toolbar and go to my favorite online EXIF reader, where I paste in the URL. The EXIF data is mostly empty, just the standard info about Huffman encoding and file sizes. My second step is usually a reverse image search. On an image like this, it may not turn up much but it is worth trying. Google tells me that this image appears on the web seven times. Most of them are on pages about badminton. I go to one of the pages and have a look at the image in comparison to the one on the cache page, just to see if there are any obvious changes, but I don't see any.

4 **Now what?** Well, we've examined the image in as many ways as we can without any special software. I right click the image and save it to my desktop. There could be a steganographic message hidden in this image, but without knowing how it was placed there, it will be difficult to extract. Most steganographic images can only be extracted using the same method used to place it there... but there isn't much here that would tell us how that happened. The simplest stegs would be those visible just by opening it with NotePad or TextEdit... wait... "note pad..." I guess there was a hint here after all.

5 **Noting my score.** I open Notepad and use it to open the image file. As expected, the file looks like gibberish at first, but it has the proper jpeg markers at the beginning. I scroll all the way to the end of the file to see if there is anything there, and I'm rewarded by a small paragraph of text that says, "You'll find the cache at N 39° 02.730, W 094 34.880. Please use stealth when retrieving, cache can handle small trackables."

6 **We have coords.** Well, we have solid coords and some idea what to look for when we get there, so we're good to go!

I've tried, over the course of this book, to make sure that all the puzzles are solvable at home, but this one is a bit difficult to simulate on a page... however, I felt like it was an important one to walk you through.

On the next page is another puzzle for you to solve on your own this time. Apply the lessons from this chapter, and you should make short work of it.

olve It Yourself!

Here are some puzzle caches for you to solve on your own. Using the skills we learned in this chapter you should be able to solve these puzzles. Take careful note of the final coordinates that you get as a solution to these puzzles, and write them at the bottom of the page. If you need a reminder of how to use the puzzle stats or hints provided, please check page 11. Good luck!

Puzzle 1 Solution:

N __ __ ° __ __ . __ __ __ , W __ __ __ ° __ __ . __ __ __

As a secondary check you should be able to answer this question: *What animal do you find at the final?*

Puzzle 2 Solution:

N __ __ ° __ __ . __ __ __ , W __ __ __ ° __ __ . __ __ __

As a secondary check you should be able to answer this question: *What animal do you find at the final?*

FIND A CACHE

 Bacon & Eggs

A cache by: CastorOyl   Hidden: 09/19/2018

Difficulty: ★★⯪☆☆   Size:
Terrain: ★☆☆☆☆

FCP0P3Y

N 32° 39.811 W 107° 09.414
In Hatch, New Mexico, USA

22 FAVORITES

The cache is NOT at the listed coordinates.
You must determine the actual coordinates by solving the puzzle below.

LOG YOUR VISIT

- View Gallery
- Watch
- Bookmark
- Ignore

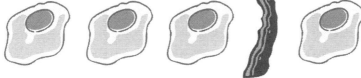

Attributes:

 **PUZZLE STATS** · **58** CHECKSUM · **BEST VIEW**

 43   143   10   131   61

FIND A CACHE

 Milk and Bread

A cache by: 49Tatankas   Hidden: 12/25/2009

Difficulty: ★★★☆☆   Size: ▪▪■■□
Terrain: ★☆☆☆☆

FCBST70

LOG YOUR VISIT

📷 View Gallery
👓 Watch
🔖 Bookmark
✖ Ignore

N 44° 25.161 W 071° 28.489

In Jefferson, New Hampshire, USA

30 FAVORITES

The cache is NOT at the listed coordinates.
You must determine the actual coordinates by solving the puzzle below.

Goodness know's I'd rather be standing at my grill making a steak, but this winter I more often fidn myself trudging to the store for milk and bread, the staples of winter living I guess. Maybe once the snow clears you can get out and find this cache.

ORANGE JUICE 4/$4.99 7oz.

DAIRY FRESH MILK $2.19 1/2 GAL.

OPEN M-F 8AM-9PM SAT 9AM-5PM SUN 2PM-9PM WE DELIVER!

UP TO 50% OFF ALL CHRISTMAS ITE

B.B.Q. SAUCE $2.94 18 OZ.

POPCORN 2/$4 6OZ. BAG

Attributes:

PUZZLE STATS

62 CHECKSUM | BEST VIEW

👆 **17**   👟 **137**   🧤 **33**

💣 **114**   ☁ **73**

Software and Hardware

Computers are an interesting thing. They've become so ubiquitous in our lives that we take all the ways that they are used and all the things that they do for us totally for granted. Even the most computer illiterate person, the 21st century equivalent of your grandmother whose VCR never stopped blinking 12:00, has several interactions a day with computers: ATMs, self check-outs, phones... even our cars, televisions, and refrigerators are computerized these days. While most of us can handle these interactions, there are more advanced users out there who know all the tricks and methods to make these computers do exactly what they want, even though they may not have been designed to do these things.

Some of that knowledge has made its way into puzzle writing as well. Some of it is as simple as looking at parts of the file that the standard user may not look at. Other parts are a bit trickier, and can be a LOT trickier if you have a sadistic CO that uses deeply obscure computer knowledge as the basis for a puzzle.

Computers are a wide and varied subject, but this chapter attempts to cover the more common ways that they can be used to create cache puzzles.

ile Types

Everyone who has used a computer for any length of time knows that files stored on a computer end in a dot followed by some letters. Those letters are the file type and let you know what program created and can open that file. A file that ends in *.doc*, for instance, is a Microsoft Word file. An image file will end in one of several types, like *.jpg*, or *.gif*. But did you know that you could easily change those file type suffixes? Changing a file type is as easy as changing the name of a file.

Think of computer files this way... Imagine a grocery store with food in tin cans. Every can has a serial number printed on the top but no other label. You have the power to label the cans any way you like, but you might be wrong. You can label a can "wax beans," but the contents would still be corn. But if you could read the serial numbers, you'd know what was in the cans, and even if it was labeled "wax beans" you'd know it really contains corn.

loss leaders

JPEGs are popular because they are small and versatile. JPEGs use a system called "compression" to lower file sizes by removing "excess" information from the file. This means that a file saved with high amounts of compression will change subtly from the original., but information is lost with each save. A file that has been saved over and over will eventually start to degrade. You can start to see a difference after as few as 10 saves.

Now, imagine deciphering a large block of text or downloading a text file on a cache page, something that looks like the gibberish I showed you inside an image file. It would be just like a can in our imaginary grocery store; without a label, you have no idea how to really use it. What is your next step? I taught you in the previous chapter about opening a file in *NotePad* or *TextEdit* in order to check for extra text at the end. This is sort of the opposite of that. Examining this "gibberish" text is just like looking at the serial numbers on the mysterious grocery store cans. Once you know what's inside, you can put a proper label on it, (a file extension) and then you'll know what to do with it.

Let's start with a JPEG, which is the probably the most common file type that will get treated this way. When you open a JPEG using a text editor, you'll see this:

```
ˇÿˇ†JFIFˇ€Cˇ€Cˇ¬Ôp"ˇƒ
ˇƒˇ)
¯ w∑„ aX∞≥s∞sÅsáÒ√úfiXqÁ¶9ÊÚÆXî
R'√`ƒä"áìéz3«cí6h≠Eh"3;¥|/K
@¶–TÔŒëvÕ°·≥î÷¨BŸùHèKt["
µûBÏbqŒF«0ı9ˆK!"XÔv9RAY"ÀNÌAZ£Íñq€™,©¥w4mXñp'3!?C"
```

Note that the circled area says **JFIF**. This is the file signature for a JPEG. This tells the computer to treat what follows as an image file. (Some rare JPEGs may use **ÿØÿà** instead.) You'll find this near the beginning of the file.

So... you have a block of text in your text editor, and you've identified it as a JPEG by reading the file signature... now what? Well, it's actually pretty simple: save the file as a text file, then change the file extension to .jpg instead of .txt. On a Mac, this is just like changing the name of a file. Click the file name, count to three then click it again. The file name will visibly change to an editable text box. Make the change, and then click 'Enter.' On a PC, it can be a bit trickier. First you have to make sure that you can actually see the file extensions. Go to 'Organize' in the desktop menu bar and choose 'Folder and Search Options,' then click the 'View' tab. Uncheck the box titled 'Hide extensions for known file types,' and click 'Okay.' Now you will be able to see the file extensions. Then you can simply click the file name and choose 'Rename.' Most computers will stop you and ask if you are sure you want to change the extension some may even warn you that the file may no longer work properly, but you just need to say yes. After you change the extension the icon will change, and you can now open the file as an image.

This method will work for GIFs, where you'll see **GIF87a** or **GIF89a**, PDFs where you'll see **%PDF,** or BMPs, where you will see **BM** near the beginning of the file.

The most common time that you will see this type of file renaming is when the CO hides a .zip or .rar file inside a jpeg. The file will look like a standard jpeg on the page, but if you change the file extension to .zip or .rar it will transform and you might find a new image, or a text document inside the .zip file.

Hidden Information

As you are learning, computer files contain far more information than they might appear to. Besides the secret information that files use to communicate with computers, most files contain something that is known as "metadata." Metadata is information about how the file was created, what program was used, the date, or even the location where the file was created.

Other information can be hidden in a file by applying user comments or tracked changes, which would be hidden to most users.

Exif Data

One of the most common forms of metadata is Exif, which stands for "Exchangeable image file format." Exif data is information that is attached to photos. This information contains the type of camera that was used to take the photo, the f-stop and shutter settings used to take the photo, the date, the pixel dimensions, and if the camera was GPS enabled, it will even contain the coordinates where the photo was taken. Photographers can also edit a "comment" section in the Exif data to add information. Exif data can be manipulated by COs to contain almost anything.

There are several methods to view Exif data. In Windows, a portion of the Exif data can be viewed by right clicking on an image file and clicking properties from the properties dialog click the Summary tab and then the Advanced button. On a Mac, basic Exif information may be viewed in the Finder by choosing "Get Info" for the file and expanding the "More Info" section.

There are also several websites and downloadable programs that will allow you to see the Exif data. These methods tend to show much more information than simply looking at the file information through your computer. (See Appendix 5 for some of these websites!)

Similar to information hidden in the source code of a page, Exif data may contain a straightforward answer, like the

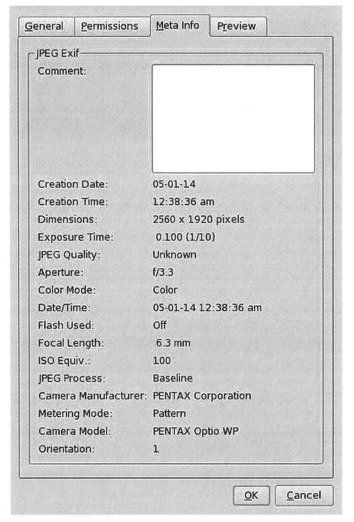

coordinates, a website, or coded information that the solver would then have to decode.

If you find an image on a cache page, right click it and choose "View Image." This will isolate the image away from the rest of the website, and give you the direct web address of the image. From there you can download the image or copy the web address to use in an online EXIF reader. Most images that I come across on puzzle pages get run through an Exif reader as a first step, just to be safe.

exif practice
Run a few photos through an EXIF reader, some that you own, and some from the web, so that you can start getting a feeling for what is standard in an EXIF return. That way, when you get an unusual return you'll know it for what it is.

One thing to be careful of is how you save the image. If you are saving the image to your computer to use an Exif reader, do it by using a right click, and "Save As" method, not by copying and pasting the image, or taking a screenshot. Copying the image rather than saving it removes the original Exif data, and begins a new chain of Exif data.

Finally, if you are convinced that there is Exif data involved in the puzzle, but you aren't seeing any, try a different method. Viewing through Photoshop may not reveal information that is available by viewing with an online reader, and vice versa.

GIFs

We've all seen animated images online, small loops of video, usually just a few seconds long. These are called "GIFs," which stands for Graphics Interchange Format. Not all GIFs move, but that is one of the advantages of the file format. That advantage can be used in another way: by creating a moving GIF that never moves. What do I mean? This is very similar to the steganography that I discussed previously. GIFs act in the same way a movie does, displaying slightly different images in rapid succession. The speed at which the frames display, and how many frames there are is at the discretion of the creator. It is possible to create a GIF that would blink to a different image for just a fraction of a second, or contain a second image... but never display it at all. There are websites and programs that will split the GIFs into individual frames so that you can examine each of them. In fact some of the Exif programs and websites will also do that.

color vision
Because GIFs use only 8 bits of storage per pixel they have a very limited color palette., only 256 colors. This means that the color might look a little grainy, but it also means that the colors are very stable. A JPEG changes color subtly every time you save it because of the compression it uses, but GIFs do not.

If you see an image on a cache page, follow the directions I've given you before to isolate the picture (right click, "View Image") to see what the file type is. If it is a GIF there might be an extra layer to the puzzle. There may be a second image embedded inside it, or the image may actually "move" in some way. One of the most clever uses of a GIF I've ever seen was an image of a water tower that had a subtly blinking light on the top. The light itself blinked out Morse code, but the rate was so slow that it took minutes, and the change was barely perceptible.

Thumbnails

Another thing that can be embedded in the metadata of a photo is a thumbnail image. For most photos, this is a scaled down version of the photo, but you might be surprised to know that the thumbnail does not necessarily have to match the actual photo. This is visible in most Exif data viewers. I have even seen a puzzle where you had to download the thumbnail image and run it separately through an Exif viewer in order to see the thumbnail of the thumbnail, which then contained coords!

PDFs

PDFs were created in the pioneering days of computers when it couldn't be certain that the operating systems between two computers would cooperate. The PDF, Portable Document Format, was created as a way to ensure that if I sent you a document, you could read it, even if we used different computers. PDFs have a couple of interesting functions that are useful for puzzle creators.

The first is that they are lockable with a password. This is an interesting twist for puzzle makers because it opens up the possibility of a puzzle solution that isn't coordinates.

The second important feature of PDFs is comments. Users can embed a comment in a PDF, and then hide the comments so that when it is initially opened, it will simply look like a photo. Viewing the comments in a PDF varies depending on the version of Adobe Reader you are using, but look under the View tab for the comments or in the Show/Hide menu. Be aware that viewing a PDF through a browser or using a program other than Reader, such as Preview on a Mac, may not be capable of showing you the comments at all!

Finally, PDFs have a feature that you would normally only find on websites: rollovers! A rollover is a caption that will only show up if you place your cursor in the right place on the image. If, for instance, the PDF contains an image of a person, there could be a rollover hidden in one of her eyes. Placing one of these rollovers can be quite precise, and can be as small as a few pixels wide! They are also completely invisible. They will be fairly difficult to discover by just moving your cursor around randomly.

If your puzzle CO has given you a PDF to download, be on the lookout for these tricks! There is a lot more to PDFs that the average image file.

# hoto Information

Photos in puzzles are FULL of way to embed puzzles. Some of them are straightforward, and others require a bit of manipulation and fidgeting with the file in order to solve.

There are two things you need to understand about image files in order to solve these puzzles, and they both pertain to construction of the files. First is the building blocks of an image file: pixels. Think of pixels as Legos, or colored blocks. They are small, square blocks of color that your computer puts into a grid to create pictures. If you zoom in very tightly on a photograph, you will start to see them, but from a distance, or when you view the full image your eye blends those tiny blocks together into smooth colors. A gradation in color is created by putting slightly differently colored blocks side by side. Imagine a block that is 100% red. Beside it is a block that is 90% red, then 80% red, then 70%, etc. This will give you gradation from red, to pink, and eventually, to white. (This isn't *quite* the true story of how color works, but it helps you get the idea for right now.)

The second thing you'll want to understand is how computer color works. Now, I'll admit that this is going to be counter intuitive. We spend a lot of our childhood learning that red, blue and yellow are the primary colors, and that yellow plus blue makes green, and red plus blue makes purple, etc. The problem is that when we talk about computer colors, that's all wrong.

The classic way that we understand color (what we learned by mixing tempera paint in kindergarten), is called "subtractive color mixing." White light contains all colors. The color we see from an object is the color of light that is reflected from it. All the other colors are absorbed by the object. Imagine being in a dark room with a flashlight that projects a rainbow. If you shine your rainbow-flashlight onto a blue ball,

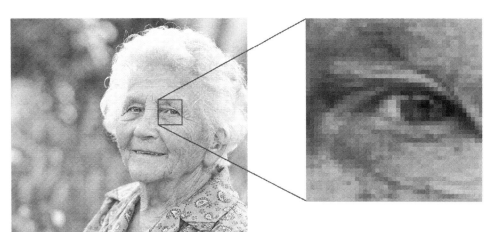

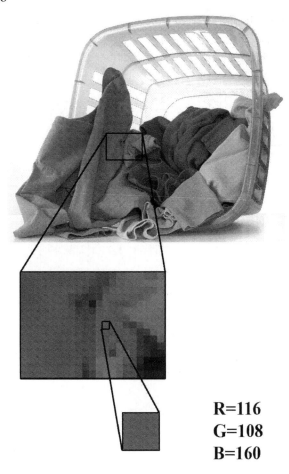

R=116
G=108
B=160

that ball will absorb the red, orange, yellow, green, and violet light from your rainbow, and the blue light gets reflected back to your eye. That's how you know that the ball is blue. The ball "subtracts" all the colors that it isn't and reflects the color that it is.

On a computer screen we have the opposite. A computer screen doesn't reflect light, it creates light, therefore, there is no "subtraction" happening. Color from a computer screen is created using what is known as "additive color mixing." Rather than removing colors to leave what your eye can see, it projects the correct color. The image of a blue ball simply uses blue light. Other colors aren't necessary.

In additive color mixing, the primary colors are red, and blue (as you are familiar with) but the third is green, instead of yellow. Red plus blue makes magenta. Red plus green makes yellow. And green plus blue makes cyan (a sort of sky blue color). All the colors together make white.

As we discussed back in Chapter 12, a computer assigns a pixel an amount of each of the three colors, which is a number from 1 to 256. When each amount of those colors comes together, they create the color you see. If all the colors are at 0 you get black. If all the colors are at 256, you get white.

Don't forget that you can use Google Image Search, or *tineye.com,* to reverse image search any photo that you might find on a cache page. You never know what sort of information this might reveal!

Photo Manipulation

Hopefully you are starting to see a few of the many ways to embed puzzles in photos. But now that you know the building blocks of digital imagery, we can start to look at how these puzzles can be solved.

What if I told you that the following image contained coordinates?

As I explained, computer color profiles rely on numbers, three values for red, green and blue. If you have the right tools you can discover those values. These type of puzzles require you to use a piece of photo editing software. The name that immediately comes to mind is Photoshop, but as anyone who works with Photoshop will tell you, it is an expensive program, and quite intimidating to learn. There are a couple alternatives out there. One is a free program named "GIMP," which is a Photoshop alternative. The other is a photo editing website, like *pixlr.com.* These will allow you to do what Photoshop does, without dropping a couple hundred dollars on the actual software.

What you will need is the Color Sample Tool, or the Color Picker, which is colloquially known as the "Eyedropper Tool," because of the icon. The process works the same in basically all of the programs we've mentioned. Choose the Eyedropper Tool, then move the cross hairs (or the cursor icon) onto the image and click in the area of one of the colors. At the bottom of the tool menu on the left, you'll see a square of color. Once you click on the image that square should change to the color of the pixel you clicked on. You've now selected that color. Now, move your cursor over to that little square and click again. You'll get a new window that pops up, There will be several things in that window, but what you want to look for is the area that tells you the RGB values. You'll get three values, just like I gave you in the image of the laundry on the preceding page.

If you are a PC user, you can also do this using MS Paint. Open your image file using Microsoft Paint (Programs -> Accessories -> Paint) and choose the "pick color" tool in the tool bar located on the left (the eye dropper). Click on the part of the image that you want to determine the RGB color value of. You should see the lower-left color indicator change to the color that you have pointed to or clicked. Now in the Menu Bar, go to "Colors - > Edit Colors…" and click "Define Custom Colors." A window will pop-up showing the Red, Green, and Blue values.

You'll recall from our discussion of coordinate formats (Chapter 2) that coordinates can also have three components: degrees, minutes, and seconds. A coordinate of 106° 35.255, could be assigned to the color values as Red=106, Green=35, Blue=255 which would give you a bright purple color in reality.

This type of puzzle tends to use GIFs rather than JPEGs because of the way that JPEGs change the colors in a file when they are saved. GIF colors are locked and won't change on a save.

A word of warning. I own a puzzle that uses this method, and many solvers have attempted use online color pickers only to discover that they are highly inaccurate.

limits of color

Because of the way RGB color works, no value in the coordinate can be higher than 256, which will limit the places that this type of cache can be hidden.

remember

When dealing with picture files on a cache page, always download them using the "Save As" option. Copying and pasting or screen-shotting the images might subtly change the content of the image file and render the puzzle unsolvable. Just a few percentage points difference in RGB values would radically alter any coords that were hidden in that manner.

Contrast

Here's another way that a block of color might work into a puzzle. I present to you another favorite of cache puzzlers everywhere. I like to call it "The Inscrutable Block of Color™!"

This puzzle takes advantage of the weaknesses in the human eyes. The color mix of the above block is Red=137, Green=137, Blue=137. Hidden inside are coordinates, but the color of the coordinates is Red=138, Green=138, Blue=138. A computer can very easily discern a difference of just one digit in each RGB setting, but the human eye would never be able to see it.

So, how do you extract the coords? The trick here is to alter the contrast between the two colors. Right now there is almost no contrast, but using one of our photo editing programs we can change that. Save the image by right clicking, and choosing "Save As." This ensures that the file won't change at all. Then open the image in the photo editor of your choice.

In Photoshop you'll find what you want under the Image menu at the top. Image → Adjustment → Brightness/Contrast. In GIMP it's in the Tools Menu: Tools, → Color Tools → Brightness/Contrast. That will get you a pop up that contains two sliders, one for Brightness, one for Contrast. Moving the slider left lessens the contrast, and moving it right increases the contrast. Go ahead and push that slider all the way to the right, and click "OK." You may need to do this a couple times to get a clear image, and it might take bumping the brightness up or down a bit as well, but eventually, you'll get something that looks like this:

The contrast between the two colors has been heightened quite a bit, and the coordinates have been revealed!

This type of puzzle can also work on photos if the photo is primarily one color, or has large areas of color. For instance a photo of a beach with a large area of blue sky may have the coords hidden in the sky, so even if it isn't just a block of a single color you may still want to try this method.

I have also seen the method called "watermarking" in some hints and puzzles, so if you see that you'll know what to do.

Indexed Color

Color Indexing is a method of saving a photo to reduce file sizes by limiting the palette of colors available. It is only available to these file types: GIF, PNG, TIFF, or BMP. GIFs will be the type that you will most commonly see.

Color Indexes can be used to create puzzles in very interesting ways. If you have a GIF, open it in the photo editor of your choice. In Photoshop go the Image menu and choose "Mode." Image → Mode. In the Mode menu you'll see an entry for "Color Table." If it is in black, your image has Indexed Color, and there is a Color Table available. If it's in gray, then there isn't.

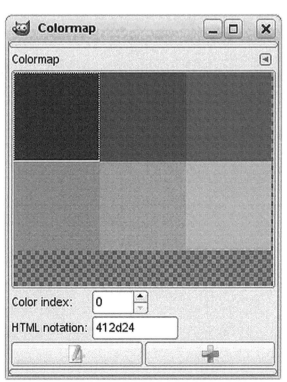

It's a bit harder in GIMP. From the image menu choose: Windows → Dockable Dialogs → Colormap, or from the Tab menu in any dockable dialog click on Add Tab → Colormap.

Once you have a Color Table or Color Map of the image you'll see a series of squares that represent every color used in the image. What you are looking for here is to see if the colors repeat. By clicking on any of those squares, you'll get the Color Picker dialogue box that will show you the RGB mix of that color. Take note of those values, and then close the box. Click on the color directly to the left or right of that. Are the RGB values identical? If so, you've got yourself a puzzle! (If not, close all these windows, and look elsewhere.)

Now... the next step will take some work. First close all the windows and pick a color from the color palette. It will appear in the square at the bottom of the tool menu on your left. Pick something bright like pink or red. Now, go back to your color table. The identical colors should be arranged in pairs throughout the table. Choose either the left one or the right one of the pairs. For my example, I'll choose right. In the first color pair click the right color. When you click it, you'll get the Color Picker dialogue box. Now move your cursor over to the color in your tool palette and click that. What you are doing is telling your computer, "I know this color is green. But I want it to be pink." Then click "Okay." All of the pixels in the image that were that color will now be pink, or whatever color you chose. Do that again for the next color... and the next... and the next. Eventually a second image should start to emerge from what you've got.

Color Notation Systems

In this chapter I introduced you to one method of writing down computer colors: RGB. In RGB notation you are given three numbers that represent the amount of red, green and blue in a color. In previous chapters I've discussed hexadecimal notation for colors, a different system. In hex, colors are presented as a 6 digit hexadecimal number. If you divide a hex number into smaller two digit pieces, each of the pieces represent the red, green and blue values.

CMYK is the system of color used by printers, standing for Cyan, Magenta, Yellow and Black.

CMY is sort of the inverse of RGB. In RGB, cyan, magenta and yellow are the secondary colors, made from mixing the primaries red, green and blue. CMY uses the colors cyan, magenta and yellow as the primaries.

HSL, HSI, and HSV are a slightly different system. Rather than noting the color based on the components that make it up, these three systems note color based on the hue (the "H" in the name), the saturation (the "S"), and either the lightness, intensity, or value. The "Hue" value is noted in degrees because it is noting the color's position around a color wheel. This system is supposed to be less arbitrary and more intuitive for the user.

YCbCr, YIQ, and YUV are color systems used by high definition color televisions. They measure things in terms of chroma, luminance and phase.

The chart at on the left shows the values for a color I am calling "Rosy Pink" in all of the different notation systems. Photoshop and GIMP can measure color in CMYK, but the other color systems would have to be found using a converter. Online converters can show you all the different notation systems of any given color, though not all converters handle all of the systems.

On a cache page, a puzzle could be as simple as converting one of the RGB color puzzles that we discussed earlier into one of these other color systems. If you see a word or sentence that is in a color other than black on a cache page, check the source code and see what the hexadecimal value for the color is. Remember it will look something like this: **<font color="#76923C">** (For more on checking source codes look back at Chapter 3!) By converting that number to RGB, or one of these other systems, values will be revealed that could be used to create coordinates.

There are also proprietary color systems like Pantone or the RAL, which have assigned numbers to colors, but they are

	Rosy Pink
CMYK	0% 45% 0% 7%
CMY	7% 49% 7%
Hex	#ee82ee
HSI	300° 36% 79%
HSL	300° 76% 72%
HSV	300° 45% 93%
RGB	238, 130, 238
YCbCr	68% 64% 68%
YIQ	68% 20% 42%
YUV	68% 28% 35%

only cataloging numbers, not references to how the colors are created.

Pixel Perfect

Pixels are the building blocks of computer imagery. Tiny squares of color that, when stacked together, turn into a whole world of pictures and images. You can imagine a very complex mosaic, thousands of differently colored tiles that are laid out in a pattern, and when you step back an image appears. Up close, pixels look like nothing but tiny squares, but from a distance, your eye blends them into a photo.

It should come as no surprise that puzzle makers can use pixels to create puzzles as well. After all, why would I bring them up otherwise? Have a look at this image.

As with the other images we've discussed in this chapter, there are coordinates hidden inside it. In fact, there are coords hidden twice! Can you spot them? Probably not. But if you take the photo into a photo editing program and use the 'zoom' tool, (which usually looks like a magnifying glass), and examine the image very carefully, you would eventually find the coords written on the bottom block, in letters just one pixel wide.

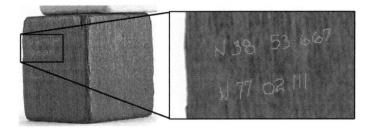

The second set of coords encoded here are probably much harder to spot. Here's a closer look:

You might start to be able to see something now, at the top of the image, close to the corner of the stack of blocks. Do you notice that the border on the image looks slightly different in that area? I'll blow it up a little more.

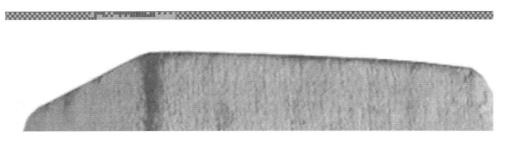

predicting the future

The word "pixel" was in use for nearly 80 years before it was used to describe an element in a digital image! Its first recorded use was in an 1888 German patent, short for "picture element." It began appearing in US patents in 1911, and came into popular use in 1965 when NASA began using it to explain to the media how images were being transmitted from the moon.

At this level, the fact that the border is broken up oddly on the left of the image is very clear. In an image editor, you'd be able to zoom in all the way to the pixel level, where you'd see this:

Tiny blocks of two different colors. We've spoken at several points in the book about codes that you could build using "binary" units, or two units that differed somehow. Looking at these squares of color, I'd go immediately there. Those binary codes could be Morse Code, Braille, Baudot, Binary... but in this case I hope you'd notice that they were arranged in grids that are two wide, and three tall, which most likely means Braille. Comparing this to a Braille chart will get you the coords of the cache!

Editing an image at the pixel level can hide all manner of clues. Even an innocent text document could have single pixel dots under certain letters, and when you read those letters in order, you'd get an answer. Learn to use that zoom tool!

About The Size Of It

The final thing I'd like to discuss about pixels is using them as a dimension. Pixels are like inches. You can say that a photograph is 8x10, meaning that it is 8 inches wide and 10 inches tall, or you can say that it is 2400x3000, meaning that it is 2,400 pixels wide and 3,000 pixels tall. Those two numbers could be used by a puzzle creator to denote the decimal minutes in a puzzle. If the photo was 455x693, and you had 38° 45.XXX, -092° 12.YYY, you could plug those dimensions into the missing spots there, and you'd have coords!

In Photoshop, you would determine that by going to the Image menu and choosing "Image Size." Image → Image Size. The top of that dialogue box will display the size of the image in pixels. In GIMP you'd go to the Image menu and then choose "Scale Image." Image → Scale Image. This is the method to change the size of an image, but when you first open it, it will tell you what the current size of the image is. (Make sure that the top is set to pixels.)

One thing to watch out for is the difference between the actual size and the display size. When an image is put into a website, you'll find something like this in the source code:

```
<img width="500" height="386" src="http://img.geocach-
ing.com/cache/f76b6cfe.jpg" />
```

This tag tells the browser two things: the web address of where the image is stored and what size to display the image. In reality the image may be bigger or smaller than this, but browser will stretch or shrink the image as needed to display it at the size indicated here.

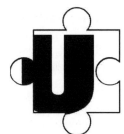PC and QR Codes

UPC codes, or Universal Product Codes, have become a ubiquitous part of life. They adorn every product, every piece of mail, even our driver's licenses in some states. What you may not realize is that there are dozens of variations of UPC code, depending on the use.

UPC codes are known as a "One Dimensional" information storage system. Most UPCs are about twice as wide as they are tall, but information is only stored in the horizontal dimension. The width of the lines is how the information is stored. The height of the lines doesn't matter to the information.

Different variations of bar code can encode different types of information. Some can only encode numbers, others can encode a limited set of characters, others can encode the full 128 character ASCII chart. Each of the codes at the right contains either the word "GEOCACHE," or the numbers "1234567890," depending on what was appropriate for the style of bar code.

It is possible to read a UPC code with the naked eye if you learn what the groupings of different line thicknesses mean, but the most efficient way to read them is, of course, mechanically. Any smartphone with a camera can download an app that uses the camera to read UPC codes. Alternatively, they can be uploaded to a website like *onlinebarcodereader.com* that will read the bar code.

QR codes, or Quick Response codes, are a new form of bar code, known as a "Two Dimensional" code. As you can probably guess, 2D codes use both dimensions to encode information. Most QR code types also use target shaped areas that help the scanner or code reader stabilize the code and place it properly in the camera.

QR codes are incredibly versatile because they contain a high amount of redundancy. 30% or more of a QR code can be missing or hidden and it will still be readable by a scanner. This means that they can wear away in the rain or be incorporated into a design and still function.

Both UPC codes and QR codes can be incorporated into geocaching puzzles. QR codes are especially useful because large amounts of information can be encoded in a very small area. Besides just traditional puzzles, QR codes could also be used in multicaches. If they are printed on business cards and left in stages, they can be read to get the coords to move on.

There are variations on QR codes. The Microsoft Code uses triangles of cyan, magenta, yellow and black to create the code. Jag Tags require the user to email or text an image of the code in order to decode it. Bee Tags use interlocked hexagons rather than squares. To make these types of tags specialized software is required, and usually a dedicated reader, so they are less frequently used.

TYPE	SAMPLE	CHARACTER SET
AZTEC CODE		All ASCII Characters
CODABAR		A-Z, 0-9, -,.*$/+%
CODE 16K		All ASCII Characters
CODE 128		All ASCII Characters
DATA MATRIX		All ASCII Characters
EAN		Numbers Only
MAXICODE		All ASCII Characters
PDF 417		All ASCII Characters
POSTNET		Numbers Only
QR CODE		All ASCII Characters
UPC A		A-Z, 0-9, -,.*$/+%

Notice that each type of code has standard characteristics, QRs have the boxes in the three corners, Aztec has a box in the center, Data Matrix has solid lines on the left and bottom, etc. If it doesn't have those characteristics, you are probably looking at something else, or will require another step to make it work.

If a block of black and white squares doesn't read with your QR reader, or doesn't have the characteristics of a QR, try treating it like a Morse code or binary code problem, white equaling on, black equaling off, or white equaling a dot and black equaling a dash. The reverse can also be true. There are puzzles out there that appear to be Morse but when they are plotted on a sheet of graph paper turn out to be a QR code.

Reading UPCs by Eye

Most of the time you'll be using either a smartphone or a website to read a UPC code, but it is possible to read a UPC by eye. Look at any standard bar code. You'll see that it is made up of black bars and white spaces between the bars. The thinnest bar or space that you see can be called "one unit wide." If you use that as your unit of measure, you'll be able to see that the bars and spaces have proportional widths of either one, two, three or four units wide. It might make you a little cross eyed, but with practice you can start to recognize the different widths.

The start of any standard product bar code will be "1-1-1." This will also appear at the end. Starting at the left, you will find a one-unit-wide black bar followed by a one-unit-wide white space followed by a one-unit-wide black bar (bar-space-bar). This is done to help scanner recognize where the code starts and stops. The numbers 0 to 9 each have a unique 4 digit code, created using an alternation of bar/space/bar/space at varying widths. The digits are encoded like this:

$$0 = 3\text{-}2\text{-}1\text{-}1$$
$$1 = 2\text{-}2\text{-}2\text{-}1$$
$$2 = 2\text{-}1\text{-}2\text{-}2$$
$$3 = 1\text{-}4\text{-}1\text{-}1$$
$$4 = 1\text{-}1\text{-}3\text{-}2$$
$$5 = 1\text{-}2\text{-}3\text{-}1$$
$$6 = 1\text{-}1\text{-}1\text{-}4$$
$$7 = 1\text{-}3\text{-}1\text{-}2$$
$$8 = 1\text{-}2\text{-}1\text{-}3$$
$$9 = 3\text{-}1\text{-}1\text{-}2$$

(Something to notice: All of these encodings add up to 7. For 1, 3+2+1+1=7, etc.)

 # Programming Languages

There are hundreds of different languages that are used to create the programs that we use on a day to day basis as well as the websites and other computer functions that we enjoy. Some of these languages are specific to certain types of application; others are broader and more general.

There are puzzles built around "debugging" certain programs written in computer languages such as Java or HTML. Programs written in these languages generally have line numbers at the left. "Debugging" is the process of finding errors in the program code and fixing them. You may also be required to interpret the results of a piece of code. Puzzles can be written in BASIC, turtle code, g code... any computer code really. Some of these, like BASIC you may be able to determine just by looking at it. Others would require you to find an emulator online and actually run the code. As you can imagine, these types of puzzles require you to know which language the program code for the puzzle is written in. Hopefully the CO has left you enough breadcrumbs to follow to the right code.

Brainf*ck and Ook!

Besides the real computer languages that are in use there is a subculture of programmers who create joke languages, or "esoteric programming languages." One of those languages is the unfortunately named "Brainf*ck." Brainf*ck was written to be a minimalist language and uses only 8 characters to create its codes: **< > . , + - [** and **]**. As the name might suggest, it is a difficult language to comprehend *because* it is so simple. Any even mildly complex task that is coded using the language results in a long series of characters to accomplish the task.

Any text can be converted to Brainf*ck, but expect a large result. Here is what just the simple word "GEOCACHE" would look like:

```
++++++++[>+>++>+++>++++>+++++>++++++>+++++++>++++++++>+++++++++>
++++++++++>+++++++++++>++++++++++++>+++++++++++++>++++++++++++++>++++
+++++++++++<<<<<<<<<<<<<<-]>>>>>>>>>>>>>-.+<<<<<<<<<<<<<>>>>>>>>>>>>>-.++
+<<<<<<<<<<<<<>>>>>>>>>>>>>-+<<<<<<<<<<<<<>>>>>>>>>>>>>+++.----<<<<<<<<<<<<<>
>>>>>>>>>>>+.-<<<<<<<<<<<<<>>>>>>>>>>>>>+++.----<<<<<<<<<<<<<>>>>>>>>>>>>>.<<<<<<
<<<<<<<>>>>>>>>>>>>>----.+++<<<<<<<<<<<<<.
```

As I said, quite complex.

A programmer by the name of David Morgan-Mar took the basic concept of Brainf*ck and translated it into what he calls "the language of orangutans." He calls it "Ook!" Rather than the eight characters that make up Brainf*ck, Ook! uses three variations of the word "ook:" One followed by a period, one followed by a question mark and one followed by an exclamation point. Two of these replaces a character in Brainf*ck. For instance **<** becomes **"Ook. Ook?"**

Standard text can be converted to Ook!, but because Ook! replaces a single Brainf*ck character with 8 characters, the resulting text is even longer than Brainf*ck.

 **ardware**

Another rich source of puzzle ideas can come from the actual hardware of computers and electronics. There are field puzzles that use arduinos, which are prototype circuit boards as well as short range radio transmitters, astronomical lasers, and all sorts of gadgets and goodies. Garmin even manufactures a short range transmitter that can be picked up by their higher end GPSrs that is known as a "Chirp."

There are also solve at home puzzles that use the wiring or components of electronics to build their mysteries. Some of these will fall into the "parts number" style of cache that we discussed a few chapters ago, but there are other variations on this style that use the wiring diagrams or knowledge of how electronics work.

LOLCode

Another esoteric programming language is "LOL Code" based on the broken English used in the popular internet meme known as "LOL Cats."

Resistors

Resistors are one of the most basic components of electronic circuits. They provide resistance to the flow of electricity and regulate the power entering a device. On the exterior, they just look like little blobs of tan or gray putty stuck on a wire, but different resistors provide different results, so you'd need a system to tell them apart. To do this, resistors are painted with stripes of color, either 4 or 5. The stripes form a code that can be read to determine the resistance of the piece.

The code is created from two pieces of information: the color of the stripe and the position of the stripe. The stripes are read from left to right, and to help you determine which end is which, there will be a gap between the group of stripes on the left and the final stripe on the right. There will be either three or four stripes on the left.

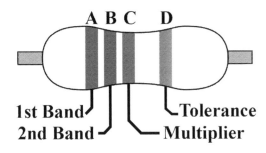

The first three stripes, or four if you have five total, refer to the ohms that can travel through the resistor. This is calculated by looking at the first two stripes, which provide a number, and then multiplying that number by the multiplier indicated on the next stripe. So, a resistor that had yellow, violet, and red stripe to the left would be read as 4700 ohms. Yellow = 4, violet =7, and red = 10^2 or 100, so 47x100. Remember that this might be three or 4 bands. The second band from the right, the first band before the gap, is always the multiplier, and the remaining stripes determine the number.

The final band at the right provides the tolerance of the resistor, which might be slightly more or less than what is advertised by the first grouping of stripes. For instance, a gold stripe signifies that the tolerance is ±5%, meaning that the actual resistance would be anywhere between 4,465 and 4,935 ohms.

A puzzle could be written that utilizes this information in a variety of ways. The most straightforward would be simply using the colors as a code (there's a chart on the next page). The other would be to determine the capacity of the resistor, either with or without the tolerance band. If the tolerance band is included then you end up with a high end and a low end number for the coords, and so you might need a bit of guess work to get to the actual final coords.

Color	Number	Multiplier	Tolerance
Black	0	$\times 10^0$	--
Brown	1	$\times 10^1$	±1%
Red	2	$\times 10^2$	±2%
Orange	3	$\times 10^3$	--
Yellow	4	$\times 10^4$	±5%
Green	5	$\times 10^5$	±0.5%
Blue	6	$\times 10^6$	±0.25%
Violet	7	$\times 10^7$	±0.1%
Gray	8	$\times 10^8$	±0.05% or ±10%
White	9	$\times 10^9$	--
Gold	--	$\times 10^{-1}$	±5%
Silver	--	$\times 10^{-2}$	±10%

You could also be asked to calculate the total resistance of several resistors on a circuit board. To do this, you would need to know if they are connected in series or parallel. The formula to find the voltage of a series circuit is simple: Just add the resistance of each piece to the next. Total Resistance = R1+R2+R3... Rn. For a parallel circuit the formula is a bit more complex 1/RT=1/R1+1/R2+1/R3... 1/Rn where RT=Total Resistance. Google "Calculate total resistance" for a more thorough explanation.

Segment Displays

Segment displays are LED number circuits, the kind that shows up on your alarm clock. The most common ones are

226

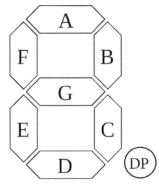

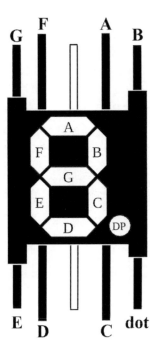

composed of seven straight line segments, sometimes with a decimal point. By lighting certain segments and leaving others dark any of the standard numbers and several letters can be created. All of the letters needed to display hexadecimal numbers can be displayed using seven segment displays.

Each of these segments has an assigned letter that is used in wiring charts. Lighting segments A, B, C, D, and G would display a 3. There is also an eighth "segment" that lights up a decimal point when this type of display is used in applications like a calculator or a gas pump.

There are 10 wiring leads that go into each number in a seven segment display. Seven of those wires provide electricity specifically to one of the segments, and the other two are used as an anode, or a cathode, the lead where electricity enters or leaves the unit. The eighth is responsible for providing electricity to the decimal point.

COs can build puzzles around 7 segment displays by indicating which segments are lit, usually by referring to the letter of the segment. For instance, saying "F, G, B, C," would indicate a 4. Another method would be to indicate which leads are receiving electricity. This could be accomplished by showing a display similar to the one at left and coloring the leads to indicate that they are either off or on, or it could be written in 8 digit binary. Arranged as ABCDEFGH, with H representing the decimal place, you would replace the leads that are off with zeros and the leads that are on with ones. So 01100110 would represent "4."

This could also be done by ignoring the decimal place and writing seven digit binary.

Seven segment displays can be arranged to display up to 128 different positions. The numbers 0 to 9 (naturally), and the letters A, B or b, C, d, E, F, G, H or h, I, J, L, n, O, P, q, S, t, U, Y and Z. The other 96 arrangements do not represent letters or numbers, per se, but could potentially be used by a puzzle creator.

Besides seven segment displays, there are also variations with nine, twelve, fourteen, or sixteen segment displays that further break up the segments and add others in order to make more characters possible in the display.

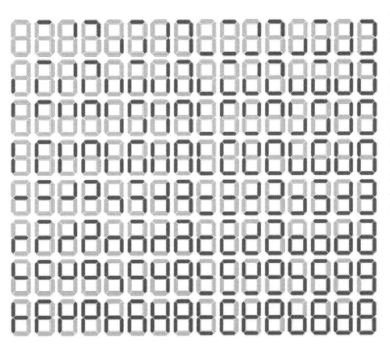

There is another way that segment displays get used in puzzles, though it has more to do with logic puzzles than the actual function of the displays. There are several variations on this puzzle, but the simplest goes like this: two digital numbers are laid on top of each other, and the segments of the display are colored one of four colors. In my example the segment is colored black if it would be lit in both numbers, dark gray if it would be used in only one number, light gray if it would be used only in the other, and white if it would be lit in neither number. Here are two examples:

Using that logic, can you determine the two three digit numbers hidden in the following image?

Calculator "Code"

Besides alarm clocks, the most common place that you would see seven segment displays is on a calculator. Because calculators have a limited number of characters available (0 to 9) kids everywhere have discovered that if you turn a calculator upside down, a certain number of letters become available. This has led to the nickname "beghilos," which is a nonsense word made up of all the available letters. The classic joke that every school boy learns is the word that 55378008 spells when you turn it upside down, but there is a limited range of other words available as well.

Three advanced calculator codes can be found by imagining the numbers being manipulated in a way other than flipping them upside down. By rotating the numbers 0 to 9 counterclockwise 90° you get O,--, N, M, J, u, b, C, ∞, and a. Rotating 90° clockwise gets you O,--, N, W, r, n, a, J, ∞, and b. Finally, mirroring the numbers gets you O, 1, S, E, y, Z, a, r, B, and e.

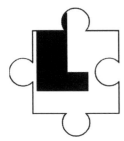

EET Speak

The final thing I'd like to discuss in this section is not any sort of official computer language or hardware, but a language of sorts that was created on the bulletin board systems, or BBSs, in the 80's and 90's. A BBS was a very early form of the internet and functioned like a very limited version of the forums that we know today. Being an "elite" user on a BBS meant that you had access to all the files and games, and could enter any of the chat rooms or areas of the Bulletin Board.

In an effort to prevent certain types of information from being passed through their bulletin boards, some owners installed text filters that would reject messages containing certain words. Users circumvented this by replacing some of the letters with numbers or symbols that simply looked like the letters. Using "$" instead of "S" for instance, or "3" instead of "E."

This became known as "LEET Speak," riffing on the term "elite." Most popularly, LEET is rendered using the numbers 1337 rather than letters. It is also referred to as eleet, leet, l33t, L337, l33t, 31337 or 3l33t.

There are dozens of ways to write each letter in 1337. For instance, here is a small sampling of the many ways that the word "Geocaching" might be represented:

930CacH1Ng   G30C4c#1N' Ge0<@(}{|n9
9e0<@<}{!|\|9   930<a<|-|1N'   9E0(A(#!|\|6

Translating information from 1337 to English is really just a matter of focusing your mind towards recognizing unfamiliar shapes and patterns that might be used to represent letters. Any alternate letter or symbol might be substituted, sometimes even changing within words if a letter is repeated, as long it remains readable. Cyrillic or Japanese characters are often used, like "д" or "ω" for "A" and "W."

Sometimes a single letter can replace an English syllable, like "&" standing in for the syllable "and" in the word st& (stand), or "8" standing in for the syllable "aight" in str8 (straight) or "ate" as in sk8 (skate).

Like most languages, 1337 progressed and certain grammar rules started to form. Some suffixes have risen, like -xor, which acts in the same way as -er, making a noun into someone who does that thing. Geocache, into geocacher in English, or Geocaxor in 1337. Words that end in S often have it replaced with a Z: geocaches becomes geocachez. Words that end in D or -ed are sometimes changed to T, so that cached becomes cach't.

Solving it

Bringing together what you've learned.

Use this checklist to help you apply what you've learned in this chapter and determine if you need an image editor or some other computer program to help solve the puzzle.

Checklist: FILES AND COMPUTERS

- [ ] If you have a text file, try opening the file in NotePad or TextEdit to examine the extensions to see if it is actually an image file in disguise.

- [ ] Open any image files in a EXIF viewer to examine any hidden information.

- [ ] Open image files in an image editing program and adjust the contrast to look for hidden information.

- [ ] Open image files in an image editing program to examine the make-up of the color pixels.

- [ ] Open image files in an image editing program to examine the image at the level of individual pixels.

- [ ] Look at how the image is attached in the source code.

- [ ] Look for UPC or QR codes.

- [ ] Look for words that may be spelled using calculator code, or LEET.

 alk-Through

So, what do you think? Can you solve a puzzle using these techniques? At right is a walk-through of how I'd go about solving this puzzle, so that you can see the techniques at work. Remember, there are no actual caches at these locations.

FIND A CACHE

 QaR Henge

A cache by: gleRrLr   Hidden: 02/26/2009

Difficulty: ★★★☆☆   Size: ▪▫▪█▪█
Terrain: ★☆☆☆☆

FCG0UL5

N 42° 08.281 W 102° 51.238
In Jefferson, New Hampshire, USA

🏅 **19** FAVORITES

The cache is NOT at the listed coordinates.
You must determine the actual coordinates by solving the puzzle below.

Out driving around today and I spotted this place and knew right away that there needed to be a cache here. Given the nature of the place I decided that it should probably be a mystery cache.

If you want to find the cache you may need to quietly read the code below. Quickly rearrange what you need and so you will be out scanning for a cache.

```
11111110101011101111111100000100011001000001
10111010110100101110110110101100101011101
10111010100100101110110000010011110100001
11111110101010101111111000000000001100000000
11110010111111001101000101001001111101000
00111111001000000110111000100110010110111
01110011100010010110100000000111100100011
11111110000110010100110000010011000000011
10111010010011111000110111010100100111010110
10111010111010101000010000010101001001001011
1111111101100010101110
```

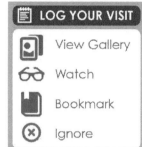

1 **Getting started.** Well, that looks like binary! I'm tempted to just jump straight to the binary, but this is a 4 star cache. I can't imagine that anyone thinks that simply decoding binary would be worthy of 4 stars. So, let's look for other clues before we dive in. The user name is standard, the date looks normal, the gallery is empty, there's no Related Web Page link, and there are no TBs that look suspicious. The title is a bit strange. I know that this area has a thing called "Carhenge" in it, a mock up of Stonehenge using junked cars, so this is probably a reference to that, but spelled very oddly with a Q and a capital R at the end. QR? It could be a QR code, but I don't see anything that looks like a QR code. Maybe that's a later step? I check for white text and look at the source code just to be sure that there isn't anything there, but find nothing.

2 **A quick read.** The description looks pretty basic. I notice that there are two Q words in the description, "quietly," and "quickly," and both of them are followed by R words, really pushing the QR hint, but I'm not seeing how it connects to the puzzle. Not yet, anyway.

3 **That binary.** That REALLY looks like binary to me, maybe it decodes a web address where I'll find a QR code. I copy it and drop it into my favorite binary decoder, that simultaneously shows me the translation in octal, decimal, Base 64, and plain text. It also automatically subdivides the binary into 8-bit sections, which saves me a few steps. The text result is unreadable, a bunch of random characters. It doesn't look like LEET or a web address. The decimal decoding at least gives me numbers: "254 187 252 17 144 110 180 187 117 149 219 169 46 193 61 7 250 175 224 3 0 242 252 232 164 250 15 228 6 226 101 183 56 150 128 121 15 248 101 48 76 3 186 79 141 212 157 174 186 161 5 73 191 236 87 0." They are definitely not coords, though. I try to compare them to an ASCII chart but I get gibberish there too: "rk&(?OD_G;Fd:^\0#9[UqQJfZ!:p'OV"tV_#3'4'30o)?&,9]i9EVk%NRXN%\ tK:!^[,#%." It could be double encoded, I try Rot47 on the ASCII but get nothing. Maybe it isn't binary after all.

4 **If it isn't binary...** What else could it be? We definitely have a "binary" set up here, so it could be Morse, 1 for dots, 0 for dashes. The problem is that Morse letters don't have a set length, so I don't know where to break these up. Morse numbers are all five characters long, so I could try that. The code stars with five 1s, that could be a 0 or a 5 depending on whether 1s represent dots or dashes. After that is 11010. So, either --•-• or ••-•-, but neither of those works in Morse. I try a Bacon Cipher and get the same results, eventually I end up with an untranslatable string. I try Tap Code, no. Baudot Code, no. Lots of dead ends here... I'm back to QR codes.

5 **That pesky QR...** QR is mentioned three times, so I expect to have some sort of QR application eventually. Maybe there's something else in the description, let's read closer. The two QR phrases stand out to me. One phrase is "quietly read." You "read" a QR code, so, possibly another QR hint. The next QR phrase is "quickly rearrange." You don't typically need to rearrange QR codes, so what could this mean? Do I need to rearrange the code somehow? Is it a transposition cipher? Or a route cipher? I quickly count the digits in the "binary," and get 441. If I'm going to rearrange something my first impulse is to rearrange it into a square. The square root of 441 is 21, so it is possible to arrange this into a square, that's good. Hmm... QR codes are typically square.

6 **Is it a QR?** QR codes typically have a square box in the two top, and bottom left corners. In the rearranged text I can see that "binary" starts with a long string of 1s, a QR could have a long string of black squares in that position. Wait... is that it?

7 **Graph it and scan it.** I break out some graph paper and mark off a 21x21 square, (you could also use Excel here if you know that program well enough) and carefully begin transposing the 1s and 0s to the graph paper. If I have a 1 I color the square in, if I have a 0 I leave it blank. It's a little bit tedious but I'm rewarded by squares in the two upper corners, just as I'd expect. After I complete the graph there's nothing left to do but whip out my smartphone and open my QR app... a "quick read" later and I have a string of numbers! 4, 2, 0, 8, 5, 3, 4, 1, 0, 2, 5, 1, 4, 7, & 6, or 42° 08.534, -102° 51.476.

(For the first time in this book there actually IS a cache fairly close to this final, but it is unrelated, I just thought the area was thematically cool.)

On the next page is another puzzle, for you to solve on your own this time. Apply the lessons from this chapter, and you should make short work of it.

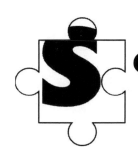olve It Yourself!

Here are some puzzle caches for you to solve on your own. Using the skills we learned in this chapter you should be able to solve these puzzles. Take careful note of the final coordinates that you get as a solution to these puzzles, and write them at the bottom of the page. If you need a reminder of how to use the puzzle stats or hints provided, please check page 11. Good luck!

Puzzle 1 Solution:

N __ __ ° __ __ . __ __ __ , W __ __ __ ° __ __ . __ __ __

As a secondary check you should be able to answer this question: *What childhood item do you find at the final?*

Puzzle 2 Solution:

N __ __ ° __ __ . __ __ __ , W __ __ __ ° __ __ . __ __ __

As a secondary check you should be able to answer this question: *What toy or game do you find at the final?*

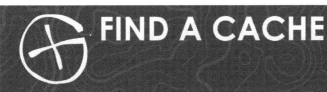

FIND A CACHE

Ripples, Guppies, Boats

A cache by: RaggedyAnimal   **Hidden:** 07/27/2005

Difficulty: ★★★☆☆   Size:
Terrain: ★☆☆☆☆

N 29° 48.360 W 094° 22.515
In Winnie, Texas, USA

15 FAVORITES

FC67WJM

LOG YOUR VISIT

- View Gallery
- Watch
- Bookmark
- Ignore

The cache is NOT at the listed coordinates.
You must determine the actual coordinates by solving the puzzle below.

I could give you 16 reasons why it might be a good idea to come out here looking for a cache. They might include the color of the sunset, the cool breezes, the color of the grass, the wildlife, or the color of the sky... but who needs sixteen reasons why you have this one reason: it's where the cache is!

Pack some art supplies to help you capture the beauty of the area and head on out!

1D3004

5E163B

Your solution will be in M D S format.

Attributes:

FIND A CACHE

 ## Wait a Minute Mr. P

FCH4B1T

A cache by: Rabbit46   Hidden: 01/27/2015

Difficulty: ★★★☆☆   Size: ▪▪■■□

Terrain: ★☆☆☆☆

N 38° 42.261 W 078° 39.839

In Quicksburg, Virginia, USA

35 FAVORITES

 LOG YOUR VISIT

 View Gallery

 Watch

 Bookmark

Ignore

The cache is NOT at the listed coordinates.
You must determine the actual coordinates by solving the puzzle below.

 Attributes:

PUZZLE STATS
63 CHECKSUM   BEST VIEW

 80   **135**   **7**

 65   **121**

Math

If you are anything like me, you probably look at this chapter and think, "UGH! Math!"

In reality, geocachers use an enormous amount of math in our pursuits, from the simple math that we all to determine how many caches we can accomplish in a day and how much gas it will take, to the highly complex geometry of the signals that travel between the satellites and our GPSr units.

Simple equations have also been a part of puzzle caches from the start, used in thousands of "Research Puzzles" around the world. These simple equations usually just have a few numbers missing that can be replaced by reading plaques or counting items found near the cache, but much more advanced math concepts are also used in caches all the time. Simply dropping some pre-Calc on a cache page would be enough to halt most cachers in their tracks and leave us scratching our heads.

While I can't teach you calculus, (or even algebra!) I hope I can show you some simple math concepts that often get incorporated into puzzle caches and how to approach them. We've already covered some basic math: units of measurement back in Chapter 5, and alternate numerical systems in Chapter 11. In this chapter, I'll expand on that knowledge base.

 # umbers

All math, of course, comes down to numbers, so let's start with that. Numbers can be broken into several categories. Some fall into more than one of those categories; others stand alone.

We start with "Natural Numbers," otherwise known as "Counting Numbers." This is 1, 2, 3, 4, 5, 6, 7, 8, 9, 10, 11, 12, etc. The first numbers that we learn as small children. You'll notice that I left zero off that list. Zero is not considered a Natural Number, but zero and Natural Numbers are all considered "Whole Numbers."

Next are "Integers." Integers are all of the Natural and Whole numbers, plus their negatives: –6, –5, –4, –3, –2, –1, 0, 1, 2, 3, 4, 5, 6, etc.

The next step up the ladder are "Rational Numbers," which includes fractions and decimals. These are not whole numbers but ratios, or parts of numbers. Rational numbers, however, only include decimal numbers or ratios. The fraction 1/2 is a rational number because it can be expressed as the decimal 0.5, and 2/3 is because while its decimal representation is an infinitely repeating series of 6's, 0.6666666666, it can be expressed as a ratio. I'll get to their opposite, "Irrational Numbers," in a bit.

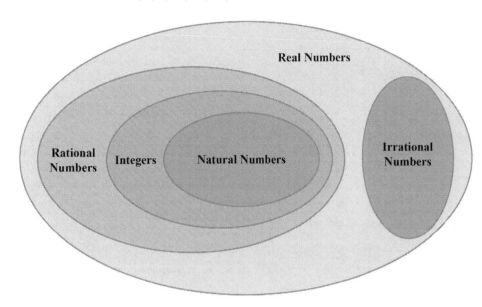

All of these fall into the subcategory of "Real Numbers," which are, for the most part, the numbers that we use in our everyday lives.

Of course, the opposite of Real Numbers also exists: "Imaginary Numbers." Imaginary Numbers are those where a negative result occurs when the number is multiplied by itself: i x i= -1. Imaginary Numbers mostly fall into the purview of mathematicians, but it's good to know they exist.

 # ther Number Types

Beyond basic numerical types, we start getting into numbers that are defined by their relationships to each other, whether or not they fit a mathematic formula based on their make-up, or how they interact with each other. Some of these types of numbers are well known, and others are more esoteric, usually only known to math geeks who like to play with the odd properties that some numbers possess. This, however, is usually where the puzzle makers start stepping in.

Primes

Prime numbers are defined as "Natural Numbers that can be evenly divided only by themselves or 1." 1 itself is not considered to be a prime number (though if you want a good bar argument, get a couple mathematicians drunk and ask them their opinions on that!) 3 is a prime number because it can only be divided evenly (meaning with no decimal remainder) by 1 and 3. On the other hand, 4 is *not* a prime because it can be divided by 1, 2 or 4. Numbers which aren't prime are referred to as "compound" or "composite" numbers.

So, where does the puzzle come in? A simple puzzle would be to give you a choice of several numbers and to tell you that the numbers that make up the coordinates will be the prime numbers. There are plenty of charts online that will show you which numbers are prime and which are not, but one easy way of eliminating a few would be to check if they are even or odd. The number 2 is the only even prime.

A more advanced version of that would be to make the coordinates a certain prime according to the order that the primes appear in. The first prime is 2, the second prime is 3, etc. For a puzzle like this, the CO may tell you that the west coords end in the 167th prime, which is 991.

Another aspect of primes to consider are "prime factors." Factors are the numbers that you multiply together to produce another number. So, in the case of 2 x 3=6, 2 and 3 are the factors of 6. A factor of a number that is itself a prime number, is called a "prime factor." In our example of 2 x 3=6, both 2 and 3 are prime, so they are the prime factors of 6. Any number can be broken down as the product of prime numbers. For a number like 147, the prime factors would be 3 x 7 x 7, or 3 x 7^2=147. If a number is itself prime, like 17, its only prime factor is itself.

There are online calculators that will give you the prime factorization of even very large numbers. If a large number, say 100,091, appears on a cache page you may want to check the prime factorization of the number. If it has only two prime factors, those two numbers could well be related to the cache coordinates. In this case the prime factors of 100,091 are 101 and 991, which could serve as the decimal minutes of a set of coords.

Squares and Square Roots

Square numbers are defined as numbers that are formed by multiplying a number by itself. For instance, 4 is a square number. It is created by multiplying 2 by 2. Because the two numbers multiplied together are whole numbers, squares are also sometimes called "Perfect Squares." A square number can end only with digits 0, 1, 4, 6, 9, or 25.

Square Roots take this idea and reverse it. You find the square root of a number by finding another number that can be multiplied by itself to get equal the original number. Take the number 25. Most of us know that 5 x 5 = 25, making 5 the square root of 25. Square roots do not have to be whole numbers, but those that *are* also whole numbers are known as "perfect roots." Fractional numbers are not "perfect" because they often only get close to the original number, not exactly arriving at it. For instance, the square root of 991 (a prime number) is 31.4801525. Multiplying 31.4801525 by itself actually results in 991.0000014, but for most purposes, it is close enough, just not "perfect."

You can also take the square root of a decimal number. For example, the square root of 1.44 is 1.2.

A puzzle could be as simple as finding the square root of a number or squaring a number to get digits for the coords.

Cubes and Cube Roots

An expanded version of this idea is the cube and the cube root. Cubes are numbers formed by multiplying a number by itself twice: 3 x 3 x 3 = 27. The cube root of a number is the number that can be multiplied by itself to equal that original number. For instance the cube root of 125 is 5. (5x5=25, 25x5=125) The first few perfect cubes are 1, 8, 27, 64 and 125.

Esoteric Number Types

The number types I've covered so far have one thing in common... their properties are actually useful, but that doesn't stop mathematicians from looking for crazier methods for linking numbers together. Math types can be truly eccentric and obsessive, and that leads to finding (and naming!) all sorts of crazy connections between numbers.

For instance there are "Happy" and "Sad" numbers. Happy numbers work like this: take any positive whole number and break it into its individual digits, square them, and add the results together. Repeat the process with the resulting number. Let's start with the number 19.

$$1^2 + 9^2 = 82$$
$$8^2 + 2^2 = 68$$
$$6^2 + 8^2 = 100$$
$$1^2 + 0^2 + 0^2 = 1$$

At the end of all that, if you end up with a 1, then that number is deemed "happy." Here are the Happy numbers that occur between 1 and 100: 1, 7, 10, 13, 19, 23, 28, 31, 32, 44, 49, 68, 70, 79, 82, 86, 91, 94, 97, 100.

When subjected to this process other numbers, like the number 4, end up going in a loop: 4, 16, 37, 58, 89, 145, 42, 20, 4, and so, these are "Sad" or "Unhappy" numbers.

Numbers can be said to be "Amenable," which means that it is possible to find a sequence of numbers that, whether you multiply or add them, will still equal the original target number. Like 6: both 1+2+3 and 1x2x3 equal 6, making 6 an amenable number.

Numbers can be "Perfect," meaning that their factors when added together, equal the original number. (In this case we mean ALL of their factors, not just the prime ones, for instance the factors of 12 are 1, 2, 3, 4, 6, and 12.) 6 is the lowest perfect number, since 1x2x3=6. (the number itself is not considered one of its own factors for this exercise.)

Numbers can be either "Abundant" or "Deficient." An abundant number is a composite number whose factors (again, ignoring the number itself) have a sum greater than the original number. For example, 12 has factors of 1, 2, 3, 4, 6, and 12. The sum of these, 1+2+3+4+6 equals 16, and 16 is greater than 12, making 12 "abundant." If the sum of a number's factors are less than the original number, then that number is "Deficient."

Numbers can be "Narcissistic." A Narcissistic number is a number than can be created using any math problem that only includes its own digits. Like so: 153=1^3+5^3+3^3.

Numbers can even be "Vampires." A Vampire number can be created by rearranging its own digits into two "fangs" that when multiplied together, equal the original number, like 1260=21x60 or 1435=35x41.

There are many of these esoteric number types. If you come to a cache puzzle that is referencing numbers with an odd name or applying an odd adjective to them, look them up on Wikipedia or at Wolfram-Alpha (a website specializing in math and numbers) to see if perhaps they are describing a particular "type" of number. COs can use these number types to help eliminate numbers from the running towards being used in the coords, or it can be used as a confirmation of a correct answer.

umber Sequences

Besides the specific types of numbers, mathematicians (and puzzle creators!) often delight in how numbers relate to each other in a sequence. One of the most popular logic puzzles, often appearing on IQ Tests, is to present the solver with a sequence of numbers and ask them to predict what the next number in the sequence is. There are several famous numerical sequences, which pop up repeatedly.

wolfram-alpha

If a puzzle cache description contains a number, or a series of numbers, try copying it and searching at Wolfram-Alpha. (*wolframalpha. com*) It will give all sorts of information about the number, including how it looks in several other bases, what it looks like in Roman Numerals, its prime factorization, whether or not it is prime... etc. etc. Wolfram Alpha can also solve equations, and give you information on number sequences.

The Fibonacci Sequence

It sounds like something from a science fiction movie, or a spy thriller, but the Fibonacci sequence is one of the most famous number sequences in math. In 1202 Leonardo Fibonacci introduced the idea of this sequence to Western math (it had been used in the East long before that.) Fibonacci's sequence is a series of numbers that are created by adding together the two previous numbers in the sequence.

The sequence starts with 0 and continues: 0, 1, 1, 2, 3, 5, 8, 13, 21, 34, 55, 89, 144, etc. The Fibonacci sequence can potentially be infinite. Numbers that appear in a Fibonacci sequence are known as Fibonacci numbers.

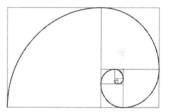

These numbers are the integral component of what is called the "Golden Ratio" or the "Golden Spiral." A golden spiral is created by using the Fibonacci sequence to define area. A square that has an area of one unit (inches, centimeters, or miles, it doesn't matter), is placed beside another. These two are then placed beside a square that has an area of two units, then four units, etc. Each square is then used to create a segment of a circle. One corner is the center of the circle, and the radius of the circle is the length of one side of the square. Together these circle segments create a spiral.

The Golden Spiral occurs quite frequently in nature. The classic example is the conch shell, which forms a perfect golden spiral, but it can be observed in artichokes, pine cones, fern leaves, how branches split off from stems, the placement of leaves on a branch, and more.

Numerically the Golden ratio is expressed as the lowercase Greek letter phi: φ. Phi is equal to 1.61803398874989484820458683... to infinity, making it irrational. (More on that shortly.)

Lucas Numbers

In the late 1800's François Édouard Anatole Lucas took the concept of the Fibonacci Sequence and expanded it to a concept that came to be known as "Lucas Sequences." Lucas' basic question was what happens if you begin a Fibonacci sequence with numbers other than 0 and 1?

The most famous example came to be known as the "Lucas Numbers." Starting with 2 and 1, the sequence is as follows: 2, 1, 3, 4, 7, 11, 18, 29, 47, 76, 123, 199, 322, 521, 843 ... etc.

Figurate Numbers

Figurate numbers are numerical sequences related to the creation of shapes or figures. The best known example of these are "Triangular Numbers." Triangular numbers are numbers that count the objects necessary to create an equilateral triangle: a triangle whose sides are all the same length. Take a handful of pennies and arrange them into triangles. The smallest you can create is a triangle with 2 pennies on a side, for a total of 3 pennies, making 3 a triangular number. If you extend two sides of the triangle and then fill in the empty spaces on the third side, you end up with a triangle that has 3 pennies on each side, for a total of 6. Then 10 pennies, then 15, etc.

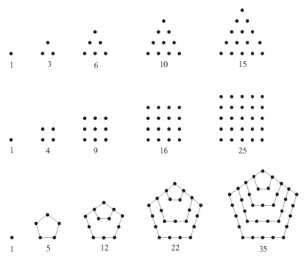

The same sequence can be created using a square, for a sequence of 1, 4, 9, 16, 25, ...

Pentagonal numbers create a sequence of 1, 3, 12, 22, 35... Hexagonal numbers (not pictured) create a sequence of 1, 6, 15, 28, 45, etc.

These numbers are known as "polygonal numbers" because they create regular polygons, but it is also possible to create non-regular shapes or even three dimensional shapes using figurate numbers.

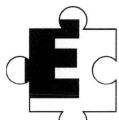ven MORE Esoteric Numbers

Believe it or not, there are some even LESS useful ways of classifying numbers, mathematically speaking anyway. They'd still make for some pretty interesting puzzles though.

Ban Numbers

Remember way back in the chapter about cryptograms I told you that you can write all of the words from 1 to 9 with just a few letters? Ban numbers divide integers by what vowels are used in writing them. Eban numbers do not use the letter "E," which leaves us with 2, 4, and 6 from the first ten digits. Coincidentally, all Eban numbers are even.

Iban numbers do not use the letter "I," leaving us with 0, 1, 2, 3, 4, and 7 from the first ten digits .

Uban numbers skip the letter "U," which just removes the number 4 from the first ten digits.

Oban numbers leave us with 3, 5, 6, 7, 8, and 9 from the first ten digits.

And finally, Aban. I'm sure you have guessed what Aban are at this point. Aban numbers keep everything up to 999, since 'thousand' is the first time an "A" appears.

The Shape of Numbers

This one started, not in the mind of a mathematician, but as a riddle that, "Even a kindergärtner could get," or so it says on lots of cache pages.

Here we focus on the shapes created when writing numbers, and the riddle is usually presented something like this: "0=1, 888=6, 531=0 How is that possible?"

The idea here is to count either the shapes or whether or not there are enclosed spaces. So 0 has a single "circle," making it equal 1, and an 8 has two circles, making it equal 2. By this logic 888 equals 6 because there are six circles, two in each digit.

There is a variation on this puzzle that references "enclosed spaces" rather than circles, which may or may not bring 4 into the mix, depending on how it is represented in the puzzle. We have two methods for writing 4, either closed like this: 4 or open like this: *4*.

irrational Numbers

I briefly mentioned irrational numbers, those special numbers that fall somewhere between fractions and decimals. Irrationals hold a special place in puzzle making due to their unusual nature as numbers that seem to go on forever without repeating.

Pi

The first irrational that most of us learn is pi. It represents the ratio of the diameter of a circle to the circumference of that circle, and the first 10 digits are 3.1415926535. We all learn that much. But pi is a miraculous number. To begin with, as far as we can calculate, it is infinite.

In 2010, a network of 1,000 computers worked for 23 days to calculate pi as far as they could and stopped at just over 2 quadrillion digits (the 2,000,000,000,000,000th digit!) with no end in sight.

Pi is also seemingly entirely random. While repeated sequences DO occur (for instance the sequence 12345 appears 5 different times within the first million digits of pi), it never repeats in a predictable way. Around the 762nd decimal place, pi reaches what is known as the "Feynman Point," a string of six 9's followed by an 8. At the 45,681,781st decimal place a string of nine 6's occur. Little random spots of numbers like this occur over and over.

Why does pi's infinite but random nature matter? Well, because pi contains... everything. Think of it this way: if we assign a numerical value to the alphabet (A=1, B=2, etc.) then look deep enough, we can find any word. My name occurs beginning at the 30160998th digit of pi! But a 5 letter name isn't very impressive. Because pi is infinite, if we could calculate far enough into it we could potentially find... the Constitution of the United States, or the entire script of Hamlet, or even the Bible! Theoretically every utterance ever made by human voice exists within pi! That's pretty cool, huh?

So how does that turn into a puzzle? Well, I've given you one

math holidays

March 14th (3/14) has been dubbed "Pi Day" by many due to its similarity to the constant. 1:59 on that date is known as "Pi Time" or the "Pi Minute" as it follows the next few digits.

June 28th (6/28) is Tau day.

Of course, these only work in America, where we list the month first rather than the day, as in Europe.

way, with the discussion of my name. There are websites online that can search within pi, up to certain digits. My personal favorite has a database of the first 200 million digits and allows you to search for up to 120 characters. A puzzle solver could give you either a number to search for, and the answer would be what digit it begins at, or you could be given the place, and then the answer would be what you find there. Another potential puzzle is the possibility of a missing number. If you are given 3.141526535 and compare it to pi, you'll see that there is a missing 9 after the first 5.

Back in Chapter 5, I mentioned a unit of measure that can be expressed in terms of pi: the radian. 360 degrees = 2 pi radians.

Tau

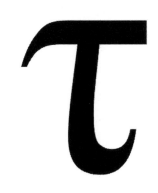

Pi is the ratio of a circle's circumference to its diameter. The diameter of a circle is a line from one side to the other that passes through the center point of the circle. For some, this seems like a cumbersome way of working with the circle, especially given that using pi in an equation to determine the area of a circle requires a square, or square root. For those people, we have pi's lesser known cousin: tau.

Tau is the ratio of a circle's circumference to its radius and is represented numerically as 6.2831853071...

Like pi, tau is infinite and seemingly random, though it hasn't been calculated as deeply as pi. Tau has a Feynman Point as well, beginning at the 760th decimal place, though it lasts for seven 9's, one longer than pi.

Puzzles with tau could work in the same way as pi, though, as I've said, tau hasn't been as deeply calculated as pi, and I am unaware of a search engine for it. The website *tauday.com* lists the first 5,000 digits.

Euler's Number

39 digits

Only the first 39 digits of pi would be necessary to calculate the circumference of the entire known universe with such precision that any error would be smaller than the radius of a single hydrogen atom!

Leohnard Euler, a Swiss mathematician and physicist is responsible for several components of our current mathematical system. One of the most famous is the irrational number that has come to be known as "Euler's Number," represented by a lower case "*e*" in equations.

I'll save you the complex mathematical discussion. You just need to know that *e* forms the basis for the Natural Logarithm and is represented numerically as 2.7182818284590452353... Note that you can memorize the first few digits of e very easily. Following the 2.7, the sequence 1828 follows twice, 2.7 1828 1828, followed by the three angles found in an equilateral triangle, 45, 90 and 45, like this: 2.718281828 45 90 45. After that it becomes a random series, similar to pi and tau. It has been calculated to over a trillion places.

Euler's number is most frequently used in calculating compound interest rates and should not be confused with Euler's Constant.

360 degrees

Appropriately enough, considering its intimate relationship with the circle, the number 360 appears in pi beginning at the 359th digit!

Irrational Roots

A number created by multiplying a number by itself is a square. The original number is its square root. Square roots come in two varieties: perfect or irrational. If a square root is a whole, or natural, number such as the square of 25 being 5, then it is a perfect square. All other square roots are irrational, those awesome infinite, non-repeating numbers we've been discussing.

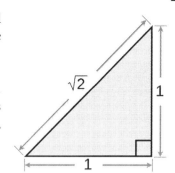

Of the irrational roots, the first few (2, 3, 5, 6, 7, 8, and 10), are probably the most studied. You can find each of these calculated online to several million places. Though the searches for numbers inside irrational roots are not quite as simple as they have been made for pi, they are still doable and available to puzzle makers and solvers.

onstants

Moving past the properties of single numbers or numerical sequences, the next thing that starts to crop up in puzzle caches are constants. Constants are numbers that remain the same, no matter what equation you put them through. Constants come in two flavors: Mathematical Constants and Physical Constants.

All of the irrational numbers that we've already discussed are Mathematical Constants. Pi is sometimes called "Archimede's Constant," the square root of 2 is sometimes called "Pythagoras' Constant," and Euler's number can be called "Napier's Constant."

Wikipedia lists nearly 50 mathematical constants on their page on the subject, which provides an enormous variety of numbers for puzzle creators to use in building geo-puzzles. They range in length from single digits to millions, billions, or even quadrillions of digits. Most of them are represented by a Greek letter or letters, as with pi and tau, but others are represented by standard letters of the alphabet. The letter 'K' for instance can be used to represent three different constants: the Landau–Ramanujan constant, Viswanath's constant, and Catalan's constant. Others are letters with a superscript or subscript number, like C_2 which represents the Twin Prime constant. If you see a Greek letter on a cache page or a person's name that you don't recognize, you might be dealing with a mathematical constant. They also have numerical values, of course.

Physical Constants refer to a fact of physics or chemistry, like the temperature at which something happens (water freezing at 32° F or 0° C for instance), or something like the speed of light, or sound. Like mathematical constants, Wikipedia has entries for a wide range of physical constants. Besides the numerical values, physical constants are referred to either by what they represent, like an electron mass, or by the name of the person who discovered them, like a Planck length. They can also be referred to by an equation like $k_J = 2e/h$, which describes the Josephson constant, or by a single letter or letter with a sub or superscript, just like a mathematical constant. $\triangle$ or 'delta' for instance.

Physical constants can also refer to the physical characteristics of something that is unlikely to change: the temperature at which something freezes or boils, the weight of an element, the circumference of a planet or a moon, or the amount of a substance that can fill a certain space.

Constants can be the outright answer to a puzzle, or they can be a base that a puzzle builds off of. Asking for the first few digits or the first few digits after the decimal place of a constant could provide the digits you need, or you may be asked to perform a slight mathematic transformation, say, subtracting the mass of a proton from the north, and the mass of a neutron from the west.

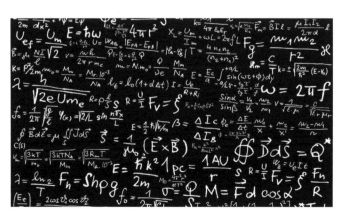

244

delta

While not a constant, another Greek letter you will often see in puzzles is delta, △, which represents the difference between two things.

ormulas

The next bit of math that we'll look at are formulas. We all went through the basic high school math education and were exposed to word problems, also called story problems, little tales of woe that we were meant to solve mathematically. "Sam lives twice as far from Joe as she does from Bob. If Sam lives exactly 5 miles from Bob... blah blah blah."

In essence, word problems are puzzles: a grouping of cryptic pieces of information that you are expected to rearrange into a semblance of order. There are several classic word problem formulas that show up quite frequently in geocaching puzzles.

The first is the classic problem of the trains that we all remember. "If a train leaves St. Louis traveling 35 miles per hour, and a second train leaves Chicago traveling 40 miles per hour, etc." There are hundreds of variations on this problem, using trains, planes, cars, bicycles, or even people walking. Numbers may be the correct answer, or an enterprising CO might combine this idea with the orienteering puzzles that we mentioned earlier and place a cache at the point the vehicles meet.

The second are ballistics equations: firing or throwing an object at a certain angle with a certain amount of thrust and determining where it lands. Again, this can be used as a straightforward equation, or combined with an actual, real world location and the answer will be the location of the cache.

These are just two common formula based puzzles. There are many different formulas that can be used in the creation of puzzle caches, just look out for the classic components of word problems.

atrices

A matrix is an arrangement of numbers in a grid. This array can be 2x2, 3x3, 2x3, or any arrangement of rows and columns.

If the matrix is a square matrix, meaning that it is the same number of columns wide as it is rows tall, then it has a special property called a "determinant." A determinant is a number that is calculated from the numbers making up a matrix via a specific formula. The determinant of a 2x2 matrix, like the example at right, is found by multiplying the upper left number by the lower right, the lower left number by the upper right, and then subtracting the second number from the first. In this case (3 x 6)-(4 x 8) or 18-32=-14. So the determinant of the example matrix is -14.

$$\begin{bmatrix} 3 & 8 \\ 4 & 6 \end{bmatrix}$$

A 3x3 matrix is quite a bit more complicated, and a 5x5 matrix usually requires the use of a specialized matrix calculator to find the determinant. I'll leave it up to you to find the methods for those if you need to.

The Plot

Another vein of mathematical puzzles would be plotting a number on a graph, either 2-D or 3-D. This is sometimes referred to as a "Cartesian Coordinate System." The 2-D version is basically the same system that we use for latitude and longitude coordinates.

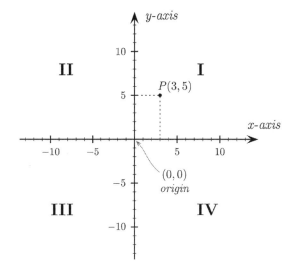

First you locate your number along the X axis, starting at the center where the two axis cross. This is known as the origin, or the 0,0 point. For a positive number, move to the right of the origin. For a negative number you move left of the origin. Next you move upward until you are even with the second number on the Y axis. Upward from the origin are positive numbers, down are negative numbers. On the example to the left I have marked the point for (3,5).

3-D coordinates add a Z axis, which would extend from the origin point toward the viewer, or into the picture plane. Think of this as having latitude, longitude, and elevation. Without the addition of the third dimension the roof and basement of a building have the same coordinates.

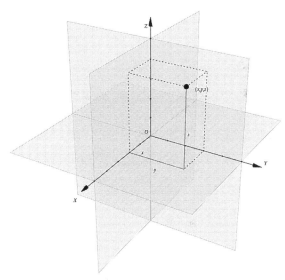

There is a third possible way to create coordinates, known as "polar coordinates." In this system, you begin from the origin point, here called a "fixed point," and measure the radial coordinate, or radius. Then you measure the angular coordinate, or azimuth, which is the angle away from the "polar axis," (marked as 0° on the example, left). On the example I have marked (2, 60°).

Puzzles that use these systems may give you a point to find within a park by giving you a grid of a certain unit size, and then a set of coordinates. For instance, Central Park in New York City is .5 miles wide by 2.5 miles tall. I could ask you to divide the park into a grid with squares that are .1x.1 miles wide, and tell you that a cache can be found at (3,15).

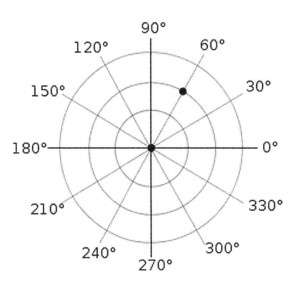

Another method would be to give you a series of grid references and then ask you to connect the dots and create numbers or a shape.

Keywords

Keep your eyes open for generally innocent geocaching words that have homophones in the math world. A "log" may refer to the cache log or a logarithm, a reference to "sign" may be a covert reference to a "sine," "pie" may mean "pi," etc. Natural logs, tangent, inverse, matrix, constant, roots... these words, and many others, could all be very innocently inserted in a cache description but have a meaning far deeper than the average description. If you think there might be a math connection to the puzzle, be on the look out for breadcrumbs like these, or if you don't know what the puzzle is about, but see some of these double meaning words, consider math!

Solving it

Bringing together what you've learned.

Use this checklist to help you apply what you've learned in this chapter and determine if you are facing a mathematically themed puzzle.

Checklist: MATHEMATICS

- [ ] Look for references to numerical types like primes, squares or cubes.

- [ ] Look for references to sequenced numbers.

- [ ] Look for references to irrational numbers like pi, tau or the square root of two.

- [ ] Examine the description for references to things that might be mathematical or physical constants.

- [ ] Examine the description for the keywords related to word problems or story problems.

- [ ] Put any numbers or fractions into Wolfram Alpha to see if they have special properties or connotations.

- [ ] Examine the description for any words that might have dual mathematical meanings, like "root" or "pie."

 **alk-Through**

Let's take a look at a few math puzzles. Here's a puzzle that uses the techniques we've covered in this chapter (combing with techniques from previous chapters). At right is a walk-through of how I'd go about solving this puzzle, so that you can see the techniques at work. Remember, there is no actual geocache at these locations.

FIND A CACHE

? Measuring Circles

A cache by: FuzzyDolphins   Hidden: 03/14/2004

Difficulty: ★★☆☆☆   Size: ▪▪■■■
Terrain: ★☆☆☆☆

N 36° 42.684 W 107° 59.116

In Bloomfield, New Mexico, USA

14 FAVORITES

The cache is NOT at the listed coordinates.
You must determine the actual coordinates by solving the puzzle below.

Doesn't it always seem like a cache is at the 17,483,228th place you look? I guess it's better than the 168,627,779th.

FCH4RYD

LOG YOUR VISIT

View Gallery
Watch
Bookmark
Ignore

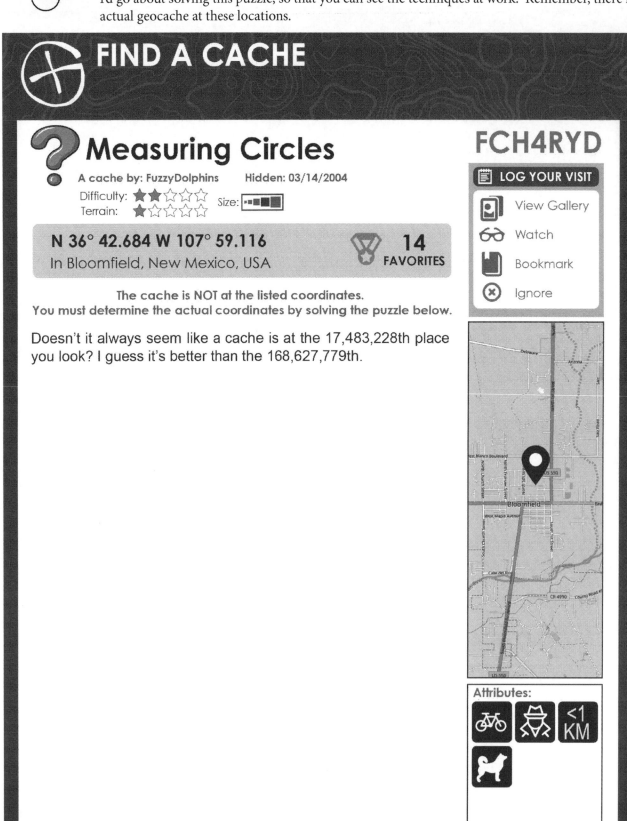

Attributes:

1 **Off the top.** We start with the classic examination of the page: Title, Placed By name, hide date, gallery, Related Web Pages, TB inventory, etc. Nothing catches my eye right away. I look at the dummy coords in street view, nothing immediately pops. I see that they are in front of a diner of some sort, named "Triangle Cafe." The name of the caches mentions circles. Maybe something about shapes? A little bit down the street is a gas station with a sign that says "2 7 11." Numbers are always useful. I'll stick a pin in those bits for the moment.

2 **In the description.** Wow. Not much of a description, just some more numbers and a joke about cache hunting. I check for hidden text, just in case, and find nothing. I look in the source code... nothing. I guess everything I need has to be here somewhere. Let me look at it again, in finer detail.

3 **Back to the beginning.** With so little information to go on, I have to look more closely at everything. When there's so little on a cache page, what you need must be well hidden, or, alternatively, very obvious but easily overlooked. So let's look at the title: "Measuring Circles." It makes me wonder, is there an actual circle that needs to be measured? There are no circles near the coordinates, like traffic circles or obvious other circles. There is a plate and a saucer on that diner sign, but they are in perspective, so they don't really look like circles, and I'm not sure how I'd measure them. While I'm looking at the streetview, I notice that there's also a piece of pie on the sign. Moving on, the cacher's name is his actual name; he didn't change it. The date is 3/14/2004. I check the logs and see that it was placed a few days before that, so the date hasn't been changed. Since I'm a giant nerd, I notice that it was placed on "pi day," which a nerdy pun on the fact that pi begins with 3.14, and March 14 is written as 3/14. Wait... pi day, and pie on the sign. Could it be about pi?

4 **Measuring circles?** If it is about pi, the title makes a little more sense. To measure a circle, you need either physical tools like a compass or you need a couple measurements, like the radius, or the circumference, and an equation, which uses pi!

5 **Back to the description.** Let's examine the description again with pi in mind. The description mentions two numbers, but neither of them is pi. It also mentions a "place," in terms of a place you might look for something, but a "place" can also mean a position in a number, like the ones place or the tens place, either in front of or behind a decimal. Pi is an infinite number, so it could potentially have something at the 17,483,228th place after the decimal, but how would I find that?

6 **Searching pi?** Turning to Google, I run a search on "search pi." Okay, the first return tells me that I can search within the first 200 million digits of pi, the second tells me that I can search 2 billion digits, and the third tells me that I can search 4 billion! Wow! I only need the 17,483,228th, not nearly that many, so I'll just choose the first one *angio.net/pi/*. The first page gives me a box with a button that says "search pi." I don't have a specific number that I am searching, but instead a specific place, so that won't work for me. To the right of that is a button that says "Digits of pi." Let's try that. There I find an entry box labeled "See 10 digits starting at position." I think this is what I need. I drop in 17483228 and get back 3642745674. Mmmm. If I stick in the appropriate spaces and decimals that could be 36° 42.745674. I can safely ignore those last few digits and have north coords! I try the second number, 168627779, and the search engine returns 1075880198. Turning that into coords I get 107° 58.801.

7 **The answer.** 36° 42.745, -107° 58.801 is a great set of coords! I'm ready to get out and start hunting! (Not a spot you can actually visit, but that's okay since there is no actual cache anyway, but thematically appropriate!)

On the next page there is another puzzle for you to solve on your own this time. Apply the lessons from this chapter, and it should be quite simple.

# olve It Yourself!

Here are some puzzle caches for you to solve on your own. Using the skills we learned in this chapter you should be able to solve these puzzles. Take careful note of the final coordinates that you get as a solution to these puzzles, and write them at the bottom of the page. If you need a reminder of how to use the puzzle stats or hints provided, please check page 11. Good luck!

Puzzle 1 Solution:

N __ __ ° __ __ . __ __ __ , W __ __ __ ° __ __ . __ __ __

As a secondary check you should be able to answer this question: *What city does that belong in?*

Puzzle 2 Solution:

N __ __ ° __ __ . __ __ __ , W __ __ __ ° __ __ . __ __ __

As a secondary check you should be able to answer this question: *What food do you find at the final?*

FIND A CACHE

 ## Triplets

FC3X4X5

A cache by: Pythagoras Hidden: 05/12/2013

Difficulty:
Terrain: Size:

N 36° 06.490 W 115° 10.358
In Las Vegas, Nevada, USA

14 FAVORITES

LOG YOUR VISIT

 View Gallery
 Watch
 Bookmark
 Ignore

The cache is NOT at the listed coordinates.
You must determine the actual coordinates by solving the puzzle below.

I present you with 4 sets of numbers. Each is made up of three whole numbers but I am only showing you two of them. Find what the number sets have in common, and find the missing number to find the cache.

$$A \sim 8 \sim 10$$
$$195 \sim B \sim 773$$
$$C \sim 24 \sim 26$$
$$228 \sim D \sim 397$$

$$N\ 36°\ A.B$$
$$W\ 115°\ C.D$$

Attributes:

PUZZLE STATS
52 CHECKSUM | BEST VIEW

22 139 102
93 32

FIND A CACHE

 ## Mr. Aerobus & Ms. Fatigue

FCUT4H1

A cache by: HikingSeaLion   Hidden: 05/12/2013

Difficulty:
Terrain: Size:

N 38° 23.620 W 086° 56.277
In Jasper, Indiana, USA

22 FAVORITES

LOG YOUR VISIT

 View Gallery
 Watch
 Bookmark
 Ignore

**The cache is NOT at the listed coordinates.
You must determine the actual coordinates by solving the puzzle below.**

Mr. Aerobus and Ms. Fatigue are very picky about the coordinates that they use for the caches that they place. Recently they teamed up to place a cache and had to compromise a bit. Mr. Aerobus was resposible for the North coords, and Ms. Fatigue for the West.

If you can determine which numbers Mr. Aerobus prefers you can get his coordinates from this list:

552849057990895

If you can determine which numbers Ms. Fatigue prefers you can get her coordinates from this list:

105225184901924

You can assume the 38 and 86.

Attributes:

PUZZLE STATS
74 CHECKSUM   BEST VIEW

 27
 47
 79
 103   **59**

Music

Much like math, music based puzzles can be intimidating because they seem like a foreign language that takes years of practice and education in order to read, but, in reality, most of the music based geo-puzzles out there are based on a few very simple musical concepts. Music theory has the potential to be very complex and overwhelmingly in-depth, but a basic understanding will get you past a lot of the geo-puzzles that have been created.

A caveat before we start... I know nothing about music. I attempted to play trumpet in 6th grade but never did very well, and I long ago forgot anything I learned then. I have consulted several people who DO know about music who helped me with this chapter. They tell me that the way I've written it might drive someone who actually DOES know about music a little crazy, but we aren't here to learn how to play piano, we're here to learn to find geocaches. With that in mind I've written this in a way that will hopefully make sense to puzzle cachers, but may not necessarily satisfy musicians. Don't expect to be able to play a sonata after reading this chapter. You have been warned.

Name That Tune

Geocaches that use music as a primary component of the puzzle can be written in dozens of ways. One of the most common comes down to simply being able to recognize music by one of several criteria. A cache page may consist of audio files that you have to listen to, portions of song lyrics, or actual lines of music written on the page. As the puzzle solver it is up to you to figure out how to get numbers from each piece. But how do you do that?

Your first task is to identify any actual musical compositions you may be presented with. In some cases that might be as simple as listening to the audio file, or researching

apps that listen to music

Smartphone apps like Sound-Hound or Shazam are capable or recognizing millions of songs and musical compositions. By activating the app and holding your phone near a speaker the app can "listen" for a few seconds and will then tell you the name and artist of the song. This can be very useful for puzzles with sound files!

the information you have been given about the piece. Smartphone apps that recognize music, like *SoundHound* or *Shazam* can be very useful for this. But if you are presented with a piece of musical notation and you don't read music you may have to ask friends or family to pick it out on a piano, guitar or a virtual keyboard (there are apps and websites that have this function), or whatever instrument they may be familiar with and have handy. Someone familiar with music may be able to look at a piece of notation and know immediately that it isn't actually playable, or that it isn't melodic, in which case you probably have a puzzle based within the actual notation. We'll get to those in a bit.

Once you've identified the tunes, consider whether there is an overall theme to the group. It could be something like Christmas songs or classical compositions, TV or movie theme songs or they may all be songs from a single group or composer, like The Beatles, or Mozart. That may help you figure out what the next step is.

Next, think about the titles of the songs... are there any numbers in there? Is one Beethoven's Fifth Symphony (that's the opening bars of it above)? Is one the Dolly Parton classic "Three Doors Down?" If it isn't as obvious as the title, look at all the possible aspects of the tunes that you can think of: lyrics in the song that contain numbers or (as we discussed in the chapter on Index Puzzles) how many awards the song won, how high it climbed on the Billboard charts, how many weeks it stayed at #1, or any number of other indexes that the song may be cataloged against.

other lands, other times, other music

This chapter is written with the assumption that you are dealing with modern, Western music. Musical notation has been handled differently in other time periods and cultures, so watch out for puzzles that might be using an older or foreign form of notation.

The key to turning it into coordinates may also lie in how the music is played or performed. Consider the number of instruments in classical pieces (for example, is the piece a duet, a trio, or a quintet), whether all the pieces are written in different keys (see later in the chapter for a discussion of how to handle this), the year it was written, etc. If the song was performed by a modern group, how many people were in the group? The Beatles were a quartet, 'N Sync a quintet, The White Stripes a duet, Earth Wind and Fire a nonet (9 members), etc. If all of the pieces are by the same composer, check to see if there is a comprehensive numbered catalog of that composer's work.

But many times, a music puzzle will consist of one or more images written in musical notation, which is not meant to be played, but is written for the sole purpose of conveying coordinates. They are right on the page in front of you, but you have to figure out how to read them, which is where a basic understanding of musical notation could come in handy.

hen You Read, You Begin With ABC...

To begin understanding musical notation you would start at the same place that a person learning to read would start. Everything begins with the basic music staff, a collection of 5 horizontal lines on which notes are written either on or in between the lines. The staff and the notes are meaningless, however, unless you are also given a "clef" sign, which orients the range of notes covered on the staff. Different clefs were designed as ways of writing the different ranges of notes for different voices and instruments. High voices and instruments (soprano, alto, flute, clarinet, trumpet, violin) use the treble clef. Low voices and instruments (bass, baritone, trombone, cello) use the bass clef. The piano uses both, usually with the right hand playing the treble clef, and the left hand playing the bass clef. These are the only two clefs that most puzzlers will ever need, but you should be aware that there are others (including the alto clef known almost exclusively by viola players). Together the clef and lines are known as the "staff."

A treble staff is marked a sort of "S" shaped thing at the beginning, known as the "treble clef," and looks like this:

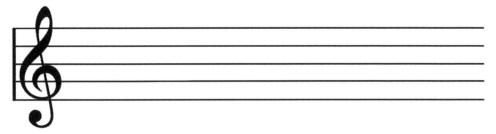

A bass staff is marked with a backward "C" shaped thing, known as a "bass clef."

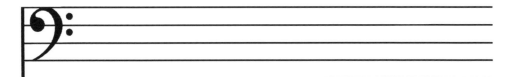

It is a clef's job to assign individual notes to the various lines or spaces on a staff. You'll notice that the treble clef has a curly bit that swirls around the fourth line down. Any note that lands on the fourth line will be a 'G.' A treble clef is sometimes known as a "G Clef" for this reason. The two dots on a bass clef straddle the second line from the top. Any note that lands on that line will be an 'F,' making a bass clef the "F Clef."

This brings us to the next component of reading music: the notes. Think of music notes as a sort of Base 7 system, where you count up to 7, and then roll back to 1 and start again. Except with music notes, there is no zero or tens place. An arrangement of ascending notes on a staff is called a "scale." As you move up the scale you also move up in pitch, and the frequency of the note also goes up. The frequency of a note has to do with how close together the individual waves of sound are. A "C" is defined as a multiple of a given frequency. Middle C on the piano (also known as C4 because it's the 4th C on the piano counting from left to right) has a frequency of a little under 262 Hz (the unit is Hertz, pronounced "hurts." Watch for that word as a breadcrumb in puzzles!). The same note an octave higher, C5, has a frequency twice as high, approximately 525 Hz. Whether notes sound pleasing to our ear when played together depends on the ratio of their frequencies.

A scale is a path of notes ascending (or descending) from one note to the same note an octave higher or lower), in 7 steps. The spacing of those steps depends on whether you have a "major" or "minor" scale. Let's start with the most basic scale, known as a "C major scale."

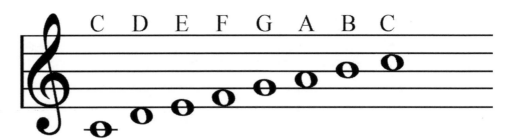

every good boy

For treble clefs, besides counting from the G indicated by the clef you can remember which notes fall where on a staff by learning two simple mnemonics.

"Every Good Boy Does Fine" represents the notes assigned to the lines, starting with E at the bottom, and going up, the first letter of each word landing on a line until you reach F at the top.

FACE tells you about the spaces. F is in the first space at the bottom, and each space gets a letter until you arrive at E in the top space.

You'll note that G lines up with the clef as we mentioned before, and we count backwards from there, placing a note between and on each line until we arrive at C, which is just below the staff on what is known as a "ledger line." On the other side of the G, we count up to B. The next highest note, in the space between lines two and three, we would start again at C.

Here is the C major scale on a bass clef with F aligning the position of the notes.

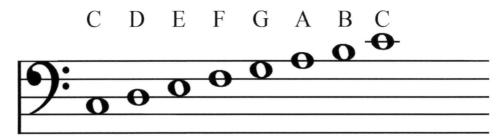

But how does this turn into a puzzle? Well, the easiest way is to transform the letter designations for the notes into numbers. A non-musical person would do a simple letter to number substitution of the type we've discussed before. A=1, B=2, C=3, D=4, etc.

A more musically minded person might approach this differently, based on the mechanics of a scale. In the case of the C major scale, C would become 1, D would be come 2, E 3, etc.

major or minor

Major scales have a lighter, brighter sound, and minor scales have a darker, more somber sound.

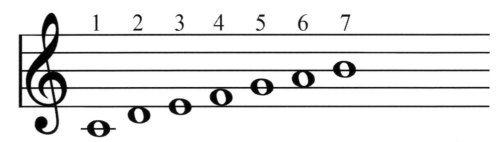

Using either system, a simple arrangement of notes would able to convey coordinates.

This arrangement says 41° 11.621, -111° 56.671, the site of a lovely sculpture dedicated to music on the campus of Weber State University in Utah.

The first note is an F, or 4. The second is a D, or 2. The third is an E, or 3, etc. This example uses the variation in which C=1.

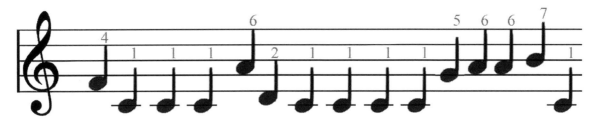

If you used the alphabet substitution method, where A=1, those same notes would give you coords of 63° 33.143, -33° 37.112, just off the coast of Greenland. (I dropped the final note, since Greenland only needs 14 digits for coords, not the 15 we needed in Utah.)

Fairly straightforward, right? That level of detail is probably enough for you to solve a large portion of music based puzzle caches, but it can, of course, get more complicated.

So far we've only looked at a C major scale, and so we began counting with C, but there are other scales that would begin the count with a different note. In order to determine what note is designated as "1" we need to know what key we are working with. To figure that out, we need to determine how many sharps and flats are in the scale. What are those? Think of the notes on a scale as the rungs on a ladder; you move one full rung in between notes. But, imagine that it was possible to place your foot in the air between rungs, taking only a half step. A half step above the note would be called a "sharp," and a half step below the note is called a "flat." A sharp is represented on a musical scale by a slanted hashtag symbol. A flat is represented by a kind of italicized lower case B.

Just after the clef sign on a musical staff, you'll often find a collection of these symbols, which tells you which key your music is in. This is called the "key signature." If you arrange all of the keys around the edge of a circle, spaced 5 notes apart, you get something called the "Wheel of Fifths." That's a bit of musical theory trivia that doesn't really help solving caches, but what it does do is create a convenient way to look at the 12 different key signatures in one handy place.

At the top you'll see the C major key signature that we've already looked at, with no further markings. This lets us know that there are no sharps or flats in the C major scale. Just to the right we find G major, which has one sharp in it.

On this scale, rather than C equaling 1, you would begin counting with G. We can easily find G based on the trick with the treble clef, the swirled portion at bottom surrounds the line that G rests on.

Looking at the inner portion of the wheel, you'll also notice a second key, signifying that each key signature represents at least two different keys, and some as many as four. The same key signature represents C major and A minor for instance. In a piece of music, there is an internal logic that governs which key the piece is being played in. Because puzzle caches aren't making an attempt to be

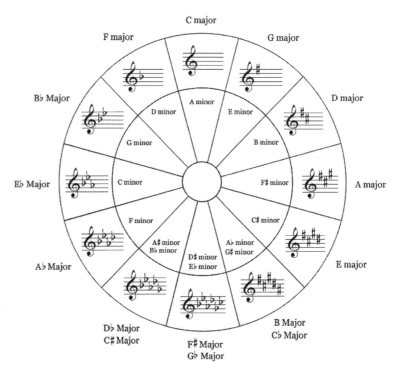

melodic, that internal structure is sometimes missing and so there really isn't a way to know which key you are dealing with. A note that would represent C (and therefore 1) on a C major scale would still be a C on the A minor scale, but would numerically be a 3, because on the A scale we start counting at A rather than C. So, if you are working with a puzzle but aren't getting the right numbers, you may consider looking at the other keys represented by that key signature to see if maybe the answer is clearer in that other key.

The key signature also means that unless you're told otherwise, the notes represented there will always be played as sharps or flats throughout the piece. So, on a G Major scale, you'll notice that the sharp symbol is in the same position on the staff that an F note would normally be, so F's will always be sharp in that scale. Otherwise sharps and flats can also be sprinkled into a piece where the key signature doesn't contain them by simply putting the symbol beside the note. The "natural" sign is indicated where a note is not intended to be sharp or flat, and takes precedence over the key signature for the measure it is in.

Natural Sign

Most people who have ever looked at a piece of sheet music will know that music notes come in a variety of shapes and forms, but they basically boil down to 5 types: whole, half, quarter, eighth and sixteenth. (You can also have thirtysecond, sixtyfourth and one-hundred-twentyeighth notes, but those are much rarer.) The different types tell you how long to continue a note when singing or playing it. The duration doesn't typically play much of a role in music puzzles, but it is good to recognize the various types.

As you can see, the stem (the line that goes off of every note smaller than a whole) can point either up or down, and eighths and sixteenths can be written either as single notes with "flags" or as joined notes

WHOLE   HALF   QUARTER   EIGHTH   SIXTEENTH

with "beams" between the two notes. Notes can also have a dot beside them, like a period, that adds 50% of the value of that note. So a half note with a dot would actually represent a 3/4 note.

The last piece of musical notation that we'll look at is the time signature. At the beginning of any musical staff are two numbers that look somewhat like a fraction. The top number tells you how many beats are in a measure, and the bottom number tells you what note equals one beat. So, if the bottom number is 4 then the quarter note would be one beat, and four quarter notes would equal one measure, two half notes would be a measure, and a single whole note would be a measure, be-

cause, like a fraction 4/4 equals 1. If the time signature was 3/4, then there would be three quarter notes in a full measure.

The staff is also divided by something called "measure lines," the vertical lines between sections of music. These close off the number of notes that, when totaled, would equal the number of notes needed to make up a measure. In 4/4, it would close off four quarter notes, eight eighth notes, sixteen sixteenth notes, or some combination of all those. Each enclosed area is called a "measure" or a "bar."

One way to use this in a puzzle would be to count the number of notes enclosed into a measure. Normally, each measure would contain an equal number of beats. If you look at a puzzle and see something like one measure with four quarter notes, but another measure with ten eighth notes, (which would represent four beats and five beats respectively, in 4/4 time) then that's probably where the puzzle is.

Above Seven

A savvy puzzle solver may have noticed a problem with all of this by now: This all only represents the numbers 1 through 7. There is no way to represent 0, 8 or 9, yet. One way around this would be to start counting up again after the notes loop. On the C major scale, B represents 7, but the next note up would be another C which could potentially be used to represent 8, and then a D which would be 9.

Zeros are easier to deal with. In math a zero represents an absence, and in music we also have a piece of musical notation that also represents an absence: a "rest." A rest is a momentary pause when performing. Like other music notes, rests have specific durations: whole, half, quarter, eighth and sixteenth. Whole rests hang under the second line of the staff from the top, half rests sit on top of the third line. The others are positioned in the center of the staff.

Another way to solve the missing numbers is with a little math. Musical notes can be joined together in a few ways. One is by "bars," which are the solid square connectors that run between notes. Another is by

WHOLE   HALF   QUARTER   EIGHTH   SIXTEENTH

ties or slurs, which look kind of like sideways parentheses. Ties and slurs actually mean something very different in the world of music, but for puzzling purposes, they would mean the same thing: that the value of the notes inside the slur would be combined.

In this example, we have two notes connected by a slur, an F and a B. Using the A=1 system, B=2 and F=6, so together they would be an 8, as 2+6=8. Slurs, ties, and bars can connect just two notes, as in the example, or several notes.

There's one other way that we can solve the problem of the missing numbers, though without jumping through logical hoops. Rather than using the notes themselves to represent the numbers, you can use the spaces between the notes.

Think of a checkerboard with 5 black squares and 4 white squares in between them. A checker placed on the board represents the note. You can place the checker either on a black square, which represents the note being on a line, or on a white square, which represents the note being between lines.

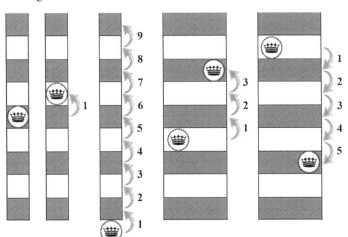

syncopation

Don't forget dotted notes when looking at how many notes it takes to fill a measure. A dotted note equals one and a half times its normal length, so a half note would be three beats rather than two. In 4/4 time, a dotted half and a quarter note would represent four beats,, and a full measure.

octal

Getting numbers 0 to 7 but not getting the coords you need? 0 to 7 would be perfect for writing a number in octal! Try converting from Base 8 to Base 10 and see if those numbers make more sense.

Moving the checker to the next square is a single step, which would represent 1. By starting at the bottom, you can get up to 9 steps. These steps can also be counted either going up or down. It doesn't matter where the start positions are; you always start counting with 1. In a complete puzzle cache, you would start counting with the intervals between note 1 and note 2, then between note 2 and note 3, note 3 and note 4, etc. If a rest follows a note, that would represent 0 since there are no steps between a note and a rest. Two notes on the same line would also represent a zero, as there is no movement between the notes.

Try your hand at this method of puzzling, to see if you can get coords that point to another music themed statue in Washington, DC.

hen You Sing, You Begin With...

As Maria from *The Sound of Music* taught us, besides the written notes, there is another way to refer to musical notes. Most people just refer to it as "do re mi," but the technical name for it is "solfège," "sol-fa," "solfa," or "solfedge." Some people also refer to is as the "Kodály Method" or the "Curwen Method." Regardless of what you call it, it works by substituting a syllable for the notes on a scale. The scale begins with the syllable "do (or sometimes 'doh,')" followed by "re, mi, fa, so (or 'sol,') la, ti (or 'si,')" and returning to "do," just as a standard scale loops back on itself. There are also solfège syllables for sharps and flats, though they are used less outside of actual music training.

As we discovered earlier, scales can start with different notes, depending on which scale we are working with, but the important part is that solfège for major scales always begins with "do," and therefore we can assume that do is equal to 1. Do = 1, re = 2, mi = 3, fa = 4, sol = 5, la = 6, and ti = 7. Solfège for minor scales always begins with "la." There is no real way to add a 0, 8 or 9 to this method as we did with the written scales.

Solfège, as a training style, also has a series of hand positions that can be used to display the notes in a visual style. These seven hand signs represent do, re, mi, fa, so, la, and ti. They help musicians in training learn to mentally hear the pitch of notes when they are first learning to sight read music. As with everything we've discussed, the hand position for 'do' can be used to represent 1, 're' to represent 2, etc.

Over the years, there have been other things associated with the various solfège syllables. For instance, Isaac Newton assigned them colors based on the 7 colors of the rainbow.

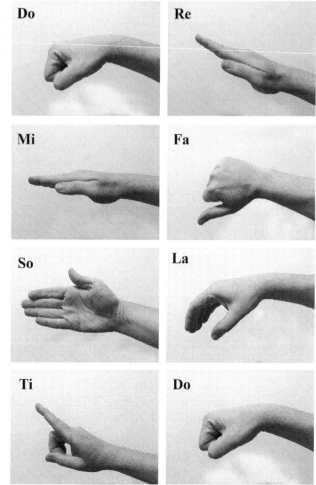

Do - Red
Re - Orange
Mi - Yellow
Fa - Green
So - Blue
La - Indigo (Blue Violet)
Ti - Purple (Red Violet)

These colors, to an extent, continue to be used today with children's hand bells. The very first set of hand bells that most kids are exposed to are color coded in a very similar way. The only difference is that they use a sky blue or aqua color for 'la' instead of indigo.

And of course there are the metaphoric representations mentioned in the song from *The Sound of Music*.

he Rest

All of this only barely scratches the surface of the world of music and musical puzzles. There are dozens, if not hundreds, of methods and musical ideas that I just don't have the room to cover. Puzzles could incorporate things like guitar or dulcimer fingerings, ancient or foreign forms of music notation, more advanced musical theory like figured bass, the sound frequency of certain notes, or any number of other things, but this should give you a base to build on, and will certainly help you solve the simpler music puzzles out there.

Is It Music?

One last thing to consider.... as I warned you in other areas, sometimes a music puzzle isn't actually about music. Watch for breadcrumbs in the title, description, or in people's logs that this may actually be the case. Could whole notes represent the dashes, and quarter notes represent the dots of Morse code? Could notes with a stem that points up represent A, and the notes with stems that point down represent B in a Bacon Cipher? Could the notes themselves take the position of dots of Braille? Or an Abacus? Or something else entirely? This kind of puzzle can actually be quite hard for people who have a music background to solve because they have to ignore the musical part of what they're seeing.

Solving it

Bringing together what you've learned.

Use this checklist to help you apply what you've learned in this chapter and determine if you are facing a musically themed puzzle.

Checklist: MUSIC

☐ Examine the title and description for keywords indicating the theme of the puzzle or method of solution.

☐ Identify any pieces of music by title and composer. For classical music, identify the key of the piece and number of instruments, or band members, if possible.

☐ Analyze images containing musical notation. Count the number of measures, notes, or chords and see if that gives you any clues as to which might be the pieces of the puzzle.

☐ Write down the names of the notes and see if they correspond to A=1, B=2, etc. Or use the key signature to count which position the note would take if you count up the scale.

☐ Count the number of notes and/or beats per measure.

☐ Investigate intervals between notes and chords.

☐ Consider that despite all appearances, the puzzle may not actually be based on music.

 alk-Through

Let's take a look at a few music puzzles. Here's a puzzle that uses the techniques we've covered in this chapter (combing with techniques from previous chapters.) At right is a walk-through of how I'd go about solving this puzzle, so that you can see the techniques at work. Remember, there is no actual geocache at these locations.

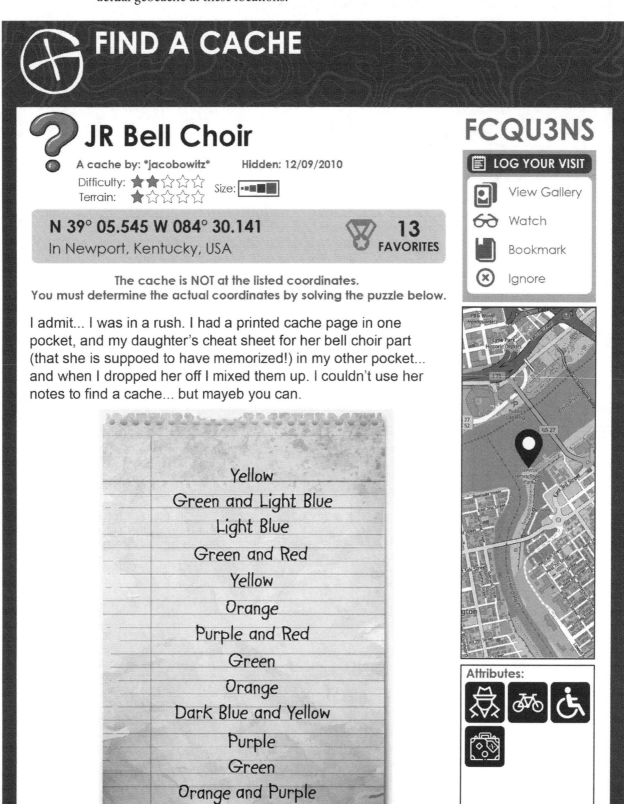

1 **You know what to do.** By this point you know where to start with the cache page, right? Nothing of note in the name, date, or at the dummy coords. No hidden text. No Related Web Pages. Nothing exciting in the gallery, no TBs in the inventory. The attributes look reasonable, probably nothing there.

2 **Describe it to me.** Short description, a cute story about the CO's daughter. He mentions bells, which are also in the title, so I'm guessing that's going to be a possible key. The biggest chunk of the description is taken up by the notebook paper image, and he practically tells us in the description that we should be able to use it to find a cache. So, I'm going to focus my attention there for a bit.

3 **Color my world.** Hmmm. Well, the list is described as being his daughter's "cheat sheet for bell choir," but it looks like a list of colors to me. Eighteen different colors on the list, but some of them are arranged in pairs. If I count that as one, and not two different colors, then there are thirteen items on the list repetitions of the same seven colors. Doesn't seem like it's one of the "magic numbers," but looking at the dummy coords, I see that the north minutes start with 05. If the CO skipped the leading zero there, then it would take thirteen digits to write the local coords, not the fourteen I'd expect. So it's possible that each color or color pair, represents one digit of the coords. There are eight different colors in the list. I'm left with two questions: What do colors have to do with bells, and what do either have to do with numbers?

4 **For whom the bell tolls.** Answering those questions will take some research. Turning to google I try "color bells." The first few results are about colored jingle bell decorations. The image search is just a bunch of coloring book pages of Christmas bells. I try "junior bells" since that's what the title says. No help there either. Most of the returns are about the bell schedules at junior high schools. I need a way to get past the coloring book pages. For that I can use a search modifier. On the image search page, I put "color bells" just as before, but I follow it up with "-coloring." This tells Google to leave out searches that include the word coloring, so it should filter out the coloring books. I click "Enter" and see that, yes, all the coloring book pages are gone. Now I have a bunch of images of multi-colored jingle bells, but also a few of multicolored hand bells. Those bells also look like the same eight colors that are on the list, a sort of rainbow arrangement from red to dark blue.

5 **Colored bells.** One last search. Staying in the images, I try "colored hand bells" to see if I can clear out the chaff of the jingle bells. It works, and I'm rewarded, not just with a bunch of bell images, but a chart that tells me what color represents which musical note! Red is a 'C,' orange is a 'D,' etc. Right beside that chart is another chart that also has numbers on it. That red 'C' is labeled '1' on this chart, and the orange 'D' is labeled 2. So I'm left with red=C=1, orange =D=2, yellow=E=3, green=F=4, light blue=G=5, dark blue=A=6, and purple=B=7. Now I have colors directly related to numbers, and I feel like I have somewhere to go with this puzzle. I love these moments.

6 **Colored numbers.** I start comparing the numbers to the list. The first color listed is yellow, which I now know equals 3. The local coords start with 39, so I think I'm good to go. The next number in the local coords is 9 though, and there was no 9 on my chart; it stopped at 7. Looking at the list I see that the next thing listed is "green and light blue," one of the items with two colors. Green is 4 and light blue is 5 according to my chart. Added together that gives us the 9 we need. I think this is it!

7 **The answer.** The next bell is also light blue, another 5. So, it looks like I was right and the CO skipped the zero in the coords. Going down the list I get 3, 9, 5, 5, 3, 2, 8, 4, 2, 9, 7, 4, and 9. Or 39° 05.532, -84° 29.749. A solid set of coords!

The puzzle on the next page is for you to solve. Remember what we've covered so far, and apply it to that puzzle.

# Solve It Yourself!

Here are some puzzle caches for you to solve on your own. Using the skills we learned in this chapter you should be able to solve these puzzles. Take careful note of the final coordinates that you get as a solution to these puzzles, and write them at the bottom of the page. If you need a reminder of how to use the puzzle stats or hints provided, please check page 11. Good luck!

Puzzle 1 Solution:

N __ __ ° __ __ . __ __ __ , W __ __ __ ° __ __ . __ __ __

As a secondary check you should be able to answer this question: *What instrument do you find at the final?*

Puzzle 2 Solution:

N __ __ ° __ __ . __ __ __ , W __ __ __ ° __ __ . __ __ __

As a secondary check you should be able to answer this question: *What instrument do you find at the final?*

FIND A CACHE

 ## GA's Music Legacy

A cache by: EssCubed   Hidden: 04/11/2011

Difficulty:    Size:
Terrain:

FCFUNSD

N 33° 29.786 W 084° 27.232
In Kenwood, Georgia, USA

🏅 **14 FAVORITES**

The cache is NOT at the listed coordinates.
You must determine the actual coordinates by solving the puzzle below.

Northern Georgia is one of the secret homes of music. Nashville, New Orleans, Portland, St. Louis, New York, Detroit... these places might get all the attention but Georgia has given us the Allman Brothers, The B-52s, REM, The Blacke Crowes, Drivin N Cryin, The Indigo Girls, John Mayer, Little Richard and dozens of others.

I'm definitely NOT a great musician or composer, but I've placed this cache in honor of those great bands and musicians. You'll need ywo solve methods to get the coords out of these two pieces of "music."

Attributes:

PUZZLE STATS
52 CHECKSUM   🧗 BEST VIEW

☝ 148   👢 123   🥊 74
💣 39   ☁ 86

FIND A CACHE

The Hills Are Alive

FCKAT13

A cache by: PatronServices   Hidden: 04/24/2014

Difficulty: ★★☆☆☆   Size: ▪▪■□□
Terrain: ★☆☆☆☆

N 46° 07.325 W 060° 12.759
In Sydney, Nova Scotia, Canada

34 FAVORITES

The cache is NOT at the listed coordinates.
You must determine the actual coordinates by solving the puzzle below.

 +

 **+**

    **+**

    **+**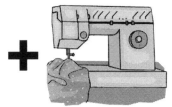

Add your solution to the following:
N 46° 0_ . _ _ _ W 60° 1_ . _ _ _

Attributes:

PUZZLE STATS
67 CHECKSUM 📷 BEST VIEW

👆 **75**   👢 **56**   🥊 **129**

💣 **30**   💥 **119**

Lateral Thinking

In 1967, a physician named Charles de Bono wrote a book called *The Use of Lateral Thinking*. In it he described the difference between what he called "vertical thinking," which is the step by step process of logical thinking: finding a predetermined order of tasks or steps that will lead to an answer (like solving an algebraic equation), and "horizontal thinking," which is imagination based, like brainstorming, and as a process is unconcerned with outcomes, implementation or answers. He suggested a third way of thinking that he called "lateral thinking." Lateral thinking rejects both the scattershot approach and the systematic approach in favor of creative thinking and unorthodox solutions.

I often describe lateral thinking puzzles as having solutions that you can only see out of the corner of your eye. These are the kind of puzzles that you solve while standing in the shower or cooking dinner and thinking of other things entirely. You have a momentary snap and the puzzle just falls into place... solved.

This chapter hopes to give you some lateral thinking tools to help you tackle these puzzle types when you run across them.

utside The Box

We've heard the phrase "think outside the box" so frequently at this point that it has lost meaning... but that's what lateral thinking is all about. So, what the heck does it mean?

Lateral thinking, or outside the box thinking, asks you to approach a problem in ways that don't seem obvious or even orthodox at first. The name comes from the classic puzzle of the nine dots that you are asked to connect using only four lines. The standard thinking would lead you to trying to attempt this by drawing a box. The puzzle, however, can only be solved if you expand your lines *outside* the box.

As cachers we use lateral thinking all the time. Think about following your GPS into the forest until it tells you that you've arrived at a cache. You find yourself arriving at tree, with a small pile of twigs on one side. The first thing you'd probably do is move that pile of twigs aside to see if there was a cache underneath. That's the "inside" the box thinking. If you don't find a cache, what do you do? This is where your lateral thinking skills start to kick in.

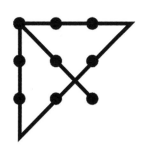

If you step a little bit outside the box, you might check the other side of the tree, look at nearby trees, look for rocks nearby, look for knotholes or hollows... all of these are starting to move away from what the average person might do.

If you still can't find the cache, and you are determined, some TRUE lateral thinking will start to unfold... You'll check for hanging caches, hollowed out twigs with micros inside, boxes with a lid disguised to look like the ground cover, micros disguised to look like tree bark, acorns or pine cones... the kinds of things that the average person, especially non-geocachers, sent to look for something hidden in the woods might never think of.

Your Thinking Cap

Thinking laterally is something you have to train yourself to do, and sometimes it isn't easy. Let's examine some classic lateral thinking puzzles so that we can see what goes into solving something like this.

Here's the first: You enter a room to find Cleopatra and Julius Caesar dead on the floor in a pool of water! Nearby is a shattered bowl... how did they die?

They may have eaten or drank something poisonous from the bowl. They may have had an extreme allergic reaction to something in the bowl. They may have spilled the water, slipped in it and broken their necks... but with no other evidence, it would be difficult to narrow it down to a specific cause, but with lateral thinking we *can* arrive at a definitive answer.

Lateral thinking puzzles take advantage of the fact that our brains tend to go in linear ways first. When presented with this scenario you are probably imaging a beautiful woman in a headdress, and a man in a toga with a laurel wreath, correct? That's the assumption that is preventing you from seeing the definitive solution.

If the solution isn't about the dead bodies, what other information are we given to solve the mystery? Other than their names and the fact that we are dead, the only other information in the scenario is the bowl and the water. Can that get us anywhere?

Think... water... bowl... water... bowl... water... bowl... at some point you have to ask yourself questions about these two items. Why is the water on the floor? Was the water in the bowl originally? What kind of bowl is it? Hopefully you'd eventually get to the point of thinking about a fishbowl, and then maybe you'd realize... they aren't people. Cleopatra and Caesar are... goldfish!

See what I mean about only being able to see the solution out of the corner of your eye? Your association with the two names as being the names of people clouded your perception and led you to assume that we were talking about the historical figures in this story, and so you tried to associate the other details with things that humans would use.

Let's look at another one... You find yourself outside a large concrete bunker with no windows or any other way to see inside. With the door closed, it is completely light proof. You are told that there are three old-fashioned light bulbs on the ceiling inside. There are three unlabeled switches on the wall outside the door. Can you determine which switch operates which bulb if you are only allowed to enter the bunker once?

Again, this puzzle plays off your assumptions about what light bulbs are, and what they can do. If you enter this puzzle thinking that the only possible way to determine whether or not a light bulb has been working is a visual examination of whether or not the bulb is emitting light, then you won't be able to come to a solution. The puzzle writer plays up those assumptions by stressing how light-proof the bunker is, and the fact that there are no windows or other ways to see inside. The key to the solution would be to determine what other qualities light bulbs have that show they've been lit. I'll leave it there for you to figure out. (There's a solution in ROT-13 at the end of the chapter.)

earning Lateral

How do you learn to think laterally? As we've seen, it's really just an exercise in relaxing assumptions. Focusing on the way you normally approach problems will probably leave you in the dark, especially if the puzzle creator has intentionally written the puzzle to exploit the typical way of thinking, or the typical assumptions, as the writer of the Cleopatra and Caesar puzzle we looked at earlier did.

A writer named Mike Michalko took an idea from a researcher named Bob Earle and created a mnemonic to help you think laterally. He called it "SCAMPER." The letters of the word are an acrostic from the first letters of Substitute, Combine, Adapt, Modify, Purpose, Eliminate, and Rearrange. Each of these provides a new way of thinking about a problem. This technique was written to use in business situations, but with some slight rethinking, we can use the same mnemonic to help us with puzzle solving.

Substitute. The classic substitution process is to think about putting a seemingly random item into the place of a more common item. Think about replacing your hiking stick with... a garden rake. Does that provide you with an advantage that a standard hiking stick wouldn't give you? In terms of a puzzle you can look for things that you can substitute, or that have already been substituted. Has something on the page been substituted for numbers? Can you substitute numbers or letters for something on the page?

Combine. Think about ways of combining puzzles or techniques to come up with a new solution. Imagine a simple word search puzzle that leaves you with a random selection of letters left in the puzzle. What can you do with those? Can you combine the idea of a word search with... a Caesar shift? A substitution cipher? Some other type of puzzle? Combining puzzle processes like scytales and Braille, or musical notes and alternate numerical bases?

Adapt. Can you adapt your way of thinking about a particular puzzle type to work with another puzzle? Do you have a systematic approach to working cipher puzzles, but fall flat on math puzzles? Can you adapt your cipher approach to tackle math?

Modify. Can you modify your typical process to make a new connection? If you have a working method for solving a Sudoku, but it isn't working, can you modify that process in some way to make headway? If you always focus on finding the 9's first, perhaps shift and focus on the 1's. Or relax your assumptions entirely. Just because it LOOKS like a Sudoku, doesn't mean that it is.

Purpose. Everything in a puzzle should have a purpose, even if that purpose is to distract you. As with the Cleopatra puzzle, the key was finding the purpose of the bowl and the water. Look for the purpose of each element. Is there an element in the puzzle that might be used in a different way? If the puzzle is full of numbers, can it actually be about the enclosed spaces within the shape of those numbers rather than the value of the numbers?

Eliminate. Can you easily eliminate part of the puzzle as irrelevant? Can you eliminate part of the normal process?

Rearrange. What if you reverse your normal order of solving a problem? What if you rearrange the order of the elements of the puzzle?

"SCAMPER" is not a hard and fast method, (that would be vertical thinking!) but if you can start looking at problems from new and unusual perspectives it may provide some answers to puzzles that have been bugging you for years.

Because there are a great variety of lateral thinking puzzles there is no real way to show you all the ways it can be used, but let's do a few so you can get a taste of this puzzling style.

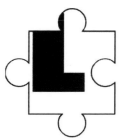ateral Puzzles

What would a lateral thinking geo-puzzle look like? Unlike crossover puzzles, ciphers, or even codes, lateral thinking puzzles could look like pretty much anything, which is what makes them so frustrating for some people. I'll present you with some examples, but keep in mind that these are really only the tip of the tip of the iceberg!

Let's start with "The Green Glass Door." This one's based on a semi-famous campfire game, so you might be familiar with it, but I've given it a geocaching twist.

Behind the Green Glass Door

It's true that behind the green glass door you'll find oodles, but not a lot. In order to find the cache, look at the following statements and find the ones that truly describe items you might find behind the green glass door.

Behind the green glass door you'll find carrots but no rabbits: N 42° 37.584'
Behind the green glass door you'll find cats but no kittens: N 42° 37.228'
Behind the green glass door you'll find a pool but no water: N 42° 37.424'
Behind the green glass door you'll find bananas but no apples: W 73° 32.093'
Behind the green glass door you'll find puppies but no dogs: W 73° 31.898'
Behind the green glass door you'll find wool but no looms: W 73° 31.506'

What do we have here? Six statements, each of which gives us half of a coord, but only the true statements give us the true coords. So, how do we determine which statements are true? Like most lateral thinking puzzles there doesn't seem to be a lot to go on at first. It could have something to do with animals, I suppose, but three statements mention animals, so that can't be it. We associate colors with some of the items orange carrots, yellows bananas, red apples, but one statement puts a banana in and an apple out... so if it's color how do we determine the right colors? That doesn't seem right either.

Let's go back to the initial statement. The puzzle begins with "It's true that..." If we trust the puzzle maker (and we have to), we know that we have at least one true statement that we can examine: that behind the green glass door we'd find oodles, but not a lot. Those two things, "oodles" and "a lot," mean basically the same thing, so it can't really be about definitions. How can we differentiate the two?

It might take some thought, but eventually we figure out that "oodles" has a double 'O,' but "a lot" has no double letters. Oh! And hey, look at that, all the words in "Green Glass Door" have double letters! I bet that's it!

If we examine the statements, we can see that both carrots and rabbits have a double letter, making that statement false. The next one, cats and kittens, puts the word with the double letter outside the green glass door, so it is also false. But a pool has double letters, and water doesn't, so that one's true! Our north coords are 42° 37.424'. Can you determine the west coords on your own?

Roll Up!

I call this next puzzle "Tumbling Dice" just because of the appearance of the puzzle pieces. The technical name for this type of lateral thinking puzzle is a "Bongard Problem," after a Soviet computer scientist of the 60's. Bongard problems set a simple challenge: the first player (in this case the CO) sets a rule, and then shows us a series of items that fit the rule, and a series of items that do not fit the rule. Then we're presented with a new set and asked if the items in that set fit the rule or not.

Examine the "dice" to the left. The first row of dice follow a certain rule, the second row does not. Below that are four other sets of dice. The row containing dice that also follow the rule will provide you with the seconds for a set of coordinates. Can you determine which?

We'll need to start with the examples to see if we can determine the rule. We can see right away that they don't look like normal dice; the pips are not in regular patterns. It isn't about the even or odd number of pips; both the 'Yes' and 'No' group contain both. It isn't about primes; the 'Yes' group contains dice with both prime and non-prime numbers of pips. It isn't a sequence, or a famous number. The pips aren't in any sort of alignment, either vertical or horizontal, and they aren't symmetrical...

So, what else can we look at? Lateral thinking is your friend here... if counting and the numbers aren't working, we have to figure out what other purposes we can apply a bunch of dots to? What is your impulse when given a series of dots? Mine is to try and connect them. Let's see if that gets us anywhere.

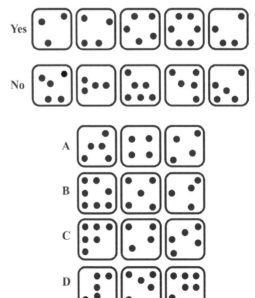

If you start drawing lines to connect the dots on each die, you might not see anything at first, depending on how you go about connecting them. But eventually you might notice that all the dots in the 'Yes' group dice form polygonal shapes when you connect them, and specifically, they form convex polygons, meaning that all of the interior angles are less than 180°. The dots in the 'No' group might form polygons, but they are not convex polygons, they are *concave* polygons.

If you know that the number of pips on the die are the number you need,

274

can you determine, using our newly discovered rule, which line gives you the coordinates?

This is just one of many ways that a Bongard problem could be presented. Keep an eye out for two sets of things being compared, or rules that you are being asked to discover or satisfy.

One on One

Here's another classic puzzle lateral thinking puzzle that at first glance would appear to be a numerical or math puzzle. Can you determine the next number in this sequence?

1, 11, 21, 1211, 111221, 312211...

Everything you need to solve this riddle can be found in the numbers you see. But be warned: The mathematically inclined tend to struggle with this puzzle.

The first assumption when presented with something like this might be that there is a mathematical sequence. For instance with the sequence 2, 3, 6, 18, 108... we would eventually determine that the next number is 1,944. Each number in the sequence is found by multiplying the two preceding numbers. However, the warning should be enough of a hint to let you know that the answer isn't to be found in math.

If it isn't mathematical, how else would you find the next number? It could have to do with how the words are spelled, for instance the sequence 1, 3, 5, 4 would follow the rule that each number is the number of letters in the number before: three letters in the word "one," five letters in the word "three," etc. It could be how many strokes it takes to write the previous number. It could be how many consonants are in the previous number. There are many possibilities.

In this case the answer comes from counting and reading aloud. If you count the objects (the numbers) you might say that the first number has "one one." If you wrote that down it might look like this: 11. Saying that aloud you'd say "two ones." Written as 21. The next is "one two one one." Got it? Lateral thinking is tricky! This is called a "look-and-say sequence" and actually has quite a history in mathematics.

Final Thoughts

There's no one way to do lateral thinking puzzles, and in some ways, every geo-puzzle is a lateral thinking puzzle. The big take away here is... *relax your assumptions.* Don't get caught up in a specific way of looking at the puzzle just because you think it's the *only* way to look at the puzzle. Find new ways to look at what you are facing, ignore the obvious, if you must, and pay attention to the finer details which may provide the keys to the puzzle.

Oh... about that lightbulb...

As promised, here is the solution to the lightbulb puzzle, encoded is ROT-13.

Ghea ba gur svefg fjvgpu sbe n zvahgr, gura fjvgpu vg bss. Gura fjvgpu ba ahzore gjb. Tb vafvqr. Gur yvtug gung vf ba vf pbaarpgrq gb fjvgpu gjb. Gur yvtug gung vf bss naq jnez vf pbaarpgrq gb fjvgpu bar. Gur yvtug gung vf bss naq pbyq vf pbaarpgrq gb fjvgpu guerr!

Solving it
Bringing together what you've learned.

Use this checklist to help you apply what you've learned in this chapter, remembering that lateral thinking puzzles cover a wide variety of puzzle types and possibilities.

Checklist: LATERAL THINKING

- ☐ Look for words that may have double meanings or that might be leading you to false assumptions about their meaning.

- ☐ Look for non-traditional applications of traditional puzzle techniques.

- ☐ Try applying the SCAMPER technique to the problem it may give you alternate venues.

- ☐ Examine the puzzle for patterns or repeated concepts that might provide a key.

alk-Through

There are hundreds of variations on the way that lateral thinking puzzles can be presented, but here's one example of a puzzle that uses the techniques we've covered in this chapter. At right is a walk-through of how I'd go about solving this puzzle, so that you can see the techniques at work. Remember, there is no actual geocache at these locations.

FIND A CACHE

... not like the others ...

FCR5VP1

A cache by: Beaux Regards   Hidden: 08/09/2009

Difficulty:
Terrain: Size:

N 43° 02.481 W 087° 59.331
In Milwaukee, Wisconsin, USA

54 FAVORITES

LOG YOUR VISIT

View Gallery
Watch
Bookmark
Ignore

The cache is NOT at the listed coordinates.
You must determine the actual coordinates by solving the puzzle below.

All of the numbers in the left hand column follow a rule. The numbers in the right do not.

YES	NO
84	16
639	38
1785	233
36	9,074
128	19
12,345	20

One of these numbers follows the same rule and will be the missing portion of the north coords: 43 02.XXX:

942   597   986

One of these numbers does NOT follow the same rule and will be the missing portion of the west coords: 87 58.XXX:

33   248   580

Attributes:

1 **Preflight check-list.** As with all puzzles I start with the basics. The date and user name look good, no hidden white text. No related Web Pages. No text hidden in the source code. Nothing exciting in the gallery, no TBs in the inventory. The attributes look reasonable, probably nothing there. There's nothing really interesting at the dummy coords.

2 **The ABCs.** Well, the description seems to lay out exactly where and what the puzzle is, so that's refreshing, no big hunt to figure it all out. Looks like a basic lateral thinking problem. We just have to examine the two series of numbers and figure out what the left column has in common that the right column doesn't share. Hmmm...

3 **Commonalities.** Both lists contain both odds and evens. The numbers on both sides have different shapes, so it isn't about round shapes vs. straight lines. They numbers vary in length, so it isn't about the number of digits or about a middle number. Let's look at spelling... all fifteen of the basic letters needed to write all the numbers 1 to 9 appear in both columns. Though looking at that does make me realize that there are no 5s in the right column. Could it be that simple? That would mean that the north coord would end in 597, but I'm looking for the number that doesn't belong in order to get the west, and I have two numbers in that group that have no 5s... so that can't be it. There must be another way to differentiate.

4 **Primes the pump.** Maybe it has to do with the type of numbers that these are. There are no primes in the left column. 19 and 233 from the right column are prime, but none of the others are. Well... if none of the numbers are prime, that means that they will have factors. The prime factorization of 84 is 2x2x3x7, so four prime factors. The complete list of divisors 1, 2, 3, 4, 6, 7, 12, 14, 21, 28, 42, 84. Looking at 639 the prime factorization is 3x3x71. That's three prime factors, so it isn't about the number of prime factors. The complete list of divisors is 1, 3, 9, 71, 213, 639. The two lists share the divisors 1 and 3. Might be something, but that seems so common that I doubt it's the answer. 1785 is the next on the list it has prime factors of 3x5x7x17. And the a complete list of divisors is 1, 3, 5, 7, 15, 17, 21, 35, 51, 85, 105, 119, 255, 357, 595, 1785. 1 and 3 appear again. Let's try the "No" list against this rule, just to check. Well, none of them have 3 as a divisor. But two of the possible answers from the possible west coords also share that trait, so that can't be it. That list of factors is interesting though. 84's list of divisors include 4, but not 8. The list for 639 includes 3 and 9 but not 6. 1785 includes 1, 7 and 5, but not 8. So the list of divisors include all the digits of the original number but one? Scanning the list I see 128... 128 probably won't fit that rule. I check, and surely enough the list of divisors is 1, 2, 4, 8, 16, 32, 64, 128. So, 1, 2, and 8 are all there, so there is no individual digit of the original number missing from the list of divisors. Is it about the position of those digits? The first digit isn't always a divisor, but the last digit is. So far at least. In other words the number is evenly divisible by its own last digit. A quick check of the "Yes" list shows that they all fit that criteria, and the numbers on the "No" list do not.

5 **Checking answers.** This rule checks out so far. Let's check the possible finals. In the north list, only 942 fulfills the requirement. So far so good. In the list of possible wests, 333 certainly fits, and 248, but 580 does not! I think we have it!

6 **The answer.** Putting our answers into the blanks gives us 43° 02.942, -87° 58.580, a nice set of coords.

Ready to try a puzzle on your own? There's one waiting for you on the next page. Remember what we've covered so far, and apply it to that puzzle.

olve It Yourself!

Here are some puzzle caches for you to solve on your own. Using the skills we learned in this chapter you should be able to solve these puzzles. Take careful note of the final coordinates that you get as a solution to these puzzles, and write them at the bottom of the page. If you need a reminder of how to use the puzzle stats or hints provided, please check page 11. Good luck!

Puzzle 1 Solution:

N __ __ ° __ __ . __ __ __ , W __ __ __ ° __ __ . __ __ __

As a secondary check you should be able to answer this question: *What animal do you find at the final?*

Puzzle 2 Solution:

N __ __ ° __ __ . __ __ __ , W __ __ __ ° __ __ . __ __ __

As a secondary check you should be able to answer this question: *What quote do you find at the final?*

FIND A CACHE

 # Debugging the system

FCR5VP1

A cache by: UnderBread   Hidden: 08/29/2003

Difficulty:
Terrain: Size: ▪▪▫▪▫

N 38° 42.693 W 104° 49.590
In Colorado Springs, Colorado, USA

101 FAVORITES

The cache is NOT at the listed coordinates.
You must determine the actual coordinates by solving the puzzle below.

2 ABOVEGROUND 2
2 ABUSIVELY 2
1 FAVOR 1
1 BOUGANVILLIAS 1
5 HOUSEBOY 5
5 BIVOUACKING 5
5 GAMBLED 5
4 ABUSING 4
9 CONTRIBUTING 9
9 BEAM 9
6 MARBLE 6
7 GRUB 7
4 MUMBLING 4
8 PLUMBING 8
4 PUBLIC 4
2 SNUFFBOX 2

Attributes:

PUZZLE STATS

58 CHECKSUM   BEST VIEW

28   108   146
67   112

FIND A CACHE

Measuring Monoliths

A cache by: Goth4mGir7 **Hidden:** 10/29/2013

Difficulty: ★★★☆☆ Size:
Terrain: ★☆☆☆☆

N 36° 50.845 W 076° 16.640
In Norfolk, VA, USA

21 FAVORITES

FCCL4RK

The cache is NOT at the listed coordinates.
You must determine the actual coordinates by solving the puzzle below.

Using the information provided here can you determine the missing measurement of the monolith? Once you have a number the following equations will provide you with coords:

(Half the height of the monument) - 345 = XXX

(The height of the monument divided by 4) + 110 = YYY

N 36 50.XXX
W 76 16.YYY

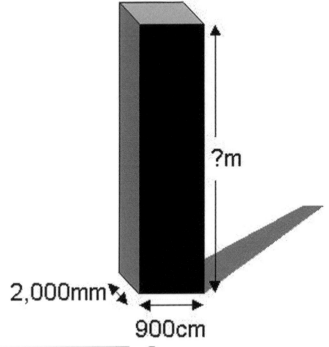

?m

2,000mm

900cm

Attributes:

PUZZLE STATS

67 CHECKSUM 📷 BEST VIEW

 52  **49**   **90**

 69   **97**

Last Resorts

You've tried it all, and nothing has worked. Now what?

You can simply ignore it, of course. *Geocaching.com* even gives you a handy way to turn a cache off so that it doesn't appear on your map. Some people just can't let that go, though. Especially if that unsolved puzzle just happens to be your nearest unfound cache to home, or a combo that you need for a Challenge cache, or if you just can't stand to leave a log unsigned. Short of cheating and getting the coords from a past finder, is there anything you can do? Well... yeah. Of course there is!

I apologize to any COs in advance, but this chapter covers methods that finders can employ as a last resort to try and find a way into the puzzle, or to find the cache itself. They probably won't be what the CO intended, but they just might work.

Be warned, however. Some COs sincerely frown upon logging a puzzle cache if you haven't actually solved the puzzle. Some will even go so far as to delete your log if they feel that you haven't satisfactorily completed all the steps and requirements of the cache. Use the methods I describe here at your own risk. If you DO choose to take any of these routes, I advise against bragging about it in your logs, or in fact, mentioning it at all. Don't try and make up a story about the hours it took you to solve. COs know what it takes to solve their puzzles and can easily spot something that's off. Short and sweet is the way to handle these logs.

Old Dogs

There it sits... unsolved... unfound... and driving you crazy. So, what to do? First, I would encourage you to email the CO. Most COs (and I will admit this doesn't extend to all of them) put out puzzle caches to be found. What is the point of having something out in the world with no one looking for it? COs generally won't give out extra hints unless the FTF (first to find) has already gone out, but as long as that has happened, take the chance and drop them a line, or approach them at an event. What have you got to lose? COs know their own puzzles and should be able to give you as big or as subtle a hint as you want.

failing up

Some cachers, inexplicably, find contacting the CO to be a failure on par with a DNF. This isn't a useful attitude. COs know their puzzles better than anyone and are happy to help you find them.

If you do contact a CO, please take a moment to tell them which puzzle you are asking about. Geocaching.com provides us several ways to contact each other, but some have features that others don't. If you use the "Send Message" or "Send e-mail" button from the COs profile, there is no information attached to the email that COs receive other than the name of the cacher who sent the email. If, however, you click the envelope on the cache page that says "Message This Owner," your message will automatically contain the information on which cache you were looking at when you decided to contact them.

Take a few lines to tell the CO what you have tried. You may have gotten close, or you may be a million miles away, but the CO has no way of knowing unless you sketch out what you've done. For instance, if you think that the puzzle has something to do with Braille but you don't tell the CO that, you might get a hint that nudges toward Braille when you are already past that point! It just leaves both you and the CO frustrated.

You may also indicate what kind of hint you want. A hint can be subtle and sly, but a hint can also be a 2x4 to the side of the head. If you just wanted a subtle nudge and the CO gives you forceful shove (or vice versa), you might come away disappointed.

But let's say that the CO fails you... or is a giant ogre that you are afraid to approach. What then? We've already talked about a few things, most notably the application of the "2 Mile Rule" and the "528 Feet Rule." Here is a map of the historic district of Newberry, SC. Imagine a puzzle that tells you in the description that the final can be found in the park near the old Opera House. Granted, it isn't a very large park, so it would be quite simple to search the entire park if you don't want to solve the puzzle, but if you look at the cache map, you'll notice that there is a cache at the corner of Caldwell and Friend Streets. If you draw a circle around the coordinates of that cache, (using Google Earth, GSAK, or any of several websites that will create the rings for you) with a radius of 528 feet, you'll create what is known as a "prox-

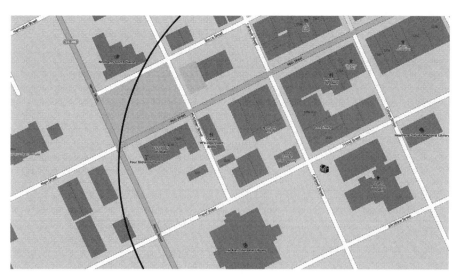

imity ring" or a "prox ring." Due to *geocaching.com's* guidelines, no other cache can fall inside that circle. I've drawn a portion of that circle on our map here, and you'll see that more than two-thirds of the park in question falls inside the prox ring of that other cache. That considerably cuts down the amount of the park that the puzzle final can reside in!

It won't always be that easy, of course. With a large park, or if there are only a few caches in an area, you wouldn't be able to use this to narrow down the area quite so much. But it might help, especially if you live in a cache rich area.

The 2 Mile Rule works in a similar way. Finals are usually within 2 miles of the initial dummy coords. If the description tells you that the cache is near water, and there is only one lake within the 2 mile radius of the dummy coords, that gives you a big clue. Or if the puzzle is themed around US Presidents and there happens to be "James Monroe Park" within the 2 Mile radius, well... I might have a look around there.

Other guidelines can also come into play. For instance, the rules at *geocaching.com* prevent cache placement inside National Parks, within 150 feet of railroad tracks, or close to schools. There are also local prohibitions to consider. The state of South Carolina has outlawed caches inside cemeteries. Other states have outlawed caches in state parks, or on state land. So, if you live in a state that has forbidden certain placements you can safely ignore those areas if they fall inside your prox rings.

Keep in mind that particularly old puzzles may have been placed before the 2 Mile Rule, and so may not be helped by this method, and that reviewers have leeway to loosen the restriction if they feel it is warranted. Also, reviewers make mistakes, and sometimes the 528 foot rule gets overlooked, especially on puzzle stages. I've found many puzzle finals that were "too close" to traditionals. Caches that get moved after placement also don't get resubmitted for review unless it moves more than 100 feet, so if it was close to the line of the prox ring, it could possibly move inside without setting off any alarm bells at the reviewer level.

Falling Off A Log

The next place to check is the logs of the previous finders. Everybody knows that when you are out on the trail and you need a little extra information, the logs are the easiest place to turn. There you might find reference to a distinct feature you need to search or reference to the size or type of container. But looking at logs can also be useful for solving puzzles before you even get to the trail.

First, and I've never really understood this impulse, a lot of finders feel the need to drop hints to the puzzle in their logs. Cache finders are often less adept at hinting than puzzle COs, so the hints will sometimes be clunky, for lack of a better word, and therefore, easier to crack. Consider the left side of this image, which seems to show just a series of lines and circles. If you were to find that on a cache page with no further hint, it might be pretty impossible to determine what the CO meant for you to do. Looking at the logs, you see that a couple finders mention something along the lines of "I was lost but then I decided to PAF (phone a friend) and realized I already had the answer." Multiple logs that mention calling someone or looking at a phone? Maybe the puzzle has something to do with phones? We can quickly see that if we lay the shapes onto a phone pad, we get an answer. The solid line lands on these numbers in order: 4400213, or 44° 00.213! The dotted line will give you the west coord.

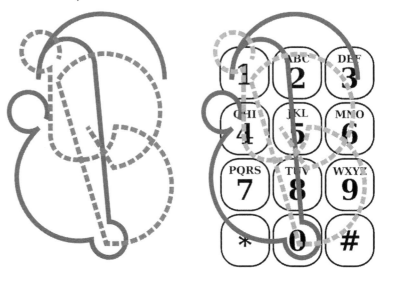

Finders will also sometimes write their logs in a ci-

ring around the rosy
See Appendix 2 for some websites and other tools that will help you create maps with proximity rings.

brute force
Finding a puzzle cache without solving the puzzle is often referred to as "brute forcing" the cache because it usually takes more effort than actually solving the puzzle! This is the reason that most geocheckers limit the number of attempts you can make within a certain period of time.

pher used in the puzzle. This is helpful because it gives you a larger sampling of the cipher to work with, which could show you something quirky about the cipher that the CO didn't exhibit, making it easier to determine which cipher is being used. For instance, a CO might carefully craft a cipher to exhibit a lot of repetitions of the letters A, D, F, G & X. This might lead a solver to decide that the puzzle was written in the ADFGX cipher. However, it might be something else entirely, and the CO intended the ADFGX as a red herring. If the finder uses the correct cipher in their log, they won't be as careful to make the red herring as prominent, giving future finders a potential clue.

Gallery Visit

Another "on the trail" trick that works when desperately trying to solve a puzzle is looking at the gallery. It's doubtful that it will give you much information about the puzzle itself, but if finders have taken photos in the proximity of the cache, you might be able to pick out a detail or a landmark in the photo that will lead you to the cache location. I know of at least one instance in my local caching community where a particularly difficult local puzzle got cracked because a finder put up a photo showing an easily identifiable sculpture in the background. If you are familiar with the area, and particularly familiar with the 2 Mile proximity ring around the dummy coords, you never know what you might be able to spot in the gallery images. Buildings, sculptures, business names, or even road signs might be visible in the gallery, and give you clues to the final location.

As we noted in the chapter on EXIF data photos can also contain GPS coordinates, and if a finder fails to remove those before uploading their photos... all the more reason to examine those gallery, photos!

Get Social

Geocaching is often a solitary pursuit, and cachers often take pride in finding things on their own, but puzzle caches in particular are often easier with more than one set of eyes on them. You might be the best lateral thinker on the block, but you might not know anything about math. Maybe you need a puzzle solving partner that can handle the math puzzles? Teaming up with another cacher gives you the opportunity to bounce ideas off each other, and it doubles the esoteric knowledge available to you. Trust me, finding that elusive partner who can recognize Aztec numerals, sight read short-hand, and decipher Morse code by ear is a miracle! Hopefully, you bring your own skills to the table, and between the two of you, smilies will roll in!

Also, try showing the cache to other people. Kids or people from a different generation than you, may be able to see something that is outside your knowledge base. Even show it to non-geocachers! You never know what knowledge

might be the key, and a co-worker or a friend might see something you've been missing. Plus, you might convert a muggle. New eyes have new perspectives and new information.

Many events also have small groups of cachers discussing the local puzzles and giving out hints and nudges, so don't hesitate to go to events and ask around. There might be previous finders in the crowd who can give you just the right piece of advice, especially if you have some info on another cache to "trade."

If you're competitive and just can't fathom the idea of giving up all your best ideas to someone local, you can also try social media. There are several Facebook groups dedicated to geocache puzzle solving, some of which have strict "help only" rules, where others will simply spoil the answers for you, so it's up to you to pick your poison on which you prefer. Personally I'd rather honor the intentions of the CO and solve it myself, albeit with a little help, than just have an answer given to me.

ew Tricks

If you are a first-to-find hound, you probably already have *geocaching.com* set up to send you notifications of new caches. You might even have them set to go to your phone in the form of text messages so that you never run the risk of missing out on that FTF. As a puzzle cacher, you should add a few new steps to your FTF routine.

First, get in the habit of watchlisting the page. Brand new puzzles, despite the best intentions of the CO, often have mistakes. It may be a problem with the puzzle itself, or it may be a problem in the description. If you look at the first few logs on a puzzle cache, you'll often see notes from the CO acknowledging an error, changing an image, or noting that they've added a new hint. Unless you have the page on a watchlist, you'll have to refresh the page in order to see that these changes have been made. (You still may not see it if the CO is sneaky and doesn't publicly acknowledge the change.)

Second, get into the habit of saving the page. When you visit a webpage, you can right click on the page (or go to the "File" menu in the upper menu bar) and choose "Save Page As." This allows you to save the HTML file to your computer. You can later use your browser to open the file and see the page. You can also save any image files separately. Treat the saved file just like you would any other document file, using the "Open" command in the File menu of the browser to open it for viewing. It will look just like the original cache page, but will not be online.

How is this useful? Again, it's all about changes in the cache listing. When a CO changes something on a page to fix a problem, or to adjust a puzzle, it can often act a clue to how to solve the puzzle. By saving the page when it is first published you have a record of what the page looked like before the CO fixed his errors. Changes in the text might also highlight which aspects of the page might be important to the solution. If the puzzle is image based, having an old version of the image can also provide vital clues to how the puzzle might be structured.

tep Away from the Cache!

If you are struggling with a cache and just can't see it... put it aside.

It sounds counterintuitive, but many problems, including puzzles, are often easier to solve if you just stop thinking about them for a while. Sometimes puzzles, especially puzzles that involve a degree of lateral thinking, will just pop into your mind, partially, or even fully solved, days, weeks, or perhaps months after you stop looking at them. I've solved puzzles while cooking, in the shower, in the middle of a hiking trail, and once in a dream! Walking away allows the mind to relax, and the ideas that you've tried to sift down, to bump up against each other, to percolate, and combine in ways that you might not have expected, or even considered.

Walking away also gives you the opportunity to learn more approaches and new methods. Early on, when I first started puzzle caching, I came across a cache that stumped me. For years it was the only unsolved cache near me. I cleared my whole county -- except that cache. I had pretty much resolved that I just wouldn't solve that cache, and that was that.

Years later I was working on a completely different cache in another part of the world, and I stumbled onto a piece of information that resolved the whole puzzle in my mind. Not the puzzle that I had been working on at the time, but that old cache that I hadn't even looked at in years!

Another puzzle in my area was solved sitting in my dentist's waiting room because I saw something in the letter column of a three-year-old copy of Smithsonian Magazine. I highly doubt I would have seen this information anywhere else. (A variation of it is used as one of the example puzzles in this book!)

You just never know when, where, or how inspiration is going to strike, or what solutions it might bring with it.

Keep At It!

On the flip-side of my previous advice is this piece of advice: keep trying. The more puzzles you solve, the more you'll be able to do. Puzzle COs are forever borrowing and recycling ideas from other parts of the world and picking up classic puzzle ideas to twist and turn into something new. Exposure to puzzle ideas will help you tackle future puzzles. You'll learn to recognize different ciphers, and you'll see different ways that information can be remixed. You will also learn the methods and quirks of your local puzzle COs. Maybe you have a local who is obsessed with the codes of World War 2 and has built multiple puzzles around those. Maybe you have a local CO who is an electrical engineer and will tend towards puzzles that involve electrical mechanisms and terms or a lot of computer programming language. Recognizing those patterns will help with future hides that those COs might place. Puzzle solving ability is just like geo-sense. The more you use it, the better it becomes, and the more likely you are to be successful.

Look around your area and check the difficulty rating of some of the local puzzles. Pick some lower rated ones and start practicing! If the COs have set the difficulty correctly (and logs will let you know if they haven't), you will start to solve some of the easier puzzles your local COs have on offer. This adds to your arsenal of tricks and builds your confidence to tackle more! Just like the terrain ratings, you wouldn't tackle a 5 Star as your very first cache, right?

There are also dozens of "Puzzle Training" cache series out there, the most famous (and most frequently copied) being the one by a CO named "ePeterso2." You can find the first in that series at GCYXZ1. The original series has sadly been archived, but he maintains a web version of the puzzles. Series like this will give you extra experience, with the added benefit of also having physical caches to log!

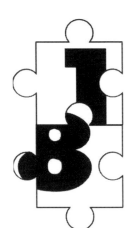

After the Solve

You've solved the puzzle.

You've done your happy dance.

Now what?

Well, if you're ready, you can get on the trail and make the find! But if you aren't... there are a few things you can do to keep track of the coords, and get yourself prepared for the next time you are out on the hunt. A few quick changes at the *geocaching.com* website or in various smartphone apps will help you keep track of your puzzles, and their solutions. This chapter shows you all those methods, plus some information on other things you can do to prepare yourself for the actual cache hunt.

eeping Track

Once you've solved the puzzles and discovered the true coordinates of the geocaches in your area, you are faced with a new challenge: finding them. If you've only solved one or two, this will be as simple as putting the coordinates into the GPS and heading out the door, but for others, those of us who solve dozens of puzzle caches at a time, it becomes a much different task. I can't tell you how many times I've solved a puzzle, hastily written the answer onto the back of an envelope or a scrap of paper on my desk, and then promptly lost the coordinates. Let's look at a few more reliable methods.

Old School

If you are an old school type who still uses pencil and paper to track your solved puzzles, there are a few tricks you can use to make that more efficient. The major one is a dedicated notebook. Unless you are a very organized person, keeping corrected puzzle coordinates on paper can get frustrating. It's hard to remember if something is solved, and when it's time to actually make the find, it can be difficult to find the correct coordinates.

One weird little trick I picked up from an experienced old school cacher was an address book. She kept (probably still keeps) all her solved puzzles in a desktop address book, alphabetized by the name of the cache. When she finds them, she crosses them out, and once or twice a year she consolidates and removes old caches, transferring what she still needs to log into a new book. It sounded like a lot of work to me, but she swore by it. Another cacher I'm aware of prints out all of their cache pages, writes the solutions on the print-outs and keeps them in three-ring binders, organized by state. Wherever he traveled, he had a binder at the ready for solved puzzles in that state.

The take-away is just this: have a system. However you choose to track your solved caches, just be consistent and build the habit of doing it the same way, every time.

At geocaching.com

Over the years, *geocaching.com* has made several changes and improvements to their system, giving us a few tools that can keep track of solved puzzles. The first, and the one that is probably the most similar to the pencil and paper method, is the bookmark list. Only premium members can create bookmarks lists, but if you have a premium membership, it is fairly simple. Your first step in creating a bookmark list is to go to your *geocaching.com* profile. At the top of that page you'll see a series of links, one of which is "LISTS." Clicking there will take you to a page where you can create a bookmark list, if you don't already own any. You can also get to this page by clicking the "Manage Bookmarks" link on the right hand navigation bar of your profile.

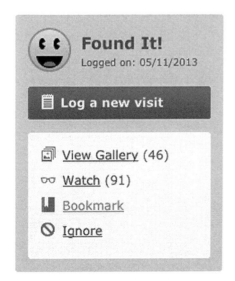

Once there, you can simply enter the name of your new bookmark list. Something like "Solved Caches" or "Solved Puzzles" works fine, and add any description you might want to apply to your list. Your bookmark list will remain private unless you click both the "I want to share this list with others" as well as "Make this list public." Once your new list is created, you can enter caches directly from the list page by entering the GC code into the box on the upper right, or you can do it from the cache pages.

On the cache pages, look in the menu on the upper right where you normally would go to log the cache and click "Bookmark." That will take you to a page where you can enter a few lines describing the cache and choose which of your bookmark lists you would like to place the cache on, if you own more than one.

Some cachers enter a little bit about how they solved the puzzle, what type of cipher was used, what the puzzle was, or any extra information that may have been revealed at the geo-checker. ONLY do this if the list is private. If the list is public, anyone will be able to access the list from the page of any puzzle that appears on it.

Your lists can contain up to 1000 caches.

Maintaining a bookmark list is in some ways very similar to maintaining a pencil and paper list. You will have to remember to remove caches that you have solved, as well as remember whether or not you have actually solved them. You may solve puzzles in another town or even on another continent, but if all you do is place them on a bookmark list, you'd have nothing outside of your own memory to remind you that you had solved them.

The second tool that *geocaching.com* provides for you is the ability to change the coordinates on a cache page. On any listing, immediately to the right of the coordinates, you will find an icon of a small pencil. Clicking on that pencil will bring up a small pop-up window that gives you a menu where you can edit those coordinates and transform them to the actual coordinates for the final, not the dummy coords of the puzzle.

In the box labeled "Change To:" you can enter your corrected coordinates. Be careful doing this. There is no check to your corrected coordinates, so if you enter a set of coordinates somewhere in the Sahara, they will be changed to somewhere in the Sahara. Be especially careful to include either the 'N' and 'W' for north and west, or to include the negative for the west if you are in the U.S. (Elsewhere you may not need this.) You can enter your coordinates in any notation system that *geocaching.com* recognizes: decimal degrees, decimal minutes, etc. The system will automatically convert them for you. Then click "Submit." The system will ask you to verify that the new coordinates are the ones you want. If you entered them in decimal degrees rather than decimal seconds, it is here that you will see the conversion happen. If the new coords look good, click "Accept."

Once the coordinates have been altered, you will see a change on the page as well. Your new coords will be underlined and italicized. The two small maps on the cache page will also now show the location of the new coords, rather than the dummy coords, and if you look at the large area map, or the map on the app the icon for the cache will have moved to the corrected coordinates as well!

If the CO has chosen to use the geochecker provided by *geocaching.com* a correct answer will automatically enter the corrected coordinates for you!

To the left are three maps. The first shows a puzzle series with no solved puzzles. The standard question mark icons for the puzzles are arranged into the geo-art of a star.

Once the corrected coordinates have been entered the question mark

Geocaching > Bookmark Lists > Create/Edit Listing

Create a Bookmark

Five Star New York

Name:

Five Star New York

For List:

Local Caches to do

Comments:

1,000 character limit; not required.

Create Bookmark

N 36° 42.684 W 107° 59.116
UTM: 13S E 233347 N 4067012
Other Conversions

N 36° 42.684 W 107° 59.116
UTM: 13S E 233347 N 4067012
Other Conversions

Corrected Coordinates (hidden from others)

Original: N 36° 42.684' W 107° 59.116'

Change To:

Submit

Print: No Logs 5 Logs 10 Logs

Download: Read about waypoint downloads

N 36° 42.789 W 107° 59.234
UTM: 13S E 233177 N 4067212
Other Conversions

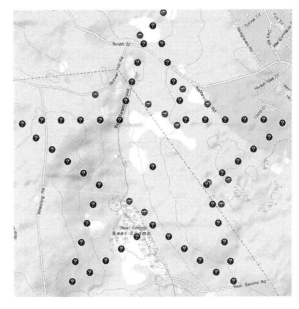

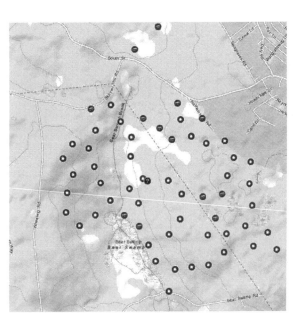

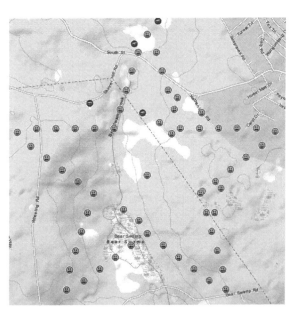

icon is replaced by a blue puzzle piece and all of the icons on the map are rearranged into their real locations, as you can see in the middle image. This makes planning a caching trip much easier, since you actually know where the caches are on the map.

Once you have logged a find on the cache the icon changes to the smiley face and goes back to its original position, at the dummy co-ords as you see in the bottom image. Only a found log makes that change. A DNF, or other log type does not.

Once you have updated the coordinates, if you want to see original coordinates or change the coords back to the original for any reason, simply click the pencil again. There you will see the original coordinates, and a small link that says "Restore" will be beside them. Clicking "Restore" will convert the coordinates back to the original dummy coords.

The most impressive thing about corrected coordinates is that they will be there in every format, whether you are printing the page, running a PQ, downloading the GPX file, or using the "send to GPS" function. They will also show up on the iPhone and Android apps.

Geocaching.com's in-house geochecker, and some third party apps and websites also have the ability to change coords for you. If the CO has used the website "Certitude" as their geochecker, and you have an account through Certitude, you can use a function there to automatically change the coordinates of any correctly solved puzzles, with little extra effort. If you enter additional waypoints on the app Cachly, it will ask if the entered apps are corrected coords. If you click yes it changes the coordinates at the website for you as well.

Finally, there is the "Cache Notes" option, which is also a premium member feature. Just below the coordinates on the cache page you'll find two boxes, a yellow box and a gray one. The yellow box is the disclaimer, but below that is a gray box that says "Personal Cache Note. Click to enter a note." Clicking this will open a pop-up that gives you a box to enter any notes that you have on the cache, which may include the corrected coordinates. Some cachers also use this as an area to keep notes on the solve method or notes on puzzle progress, if it is a complex puzzle with several steps, or a puzzle that you have not completed yet. These notes will be visible any time you visit the cache page, but are visible only to you.

This is also a very useful spot to put any extra information revealed at the geochecker. Frequently, COs will place extra hints, hide spoilers, or parking coords into the geocheck response. Certitude also automates this function and transfers any notes left by the CO directly to this area.

Placing a personal cache note does not alter the position of the icon on the map, nor does it show up in PQs or GPX files; however, several third party apps and websites use coordinates placed in the notes section as a way to track updated coordinates.

Personal Cache Note Click to enter a note

Personal Cache Note After you type your notes here they will be visible on the cache page any time you visit.

The Geocaching App

A good number of cachers these days use the official *geocaching.com* app as their primary caching tool rather than GPS units. Some of us use it as just a supplement to our GPS, a way to look up extra information in the field, or find nearby caches during a spur of the moment cache hunt. Whichever camp you fall into, there are several useful tools in the app for puzzle hunters who have a couple solved puzzles to log.

If you used the feature on the website to change the coordinates, then those corrected coordinates should be carried over to the app automatically. In the app you will see the same puzzle icon on the map that appears on the website. Like the website, once you enter a found log the icon will return to its original place.

If you are working on a field puzzle or solve a simple puzzle while you are in the field, there is also a way to correct the coords on the fly.

On a puzzle cache page, if you click "Start" on the cache page to begin the navigation for the cache, you will get a pop up menu that includes "Enter Solved Coordinates." Clicking there takes you to a screen that includes your current coordinates, and the posted coordinates. At the top is an area to enter the new coordinates using a telephone like pad at the bottom of the screen. Once you have entered the coordinates you want, click "Save" at the upper right and the app will begin navigating you to these new coords.

pq?

PQs, or "Pocket Queries" are downloadable files from *geocaching.com*, a function available to premium members. PQs are searches resulting in lists of caches tailored to a given set of specifications. You can search with advanced parameters, eliminate certain cache types, or focusing certain cache criteria like placement dates, recent finds, or location. You can also search caches along a specified route, making cache planning for a trip very easy.

You can also add waypoints to multicaches using a similar method, though the app begins navigation immediately and you have to click "More" to get the option to add a new waypoint. If for some reason you need to add a waypoint to a traditional cache you must scroll to the bottom of the page to the Waypoints menu, then click the '+' by "My Waypoints."

Keep in mind that all of these functions require you to be connected to your cell service in order for them to work, which sometimes isn't available if you are deep in the woods. You have to remember to do this while you are in an area that has cell coverage. You cannot add a new waypoint or a corrected waypoint without cell coverage.

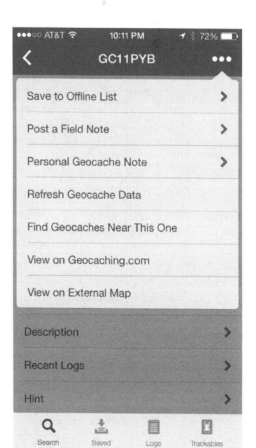

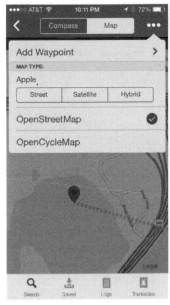

Other Apps

There are dozens of other smartphone apps that can be used for geocaching, that have benefits for the puzzle cacher. Two that I'll discuss in particular are Cachly and C:Geo.

Cachly is an iPhone only app that currently costs $4.99. The greatest benefit to Geosphere is that the maps that come up when you search for local caches will display pins for any caches that you have corrected coordinates entered for. Those pins will be in their in their corrected positions. This is very useful for the armchair solver who might solve several puzzles without actually going to find them. When the time comes to actually search, they can easily find corrected caches in an impromptu manner, without having to make special plans or coordinate their trips to look for the puzzles. If there just happens to be a solved puzzle in the area, it can be found as easily as a traditional.

C:Geo brings this same functionality to the Android user. C:Geo is a free app, but is only available to Android users. Just like Geosphere, it automatically imports caches that have corrected coordinates and adds pins to the search map for the corrected locations. C:Geo also leaves pins in place for the dummy coords.

Many other geocaching apps feature these functions, and others that could be useful to the puzzle cacher. Spend some time in the iTunes App Store, or the Android Marketplace exploring other geocaching apps and what benefits they may offer.

GSAK

GSAK, which stands for the "Geocaching Swiss Army Knife," is a tool that many geocachers love. It is a PC only application (there is no Mac version at the moment) that works with the *geocaching.com* database and PQs to perform very specific searches, even more exacting than can be performed with PQs alone. GSAK can then be used to load the results of the search onto your GPSr.

GSAK downloads both corrected waypoints and cache notes from the website and includes them in any calculations you make with the program. When loading waypoints onto a device from GSAK, it defaults to loading the corrected coordinates, and cache notes are displayed as a log on the device.

getting GSAK
GSAK can be downloaded from *gsak.net*. It has a 21 day free preview period, but then begins displaying a nag screen, asking you to pay for registration. . The program continues to function, but you must pay to eliminate the nag screen. Registration is currently $30.

GSAK is a very useful tool for those who enjoy challenge caches, the subset of mystery caches that require you to have found a certain number of other caches, or to have performed a certain type of caching feat before logging. It is also capable of creating proximity rings on maps to check the 528' and 2 Mile rules.

In truth, GSAK is a very powerful program, and I've barely scratched the surface of what it can do. There could almost be an entire book just on various aspects of GSAK. The good news is that they have a very responsive development team, and a very active user base that answers questions in their forums and creates macros for performing the specific types of searches that it is capable of. There are currently over 1500 macros available for download at the website. Keep in mind, however, that GSAK is not the most intuitive program to use. It is best suited to those with some advanced computer knowledge and a will to do some experimenting and tinkering in order to make the program the search you want.

Project GC

The website *project-gc.com* is another incredibly useful tool for the puzzle solver. It has many of the functions that GSAK does but functions entirely on the web without a downloaded program. This makes it especially attractive to Mac users who cannot use GSAK.

Project GC functions by accessing your profile at *geocaching.com*. You must sign into Geocaching through the Project GC website, a function they call "authentication." Although you appear to be logging into *geocaching.com* with your regular name and password, that information is NOT shared with Project GC. It is only being seen by the *geocaching.com* website. Once you have authenticated, you can search your finds or search other caches using filters to remove cache types, or to narrow your search to very specific types. It also allows you to look at the statistics for any other cacher, and has several "Challenge Checkers" to see if you qualify for certain challenge caches. For some challenges, it also offers the ability to locate caches that will help you fill those challenge criteria.

Some of the applications that are most useful to the puzzle solver are in their members section. The price for membership is €18, which is currently about $30 US. Once you have a membership, you can access a function they call "Solved Mysteries." This function looks at the geocaching database and finds any caches that have coordinates in the cache notes. It then allows you to plot a map using those coordinates that can be downloaded as a GPX file and placed onto a GPSr.

Consistency

The best advice I can give you is to simply find a method that works for you and stick with it. You don't want half your solved coordinates in a notebook and another half placed as corrected coordinates on the website. Once you've tried a couple different methods and you've picked the one you like, build a habit around storing your solved coords in that way. It will only help in the long run. The goal of all of this is to help you find more caches after all, not to make you frustrated by having solved caches that you still can't find because you have misplaced the corrected coordinates!

# et Out There!

Hopefully you've picked up some hints, tips, and knowledge that you didn't have before we started this journey, and you feel a bit more prepared to tackle the world of mystery and puzzle caches!

Just remember, as with all things geocaching related, the idea is to **have fun!** Mystery and puzzle caches just offer a slightly different way to achieve that goal, and add a new level of enjoyment to your caching experience. The more you solve, the better you get, and the better you get, the more you solve! Good luck, and CACHE ON!

APPENDIX 1

Following are the hints for the "Solve It Yourself" puzzles. See page 11 for how these get used.

1
Hccre pnfr ner uvtu.

2
The title is a clue.

3
Gel fngryyvgr ivrj.

4
The title is a clue.

5
Gur ahzoref ba gur obkrf znexrq N,O, P rgp pna or neenatrq vagb pbbeqf.

6
The coords are fully visible.

7
Vg'f n glcr bs one pbqr.

8
The name is a reference to "ty-pos."

9
The name you need is in the cache description.

10
Ybbx ng n Onpba Pvcure.

11
Lbh arrq gb cebwrpg va gur bc-cbfvgr qverpgvba.

12
Gjb yrggref sebz rnpu jbeq znxr gur npebfgvp.

13
The coords are fully visible.

14
Playfair with keyword "sports-manship."

15
Those are some strange units.

16
Gel "Jung 3 Jbeqf."

17
There is a hint in the description.

18
There are 14 songs.

19
Pbaireg gur urk gb ETO.

20
No left turns, no u-turns.

21
What number system is that?

22
The title has a hint.

23
Gur jbeqf "ahzoref" naq "fuvsg" ner n uvag.

24
The title is an important clue.

25
Ahzoref va NFY.

26
Lbh zvtug or noyr gb thrff n srj rkgen ahzoref onfrq ba jurer gurl ner va gur pbbeqf.

27
The names are important.

28
The title is a clue.

29
Ybbx ng gur funcrf bs gur yn-aqznexf ng rnpu ybpngvba?

30
Gur vzntrf eryngr gb Qb Er Zv

31
Lbh abj unir n ornevat naq n qvfgnapr.

32
Clguntberna gevcyrgf

33
Jurer vf gur tevyy?

34
Vg'f n sbez bs npebfgvp.

35
Ybbx ng gur genpx ahzoref sbe gur fbatf.

36
Gur pbaprcg vf obarf.

37
Projecting along the bearings you have won't help.

38
Qb nggevohgrf unir nffbpvngrq ahzoref?

39
Sbe Abegu pbhag fgrcf orgjrra orngf.

40
Gurer ner n ybg bs zvfgnxrf va gur grkg.

41
Ybbx hc alcgbtencul.

42
Znxr n ybbc nebhaq gur fznyy fdhner arne pragre.

43
The visual is a clue.

44
Do these titles have anything in common?

45
Vg'f n Cynlsnve pvcure.

46
View the Additional Waypoints in Google Earth or Google Maps.

47

What is weird about the names?

48

The CO's name is a clue.

49

ZZ naq PZ ner Ebzna ahzrenyf.

50

Yrggre gb ahzore fhofgvghgvba.

51

Pna urk or pbairegrq vagb punenpgref?

52

The number you need is already there.

53

Look past the knots.

54

Gur mreb vf vzcbegnag.

55

Zbfg bs gur zvfgnxrf ner zvffvat yrggref.

56

Do the images sound like anything?

57

Gur xrljbeq vf va gur qrfpevcgvba.

58

There is an acrostic hint.

59

Vona naq Bona ahzoref

60

Yrsg gb evtug, gbc gb obggbz. C=1, N=2, E=3, P=4... rgp.

61

Yrggre gb ahzore pbairefvba.

62

Gur pbbeqf ner va qrpvzny qrterr sbezng.

63

Trbpnpuvat Gbbyobk unf n gbby sbe lbh.

64

Does the number 3 connect to anything?

65

Rnpu yvar vf bar qverpgvba.

66

The symbols are the coords in

another form.

67

"Qroht" vf gur zbfg vzcbegnag pyhr.

68

Nqq be fhogenpg 180 nf erdhverq naq cebwrpg.

69

Those aren't measurements.

70

Gur nyohz gur fbat jnf bevtvanyyl ba vf vzcbegnag.

71

Pbaireg gb zvyrf naq qrterrf.

72

Gur ynaqznexf ng rnpu ybpngvba ner funcrq yvxr ahzoref.

73

Gur cbfvgvba bs gur erpgnathyne synxrf erirny gur ahzoref.

74

Sbe Jrfg pbhag gur orngf.

75

A song will help.

76

Purpx gur nggevohgr ahzoref ntnvafg gur yvfg.

77

Lbh jvyy unir gb pebff gur fnzr cngu gjvpr.

78

Pneebyy unq n fcrpvny nycunorg.

79

N ybg bs ibjryf va gubfr anzrf.

80

The title has a hint.

81

Qba'g sbetrg gung cyheny znggre.

82

The title is a clue.

83

There is a solid concept here.

84

The markings are important.

85

Znxr n cebwrpgvba hfvat gung orevat naq qvfgnapr.

86

Lbh arrq zber?

87

The letters in center are the coords in another form.

88

Gur pbybe anzrf ner va urk.

89

There are (currently) no spaces between things.

90

Gur ahzoref ner gurer gjvpr.

91

The title is a clue.

92

Svaq rnpu zvffvat yrggre naq jevgr bhg gur erfhygf.

93

Tbbtyr gur PB anzr naq gur gvgyr gbtrgure.

94

Each song is one digit.

95

You will need a tool or a website.

96

Ybbx ng flzobyf ba n xrlobneq.

97

Jung vf Z va Ebzna ahzrenyf?

98

The title contains a hint.

99

Solve as if it were a traditional numerical sudoku.

100

Pbhag yrggref va rnpu obar anzr.

101

Urk gb NFPVV

102

Vg pragref nebhaq n glcr bs ahzore.

103

Rnpu anzr vf zvffvat bar ibjry.

104

Ubj qb lbh trg n ahzore sebz n fbat?

105
3 is not a "magic number."

106
Ner gur flzobyf snzvyvne?

107
You will need to do unit conversions.

108
You need a reason to remove some words.

109
Guvf chmmyr vf n sbez bs erfrpgvba.

110
Lbh'yy arrq gb qb n pbairefvba.

111
Change the letters to numbers, it's probably easier that way.

112
Erzbir nyy gur jbeqf gung pbagnva "OHT."

113
Ragre rnpu jbeq, va beqre, ng Jung 3 Jbeqf.

114
Gur onaqf nobir naq orybj sbe gur tevyyf.

115
The numbers help at first... but that lessens after a while.

116
The word "last" is important.

117
The cache name is a pun.

118
Jung pna lbh fhofgvghgr sbe gubfr yrggref?

119
Qb = 1, Er = 2, rgp.

120
Erzbir nyy gur yrggref orgjrra gur svefg naq ynfg.

121
Cbfgrag pbqr jvgu fbz cnqqvat.

122
Have a look at those "Additional Waypoints."

123
Top is North, bottom is West.

124
Gur znexvatf ner ahzoref.

125
Qb nyy gur zbivrf orybat gb n pbyyrpgvba?

126
Gur unaqf sbez gur pbqr.

127
Qvq Yrjvf Pneebyy gel gb ernq va gur qnex?

128
Gur Oheebjf-Jurry Genafsbezngvba.

129
Fbzr zngu vf erdhverq.

130
Gur erdhverzragf ner nyy ngtevohgrf.

131
Rttf ner bar, onpba vf gur bgure.

132
Pevgrevba Pbyyrpgvba zbivrf unir ahzoref nffvtarq.

133
You'll need to do a conversion.

134
The title is a clue.

135
You can do it with a tool.

136
Lbh fubhyq or pbhagvat.

137
The 9th word is important.

138
Ynfg jbeq va rnpu pyhr.

139
The CO name has a hint.

140
You'll need a keyword.

141
Gur Pevgrevba Pbyyrpgvba.

142
Each paragraph contains a concept word.

143
It's a cipher type.

144
Rtlcgvna Uvrengvp ahzoref.

145
Gur pbbeqf ner va qrterr, zvahgf, frpbaqf.

146
Qb gur jbeqf unir fbzrguvat va pbzzba?

147
Google the CO in combo with the theme.

148
There are two encryption methods.

149
Gur xabgf ner n erq ureevat.

150
Those cache requirements sound familiar.

GPS and Coordinate Related Websites and Tools

Many aspects of geocaching and geocache puzzles require manipulating coordinates in one form or another. The following websites provide strong tools for geocachers to use for mapping, coordinate manipulation, and GPS functions.

boulter.com
Written by a geocacher, this website has tools for coordinate conversion, a distance calculator, coordinate scraping (pulling all of the coords off a webspage and creating a .loc file, to be used with GPS units. Useful for multicaches, or caches with multiple waypoints.) It also has functions to map solved geocaches, and a few puzzle solving tools.

convert-me.com
One stop shopping to convert almost any measurement into another format. Of particular interest to geocachers is the section on distance, which includes many archaic and ancient distance formats, as well as distances from other countries and societies.

fizzymagic.net
Home of the PC-only "Fizzy Calc" program which calculates distances, converts coords, creates and solves coordinate checksums and digital roots, and converts GC numbers into decimal.

flashearth.com
Displays a satellite photo of an area with a cross-hair at center, to the left are the coordinates of the cross-hairs, which change as you drag the map beneath them. Useful for determining the coordinates of objects in satellite view.

freemaptools.com
Calculators to determine many measurements regarding maps and coordinates. Includes an antipode calculator, distance calculators, radius creators, proximity map creators, and a tool that allows you to measure the area of an enclosed shape on a map.

geocachingtoolbox.com
Written by a geocacher, this website has tools for coordinate conversion, a distance calculator, waypoint projection, and tools to find intersections of lines, intersections of circles, midpoints of lines, and a bearing calculator. It also has the ability to create a map that shows all the possible locations for incomplete coordinates, if you have a partially solved puzzle. There are also many cipher and puzzle solving tools.

geomidpoint.com
Calculators to determine the midpoint between two coordinates, distance and bearing between waypoints, and centroids of multiple waypoints.

geoplaner.com
Online mapping tool that allows input in a variety of coord formats, including mixed formats. Useful for creating maps of multiple locations.

gpsvisualizer.com
Under their "Calculators" tab you will find functions to create proximity circles, to convert coordinates between notation methods, to project waypoints, and distance calculators.

gc-gpx-viewer.vaguelibre.net/
Online GPX file viewer. Plots GPX files against a map to help plan trips or lay out caching destinations.

gsak.net
Home of the PC-only "Geocaching Swiss Army Knife," a program with hundreds of geocaching applications, including distance calculations, coordinate conversions, waypoint projection, map creation, sending/receiving waypoints to GPSr, and many statistics macros.

jimcarson.com/macfizzycalc/
Home of the Mac version of "Fizzy Calc," a program which calculates distances, converts coords, creates and solves coordinate checksums and digital roots, and converts GC numbers into decimal.

maccaching.com
A Mac-only waypoint manager for sending/receiving waypoints to GPSr, map creation, and the ability to manipulate PQs, including changing the sorting, and editing.

Puzzle Related Websites and Tools

There are hundreds of puzzle types and hundreds of websites devoted to solving them or aiding in their solves. This appendix will endeavor to list some of the ones that cross over with geocache puzzle solving more frequently. For ciphers and codes, please see the next appendix.

General Puzzles

puzzlesolver.com
Solutions for dozens of three dimensional and physical puzzles that are sometimes encountered as field stages in geocaching puzzles.

logicville.com/tansol
Solving instructions and solutions for tangrams.

Number Puzzles

a.teall.info/nonogram/
Nonogram or Griddler solver.

iread.it/cryptarithms.php
Alphametics solver.

kakuro-online.com
Kakuro solver. (NOTE: Requires a free account.)

mlsite.net/neknek/
Ken Ken solver.

subidiom.com
Search engine for searching within irrational numbers, including pi, e, phi, and the square root of 2.

sudoku-solutions.com
Sudoku solver.

sudokuwiki.org/anagram/
Instructions and solving strategies for hundreds of different variations on sudoku puzzles.

wolframalpha.com
The most powerful search engine and toolbox online for all things mathematical and numerical.

Photo Based Puzzles

hidden-3d.com
"Magic Eye," or autosterogram puzzle solver.

magiceye.ecksdee.co.uk
"Magic Eye," or autosterogram puzzle solver.

regex.info/exif.cgi
Exif viewer.

tineye.com
Reverse image search engine.

Word Puzzles

anagram-solver.net
Very powerful anagramming tool.

the-crossword-solver.com
A solving engine for crosswords, helps with words with missing letters, anagrams and standard crossword clues.

omniglot.com
Alphabets and numbers for thousands of languages, both real and fictional. Also has a cryptogram solver.

quipqiup.com
Cryptogram solver.

rumkin.com/tools/cipher/
Besides numerous cipher tools, this site includes a general Cryptogram solver that displays all possible solutions on one page.

wordsmith.org/anagram/
Very powerful anagramming tool.

zompist.com/numbers.shtml
The words for numbers in over 500 languages.

APPENDIX 4

Cipher Related Websites and Tools

These websites represent some of the most useful sites online regarding simple ciphers and cipher tools. I have broken them into sites that deal with multiple ciphers, and sites that deal with single cipher types.

General Cipher Sites

These sites contain tools for multiple ciphers and code types in a single location, as well other cryptanalysis tools.

acaencodedecode.appspot.com
Decryption tools for many ciphers.

ackgame.com/crypto.htm
Cryptanalysis tools to identify ciphers, including index of coincidence at various periods, letter counts, frequency counts, Normor score, etc.

alltextencryption.com
Keyed encryption and decryption.

altamatic.com
A simple website for substitution, transposition, and numeric ciphers, and Morse and digital decoding.

bionsgadgets.appspot.com
Decryption tools for many ciphers. Analysis to help ID ciphers.

braingle.com
Under the "Brain Teasers" tab you will find several decryption tools for many of the most common ciphers including Caesar, Atbash, Vigenère, Playfair, Bifid, Trifid, and many others.

cryptii.com
Many encryption systems including Enigma Machine.

cryptool-online.org
Decryption tools for many of the most common ciphers including ADFGVX, Alberti, Bifid, Caesar, Enigma, Four-Square, Freemason, Navajo, Nihilist, Playfair, Vigenère, and many others. Also includes tools for cryptanalysis such as frequency analysis.

dcode.fr
Decryption tools for many ciphers. (NOTE: This website is in French, however it includes decryption tools for several ciphers and codes not found anywhere else on the net.)

easyciphers.com/
Educational site about ciphers.

geocaching.dennistreysa.de/multisolver/
Checks cipher text against several cipher types at once.

geocachingtoolbox.com
A geocacher's go to for encryptio and decryption.

guballa.de
Decryption codes specifically for cachers, works in German, French, Spanish and English.

luthorien.altervista.org/Tools/
Decryption tools for many of the most common ciphers, as well as reference charts for many common alphabets and codes. Also includes references for common puzzles. Has a great link library for puzzle reference. (NOTE: This website has an incredibly annoying color scheme but the color can be changed in the upper left corner.)

mygeocachingprofile.com
A Vigenère breaker, and several other decoders.

quipqiup.com
Cryptogram solver.

ref.wikibruce.com
Comprehensive code set and conversion tools. Includes many obscure codes.

rumkin.com/tools/cipher/
Decryption tools for many of the most common ciphers including Affine, Atbash, Baconian, Base64, Bifid, Caesar, Columnar Transposition, Gronsfeld, One Time Pad, Playfair, Railfence, and Vigenère, as well as others. Also

includes a general Cryptogram solver.

theblob.org/rot.cgi
A ROT-All decoder.

tholman.com/other/transposition/
Transposition Cipher solver.

Specific Cipher Sites
These sites contain tools for a single cipher or code type.

asciitohex.com
Tools to convert between several bases including binary, hex, and decimal, as well as converting to text formats like Base 64 and ASCII, as well as Rot 13.

binaryhexconverter.com
Tools to convert between several bases including binary, hex, decimal, octal and ASCII.

morsecode.scphillips.com
Morse code decoder and encoder, including sound tools.

myallpage.com/pager/pagercodes.htm
Remember pagers and beepers? This site records a number of message codes used during that era.

namesuppressed.com/kenny/
Kenny code.

pbs.org/wgbh/nova/decoding/virtwave.html
A simple Enigma Machine emulator.

people.physik.hu-berlin.de/~palloks/js/enigma/index_en.html#s6
A more advanced Enigma Machine emulator.

phonespell.org
Returns possible words that can spelled using phone numbers.

planetcalc.com/1434/
Displays the results of all possible Caesar rotations on a single page.

rot47.net
A Rot 47 encoder and decoder.

senses0.org.mv/popzees/rot/rotn.php
A Rot 47 encoder and decoder.

smurfoncrack.com/pygenere/
A Vigenère decoder, especially useful if you do not know the keyword. The site can guess the keyword based on a random word length, adjustable by the user.

tholman.com/other/transposition/
Transposition cipher decoder.

Cipher Tools
home.comcast.net/~acabion/refscore.html
This website can "look" at a section of cipher text and return useful information for breaking the cipher, in some cases identifying which cipher is being used.

secretcodebreaker.com
Several cipher tools, including downloadable tools (PC-only) for cryptograms, polyalphabetic ciphers, transpositions ciphers, and steganography.

sites.google.com/site/cryptocrackprogram/
Home of the PC-only program "Crypto Crack," which can decipher most enciphered text, even if it requires a password. The program also IDs ciphers from the text, and can determine passwords.

APPENDIX 5

Other Useful Websites and Tools

These websites represent some of the most useful sites online regarding simple ciphers and cipher tools. I have broken them into sites that deal with multiple ciphers, and sites that deal with single cipher types.

Bar codes and QR codes

onlinebarcodereader.com
Supports UPC-A, UPC-E, EAN-8, EAN-13, Code 39, Code 128, QR Code, Data Matrix, PDF 417 and ITF.

onlinebarcodereader.com
Supports most standard bar codes, as well as QR codes, data matrix codes, and postal bar codes.

webqr.com
Online barcode and QR reader

zxing.org
Supports most standard bar codes, as well as QR codes, data matrix codes, Aztec codes, and codabar.

Computer Languages

calormen.com
Online emulator for several computer languages including Logo, Basic, and Lisp.

w3schools.com
Primarily web page building tutorials, but also includes lists of coding for characters and colors used in HTML , as well as HTML tags.

Geocheckers

certitudes.org
evince.locuprime.net
geocheck.org
geochecker.com
nmgeocaching.com/check.php
Each of these geocheckers works in much the same way, though each has its own quirks. I suggest investigating them all to see which will work best for you.

Geography

50states.com
US states broken down by state tree, state flower, state bird, state songs, as well as the major newspapers, radio stations, highways, area codes and much more. Includes statistical and geographic information like population, major rivers, the geographic center and much much more.

flagid.org
Online flag identifier. Users are guided through a series of illustrated multiple-choice questions of features of flags to arrive at an identification.

world-airport-codes.com
Provides letter and number codes for any airport, worldwide.

zip-codes.com
Look up tool for zip codes in the US and Canada.

Letters and Alphabets

bennettroesch.com/Tools/QwertyToDvorak/
Online converter for switching text typed in DVORAK to QWERTY, and vice versa.

identifont.com
Online typeface identifier. Users are guided through a series of illustrated multiple-choice questions of features of a font to arrive at a font identification.

omniglot.com
Alphabets and numbers for thousands of languages, both real and fictional.

wbic16.xedoloh.com/dvorak.html
Online converter for switching text typed in DVORAK to QWERTY, and vice versa.

Math

hyperphysics.phy-astr.gsu.edu/HBASE/traj.html#tracon
Online calculator and equation solver for equations involving trajectory: freefall, vertical freefall, ballistics, range, launch, and many variations on those equations.

kaagaard.dk/service/convert.htm
Convenient website for converting between number bases, can handle everything from unary (Base 1) to hexatridecimal (Base 36).

numberworld.info
Online calculators, equation solvers, factoring calculator, prime number checker, Fibonacci checker and more.

subidiom.com
Search engine for searching within irrational numbers, including pi, e, phi, and the square root of 2.

wolframalpha.com
One-stop-shopping for all things math related, including information about individual numbers, equations and math concepts. Has equation solvers and calculators.

zompist.com/numbers.shtml
The words for numbers in over 500 languages.

Photo and Image File Manipulation

exif.regex.info/exif.cgi
EXIF data viewer

exifdata.com
EXIF data viewer

ezgif.com/split
Splits animated gifs into individual images, making it easier to see puzzles that may be hidden within the animation, or single frames of the gif that may hide coords.

gimp.org
The home of GIMP a free photo manipulation program similar to Photoshop.

huddle.github.io/Resemble.js/
Can compare two images to see if there are differences between them. Good to check image from cache pages that appear elsewhere on the web.

onlineexifviewer.com
EXIF data viewer

pixlr.com
An online photo manipulation program.

Puzzle practice

geocachingpuzzleoftheday.blogspot.com
4 years (at the time of this writing) of featured geocaching puzzles curated by infamous Upstate New York puzzle cacher TeamAJK. There are no answers, or solve methods, but a collection of puzzles that have been deemed "interesting" by a prominent puzzler is always worth looking at.

parmstro.weebly.com
Parmstro's Puzzle Solving Pages is a collection of hints and how-tos for puzzle solving, which features links to puzzle caches that feature the discussed method, as well as some "dummy" puzzles.

Puzzle Solving 101 by ePeterso2
A collection of ten puzzle caches by a cacher named ePeterso2, in and around Fort Lauderdale, Florida. The caches are all solvable remotely, and ePeterso2 has travelbug that can be logged remotely upon completion of the series. Begin at GCYXZ1 (http://coord.info/GCYXZ1). You will find links there to the rest of the series. Many cachers have copied these caches in their own areas, so look around your area for a "Puzzle Solving 101" series.

Science

webelements.com
One stop shopping for all the information you could need about the periodic table, and elements.

Sound

audacity.sourceforge.net
Home of the computer program "Audacity," used to manipulate and edits audio files. This program can be used to find spectrographs in sound files, which might contain puzzle info.

Steganography

futureboy.us/stegano/decinput.html
geocachingtoolbox.com
jjtc.com/Security/stegtools.htm
kwebbel.net/stega/enindex.php
manytools.org/hacker-tools/steganography-encode-text-into-image/
mobilefish.com/services/steganography/steganography.php
quickcrypto.com/free-steganography-software.html
silenteye.org
sourceforge.net/projects/stegostick/
steghide.sourceforge.net/

Just a sampling of the MANY steganography options on the web. Some of these are online tools, some are links to downloadable programs. Again, my best advice in this instance is to ask the CO what tool he would suggest since some of these tools are very specific and only the tool used to encode an image will decode that image.

APPENDIX 6
Puzzle Solving Smartphone Apps

Beyond the dozens of apps that have been created to aid in geocache navigation and finding I would suggest the following apps for use in puzzle solving.

Convert Everything
Converts over 80 units of measure, as well as acting as a translator via Google Translate.

ConvertPad
Converts units of length and measurement, scientific units, electricity, light, cooking, time, angle, and many, many more. This app covers more than 100 different unit types with high precision.

GCTools
GCTools is a very versatile puzzle solving tool, it includes unit convertors, some basic cipher tools for field use, including Caesar Ciphers, a Vigenère decoder, and others, as well as some data tables on resistor colors, prime numbers, digits of pi and cross sums, but it's most important feature is its ability to manipulate coordinates. GCTools can calculate projections, the distance between two coordinates, and the intersection of two lines in the free version. For a small in-app purchase you can add the ability to calculate the intersection of a circle and a line, or the intersection of circles. Several more advanced cipher types are also available for purchase.

Geocache Calculator
A feature packed app that includes hundreds of informational tables, cipher and code charts, a well as checksum calculators, and other useful tools.

Geocaching Toolkit iGCT
iGCT includes a variety of waypoint manipulation tools including coord conversion, projection, line intersection and circle intersection. Also has tools for ROT-13 hint decryption, and text calculations.

Morse Decoder by HotPaw
Decodes audio Morse by "listening" to the audio and providing a text translation. The developer has several other Morse based apps, including one that does translation by tapping the phone screen.

Morse Decoder for Ham Radio
Decodes audio Morse by "listening" to the audio and providing a text translation.

Puzzle Sidekick
Originally designed for Alternate Reality Gaming, this app includes dozens of cipher and codes charts, as well as informational tables and interactive cipher decryption tools. Useful for field puzzles, and on-the-fly puzzle solving.

Qrafter
Scans QR Code, Datamatrix and Aztec Code and also works well with colorful and reversed QR Codes.

Scan
Very fast and very user-friendly, this app scans QR Code or barcode automatically when you point the device at it.

Shazam
This app recognizes songs and musical compositions by "listening" to the audio and searching the internet for a match. Provides band and album information for the songs.

Sound Hound
This app recognizes songs and musical compositions by "listening" to the audio and searching the internet for a match. Provides band and album information for the songs.

ZBar
Robust QR Code, EAN, and barcode reader.

Cipher and Code
Determination
Flowcharts

On the following pages are four flowcharts that will help you determine which code or cipher you might be working with. These charts are NOT definitive, and do not include every possible cipher, but will give you a place to begin, and will hopefully help you build the mental ability to recognize ciphers and codes. Think of the charts as training. The questions on these charts are the type of questions that I ask myself when I am faced with an unknown cipher.

Before beginning the flowcharts, examine the cache page very closely. You are looking for characteristics of the code: what is the code comprised of? Does it use symbols? Does it use letters? Numbers? Both? Does the cache page mention a keyword? A grille? A code text?

If the cache page includes an encoded text that is only symbols or strange characters that you don't recognize try comparing those to the codes in Appendix 8, or using the trick of substituting letters and treating the text as a cryptogram.

CIPHER AND CODE DETERMINATION FLOWCHART 1

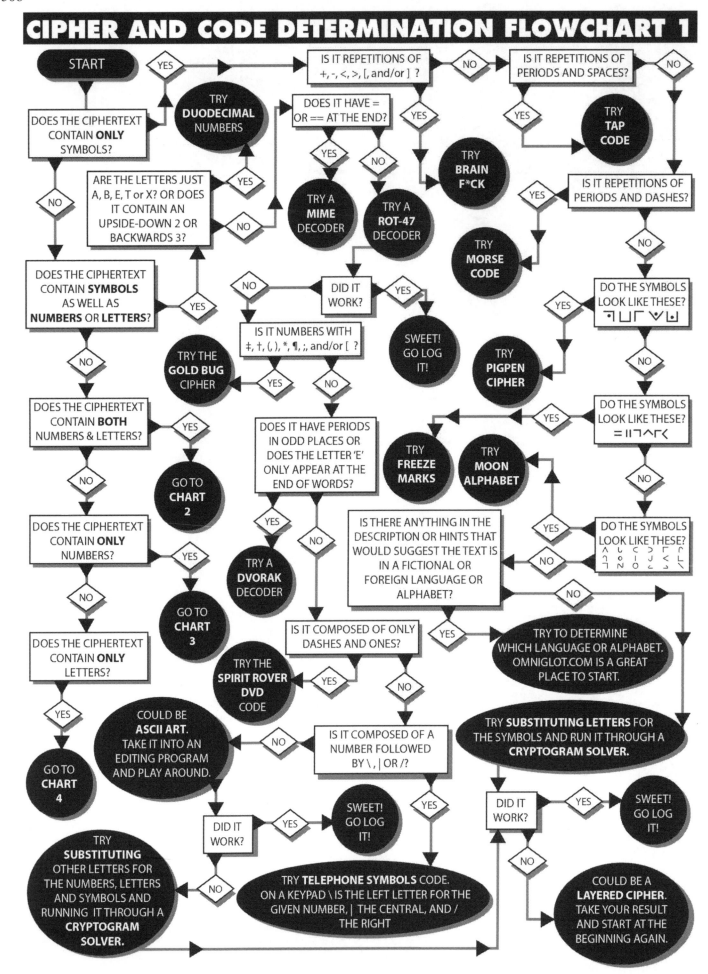

CIPHER AND CODE DETERMINATION FLOWCHART 2

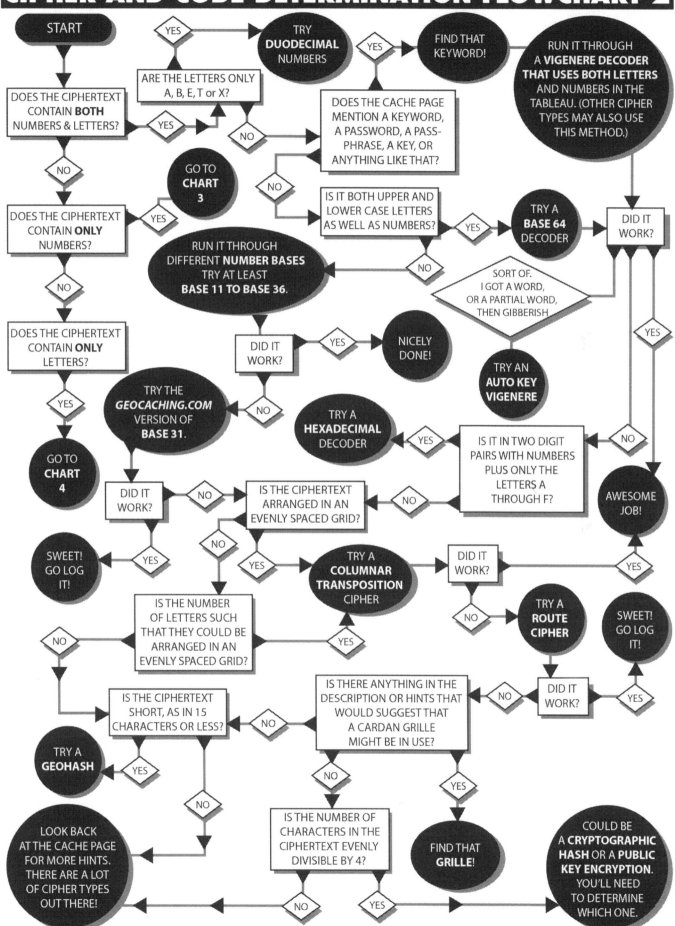

START

DOES THE CIPHERTEXT CONTAIN **BOTH** NUMBERS & LETTERS? — YES → ARE THE LETTERS ONLY A, B, E, T or X? — YES → TRY **DUODECIMAL** NUMBERS

ARE THE LETTERS ONLY A, B, E, T or X? — NO → DOES THE CACHE PAGE MENTION A KEYWORD, A PASSWORD, A PASS-PHRASE, A KEY, OR ANYTHING LIKE THAT?

DOES THE CACHE PAGE MENTION A KEYWORD... — YES → FIND THAT KEYWORD! → RUN IT THROUGH A **VIGENERE DECODER THAT USES BOTH LETTERS** AND NUMBERS IN THE TABLEAU. (OTHER CIPHER TYPES MAY ALSO USE THIS METHOD.)

DOES THE CACHE PAGE MENTION A KEYWORD... — NO → IS IT BOTH UPPER AND LOWER CASE LETTERS AS WELL AS NUMBERS?

IS IT BOTH UPPER AND LOWER CASE LETTERS AS WELL AS NUMBERS? — YES → TRY A **BASE 64** DECODER → DID IT WORK?

IS IT BOTH UPPER AND LOWER CASE LETTERS AS WELL AS NUMBERS? — NO → RUN IT THROUGH DIFFERENT **NUMBER BASES** TRY AT LEAST **BASE 11 TO BASE 36**.

RUN IT THROUGH DIFFERENT NUMBER BASES... → DID IT WORK? — YES → **NICELY DONE!**

DID IT WORK? — NO → TRY THE *GEOCACHING.COM* VERSION OF **BASE 31**.

DOES THE CIPHERTEXT CONTAIN **BOTH** NUMBERS & LETTERS? — NO → DOES THE CIPHERTEXT CONTAIN **ONLY** NUMBERS?

DOES THE CIPHERTEXT CONTAIN **ONLY** NUMBERS? — YES → GO TO **CHART 3**

DOES THE CIPHERTEXT CONTAIN **ONLY** NUMBERS? — NO → DOES THE CIPHERTEXT CONTAIN **ONLY** LETTERS?

DOES THE CIPHERTEXT CONTAIN **ONLY** LETTERS? — YES → GO TO **CHART 4**

DID IT WORK? (Vigenere) — YES → **AWESOME JOB!**

DID IT WORK? (Base 64) — SORT OF. I GOT A WORD, OR A PARTIAL WORD, THEN GIBBERISH → TRY AN **AUTO KEY VIGENERE**

DID IT WORK? — NO → IS IT IN TWO DIGIT PAIRS WITH NUMBERS PLUS ONLY THE LETTERS A THROUGH F?

IS IT IN TWO DIGIT PAIRS... — YES → TRY A **HEXADECIMAL** DECODER

IS IT IN TWO DIGIT PAIRS... — NO → IS THE CIPHERTEXT ARRANGED IN AN EVENLY SPACED GRID?

TRY THE GEOCACHING.COM VERSION OF BASE 31 → DID IT WORK? — YES → **SWEET! GO LOG IT!**

DID IT WORK? — NO → IS THE CIPHERTEXT ARRANGED IN AN EVENLY SPACED GRID?

IS THE CIPHERTEXT ARRANGED IN AN EVENLY SPACED GRID? — YES → TRY A **COLUMNAR TRANSPOSITION** CIPHER

IS THE CIPHERTEXT ARRANGED IN AN EVENLY SPACED GRID? — NO → IS THE NUMBER OF LETTERS SUCH THAT THEY COULD BE ARRANGED IN AN EVENLY SPACED GRID?

IS THE NUMBER OF LETTERS SUCH THAT THEY COULD BE ARRANGED IN AN EVENLY SPACED GRID? — YES → TRY A **COLUMNAR TRANSPOSITION** CIPHER

IS THE NUMBER OF LETTERS... — NO → IS THE CIPHERTEXT SHORT, AS IN 15 CHARACTERS OR LESS?

TRY A **COLUMNAR TRANSPOSITION** CIPHER → DID IT WORK? — YES → **AWESOME JOB!**

DID IT WORK? — NO → TRY A **ROUTE CIPHER**

TRY A **ROUTE CIPHER** → DID IT WORK? — YES → **SWEET! GO LOG IT!**

DID IT WORK? — NO → IS THERE ANYTHING IN THE DESCRIPTION OR HINTS THAT WOULD SUGGEST THAT A CARDAN GRILLE MIGHT BE IN USE?

IS THERE ANYTHING IN THE DESCRIPTION OR HINTS... — YES → **FIND THAT GRILLE!**

IS THERE ANYTHING IN THE DESCRIPTION OR HINTS... — NO → IS THE NUMBER OF CHARACTERS IN THE CIPHERTEXT EVENLY DIVISIBLE BY 4?

IS THE CIPHERTEXT SHORT, AS IN 15 CHARACTERS OR LESS? — NO → IS THERE ANYTHING IN THE DESCRIPTION OR HINTS...

IS THE CIPHERTEXT SHORT, AS IN 15 CHARACTERS OR LESS? — YES → TRY A **GEOHASH**

IS THE CIPHERTEXT SHORT... — NO → LOOK BACK AT THE CACHE PAGE FOR MORE HINTS. THERE ARE A LOT OF CIPHER TYPES OUT THERE!

IS THE NUMBER OF CHARACTERS IN THE CIPHERTEXT EVENLY DIVISIBLE BY 4? — YES → COULD BE A **CRYPTOGRAPHIC HASH** OR A **PUBLIC KEY ENCRYPTION**. YOU'LL NEED TO DETERMINE WHICH ONE.

IS THE NUMBER OF CHARACTERS... — NO → LOOK BACK AT THE CACHE PAGE FOR MORE HINTS. THERE ARE A LOT OF CIPHER TYPES OUT THERE!

CIPHER AND CODE DETERMINATION FLOWCHART 3

START

DOES THE CIPHERTEXT CONTAIN **ONLY** NUMBERS? — YES →

DOES THE CIPHER TEXT APPEAR TO USE ALL OF THE NUMBERS 0 TO 9? OR ARE THE NUMBERS LIMITED TO JUST A FEW? — 0 THROUGH 9 →

ARE THE NUMBERS ARRANGED IN TRIADS OR QUADS, AND SEPERATED BY COMMAS OR DASHES? LIKE THIS: 23 - 45 - 234

NO →

DOES THE CIPHERTEXT CONTAIN **ONLY** LETTERS?

LIMITED →

SOUNDS LIKE AN **OTTENDORF** OR **BOOK CIPHER**. YOU'LL NEED A KEY TEXT.

YES ←

ARE THE NUMBERS ONLY 0 OR 1? — YES →

TRY A **TRIDIGITAL** CIPHER

NO →

ARE THE NUMBERS ARRANGED IN PAIRS? LIKE THIS: 15 36 89 43?

YES →

GO TO **CHART 4**

TRY A **BINARY** DECODER ←

ARE THE NUMBERS ONLY 1, 2 AND 3? — YES →

NO →

ARE THE NUMBERS ONLY 1 THROUGH 5? — YES →

ARE ANY OF THE NUMBERS HIGHER THAN 26?

NO →

LOOK FOR CIPHERS THAT USE A **POLYBIUS SQUARE**. YOU MAY NEED A KEYWORD.

IS IT JUST MISSING THE NUMBER 0 or 1?

TRY THE **NIHILIST SUBSTITUTION** CIPHER

TRY A **NUMBER TO LETTER** CONVERSION

TRY A **TELEPHONE KEYPAD** CIPHER ←

YES ←

IS IT ONE LONG NUMBER, OR BROKEN INTO GROUPS OF 5?

DID IT WORK?

ARE THE NUMBERS ONLY 1, 2, 3, AND 4? AND IS THE NUMBER OF CHARACTERS EVENLY DIVISIBLE BY 4?

NO →

YES →

W00T! GO FIND IT!

YES →

SOUNDS LIKE **UPC CODE** CHARACTER ENCODING

TRY A **MORBIT CIPHER**

NICELY DONE!

NO →

IT MAY STILL BE A **NUMBER TO LETTER** CONVERSION, BUT WITH A **MOD FUNCTION** APPLIED TO THE NUMBERS. LOOK FOR HINTS AS TO WHICH MOD.

NO →

DID IT WORK?

YES →

DOES THE CACHE PAGE MENTION A KEYWORD, A PASSWORD, A PASS-PHRASE, A KEY, OR ANYTHING LIKE THAT?

YES →

IS THE KEYWORD 9 LETTERS LONG?

NO →

IS THERE ANYTHING IN THE DESCRIPTION OR HINTS THAT WOULD SUGGEST THAT A CARDAN GRILLE MIGHT BE IN USE?

TRY A **GRANDPRE CIPHER**

NO →

TRY A **ROUTE CIPHER**

NO →

RUN IT THROUGH DIFFERENT **NUMBER BASES**. TRY **BASE 2** THROUGH **BASE 9**.

YES →

TRY A **MORBIT CIPHER**

NO →

FIND THAT **GRILLE**!

YES →

YES →

LOOK BACK AT THE CACHE PAGE FOR MORE HINTS. THERE ARE A LOT OF CIPHER TYPES OUT THERE!

TRY A **MONOME-DINOME CIPHER.**

YES ←

ARE THERE THREE KEYWORDS, EACH 8 LETTERS LONG? — NO →

ARE THERE N KEYWORDS, EACH N LETTERS LONG? — NO →

CIPHER AND CODE DETERMINATION FLOWCHART 4

START

DOES THE CIPHERTEXT CONTAIN **ONLY** LETTERS?

— YES → DOES THE CIPHER TEXT APPEAR TO HAVE A FULL ALPHABET OR ARE THERE JUST A FEW LETTERS REPEATED?

— NO → Hmmmm. SOMETHING HAS GONE AWRY. YOU NEED TO GO BACK TO THE BEGINNING.

PARTIAL ALPHABET → ARE THE LETTERS ONLY A OR B?

— YES → SOUNDS LIKE A PARTIALLY ENCODED **BACONIAN CIPHER**. TRY THAT.

— NO → ARE THE LETTERS ONLY A, D, F, G, V OR X?

— YES → TRY THE **ADFVGX** CIPHER

— NO → IS IT JUST MISSING THE LETTER E?

— YES → TRY A **DVORAK** DECODER

GET OUT THE GPS!

FULL ALPHABET → RUN IT THROUGH ALL 25 **CAESAR SHIFTS (ROT EVERYTHING)**

RUN IT THROUGH A **CRYPTOGRAM SOLVER**

SWEET! GO LOG IT!

— YES → DID IT WORK?

— NO → IS IT MISSING A SINGLE LETTER, LIKE J OR Q?

— YES → LOOK FOR CIPHERS THAT USE A **POLYBIUS SQUARE**. LIKE A **BIFID** OR **TRIFID CIPHER**. YOU MAY NEED A KEYWORD.

DID IT WORK?

— YES →
— NO → LOOK BACK AT THE CACHE PAGE FOR MORE HINTS. THERE ARE A LOT OF CIPHER TYPES OUT THERE!

SPACES → DID IT WORK?

— YES → AWESOME!

— NO → DOES THE CIPHERTEXT HAVE SPACES AND WORD LENGTHS SIMILAR TO REGULAR TEXT? OR IS IT IN AN EVENLY SPACED GRID? OR ARRANGED IN PAIRS? OR SINGLE LETTERS?

SINGLES →
PAIRS → TRY A **PLAYFAIR CIPHER**

TRY THE **FOUR SQUARE CIPHER**

FIND THAT **GRILLE**!

IF YOU GOT A PARTIAL RESULT, TRY STRIPPING AWAY THE PART THAT DECRYPTED PROPERLY. THEN GO BACK TO THE BEGINNING AND TREAT WHAT REMAINS AS A NEW CIPHER TEXT. IT SOUNDS LIKE A LAYERED CIPHER.

GRID → TRY A **COLUMNAR TRANSPOSITION** CIPHER

DOES THE CACHE PAGE MENTION A KEYWORD, A PASSWORD, A PASS-PHRASE, A KEY, OR ANYTHING LIKE THAT?

DID IT WORK?

— YES → ANOTHER PUZZLE SOLVED!
— NO → TRY A **ROUTE CIPHER**

DID IT WORK?

— YES →
— NO →

— YES → RUN IT THROUGH A **VIGENERE DECODER**

— NO →

FIND THAT KEYWORD!

AWESOME SAUCE!

— YES → DID IT WORK?

— NO → IS THERE ANYTHING ON THE CACHE PAGE THAT WOULD SUGGEST A **CARDAN GRILLE** MIGHT BE IN USE?

TRY AN **AUTO KEY VIGENERE**

SORT OF. I GOT A WORD, OR A PARTIAL WORD, THEN GIBBERISH

IS THE KEY COMPOSED OF NUMBERS?

— NO → IS THE KEY COMPOSED OF A LARGE BLOCK OF TEXT? ONE THAT IS AS LONG, OR LONGER, THAN THE CIPHERTEXT?

— NO → TRY A **KEYED CAESAR**

DID IT WORK?

— NO →
— YES → TRY A **KEYED VIGENERE**

DID IT WORK?

— NO →
— YES → GO GET IT!

— YES → TRY A **GRONSFELD OR BAZERIES** DECODER

— YES → TRY A **ONE TIME PAD**

GOOD PUZZLING!

Code Charts

On the next few pages are some of the hundreds of codes and alphabets that have been created over the years, either

for practical reasons, or for pop culture fixtures like video games, comic books, toys, literature, or television shows. There is even one code represented here that was created for an amusement park ride!

The charts encompass A to Z, an numbers 0 to 9. Some codes will have missing characters, usually a "J" or "W," in which case blank spots have been left in the chart. If the alphabet does not have numbers those spots will also be empty. Some codes, such as Moon, Braille and Semaphore would traditionally have a "number sign" in front of the numbers to denote that the symbol represents a number rather than a letter. I have not represented those in the chart. Some COs will use the "number sign" but others will not.

A few of the codes have been marked with an asterisk (*). These codes have characters that represent sounds or letter combinations not represented in the normal 26 letter alphabet. In some cases this denotes that there is both an upper and lower case version of the alphabet, but in other cases there are single characters for sounds like "TH," "CH," "NG," or different symbols for long vowels and short vowels. In these cases I encourage you to google the name of the code to find the complete code chart.

Many of the codes have different names beyond the ones I have listed. For instance, the code I have named simply "Pokemon," is also known as the "Unknown Alphabet." Others, like Klingon, have an "in-universe" name (in this case "Klinzhai"). In all cases though a full chart should be available online by searching the name I have given, plus "alphabet."

Almost all of these codes are very simple one-to-one substitutions, where the normal English language letter is represented by a single character in the alternate alphabet. These could all be cracked using the trick of substituting letters and treating the text as a cryptogram. If you do not find a code represented here that matches what you have on the cache page I would encourage you to use that method on what you have.

To use these charts try to guess what the first letter of your encoded text might be. As geocachers we have an advantage in this regard because most of the time the encoded text will be coordinates. If you live in North America you can begin with the assumption that the coords will probably start with an "N" or the word "North." If there is no matching character on the chart for the letter "N," then try the first letter of the local coords, "F" for "Forty," or "T" for "Thirty." If neither of those tactics work, then focus on the characteristics of the alphabet, and compare those to what you find in the chart. For instance, all of the letters in Pokemon feature a circle somewhere. Mandalorian text is tall and thin, with pointed ends. Once you find a match you can begin your decoding.

One other thing to consider is that text encoded with an alternate alphabet may also have been encoded with other methods like a ROT-N cipher, or a Vigenère Cipher. If your text is not decoding to something you recognize, and you are sure that you have the correct alphabet, consider that it may have a cipher layered onto it as well.

	A	B	C	D	E	F	G	H	I	J	K	L	M	N	O	P	Q	R
KRYPTONIAN																		
KLINGON*																		
INTERLAC																		
ILLUMINATI																		
HYLIAN* (SKYWARD SWORD)																		
HYLIAN																		
HEIROGLYPHS*																		
GNOMMISH*																		
GARGISH																		
FUTURAMA																		
FORBIDDEN EYE																		
FINGERSPELLING (BRITISH)																		
FINGERSPELLING (AMERICAN)																		
ENOCHIAN																		
DRACONIC																		
DOVAHZUL*																		
DORABELLA																		
DOOP SPEAK																		
DAGGERS																		
DAEDRIC																		
D'NI*																		
COVENANT																		
BRAILLE																		
AUREK-BESH*																		
ATLANTEAN*																		
ARCADIAN																		
ANCIENT																		
AL-BHED																		

	S	T	U	V	W	X	Y	Z	0	1	2	3	4	5	6	7	8	9
KRYPTONIAN																		
KLINGON*																		
INTERLAC																		
ILLUMINATI																		
HYLIAN (SKYWARD SWORD)*																		
HYLIAN																		
HEIROGLYPHS*																		
GNOMMISH*																		
GARISH																		
FUTURAMA																		
FORBIDDEN EYE																		
FINGERSPELLING (BRITISH)																		
FINGERSPELLING (AMERICAN)																		
ENOCHIAN																		
DRACONIC																		
DOVAHZUL*																		
DORABELLA																		
DOOP SPEAK																		
DAGGERS																		
DAEDRIC																		
D'NI*																		
COVENANT																		
BRAILLE																		
AUREK-BESH*																		
ATLANTEAN*																		
ARCADIAN																		
ANCIENT																		
AL-BHED																		

	0	1	2	3	4	5	6	7	8	9	10	11	12	13	14	15	16	17
D'NI NUMBERS																		
ZENTRADI																		
VISITOR 2009*																		
VISITOR 1984																		
VIKING RUNES*																		
UTOPIAN																		
URUK RUNES*																		
UNITOLOGY																		
THEBAN																		
SEMAPHORE																		
RUNIC*																		
ROMULAN																		
QUADOO																		
POKEMON																		
OGHAM*																		
NYCTOGRAPHIC																		
NAZCAAN*																		
NAUTICAL FLAGS																		
NATO	ALPHA	BRAVO	CHARLIE	DELTA	ECHO	FOXTROT	GOLF	HOTEL	INDIA	JULIETT	KILO	LIMA	MIKE	NOVEMBER	OSCAR	PAPA	QUEBEC	ROMEO
MORSE																		
MOON*																		
MATORAN																		
MANDALORIAN	A	B	C	D	E	F	G	H	I	J	K	L	M	N	O	P	Q	R

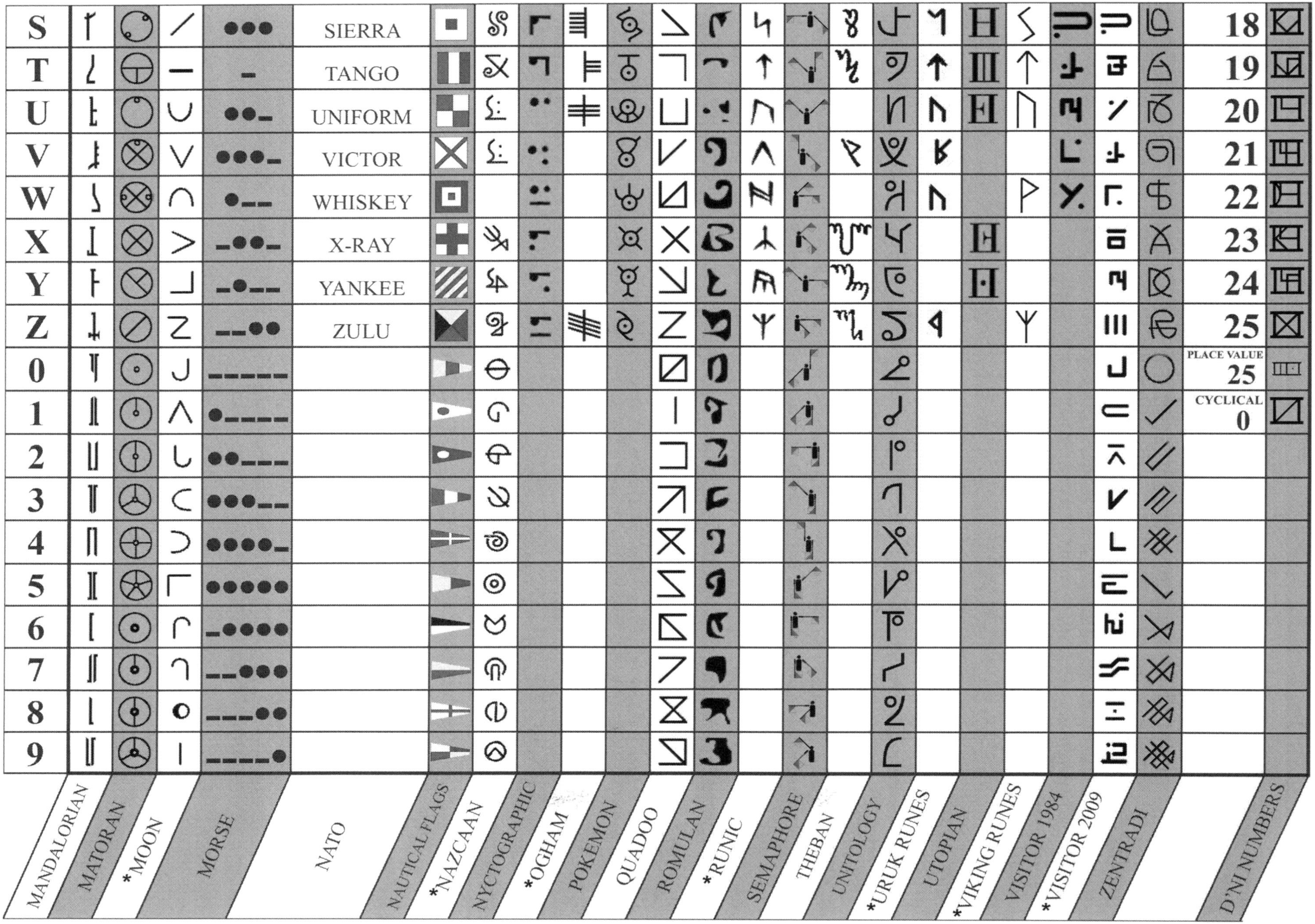
MANDALORIAN
MATORAN
*MOON
MORSE
NATO
NAUTICAL FLAGS
*NAZCAAN
NYCTOGRAPHIC
*OGHAM
POKEMON
QUADOO
ROMULAN
*RUNIC
SEMAPHORE
THEBAN
UNITOLOGY
*URUK RUNES
UTOPIAN
*VIKING RUNES
VISITOR 1984
*VISITOR 2009
ZENTRADI
D'NI NUMBERS

Character	Morse	NATO	D'NI Numbers
S	•••	SIERRA	18
T	–	TANGO	19
U	••–	UNIFORM	20
V	•••–	VICTOR	21
W	•––	WHISKEY	22
X	–••–	X-RAY	23
Y	–•––	YANKEE	24
Z	––••	ZULU	25
0	–––––		PLACE VALUE 25
1	•––––		CYCLICAL 0
2	••–––		
3	•••––		
4	••••–		
5	•••••		
6	–••••		
7	––•••		
8	–––••		
9	––––•		

APPENDIX 9

Browser Step-Through

Below are some of the basic browser functions that will help you interact with puzzle cache pages at geocaching. com so that you can more easily solve puzzles. The method for each of these is slightly different depending on which browser you are using.

Check Background Image

The "background" area of the cache page is the area to the left and right of any cache listing. The default image will be white, but a CO can place any image they wish into that area when they build the cache listing. If a puzzle cache has a background image it may be part of the puzzle, or it may just be decoration for the page.

Chrome

Unfortunately there is no direct way to complete this function in Chrome. There are third party extensions that can be added to Safari to enable this function. Alternatively, the URL for the background image can be found by reviewing the source code. It is usually around line 80.

Internet Explorer

Internet Explorer varies highly by version. Some older versions have the option to "Save Background Image" that is viewable by right-clicking the image. In newer versions of Explorer this function has been disabled, but you can find the URL for the background image by reviewing the source code. It is usually around line 80.

Firefox

Right click in the "background" area of the cache and choose "View Background Image." The image will open in the window and the URL of the image will be in the address bar.

Safari

Unfortunately there is no direct way to complete this function in Safari. There are third party extensions that can be added to Safari to enable this function. Alternatively, the URL for the background

image can be found by reviewing the source code. It is usually around line 80.

Find the URL for an Image

In order to reverse search an image, or use an online EXIF viewer you will need to have the URL for the image itself, rather than the URL for the web page. Isolating an image will reveal that URL, which you can then cut and paste to enter into the search box at Google or TinEye.

Chrome

Right clicking an image in Chrome gives you two useful options here. The first is "View Image in New Tab." That tab will have the URL for the image, and will have the image isolated away from the rest of the cache page.

If all you need is the URL, then the second option is just as useful. Choosing "Copy Image URL" will place the URL of the image in your clipboard, which can then be pasted into the search function at Google, or TinEye.

Internet Explorer

Internet Explorer varies highly by version. Some older versions have the option to "View Image" which is located by right-clicking the image. In newer versions of Explorer this function has been disabled, but you can find the URL for the image by reviewing the source code. It is usually around line 80.

Firefox

Firefox provides two options for this function, both of which are available through the pop-up menu found by right clicking. The first is "View Image," which will reload the webpage so that only that image is visible. The direct URL for the image is in the address bar. The second option is "Copy Image Location," which will place the URL of the image in your clipboard, and it can then be pasted into the search function at Google, or TinEye.

Safari

Safari provides two options for this function, both of which are available through the pop-up menu found by right clicking. The first is "Open Image in New Tab." That tab will have the URL for the image, and will have the image isolated away from the rest of the cache page.

If all you need is the URL, then the second option is just as useful. Choosing "Copy ImageAddress" will place the URL of the image in your clipboard, which can then be pasted into the search function at Google, or TinEye.

Save an Image

The most basic function for any puzzle cache image is simply saving the image. You may need this for searching, printing, or to save the image in case it changes.

Chrome

Right click and choose "Save Image As."

Internet Explorer

Right click and choose "Save Image As."

Firefox

Right click and choose "Save Image As."

Safari

Right click and choose "Save Image As..." or "Save Image to Desktop..."

Save a Page

Saving the page as a document might be helpful for comparison if the cache page later changes.

Chrome

From the "File" menu in the menu bar choose "Save Page As." This will save a file to your desktop that you can open using the "Open" command in your browser's "File" menu, just as you would any computer file.

Internet Explorer

From the "File" menu in the menu bar choose "Save Page As." This will save a file to your desktop that you can open using the "Open" command in your browser's "File" menu, just as you would any computer file.

Firefox

From the "File" menu in the menu bar choose "Save Page As." This will save a file to your desktop that you can open using the "Open" command in your browser's "File" menu, just as you would any computer file.

Safari

From the "File" menu in the menu bar choose "Save As..." This will save a file to your desktop that you can open using the "Open" command in your browser's "File" menu, just as you would any computer file.

View Source Code

Many geocache puzzles are as simple as looking into the source code to see what the CO may have hidden there. For an in-depth discussion of this see Chapter 2.

Chrome

Right click and choose "View Page Source." This will open a new tab where the source code will be visible.

Internet Explorer

To view the HTML source code for a Web page using Internet Explorer 3.x and later, click Source on the View menu. In Explorer 10.x and later you will need to use the "Page" menu on the menu bar. Click there, then choose "View Source."

Firefox

Right click and choose "View Page Source." This will open a new window where the source code will be visible.

Safari

If you are using Safari and have never done this before, you will first need to activate the "Develop" menu. To do that, click on "Safari" in the top menu bar, then go to "Preferences." In that pop up menu, click the "Advanced" tab and then click the check box next to "Show Develop." Then you should be able to right click on a page and select "View Page Source."

Index

Special Thanks

I'd like to extend a very special thanks to Brett Rogers (addisonbr) for helping with the initial outline for this book, providing a sounding board for many of the sections, and for inspiring me to get involved in puzzle caching in the first place. I owe an enormous debt to Jenn Kidder (teamajk) who helped me with incredibly detailed critiques of all the chapters, as well as beta-testing the puzzles and codes. Marc Blatchford (mblatch), Ruth Kramer (ruthny) and Caitlin Stork (caitlin535) were also instrumental in beta-testing the book, and providing feedback. Thanks to Matt Pickens for being my test "muggle." A hearty thanks to Vanessa Leonardo for providing grammar feedback! Thanks to Sonny and Sandy Portacio for their heartfelt foreword, and for some feedback on early chapters.

Acknowledgments

All maps used in this book were provided through the great work of the people at Open Street Maps (*openstreetmaps. org*) and those maps are © OpenStreetMap contributors. All Open Street Map data is available under the Open Database License and the cartography is licensed as CC BY-SA. Screenshots and images of the *geocaching.com* website, and the Geocaching app, are copyright Groundspeak, Inc. dba Geocaching. The Geocaching logo is a trademark of Groundspeak, Inc. Used with permission. "Travel Bug"® is a registered trademark of Groundspeak Inc. Used with Permission. All rights reserved. Terracaching logo is used with permission. Navicaching logo is used with permission. The Geocaching Australia logo is used with permission. Open Caching US logo is public domain. Cachly logo is used with permission. The "GX" geocaching logo is an open source logo originally created by the cacher Leatherman, and was provided to the public domain. The Android robot is modified from work created and shared by Google and used according to terms described in the Creative Commons 3.0 Attribution License. The Apple logo is a trademark of Apple Inc., registered in the U.S. and other countries. Screen shots from GIMP are used with permission. Geocheck.org screenshot courtesy of Samuel Thrysøe. "How To Puzzle Cache" is an independent publication and has not been authorized, sponsored, or otherwise approved by Apple Inc., Google, Android, Groundspeak, Garmin Ltd., or any of the other entities, businesses, corporations, websites or publications mentioned within.

Many of the illustrations in this book are adapted from illustrations found through Wikimedia Commons. I encourage all Wikipedia/Wikimedia users to contribute to their cause.

Photo Credits

All photos in this book were used with permission from the photographers, where applicable. Other photos were released to the public domain. Cover, ©Tatiana Popova/123RF; Pg 9, ©Marc Briggs (gotfish at *geocaching.com*); Pg 11, ©Marcin Balcerzack/123RF; Pg 13, ©Gilles Paire/123RF; Pg 19, ©123RF; Pg 31 ©JeeperMTJ (*JeeperMTJ.com*); Pg 33, ©123RF; Pg 41, belchonok/123RF; Pg 59, ©Oregon Bureau of Land Management (blm.gov); Pg 69, ©dvortygirl through Wikimedia Commons; Pg 70, ©cardiograph through Wikimedia Commons; Pg 71, ©cardiograph through Wikimedia Commons, Pg 77, ©Ruth Harrison; Pg 80, all presidential portraits are public domain; Pg 89, ©John Martin; Pg 90, ©Pavel Streznev/123RF; Pg 97, ©*TimKellerPhotography.com*; Pg 101, ©Kirill Kirsnakov/123RF; Pg 121, ©Omar de Armas (*omardearmas.com*); Pg 140, ©Chris Mills through Wikimedia Commons; Pg 149, ©CatCorner on Flickr.com; Pg 161, ©Arnold Rhinehold through Wikimedia Commons; Pg 171, ©Louise Bell; Pg 172, through Wikimedia Commons; Pg 189, ©natika/123RF; Pg 182, ©lightpoet/123RF; Pg 185, ©David McNeish; Pg 190, ©lammeyer/123RF; Pg 190, ©Patricia Phillips/123RF; Pg 203, ©*istockphoto.com*; Pg 209, ©Cully Long; Pg 212, ©iqoncept/123RF; Pg 216, ©Elina Elisseeva/123RF; Pg 233, ©Cully Long; Pg 239; ©Rebecca Altman; Pg 240, ©Rancz Andrei/123RF; Pg 241, ©Luka Godja/123RF; Pg 242, ©Tomasz Stasiuk; Pg 243, ©Jorge Hernando/123RF; Pg 251, ©cachemania; Pg 257, ©Sarah Happel Photography; Pg 262, ©scanrail/123RF.